About Thinking

W. Ward Fearnside
Babson College

PRENTICE-HALL, INC., Englewood Cliffs, N.J. 07632

Library of Congress Cataloging in Publication Data

Fearnside, W Ward.
    About thinking.

    Includes bibliographical references and index.
    1. Logic.   I. Title.
BC71.F4   160   79-20345
ISBN 0-13-000844-3

Printed in the United States of America

10 9 8 7

Editorial/production supervision by Les Bodian and Virginia Rubens
Interior design by Les Bodian
Cover design by Infield/D'Astolfo Associates
Manufacturing buyer: John Hall

PRENTICE-HALL INTERNATIONAL, INC., *London*
PRENTICE-HALL OF AUSTRALIA PTY. LIMITED, *Sydney*
PRENTICE-HALL OF CANADA, LTD., *Toronto*
PRENTICE-HALL OF INDIA PRIVATE LIMITED, *New Delhi*
PRENTICE-HALL OF JAPAN, INC., *Tokyo*
PRENTICE-HALL OF SOUTHEAST ASIA PTE. LTD., *Singapore*
WHITEHALL BOOKS LIMITED, *Wellington, New Zealand*

To Students
for whom this book is written

Contents

part four
Language   281

part five
Evidence   313

Introduction

When Archimedes ran through the streets shouting "Eureka!" he was rejoicing in having solved a practical problem by logic. *About Thinking* is concerned with practical problems. It offers some rules for improving the quality of thinking. It explains induction and deduction simply. It treats the common fallacies so that their shoddy arguments can be spotted and rebutted. Evidence, statistics, and language are taken up briefly and, we hope, usefully.

Many of us are not as skilled in the reasoning process as we think we are. Though we do learn something about sound reason just by growing up, still, many adults are illiterate in logic. They make glaring errors. This is because they never have examined the reasoning process at any length—a fact that I find strange considering how often we are told that "learning to think" is the essence of education.

Perhaps "learning to think" is assumed to be a by-product of studying other subjects. If so, long teaching experience convinces me that this assumption is only partly justified. Possibly logic is viewed by many as a numb subject, devoid of pictures or promise of material gain. As a liberal arts teacher, somewhat beleaguered these days, I like to point out that the two most practical subjects in anybody's college education both happen to be in the liberal arts field: English Composition and Logic. Whatever one does, one will have to express oneself and, occasionally, think.

About Thinking deals with questions that *have to be* answered to evaluate argument. Is this generalization well supported? How do I evaluate this analogy? Can I conclude that there is a causal relationship here? Is this a statement by a qualified authority? What should I look for in weighing evidence of this type? What information should accompany these statistics?

Logic has its limits, of course. No one contends that the human mind is always rational, nor will logic tell us such things as the purpose of life or whom we should love. The reasoning process is a tool, a procedure for reaching supported conclusions. Once you have learned it, you will use it every day in evaluating argument, unlike some subjects which may not enter the mind for days at a time.

Acknowledgments

About Thinking is written for students. Above all, I have strived to make its exposition clear and its contents of practical use. It is both accurate and fitting for me to acknowledge first my debt to the many classes of logic students who showed me what their interests are and what points give difficulty.

No one writes a textbook without great debts to the thinkers of the past, to writers of other textbooks, and to colleagues and friends who contribute ideas. I should mention specifically Beardsley, *Practical Logic*, Little *et al.*, *Applied Logic*, and Cohen & Nagel, *An Introduction to Logic and Scientific Method* as prominent influences among the many logic texts that I have read.

Individuals who have helped are legion. I thank Walter Bordewieck, Margaret Fearnside, Tracy Fearnside, Edward Kingsbury and William Rybolt for generously reading and commenting upon the entire manuscript. Anonymous reviewers made helpful suggestions, while Les Bodian, Charles Place, Virginia Rubens and Norwell Therien of the staff of Prentice-Hall, Inc. worked effectively to edit the book. Janet Manter, secretary and friend, contributed her skill and efficiency in typing and retyping the manuscript.

Finally, I wish to thank the following publishers, businesses and individuals for permission to quote from or use copyright works: American Electric Power Co., Appleton-Century-Crofts Co., Ashland Oil, Inc., The Conference Board, Doubleday & Co., Inc., Elsevier Scientific Publishing Co., Grosset & Dunlap, Inc., Harcourt Brace Jovanovich, Inc., Harper & Row, Publishers, Inc., *Harvard Business Review*, Harvard Law Review Assn., Professor Roger W. Holmes, Mrs. Winston W. Little, McGraw-Hill Book Co., Merrill Lynch, Pierce, Fenner & Smith, Inc., *Journal of the National Cancer Institute*, The *New Republic*, Newspaper Enterprise Assn., Planned Parenthood Federation of America, Prentice-Hall, Inc., G. P. Putnam's Sons, Random House, Inc., Rhode Island Department of Economic Development, Saturday Review Magazine Corp., Scott, Foresman & Co., *The Wall Street Journal*, and *The Washington Monthly*. The material from these various sources is acknowledged in footnotes at the places where it is used.

part one

Fallacies

chapter 1

The Nature of Fallacies

It would be a very good thing if every trick could receive some short and obviously appropriate name, so that when a man used this or that particular trick, he could at once be reproved for it.

Schopenhauer

Logic can be fun. It's a challenge to figure out whether an argument hangs together or not, whether an appeal is cogent or fallacious. Logic does not supply the materials that go into argument, nor does it make value judgments. It is a process for sound thinking, and if a conclusion turns out to be a poor one even though the requirements of logic were complied with in reaching it, then the fault was in the material or the value judgments and not in logic. It is not too much to say that the application of logic has played a central part in man's rise from savagery. And the spirit of scientific inquiry, which permeates the modern world, has at its heart an approach to truth in accord with the rules of logic.

Logic can be pictured as a coin with two sides. One side is positive; it is concerned with the requirements for sound thinking. The other side is negative; its province is mistakes in reasoning—that is, fallacies. Though our main concern will be to present the positive requirements for sound argument, we shall start off by considering common fallacies.

Why begin with fallacies? After all, many logicians have little time for fallacy as a subject, looking upon it as a sort of briar patch of naive, vicious, or whimsical errors. Better attend to the rules for valid reasoning which can be classified and cultivated in an orderly garden. The mind skilled in logic will not be taken in by fallacies—there is much truth in this. Yet fallacies make a good beginning point because they are so evident: one finds them intoned in speeches, hawked in newspapers, flashed on TV screens, vended in every marketplace of public discussion. It is well to know the names and faces of these shoddy practices. Some fallacies have well-established names coming down from the days of the Greeks and Romans; others lack a venerable or consistently used designation. In any case, it is more important to be able to point out in one's own words what is the fault in something offered as reasoning than it is to cite any special nomenclature. Knowing an appropriate name is helpful, though, because we think with words. One way that the terms in our vocabulary influence our thought is by guiding us to look for those phenomena for which we have names.

What is an argument and what is a fallacy? "Argument" has several meanings and one of its most common is "disagreement," a yak-yaking and a raising of voices. This is not the meaning of the word as used in this book and, to keep things clear, the word "dispute" will be used whenever this meaning is to be expressed. "Argument" as used in logic refers to a chain of reasoning: *an argument is the reasoning alleged to support a conclusion.* The notion of the "argument" as a chain of reasoning includes the conclusion reached, as is shown by the usage, "The conclusion of his argument was so and so." If the argument conforms to the rules of logic we call it "valid" or "reliable." If it does not, we declare it "invalid" or "unreliable" or, what amounts to the same thing, we may label it "fallacious."

"Fallacy" also has more than one meaning in general use. People often use the term to mean that a conclusion is not true; e.g., the retort "That's a fallacy" may be the speaker's way of saying, "That conclusion is false." In logic, however, "fallacy" is reserved for *an error in the reasoning process,* and although a weird and mistaken argument is likely to lead to the wrong conclusion, it does not *necessarily* do so. For example, suppose someone says, "It was sunny and warm for the whole week we were in Atlanta. That place must have a wonderful climate." With the slightest thought, anyone can see that a particular week in a particular season is not a sample that will properly support a conclusion about the climate of any city. Clearly, it is a fallacy, a mistake in reasoning, to base a conclusion on such slim and unrepresentative material. Yet Atlanta may indeed happen to possess a good climate. So you see, a conclusion may be true even though it is based on faulty reasoning.

In this book, when the word "fallacy" is used we mean only that the argument is faulty. When we want to talk about whether a conclusion is in fact true, we will use the words *true* or *false* or, perhaps, *reliable* or *unreliable*. Would that the problem of keeping the meaning of "fallacy" clear were so readily solved! Alas, impressions created by the different senses in which fallacy is employed in ordinary speech leave a lingering feeling that somehow poor reasoning indicates a false conclusion. So, to restate the nature of fallacy: where one notices a fallacy, then one knows that the fallacious argument does not support the conclusion as it claims to do. One simply does not know, however, whether other arguments and other evidence might show that the conclusion is true.

Schopenhauer is right in saying that knowing short and appropriate names for common fallacies aids in spotting and denouncing them. When he styles fallacies as "tricks" he is only half right. Sometimes a mistake in reasoning is consciously made and is indeed an unscrupulous trick. The speaker who uses character assassination instead of decent reasons to support his position may be a case in point. Yet fallacious argument often is the product of a blundering mind; the person may know no better and he may think his argument is good. Motive makes no difference; *a fallacy exists wherever the reasoning is mistaken.*

Fallacies do not classify neatly. This isn't surprising when one considers the great variety of ways in which people twist their reasoning. I suspect that any classification offered can be criticized for overlapping categories or for inelegance in its structure. Fortunately, it is not some overall pattern but rather the ability to recognize and refute individual fallacies as they occur that is the useful result of studying the common mistakes in reasoning. One builds up, piece by piece, a suit of intellectual armor against being fooled. So, when you come to the exercises you will find that all the questions concern understanding particular fallacies; there will be no stress placed upon recalling just how one or another fallacy can be classified. Still, in order to present fallacies in a coherent pattern, we have presented them in three groups that bring together those of similar nature. The groups are:

    I. Psychological fallacies
    II. Material fallacies
    III. Logical fallacies

This arrangement can be illustrated by a figurative analogy. Suppose we compare argument to a manufacturing process which uses a machine, an operator, and raw materials. If the operator is efficient, the materials up to standard, and the machine running smoothly, the finished product will probably pass inspection. However, three kinds of things can go wrong. The operator can make a mistake—get sleepy or be distracted and turn the wrong knob. The materials can be below standard or poorly prepared. And the machine itself can break down or misfunction. If the trouble lies with the operator, we call it *psychological*; if with the material, we call it *material*; if with the machine, then *logical*. The analogy gives an idea of the emphasis in each section. Under the psychological heading we discuss common errors that cause the audience to be carried away, as, for example, fallacies involving the use of personal attacks and emotive language. Under material fallacies we discuss such errors as faulty generalization and other instances of inadequate or shoddy material. The processes of logic follow rules rather like a machine conforming inexorably to natural laws; thus the logical fallacies are those which involve failure to conform to the rules that produce valid arguments.[1]

---

[1]This organization follows W. Ward Fearnside and William B. Holther, *Fallacy: The Counterfeit of Argument* (Englewood Cliffs, N.J.: Prentice-Hall, 1959). Passages reused from this book will not be presented as quotations or paraphrases.

SUMMARY

Argument in logic is the reasoning alleged to support a conclusion. The conclusion itself is considered part of the argument.

A *fallacy* is a mistake in argument.

Fallacy exists wherever a mistake in reasoning is made, regardless of whether the party employing fallacious argument knew better or not.

Spotting a fallacy does not establish that the conclusion is false. Where there is a mistake in argument, then *that* argument is not a reason for believing the conclusion true. Other evidence might show the conclusion to be true or to be false.

EXERCISES FOR CHAPTER 1
pages 3–6

I. Answer **T** for "true" or **F** for "false":

_____ **1.** A fallacy is a mistake in reasoning.

_____ **2.** Wherever a fallacy is spotted, one knows the conclusion is false.

_____ **3.** In order to understand a fallacy, one must know an appropriate name for it.

_____ **4.** An "argument" in logic is the reasoning alleged to support a conclusion.

_____ **5.** A fallacious argument always is an intentional trick.

_____ **6.** Wherever a fallacy is spotted, one knows for sure that *that* argument does not support the conclusion.

_____ **7.** Knowing an appropriate name for a fallacy helps to make one aware of that particular fallacy.

_____ **8.** It is possible for an argument to contain a fallacy and yet for the conclusion to be true.

_____ **9.** The speaker's motive has no bearing on whether or not his argument is fallacious.

_____ **10.** There can be no complete list of fallacies.

II. Explain how an argument may be fallacious even though the conclusion it reaches is true. Provide an example of your own.

chapter 2

Psychological Fallacies

Psychological fallacies are those that mislead the audience by taking advantage of psychological factors. One could call them fallacies of the audience.

1. PERSONAL ATTACK: *ad hominem* argument

A personal attack seeks to discredit the source of argument by charging personal shortcomings that are irrelevant to the issue to be decided.

The ancient name for personal attack—*ad hominem*, or "to the man"—is still used, as are the terms "name calling" and "character assassination." It is a device easily and effectively used by unscrupulous persons, quick to vilify opponents and forget their arguments. The armory of personal abuse is inexhaustible: no one readily forgets the doubts engendered when someone is represented as being dishonest, crafty, selfish, perverted, conceited, arrogant, or simply foolish. Charging unorthodoxy of political, religious, or moral views is another means for discrediting a source in the eyes of an audience that does not countenance such views. Personal attacks may cite misconduct that can at least be said to be factual, or they may be mere vague abuse, impossible to refute. For example, when Representative Collo was expelled from the Massachusetts Convention of 1978 after disregarding three warnings not to interrupt speeches, he charged that the president of the Convention was "dictatorial" and had "set him up."[1]

[1]*Boston Globe*, June 27, 1978.

8

How, then, can a person take account of the character of a party presenting an argument without himself falling into fallacy? There is no fallacy in not accepting uncorroborated statements from a party whose character or motives cast doubt on his credibility. Statements from an unreliable source are suspect, obviously. But there is a difference between "suspect" and "false." And there is a difference between taking into account the reliability of a witness and blindly assuming that personalities dispose of issues. One should assume a judicial attitude where discrediting allegations are made against the source. Where the discrediting allegations appear clearly irrelevant to the matter under consideration, one may fairly doubt the ethics of the party engaging in them. For instance, when a firm representing General Motors placed Ralph Nader under surveillance in the hope of discovering some scandal in his private life, this constituted a notorious attempt to make a personal attack. Had any personal shortcomings of Mr. Nader been found (none were), misgivings about his personal life would *not* refute his observations about the safety of cars.

Sometimes personally discrediting facts are relevant to the decision being made, and what is relevant can never be a fallacy. To bring up a person's moral shortcomings when he speaks in favor of widening a street is one thing; to bring out the same information when he seeks to become pastor of a church is another. In other words, the fallacy is confined to charges of shortcomings *that are irrelevant to the issue to be decided.* The limitation is important. The candidate for political office or the applicant for a job has put his/her character in issue insofar as honesty and some spheres of his/her beliefs are proper considerations in judging whether to elect or appoint.[2]

2. DAMNING THE ORIGIN, CEREMONY, AND SETTING

These three fallacies are simple and they lend themselves to a combined discussion. Like a personal attack, each is an invitation to consider the source rather than attend to whatever evidence may support the argument. In fact, *personal attacks* could be placed as a sort of special case under *damning the origin.*

Damning the origin is to claim that the origin of an argument is unimpressive, with the suggestion that it should not be accepted for this reason.

Damning the origin suggests disregarding an argument because the source is unimpressive in some way: young, inexperienced, foreign, and so on. To be sure, there is no fallacy in noting meager qualifications if the person advancing

---

[2]Since maintaining "his/her" references in all cases would be a compositional atrocity, henceforth I will employ the masculine pronoun to include feminine instances also where this is an appropriate interpretation.

the argument takes the line that his word is to be accepted as authoritative. However, this rarely is the case where damning the origin pops up. In the usual situation, some characteristic is brought up to damn the origin as if it weakened a *factual* argument. A mother, for instance, may be neither a manufacturer nor an engineer, but this is no reply to factual observations she makes concerning the safety of toys.

Sometimes a source is highly unpopular or philosophically unacceptable and, therefore, suspect. Even justified revulsion against a source does not in itself dispose of argument, though it properly puts us on guard to check evidence from such a source. For example, pronouncements of the John Birch Society or of the Socialist Workers Party are not rightly dismissed on account of their origins. A garden full of weeds may contain some flowers, so one must judge each plant on its merits.

One common variation of the fallacy of origin comes close to home, and all of us have experienced its overwhelming psychological power. It has the classical name *tu quoque*, meaning "you also." People are quick to notice when a person advocates what he does not practice. Yet the soundness of an idea is not diminished through the source's personal failure to exemplify it. For instance, an argument that dwindling oil supplies make it desirable for people to restrict oil consumption is not rebutted by an observation that the remark comes from one who himself drives a gas-guzzling car. A mother may advise her daughter not to marry at 18 even though she did so herself. No need to be flawless ourselves before we can stand up for an idea in this world—no need in logic, that is. Yet a devastating psychological resistance is stirred when someone fails to practice what he preaches. Thus the adage "People who live in glass houses shouldn't throw stones" is cited as impelling argument. Another favorite reminds us that "The pot shouldn't call the kettle black." Why not? What is the pot to call the kettle if the kettle *is* black? Do saints alone have a right to throw well-aimed stones of criticism? The adages are absurd in logic. Their psychological cogency is another matter.

The power of example is particularly noticeable in dealing with children. Injunctions to be honest are unlikely to impress the child who sees his parent deliberately pocket an excess of change given in error, nor will the young driver be persuaded by reasoned argument to do better than his parental models who have driven him for years in the family car. And so it is with nonsmoking, nondrinking, or any other virtues we might wish our impressionable children to possess when we do not. Every adult needs to identify the "glass house," "kettle black," and "practice what you preach" rejoinders for the intellectual rubbish they are, so that he will never *himself* use them to shrug off sound advice. And every adult needs also to recognize the psychological power of example.

The fallacies of ceremony and setting refer to the psychological influence of the pomp and circumstance of ceremony, or by the bedazzlement or drabness found in setting.

Sometimes argument is surrounded with a ceremony or setting calculated to enhance its dignity; at other times an unimpressive setting tempts the audience to give scant heed to the argument. Whenever such externals influence the audience's receptivity to an argument, a fallacy has occurred. Though truth is not really affected by whether it is propounded from a rostrum or a soapbox, in the practical world we know full well that surroundings make a difference. The salesperson who must sell to business executives cannot afford to go around in old clothes lest he be sized up as unsuccessful. If he dresses well and stretches his budget for a late-model car, is he guilty of fallacy? Must he be damned if he doesn't and damned if he does? Well, the logician is not trying to convict anybody. Fallacy occurs wherever reasoning is mistaken, no matter whether the error is willful or not. It is simply true that a psychological fallacy has occurred whenever the setting or ceremony has influenced the reception of argument.

Sometimes setting is organized to an extraordinary degree so that there is a real assault on the emotions. Consider the psychological purpose behind mass meetings organized for May Day in Red Square or for the inauguration of American presidents.

3. MISUSE OF AUTHORITY

Misuse of authority is claiming expert standing for a source that is not qualified.

In this day of specialization, we all must rely upon authority to guide our actions in all sorts of matters in which our personal knowledge is inadequate. We consult lawyers, golf instructors, auto mechanics, speech therapists, or zither players according to our needs. The man with twenty years' experience in the pickle business is just the fellow to ask—about the pickle business. Reference to authority is a sort of delegation of a problem for solution by another where one's own knowledge is inadequate. It's modest and reasonable conduct. There is, however, no good reason to be impressed by opinions given by those who *don't* have special knowledge of the subject. A great reputation in some other field or, worse, mere notoriety, is not a sound basis for accepting the opinions such sources offer. Nor should statements in outmoded books or pronouncements by great people who lived in earlier times be taken as authoritative opinions applying to today's problems. What goes on in misuse of authority?

The principal ingredient in misused authority seems to be the psychological dazzlement that gathers around prominent people. The advertising world capitalizes on this by sending out a tidal wave of athletes and actresses quoted out of their fields. Also the prestige of leaders lingers on after their day so that outdated pronouncements of Thomas Jefferson and like idols still find a ready market. Finally there is the "plain folks" appeal as an interesting variant, in which conspicuous *non*-authorities are used to give plain folks endorsements for those who trust advice from others like themselves.

In Chapter 20 we will take a careful look at how an authority is properly qualified. For the present we have seen that fallacy exists wherever unqualified sources are urged as authoritative. In every case one must ask, "What knowledge can I presume *this source* to have about the problem?"

4. IMPRESSING BY LARGE NUMBERS: bandwagon

Impressing by large numbers is buttressing argument by citing its adoption by large numbers of people who are in fact not specially qualified to judge the problem.

This fallacy is the old bandwagon technique; lots of people do this or believe that, ergo, you may safely follow along. The numbers are used as a sort of pseudo-authority. You should buy this brand, support this candidate, hold this belief because so many people do. Though it is pleasant and psychologically reassuring to be in step, truth is not always democratic, and even unanimity is not infallible.

The authority of mere numbers of people who are in no special position to judge amounts to no more than mass suggestion or unquestioning acceptance of tradition. Obviously, what "everybody knows" is not necessarily true—once "everybody" knew that the earth was flat, that disease was caused by evil spirits, that slavery was necessary. Informed support of democracy today doesn't rest on a belief that the majority always is right. Indeed, one argument for democracy is that where majorities are wrong the resulting mistakes will become evident and the system will provide the self-correcting feature of later free choices.

Of course, everything else being equal, large numbers often do have a wisdom and authority. For example, when numbers of experts—those who are qualified to judge—take a particular position in some matter, it is sensible to be impressed by their opinion. There are occasions, too, when it is sensible to take into account the numbers of laymen holding an opinion in a matter in which experience without special training makes one capable of judging. For example, we know that before the Berlin Wall effectively stopped the movement, some 2 million Germans "voted with their feet" by leaving Eastern Germany to become displaced persons in Western Germany, while the movement from Western to Eastern Germany remained negligible. The pattern has been repeated in Communist countries—streams of exiles flow out and only a few seek to enter or re-enter. Is it a *fallacy* to be impressed by large numbers in such cases? Perhaps one should concede that individuals who have *lived* under Communism are rather like experts in the life it offers to them. It would be too much to conclude from these figures that Communism is inefficient, unworkable in the long run, or even undesired by the majority of those who come to live under it. Yet the numbers do seem to support the argument that significant numbers of people find life under Communism unsatisfactory to the point where they will accept great disadvantages to escape it.

5. APPEAL TO TRADITION: tried and true

When a tradition is questioned on its merits, it is a fallacy to argue that raising the question is revolutionary, scandalous, or irreverent, or to merely restate the tradition without showing its desirability.

Nations, cultures, groups, even families develop traditions: the force of tradition often is strong and highly significant. The British Constitution is an extraordinary example of the part tradition can play in government since, though largely unwritten, nevertheless it is scrupulously followed. The people of Britain support overwhelmingly the maintenance of their institutions—just as the great majority of Americans support the U.S. Constitution. Such traditions are vital in maintaining orderly government, and, alas, all are familiar with the instability of governments that possess no strong support in the traditions of their peoples. Churches, businesses, and all sorts of organizations acquire traditions in the course of their operation which their supporters come to expect them to follow. Further, traditions are preserved by cultural habit as, for example, the taboo against eating horse flesh. It is not uncommon for a taboo to become reinforced by psychological reactions which tend to sustain it long after the original justification, if ever there was one, has passed.

It is always proper to suggest that a particular tradition be discarded because it is obsolete or inapplicable. Such a suggestion may appear scandalous or even revolutionary when the tradition questioned is deep-seated and generally accepted. Those defending the tradition may contend that it serves a purpose, or they may point to the inherent value of maintaining stability by following an established way of doing things. Yet harping on the age of the tradition or mere reiteration that tradition has value may be carried to the point of fallacy, especially when advantage is taken to play up the idea that challenging the existing order is wrong. Dwelling upon the notion that the tradition is fundamental or hallowed by usage and loyal observance only obscures the issue. When a tradition is being frankly challenged, attention should focus on a re-examination of the commitment on its merits.

A classic instance of obscurantist repetition of tradition is that of the debates held over President Wilson's proposal that the United States ratify the Covenant and become a member of the League of Nations. The tradition of isolationism was strong in the country, and it had been both applicable and followed with success throughout the nineteenth century. Isolation for an agricultural nation in a world of sailing ships is not the same as isolation for an industrial state in an age of steam and expanding communication by air. So, what was needed was to consider the appropriateness of isolationism for the United States in the twentieth century. The debate was marred by unceasing reiteration of the tradition of isolation, together with frequent citations from the obsolete authority of George Washington's Farewell Address. National sovereignty was another tradition given prominent place in the League of Nations debate and, of course, this tradition remains as one of the strongest political forces the world over. Perhaps we should debate again whether some modification of this tradition is needed in an age of H-bombs and rocket propulsion? After all, the human race is treading on new ground, and it is just possible that the result of too many people holding outmoded traditions for too long will be the undoing of all.

6. POPULAR APPEALS: *ad populum* argument

Ad populum appeals seek to win friends for an argument by playing upon the likes and dislikes of the audience.

One way of gaining favor with an audience is to tell it what it wants to hear. This device, called an appeal "to the people" (*ad populum*), is psychologically effective with any individual whose thinking is no deeper than his prejudices. Bacon named it "idols of the marketplace," thereby marking the trick for its link with common belief. The demagogue assures us of his patriotism, of his belief in "the American way," of his distrust for "mere theories," his faith in democracy (*yes*), his opposition to the "privileged few" (*Yes*), contempt for "pseudo-intellectuals" (*NATURALLY!*), "We don't need outsiders to tell *us* what to do" (**NO! NO!**).... The list is endless. He who uses *popular appeals* will have to know his audience, for the popular idols will differ from group to group. Denouncing "irresponsible unions" may appeal to an audience of bankers, being against "the Establishment" may catch the fancy of some people, trumpeting the menace of "imperialists" may sell in Red Square. Obviously, the more homogeneous the group, the easier to find beliefs that will be acceptable to all. Then there is the case where the group shrinks down to a single individual whose confidence may be won by espousing his particular prejudices. If *ad populum* seems inappropriate for an appeal to some individual idiosyncrasy, one might give the name "attitude fitting" to the device. No matter. The psychological base of flattery by agreement remains the same.

Numerous textbooks cite the funeral oration Shakespeare puts in the mouth of Mark Antony as the classic example of the *ad populum* appeal. It's too good to miss. Antony first reminds the audience members that they once loved Caesar:

> You all did love him once, not without cause.
> What cause withholds you then to mourn for him?

exhibits Caesar's bloodstained mantle,

> Through this the well-beloved Brutus stabb'd

implies that the conspirators' motives were personal,

> What private griefs they have, alas, I know not, that made them do it:

assures the audience that he, Antony, is an ordinary and guileless man,

> I am no orator, as Brutus is:
> But, as you know me all, a plain blunt man,

and, to cap his case, alleges that Caesar's will leaves his property to public uses,

> To every Roman citizen he gives,
> To every several man, seventy-five drachmas.

Self-interest, perhaps the strongest appeal of all, sends the mob on its way to avenge Caesar. Not a word had been said about the issues that faced the Roman public at that time. These issues were: (1) Had Caesar been guilty of conspiring to overthrow the Republic? and (2) Should action be taken against his assassins?

7. FORESTALLING DISAGREEMENT: poisoning the well

Forestalling disagreement is prejudging the issue by presenting the argument in a way that makes it embarrassing to disagree or makes it apparent that disagreement will arouse the personal ill will of the speaker.

Adults usually have learned to avoid needless quarrels and to steer clear of embarrassment. So they are silenced by the implied threat contained in assertions that are phrased to make disagreement embarrassing, and in turn they develop skill in phrasing their ideas in ways that will forestall disagreement. Many expressions such as "it is obvious," "everybody knows," "clearly," "of course," "as anyone can see" serve the double purpose of assuring the audience that it is not necessary to think about the problem and cowing those who remain unpersuaded. The person who protests, "It isn't obvious to me!" runs the danger of appearing ignorant or boorish.

One need not take notice of mild phrases which, though used to make agreement easy, are hardly enough to preclude polite disagreement. On the other hand, sometimes highly prejudicial statements are designed to intimidate opposition: "Only a muddle-headed person would suggest... ," "All loyal Americans support... ," "Every right-thinking person believes... ," and so on. Massive poisonings of discussion are being injected here. Standing up against intolerance, like the defense of freedom, requires courage.

8. CREATING MISGIVINGS

The fallacy of creating misgivings involves making unfounded or distorted charges to arouse lingering suspicion in the mind of the audience.

The suspicion that follows charges of immorality, corruption, or disloyalty is notoriously hard to clear away. Those close to a person who has lived down such a charge may be able, through their knowledge of the facts, to hold him in undiminished regard. Others, long after they have forgotten the nature of the charge, to say nothing of whether or not it was substantiated, tend to retain lingering suspicions. "Where there's smoke there's fire" voices our willingness to give credence to suspicion.

Character assassination probably is the most powerful use made of this fallacy (see #1, *Personal Attack*). Because personal charges leave lasting impressions, the ethical person does not make them unless they are both well-founded and necessary to state. Quite the contrary for the demagogue: by creating misgivings, he builds a leverage point for his work. Senator Joseph McCarthy made his name a byword with distorted charges, and Adolf Hitler wrote a famous analysis of the problem:

> ... in the size of the lie there is a certain factor of credibility, since the broad mass of people will be more easily corrupted in the depths of their hearts than they will be consciously and intentionally evil. Consequently, with the primitive simplicity of their feeling they fall victim more easily to a big lie than to a small one, since they themselves occasionally lie in small matters but they would be ashamed to tell great lies. Such a falsehood will not enter their minds, and they will also not be able to imagine others asserting the great boldness of the most infamous misrepresentation. And even with the explanation of the matter, they long hesitate and vacillate and accept at least some ground as true; consequently, from the most bold lie something will remain. . . .[3]

Hitler's "big lie" technique has illustrations from before the time the Greeks dreamed up the Trojan Horse. For a modern instance one might cite the "doctors' conspiracy" fabricated by Stalin to start hysteria that would sustain the purges. Yet the ultimate effect of lying makes interesting speculation. Hitler may

---

[3] Adolf Hitler, *Mein Kampf* (Munich: Franz Eher Nachfolger, 1934), pp. 252–53. English translation by W. Ward Fearnside.

well be right in arguing that the very boldness of the "big lie" gives it credibility—initially. But perhaps his own career illustrates the shortsightedness of this sort of Machiavellianism. At least, his repeatedly making promises that turned out to be "big lies" (for example, the Munich Pact and his assurance that "This is my last territorial demand in Europe") finally convinced millions of people—statesmen and ordinary people alike—that it was pointless to make agreements with him at all. In other words, confidence in communication broke down, and the conviction grew that further appeasement would lead only to further demands. This conviction hardened resistance to Hitler's aggressions and turned his demand for Danzig into a world war instead of another diplomatic concession. The crude unscrupulousness of the "big lie" may boomerang in the not-so-long run. Talleyrand might have dismissed the device with his dictum, "It is worse than a crime, it is a mistake!"

Whether misgivings arise from a "big lie" or from more modest charges or innuendoes, fairness demands that we look for sound proof and, if it is not forthcoming, seek to put the allegations out of mind and not be influenced by them.

EXERCISES FOR THE FIRST HALF OF CHAPTER 2
pages 8–17

I.   Answer **T** for "true" or **F** for "false":

_____   **1.** To bring up personally discrediting material in argument always is a personal attack of the fallacious or *ad hominem* sort.

_____   **2.** Material that is relevant to the decision being made, even though damaging, is not a fallacious personal attack.

_____   **3.** Where the discrediting allegations are irrelevant to the matter under consideration, it is clear that a personal attack has been made.

_____   **4.** Argument from an unimpressive source is properly disregarded.

_____   **5.** It is irrelevant in logic whether or not the party making an argument "practices what he preaches."

_____   **6.** An audience should notice where setting is contributing to an atmosphere of respect for the speaker or where it is unimpressive to the point of creating scorn. The critical thinker in such an audience should shape his opinion according to the setting he observes.

_____   **7.** By definition, to be an authority in a field means that one is a good original thinker.

_____   **8.** It is a fallacy to be impressed by the numbers who hold a certain belief only if the belief concerns a matter that the large numbers are not especially qualified to judge.

_____   **9.** Only opinions by very distinguished people can be accepted as statements by an authority.

_____   **10.** When a tradition is questioned, there should be a re-examination of the commitment on its merits.

_____   **11.** When the existence of a tradition is a stabilizing political fact or a source of security or pleasure, it is not a fallacy to take these matters into account in deciding whether the tradition should be upheld.

_____   **12.** It is always a fallacy to imply that the questioning of a tradition is scandalous, unpatriotic, or immoral.

_____   **13.** Flattery by agreement is the psychological basis for *ad populum* appeals.

_____   **14.** *Ad populum* appeals are the same for every group.

_____   **15.** "Creating misgivings" can be termed a fallacy only when the fears created are groundless or exaggerated.

II.   In the Appendix beginning on page 392 you will find a *Checklist of Fallacies* to provide a brief description for all the fallacies discussed in this book. Get acquainted with this checklist by using it to review the eight fallacies you have studied so far.

III.   Provide short answers to the following questions:

1. Sometimes it is proper to bring out facts that reflect unfavorably on the character of a party advancing an argument. On other occasions it is a fallacy of personal attack or *ad hominem* argument to allege flaws in the character of a party to the argument. Differentiate between these two situations.

2. There are occasions when it is sensible to regard the numbers of people holding certain opinions as evidence of the correctness of the widely held opinion. When may one do this without being a victim of the bandwagon fallacy?

3. "You should practice what you preach" expresses a common attitude. Yet this injunction is irrelevant in logic. Explain how this is so.

4. Logic aside, if one wishes one's advice to be heeded, it may be highly important to "practice what you preach." Explain.

5. There's nothing wrong about defending a tradition. So how can a fallacy of "appeal to tradition" occur?

IV.   Each of the following passages contains a clear instance of one of the fallacies discussed so far. Spot the fallacy in each case and fill in the blank from memory. If you cannot recall the name applied to the fallacy in this book, *make up an appropriate name of your own.* Be prepared in each case to explain how the fallacy occurs in the passage.

1. Now that I have become head of the government, I want to say plainly that you should expect no tricks or fancy arguments from me. It is not for me to ape the vocabulary of a professor or the finesse of a lawyer. I propose simply to do my duty and my best.

2. Introducing a new product line sometimes is a good idea. But I'll be darned if I'm impressed when the suggestion comes from a young fellow who hasn't been in the business for six months.

---

3. More people use *Covermor* paint than any other brand. You're safe when you use *Covermor*.

---

4. It is the policy of this company to carry on a mail-order business. And now some people in the new management want to phase out the mail-order side of our operation. It really is an outrageous suggestion, considering that the company has been known for selling by mail-order ever since it started.

---

5. As long as I am your Congresswoman, there will be no politics, no favoritism, no privileged few.

---

6. You're a fine one, Karl, to advise me to give up smoking. Why, you can't seem to quit yourself!

---

7. Let me tell you about the man who opposes building a Veterans' Hospital on Elm Street. *He* never risked his life in a war. When others were dying in Vietnam, he stayed home and made money.

---

8. As we know, the medical examiner says this child died as a result of eating ice cream containing peanut oil. The child was extraordinarily allergic to peanuts and the fact that the ice cream contained peanut oil allegedly was not on the label. But before we jump to the conclusion that manufacturers ought to be required to put every ingredient on the label, do we *really* know why this child died? When you consider the many times this case is cited, don't you become suspicious that it's being blown out of proportion?

---

9. Every right-thinking person knows that strip mining ought to be banned.

---

9. APPEAL TO PATHETIC CIRCUMSTANCES: crybaby

The appeal to pathetic circumstances is an attempt to substitute feelings of sympathy and mercy for a cold weighing of the merits.

The ancients named this device the *argumentum ad misericordiam*. Indeed, influencing decisions by urging human considerations must always be with us. Is there anyone with a soul so dead that he has never succumbed to an irrelevant appeal to pathos, sentimentality, human sympathy? Can one, in the name of logic, seriously turn a deaf ear to all human considerations? Well, differences in degree may on occasion make differences in kind. Still, we need to know what we are doing, for appeals to sympathy can be abused and demands for special consideration particularly recommend themselves to unscrupulous pleaders, since they work by taking advantage of the audience's feelings of decency and common humanity. After all, if there is a case for sympathy, should there not also be a solid case on the merits supported by evidence? If there is, we will not have to rely on sympathy.

The fallacy lies in *taking advantage* of pathetic circumstances. The beggar wears rags and the brochure of a charitable foundation exhibits the picture of an emaciated child. If these are typical and not prearranged for show, then they are legitimate evidence of the need for aid which is the heart of the problem, but when such evidence is overdrawn or fabricated, then there is an attempt to take advantage of our emotions. If the beggar or the charity seek to stir sympathy, at least the situation is one in which human considerations are relevant. On other occasions, however, it is simply improper to take account of pathetic circumstances. Take the criminal prosecution in which conviction will mean great hardship for the accused and his family. The jurors have sworn to make a finding of "guilty" if and only if guilt is shown by evidence beyond reasonable doubt; otherwise they are to find "not guilty." Appeals to pathetic circumstances are not a proper way to influence the jury's determination of guilt, and some of the rules of evidence are framed to limit their use. Since a trial at law is often closer to a dogfight than a search for truth, one may expect to find counsel for the defense busy making appeals to sympathy wherever possible. And the jury, unfortunately and despite all oaths, may well be swayed by these considerations irrelevant to the question "Did the accused do the act charged?" Incidentally, where a defendent is found guilty and special hardships are involved, these are proper matters for the judge to take into account when choosing between the alternatives of fine, imprisonment, or suspended sentence. The law provides counsel with opportunity to bring out mitigating circumstances *after* the question of guilt is decided.

10. THE ARGUMENT FROM IGNORANCE

The argument from ignorance is a claim that inability to prove something establishes that the opposite is true.

When something cannot be proved, then the truth about the matter remains unknown. This appears so obvious that one might wonder how anyone could be misled about the consequence of not being able to prove something. At times, however, people mistake a failure to prove one thing as establishing that the opposite must be true. This does not follow, and the error has been known for centuries as *the argument from ignorance.*

Belief in God, for example, rests upon faith, since there is no satisfactory proof for God's existence. One cannot settle the question by reasoning, "There is no proof for the existence of God; therefore He does not exist." Nor can one reason soundly, "There is no way to disprove the existence of God which shows that He does exist." As you can see, in these unwarranted conclusions reached by the argument from ignorance, everything depends upon where one starts.

Under our law a person charged with crime must be proved guilty before he may be punished, and if guilt is not proved to the satisfaction of the jury it will bring in a finding of "not guilty." Such a finding does not mean that the accused has been shown *not* to have committed the offense; it signifies merely that his guilt was not proved. He may be guilty in fact or he may be innocent, but whichever he is, the evidence to show guilt is inadequate. Since we punish only those proved guilty of wrongdoing, where proof fails, a defendent is not guilty in a legal sense and we misleadingly announce "not guilty" where we may mean "not proved." Perhaps this generous confusion is just as well—even though not strictly logical—for no one wants to fall for the fallacy of *creating misgivings* (see #8). Although it may seem unchivalrous, the truth of the matter is that so long as one has not followed the evidence to make his own evaluation, the situation calls for withholding judgment.[4]

Now suppose a society placed the burden of proof the other way around by requiring an accused party to prove that he did not commit the offense with which he is charged. A person sent to jail under this system might be in fact the offender or he might be just an unlucky fellow who couldn't produce evidence to prove he had not committed the act charged. An inability to prove oneself *not guilty* does not support the opposite conclusion—to wit, that guilt is established.

When one comes to proof of existence, it's easy to become confused about proof and failure of proof. Don't we say, for instance, that unicorns do not exist because no one has succeeded in proving that they do? Not quite. The situation

---

[4]A defendent may have a strong defense which amounts to a showing that he was not connected with the offense charged, or he may base his defense upon showing that the state has failed to prove its case beyond a reasonable doubt. The verdict "not guilty" does not distinguish these possibilities. In Scottish law a verdict of either "not guilty" or "not proven" can be returned to distinguish the two situations.

can be likened to the search for a missing part when a box is unpacked. Clearly, a careful search of the box and the packing material becomes proof that the part was not in the box. With unicorns, alas, having visited every suitable part of the world we have, in effect, amassed overwhelming evidence that the unicorn does not exist. Thus we dismiss unicorns on this evidence and not upon a failure to prove the unicorn does exist. If the Loch Ness monster appeals to you, well and good. Eventually, the monster will be found or its "box" of Loch Ness will become sufficiently explored to demonstrate its nonexistence.

11. MISUSE OF HUMOR AND RIDICULE: lost in the laugh

Misuse of humor and ridicule are diversions to avoid argument or to put the audience in a mood unreceptive for serious discussion.

Heaven help us if we don't enjoy humor! Yet continuous humor or witticisms injected at serious moments in discussion is diversionary. So also sarcasm, parody, mimicry—all the various forms of ridicule—are impertinent intrusions in argument; they tempt us to get lost in the laugh. As audience members we will want to enjoy any good sallies—and then scrutinize the argument.

The politician who can entertain his audience by getting off good jokes and witty barbs against his opponents will gain many votes. Humor is an asset for the lawyer, too, for all enjoy a ready wit, and the personal appeal of the person who is entertaining certainly doesn't turn one against his arguments. One can credit the skillful attorney with the judgment not to break the continuity of thought about serious points of his own case with quips and funny stories. Distraction is no friend of careful thought.

Though added discussion of this simple fallacy hardly seems necessary, it would be a dull thing to leave the fault unillustrated. A politician in the French Chamber of Deputies, when speaking in favor of women's rights, declared "There isn't much difference between men and women." A cry of *Vive la différence!* dissolved the Chamber into laughter, thereby destroying the mood of listening to argument.

12. OBFUSCATION, PETTIFOGGING, AND CLAMOROUS INSISTENCE UPON IRRELEVANCIES

This array of diversions is grouped together because they are cousins. Pettifogging and clamorous insistence upon irrelevancies amount to special types of obfuscation.

Obfuscation is any confusing of argument by verbose or unclear discussion or by magnifying trifles and quibbling over details.

We hope the definition is broad enough. To start off, we should remind ourselves that fallacy need not be the result of a willful trick or knowing misuse of argument, for obfuscation has its unintentional as well as its willful practitioners. It may result from deliberate desire to confuse, true enough, as where a competent individual decides to talk a proposal to death, to evade an answer by disappearing into a cloud of words, to magnify trifles and stall discussion on every detail. Then there is the bumbling fellow who does not know the shape of relevant argument, and the bore whose intellectual brakelinings are so worn that he rambles on and on. These will leave discussion more confused than they found it.

The pettifogger makes much of little. His hallmarks are quibbling over definitions that are unneeded, insisting that matters that are reasonably established have not yet been proved, weighing the evidence on an uneven scale, and announcing solemnly that an important action should not be undertaken because some slight interest would suffer.

Clamorous insistence on irrelevancies means just that. One way of hiding the weakness of a position is to draw noisy attention to a side issue. The side issue may be the character of the opponent, who is damned vigorously while the argument gets lost in personalities (see #1, *Personal Attack*), or it may be some movement or group that serves as a whipping post. This, the red-herring technique, is the tactic made familiar by speakers who, instead of meeting the real question, turn their talk into attacks on bureaucracy, foreign aid, or whatever else may be a handy *ad populum* appeal to deflect the attention of the audience (see #6, *Popular Appeals*). Perhaps we are being hard on lawyers in this book and yet it is true that at least some of the sawing of the air and trifling argument that takes place in courtrooms results from being caught in a case for which good reasons are scarce. Then clamorous insistence on irrelevancies, of necessity, becomes the patron saint of one who is being overwhelmed in argument.

13. THE BARRAGE OF OBJECTIONS and THE CALL FOR PERFECTION

Again we have a pair of fallacy cousins. They may even be thought of as second cousins of the devices of *obfuscation*, which we just considered.

A barrage of objections seeks to paralyze action by stressing all possible objections without fairly weighing the advantages offered by action.

No one suggests, of course, that objections of substance should not be raised. The fallacy lies in a one-sided focus on objections so that the positive side of the case becomes smothered. To play upon the fear of action raises doubts in the minds of the timid. Thus the fallacy, when successful, owes its effectiveness to psychological weakness of the audience. The campaign against Medicare illustrates the use of a barrage of objections. The public was told the plan would be "ruinously expensive," would "overcrowd the hospitals," "lead to inferior medical service," "restrict the patient's choice of a physician," "violate confidential patient–doctor communication," and so on. Even if there were justification for some of these fears, their presentation without fair discussion of medical care for the elderly as it existed in the absence of Medicare was a distorted treatment of the problem.

The logician Richard Whately has analyzed at length the nothing-but-objections technique and summarized the problem thus:

> There never was, or will be, any plan executed or proposed, against which strong and even unanswerable objections may not be urged; so that unless the opposite objections be set up in the balance on the other side, we can never advance a step.

A call for perfection proposes to defer a practical action until some impossible or, at the least, unlikely change is first achieved.

In a discussion concerned with reducing theft in a locker room, all would recognize the suggestion, "If people were taught to be honest, we would need no locks" as mere idle musing. In less obvious situations, the contention that people should first be changed or perfected in some way is mistaken for serious argument and allowed to dull the blade of action. Where a call for perfection is urged, there generally seems to be an assumption that problems are to be solved when ideal conditions exist. In real life, action cannot await the ideal and many problems are best dealt with by several approaches at once. For example, it is true that racial discrimination cannot be ended by law alone; it will persist as long as belief in it exists in the prevailing culture. Yet to suggest that the various devices by which discrimination is practiced should be allowed to continue until such time as people have been educated not to desire to discriminate is to suggest replacing practical action with a call to perfection. *Both* education and law are available to deal with this problem, and neither one need await the full accomplishment of the other.

14. POINTING TO ANOTHER WRONG

Pointing to another wrong is claiming that one wrong justifies another.

So common is the practice of claiming justification for one wrong by citing another that the adage "Two wrongs don't make a right" exists to rebut it. Yet most of us are tempted to mitigate wrongs on one side by pointing to those on the other. Justice seems to demand that one who complains of wrongdoing should himself have "clean hands." It is all too easy to turn attention away from charges that are difficult to answer and to focus attention instead upon a claim that the accuser himself is guilty of misconduct. Yet even when the counter-charges are deserved, all that is demonstrated is that *neither* side is right. For example, AFL-CIO President George Meany countered consumer criticism of excessive plumbers' wages with the story of a lawyer who was billed $50 for 15 minutes of plumbing work. Protests the lawyer, "But I earn only $100 an hour!" The plumber shrugs and says, "That's what I used to get when I was a lawyer."[5] By charging in effect another wrong of a different group, Meany is diverting attention from the issue of whether plumbers' wages are out of line.

It would be nice if situations always were clearcut. But there is the difficult problem of the rule-of-the-game approach, in which the "other wrong" actually is a fair response to prior wrongdoing. For instance, when during an Arab-Israeli armistice, one side built fortifications to improve its position in violation of the agreement, then it became proper for the other side to take *appropriate* countermeasures. One could argue that the first breech was serious enough to terminate the agreement so that the countermeasures were not violations, but this does not cover the situation since the armistice continued in effect. In any case, only an appropriate countermeasure could be justified. After all, even in the stress of war it becomes another wrong to offset one life with a hundred.

It is unfortunate that the fallacy of *pointing to another wrong* is confused by special situations for which legitimate connections between the actions cannot be ignored. Still, everyone needs to resist indiscriminate claims that one wrong is to be excused on the grounds of another, for by such reasoning gross crimes by individuals and by states are condoned or even praised on the ground of other misdeeds. A vendetta mentality perpetuates evil in the world. Too often the human propensity to harbor memories of other wrongs creates a sort of tradition of hatred that bedevils human relations by piling wrong upon wrong for decades or even centuries. Whole peoples nourish traditional hostilities on a diet of past grievances—witness Ireland and England, the Arab states and Israel, Turkey and Russia, Cambodia and Vietnam, Korea and Japan.

15. THE ARGUMENT OF THE CLUB: *argumentum ad baculum*

In this fallacy, one seeks to induce action by threatening some disadvantage either expressly or by implication.

"Your money or your life" isn't an argument. It works, though. Clubs have their place in this world, right enough. "Come to supper *now*, or get a spanking." "Trespassers will be prosecuted." We needn't linger over cases in which

[5]Cited in *The Wall Street Journal*, July 24, 1978.

the threats are palpable, for it is evident to all that reasoning is at an end here. The traditional name for the fallacy, *argumentum ad baculum* (argument of the club), suggests these gross cases.

Though hardly subtle in any case, threats can be veiled, and the disadvantage to be suffered need not be physical. For example, a storekeeper's prudent decision not to take sides in a local political issue that divides his customers is a case of the club of public opinion restraining argument. One recalls the sequence "He who cannot reason is a fool. He who will not reason is a bigot. He who dares not reason is a slave." On occasion, all are slaves to the argument of the club.

Self-interest is not commonly identified and discussed as a fallacy. Yet the argument of the club really is a part of this wider fallacy of influencing an audience through appeals to self-interest. Schopenhauer, lampooning the level of public discussion in his day, advised, "Instead of working on your opponent's intellect by argument, work on his will by motive; and he, and also the audience, if they have similar interests, will at once be won over to your opinion, even though you got it out of a lunatic asylum." Yes, our minds do rationalize along the channel of self-interest. We can only hope knowledge of logic will reduce this human weakness by making it harder to fool ourselves with distortions. Self-interest and the *argument of the club* need to be recognized as base invitations to stifle reason.

16. EMOTIVE LANGUAGE: colored words

Emotive language refers to the psychological distraction produced by the connotative suggestions of words.

The use of *emotive language* is the most pervasive of all fallacies. In fact, this fallacy is one that nobody succeeds in resisting completely.

"Emotive" is a not-so-common word. It would be easier to employ "emotional," but that word applies too specifically to strong feeling. The initial step in understanding the emotive nature of language is to notice the two levels of meaning found in many, probably in most, words. First, there is the *denotative* meaning. This is what the word designates: thus "bed" designates a certain article of furniture that anybody can point to. Second, there is the *connotative* meaning. This refers to the feelings that the word stirs up in our minds: "bed" may connote warmth, comfort, safety. So we see:

Denotative   "bed"   designates

Connotative   "bed"   arouses thoughts of *warmth, comfort, safety*

The simplest kind of denotation occurs with a physical object that presently exists as a single entity distinct from everything else in the world, say the Taj Mahal. One may go there and point to it; "Look, that is what I mean when I say *Taj Mahal.*" Nice thought. Then there are words like "bed," Plato's famous example. Though one can point to this bed and that bed readily enough, it is out of the question to point to all past, present, and future beds. No matter. The denotation is clear. It includes every object that ever has or will fulfill the notion of bed. Now we move to the cases of entities that have existed in the past—for instance, Vercingetorix, a man now long dead. We cannot tramp through the forests of Gaul to meet and fight with him as Caesar did. We simply have arrived too late for the show, but we can gather what the show was about from reports of those who saw it. The name denotes a man who did certain things that we know about. The denotation is this Gallic leader whom we will never see. If we want an image we will have to resort to an artist's conception. When we come to words for nonexistent beings, such as mermaids, the denotation still remains simple, but, since we have entered a land of fancy, we will have to rely on verbal descriptions and artists' conceptions. *What* is denoted is clear, even if the world is a poor place lacking these particular delights. Abstractions give more trouble. Take "thinking" and "poverty" for examples. The denotations for these cannot be represented directly, though sometimes statues or pictures are made to represent situations which we associate with these intangible ideas. The chief avenues for understanding them are our personal experiences, and whatever verbal explanations we may have come across. Despite difficulties, the denotation *is the object or the idea indicated by the word.*

Connotative meaning is more personal. It refers to the stirrings within us suggested by words. These stirrings, though not exactly the same for any two people, usually correspond reasonably closely. I suppose any woman feels pleasantly flattered when she is called "slender," while the fellow she catches calling her "skinny" rouses a different reaction and she may let him know. The two words may have the same denotation—same girl, same curves. But the connotation! There are many such words carrying strong connotations even without a context. Consider *snooper, lame duck, nigger, Uncle Tom,* and so on. Or *staunch, succulent, resolute, Mutual Benefit Savings Bank, patron,* and so on. No one has to be told which series is laudatory and which derogatory.

Many words are neutral and have no strong coloration: *street, walking, blue, fifteen, transportation, glass, tape measure, structure,* and so on. To me at least, these words arouse little connotative reaction when they are listed without a context. But within a context such normally neutral words often take on emotive overtones, as in the sentence, "The family was put out into the *street.*" Here "street" carries the emotive overtones of a hard, friendless world. "The dog *barked at* the cat" seems neutral enough, while "The governor's critics *barked at* the reform as was to be expected" obviously derides the critics by choosing words connoting an ineffective and often unprovoked action. Terming the change a "reform," a description the critics surely would not accept, is a further use of connotation to turn us against the critics who are only doing what "was to be expected." So we see, some words rouse emotive reactions even without a context while others are neutral when standing alone.

Bertrand Russell had some fun contrasting emotive terms in his mock "conjugations" of "irregular verbs." One of the most famous of these runs:

> *I am firm.*   *You are obstinate.*   *He is pigheaded.*

Note that these three descriptions all could apply to the same decision. Perhaps you would enjoy making up some examples. Try your own conjugations beginning with: "I protested," "I ate a hearty meal," "I am fastidious."

This summary investigation of the denotative and connotative aspects of language has sought to keep these two levels of meaning separated clearly. Let's not make the simple complicated: they are separate levels. However, denotation sometimes does affect connotation. "Murder," "slave," "cancer" designate evils and arouse emotive revulsion at the same time. No circumlocution will describe these conditions in a way that is accurate and neutral. Thus, some of our emotive reaction originates in the response to the designation of the word.

Grasping both the denotative and the connotative meanings for the words and phrases of a language is part of the process of learning the language itself. After all, one does not learn a language by looking up dictionary definitions. Mostly we hear words in use from childhood on, and these hundredfold and thousandfold encounters build up concepts of how each word is appropriately applied. We come to know the area in which each word may be used *both* for its denotation and for its connotation. With the mother tongue the process is early and painless. The child runs his electric train and yet does not know how it runs; he also chooses his words for emotive suitability long before he can explain what he is doing.

There is more to the emotive side of language than the connotative feelings found in isolated words and phrases. Rhythm and cadence are strong forces. Aldous Huxley suggests how strong:

> No man, however highly civilized, can listen for very long to African drumming, or Indian chanting, or Welsh hymn singing, and retain intact his critical and self-conscious personality. It would be interesting to take a group of the most eminent philosophers from the best universities, shut them up in a hot room with Moroccan dervishes or Haitian Voodooists, and measure, with a stop-watch, the strength of their psychological resistance to the effects of rhythmic sound. . . . What a fascinating, what a fruitful field for experiment! Meanwhile, all we can safely predict is that, if exposed long enough to the tom-toms and the singing, every one of our philosophers would end by capering and howling with the savages.[6]

Though spoken language does not go to this extreme, dramatic arrangement of

[6]Aldous Huxley, *The Devils of Loudun* (New York: Harper & Row, 1971), pp. 351–352.

the parts of a sentence and the rhythmic affect of language itself do sway the emotions. "Four score and seven years ago, . . . "—would "eighty-seven" have done as well? Appropriate use of words for their emotive affect is of the essence in poetry; take this away and there is no poem. Fancy transposing Thomas Gray's

> The curfew tolls the knell of parting day,
> The lowing herd wind slowly o'er the lea,

into

> The curfew sounds indicating the end of the day
> The herd of mooing cows walks slowly over the pasture.

We want to enjoy poetry, we want to hear speeches which stir us with the dramatic skill that comes from a good arrangement of the parts as well as choice of words, we want to read descriptions that do not put us to sleep but excite us with the emotive resources of language. Is all this to be called *fallacy* and therefore not done?

We declared at the outset that nobody is immune to the beguilement of emotive language. Though bold, I think the statement is correct. Where the task is *to reason* about a problem, it is best not stated in poetry, in impassioned oratory, or urged with any sort of emotive embellishment. Dean Acheson, former Secretary of State, illustrated the point with a wry tale:

> Some years ago, a colleague in the State Department wrote papers in such beautiful prose that I found myself influenced toward conclusions which, when challenged, I could not justify. Protection against this siren proved simple. Another colleague rewrote the paper in telegraphese, leaving out most adjectives, inserting the word "stop" for periods. This exorcised the magic. Too much art in the mixture and, in Sir John Seeley's contemptuous words, "history fades into mere literature."[7]

In short, the rich resources of emotive language are there for legitimate enjoyment when reason is not the chief concern.

When we first defined a fallacy as a *mistake in argument* we pointed out that fallacy occurs whether or not there is an intent to use faulty reasoning. We all choose the words that seem to us emotively appropriate and, as audience members, we may be carried along by the emotive overtones. Sometimes a calculated use of emotive language is made to create the reaction that the speaker wants. Calling the police "pigs" or nonstrikers "scabs" are gross instances in which the emotive terms are used as a device for incitement. A Ford assembly-line worker put the matter well when he declared, "If a word can cause a given reaction, just the word, and somebody knows that, they can just use your mind like it's got a

---

[7]*Time*, April 6, 1966, p. 42.

steering wheel."[8] All too often our minds are directed by this "steering wheel" effect of the choice of words.

The language of scholarship generally avoids highly emotive descriptions. Here the search is for truth. The audience is, one hopes, intellectually sophisticated and displays of emotion or forensic skill would seem out of place, so the vocabulary chosen tends to be in neutral terms. Should we conclude that whenever the ideal is to reach truth through reason, that language should be kept as free from emotive suggestion as possible? No. A neutral vocabulary may be inadequate to a situation. In this world there are slave-labor camps and massacres, acts of heroism and tender selflessness. Shall speakers always find euphemisms? What polite word should Hobbes have substituted for "fools" in his fine sentence, "Words are wise men's counters—they do but reckon by them; but they are the money of fools"? *To the extent that connotative overtones form part of an appropriate description of the event*, then truth may be served by frankly emotive language.

[8]Patricia Sexton and Brendan Sexton, *Blue Collars and Hard Hats: The Working Class and the Future of American Politics* (New York: Random House, 1971), p. 76. Copyright Random House, 1971.

EXERCISES FOR THE SECOND HALF OF CHAPTER 2
pages 21–31

I.   Answer **T** for "true" or **F** for "false":

_____   **1.** Several politicians were indicted in a milk fund scandal. One politician, after he was found "not guilty," declared, "I have been certified innocent by the jury."

_____   **2.** Though humor may make a good point, still the laughter evoked by humor always is a diversion in argument.

_____   **3.** If confusion results from obfuscation, whether it was intentional or not, a fallacy has been committed.

_____   **4.** A call to perfection is sound argument because the solution of a problem will be easier if people are first improved.

_____   **5.** The adage "Two wrongs don't make a right" is sound in logic.

_____   **6.** Where one party to an agreement commits a wrongful breach, then appropriate countermeasures may not be "another wrong."

_____   **7.** *The argument of the club* refers to pressure to make a decision according to personal expediency rather than according to sound reason.

_____   **8.** One who understands the emotive response that words evoke never will be a victim of emotive language.

_____   **9.** "Connotative meaning" refers to the stirrings within us suggested by words.

_____   **10.** The fallacy of *appeal to pathetic circumstances* (*argumentum ad misericordiam*) occurs wherever pity or human sympathy is allowed to enter into the making of a decision.

II.   Provide short answers for these questions:

1. Does the listing of the *appeal to pathetic circumstances* (*argumentum ad misericordiam*) as a fallacy mean that human considerations can have no place in argument? Defend your answer.

2. Explain and give your own illustrations of "denotation" and "connotation" in language.

3. Since the emotive element in language exerts a "steering-wheel" effect that is a constant influence toward fallacy, does this mean that fine writing and poetry should be eschewed? Does it mean that emotive language should be avoided in argument? Justify your positions.

4. Hobbes wrote, "Words are wise men's counters—they do but reckon by them; but they are the money of fools." Explain what the comment means.

5. Though citing one wrong as justifying another is a common fallacy, there are occasions in which a "wrong" by one party may justify a reaction by the other party which, if done without provocation, would be counted as a "wrong." This possibility clouds the clarity of the *pointing to another wrong* fallacy. Provide an instance of the fallacy and an instance of a situation in which the reaction would not be termed another "wrong."

III.   Each of the following passages contains a clear instance of at least one of the fallacies discussed so far in this book. Some passages contain two fallacies. Spot the fallacy or fallacies in each case and fill in the blank from memory. Do not strain to find fallacies that are, at the most, only barely committed. It is an error to complain of a fallacy that is not really committed. If you cannot recall the name applied to the fallacy in this book, make up an appropriate name of your own.

1. You say that the United States is a democracy. I don't think we can assume that. What does "democracy" mean, anyway?

_____   _____

2. Mr. A complains, "That company sure did a sloppy job of fixing my furnace." Mr. B replies, "Well, look who's talking! I happen to know about a few shortcuts you've taken in your work."

_____   _____

3. Disarmament is desirable. That's true. I say when we *know* we aren't going to be attacked, then it will be time to negotiate about disarmament.

_____   _____

4. If you are wise, you will be mighty careful about arguing that point with the city government. You've heard the saying "Don't fight City Hall." People learned that long before you and I were around, and there's good reason for us to keep it in mind.

_____   _____

5. Only a person dead to all shame would agree to this dishonorable compromise of our rights.

_____   _____

6. There's been a lot of uninformed prattle about the danger of drug abuse. Some of these self-styled experts would have us think they know just how to handle a problem which no government with years of study and experience has been able to deal with successfully.

_____   _____

7. We should oppose this legislation, which would compel arbitration of jurisdictional disputes between labor unions. Our right to strike was hard-fought and hard-won in this country. In supporting that right unfettered and untrammeled, we follow in the footsteps of Franklin Delano Roosevelt and John Fitzgerald Kennedy.

_____   _____

8. When denied entry into the United States, a member of a terrorist organization declared, "I never expected the United States to stoop to take orders from a foreign state."

_____   _____

9. There isn't any reason for all this fuss over the damage our new city dump may do to that residential section over in Bayville. Let me ask you how much attention those Bayville people paid when we tried to get them to locate their waterworks in another place? They didn't give our request a second thought.

_____   _____

10. The talk about safer cars misses the mark. When we get safe drivers we'll have the accident problem licked, and not until then.

_____   _____

11. Softly, softly she sleeps on her *Oceanpearl* mattress. Years of careful craftsmanship have made *Oceanpearl* the perfect complement to slumber.

_____   _____

12. I thought it showed a lot of nerve for one of our national magazines to run that article on the slums of Rio de Janeiro. We'd do well to look at our own back yard, and we got a prompt answer when a Brazilian newspaper published similar pictures of the USA. I hope our editors have learned that pots shouldn't call kettles black.

_____   _____

13. Every unbiased observer recognizes the important contribution this company has made to safer mining.

_____   _____

14. Since nobody can show that the new policies account for the upswing in business, we'll have to find some other explanation for the improvement.

_____   _____

15. Gentlemen of the Jury, before you bring in a verdict of "guilty" against these young defendants, think of some of the things you may have done when you were their age. And even more, think of what it would mean to you if you were their parents, or of how it would be if the word "felon" were stamped on your good name.

_____   _____

chapter 3

Material Fallacies

Material fallacies have in common the urging of a conclusion on the basis of faulty or inadequate material. Here one is invited to accept some sweeping conclusions after the citation of a few facts or, perhaps, a lot of facts which, by not being representative, give a lopsided picture. Or, one may be asked to accept an oversimplification, or to assume that language always describes some meaningful reality: these are but a few of the instances in which the fallacy consists of faulty material. As with the psychological fallacies, it may help to keep in mind the common thread of *weakness in material* that runs through all fallacies in this group. But again, the most practical aid in spotting fallacies is knowing some appropriate names for the individual errors and understanding the way each error works.

17. FAULTY GENERALIZATION

Faulty generalization includes two different sources of error:

1. In hasty generalization, a generalization is formed without enough cases to support it.

2. In unrepresentative generalization, a generalization is formed on the basis of cases not typical of the whole area it covers.

Every person on earth has to generalize his experience by noticing things that happen and forming general rules summing up his experience. These general rules are used to guide future conduct—remember the proverbial burned child who learns to avoid the stove. What is the child's reasoning? He has made a rule, a generalization, which very likely runs like this: "All cases of touching that stove will be painful to me." If this is his rule it is wrong, and he will later learn refinements as to when and how he may touch the stove. When the child grows up to be a scientist, a stock market analyst, a farmer, or whatever, he will still be trying to figure out general rules to guide him in what he is doing.

"That's only a generalization." When this comment indicates, as sometimes it does, the speaker's belief that *all* generalizations are somehow suspect and unreliable, then the comment shows ignorance of what generalizing is all about. If the comment is a protest against sweeping statements made without respectable factual support, then the protest has great merit, though we must forgive the speaker's lack of art in stating his objection. Now let us take a look at what makes a generalization justified. We will do this by imagining a simple situation.

Suppose I hold a hat above you, saying, "Please reach in and take out whatever object you first touch." You know nothing about what is in the hat. Oh, there are negative limits: you know there are no elephants, and your confidence in me has not yet fallen to the point of suspecting the presence of a delicately set mousetrap. So you reach in. The object you first touch and faithfully take out proves to be a white bean. Anticlimax. Now I ask you, "What else is in the hat?" If you are wise, you respond that you don't know. Should you say, "Why, the hat is full of white beans," you have committed the fallacy of hasty generalization even if it turned out you were right. Drawing out and identifying the first thing you touched doesn't entitle you to conclude what all the other objects in this universe—that is, in this hat—will be. Now we can play this game a while longer. You draw out object number two and it is a white bean; number three is a white bean; number four, again, a white bean; number five, a white bean; numbers six through thirty—all white beans. Well, giving you credit for being reasonably bright, you're beginning to suspect that drawing number thirty-one is likely to produce a white bean. Maybe you have been saying to yourself, "Let's get on with it. Anyone can see that the hat is full of white beans." If you are a patient conservative and the thought hasn't yet occurred, I'll guarantee that conclusion will suggest itself somewhere along the line. And when you do form a conclusion about the contents—all the contents—of the hat on the basis of observing *some* of those contents only, you will have taken the *inductive leap*. The inductive leap is the process of generalizing and may be defined as follows:

Making the inductive leap is forming a conclusion about all cases included within a generalization on the basis of observing some of those cases only.

Now, assuming that after the thirtieth drawing you took the inductive leap to conclude "This hat is full of white beans," then again you committed a fallacy.

It's discouraging. This time we'll assume that you have enough cases to avoid the charge of hasty generalization. All the same, you followed instructions to take out the first thing you touched so you sampled only the top layer of whatever is in the hat. If your statement had limited the universe to "objects resting in a position to be touched from the top of the hat," then I would allow your generalization as reasonably well supported. But if you are going to make a conclusion about the entire contents of the hat, and not just the top layer, then you will have to get a sample that is representative of all objects in the hat wherever they may be located. Your device, stirring or reaching around under the top layer or whatever it is, will have to give every object in the hat an equal chance of being selected.

No matter how many objects you draw out, your generalization might turn out to be not quite correct. After drawing 999 white beans out, the 1,000th and last drawing might still produce a black bean or a penny. In other words, the process of taking the inductive leap may approach certainty but will never reach that goal. Logicians attend carefully to the lack of certainty that characterizes induction. We shall come back to the subject. Fortunately, the philosophical uncertainty of induction does not mean there is uncertainty in practical terms— not always, at least. After all, the law of gravity rests upon induction.

Most problems that occupy our thinking are neither as simple as a hat filled with small objects nor as fantastically broad-based as a natural law. Instead of classifying into bean or non-bean, we may be concerned with a less obvious group, say, people who have schizophrenic tendencies. It may be that the cases available for study are not numerous or that their characteristics are not easily measured. Whatever the difficulties, there is no excuse for not knowing what it takes to give **reliable** support to a generalization. So we will state the requirements again:

1. There must be a *sufficient number* of cases to justify taking the "inductive leap."
2. The cases must be *fairly representative* of the generalization made.

It is a fallacy to violate either requirement, and the names chosen direct attention to which requirement is violated:

1. *Hasty generalization* is generalizing without enough cases.
2. *Unrepresentative generalization* is generalizing on the basis of cases that are not representative or typical.

We will come back to the problem of sound generalization for, as you may have noticed, nothing has been said about the situation where the cases are not all one way, or how many cases may be "enough," or by what devices representative cases may be secured. These matters are taken up in Chapter 13. For now, we have said enough to identify faulty generalization in its two branches: hasty generalization and unrepresentative generalization.

18. ASSUMING THE CAUSE: *post hoc* reasoning

Assuming the cause is taking the mere fact that one event precedes another in time as a sufficient proof of a causal relationship between the two events.

This fallacy has been described traditionally with the phrase *post hoc, ergo propter hoc* meaning "after this, therefore on account of this." So we have *post hoc* surviving as a Latin relic in the language. Here is an example of this venerable fallacy at work in the Middle Ages. In about 1350, a perfectly preserved statue by the Greek sculptor Lysippus (c. 372–316 B.C.) was found where it had been carefully buried near Siena, Italy. According to a contemporary account, "Everyone . . . praised it; to each of the great painters that were in Siena at that time it appeared to be of the greatest perfection." But after a short time Siena met with adversity in a war with the Florentines, and the Sienese citizens met in council. "One citizen arose and spoke in this vein of the statue: 'Signore, citizens, consider that since we found this statue we have always been overtaken by misfortune. . . . I am one of those who would recommend taking it down, destroying it entirely, and smashing it, and sending it to be buried in the land of the Florentines.'"[1] And so it was done. The sculpture was lost, alas, because though it had been hidden from barbaric wantonness, it was found again before man's mind had cleared.

Although causes always do precede their effects in time, it is a common error to suppose that a causal relationship is shown just by pointing out that one event followed another. Only a naively ignorant person would believe that the display of a statue was a cause for military reverses. But if a friend, for example, told us that a medicine called "Sniffleless" had cured his cold because he felt much better the day after he had taken some, then we would be better impressed with his argument. Why? Obviously, we are better impressed because taking medicine fits our conception of what may be causally related to recovery. Yet the Sniffleless case no less than the statue case is a clear instance of *assuming the cause*. After all, in the cold situation time went by, and the body cures itself in most cases if left alone. Besides, presumably our friend had supper, kept warm, got a good night's sleep—to list only reasonably relevant things. If Sniffleless scoops up the credit it is because the mind focused on this fact out of several, so there was an *assumption* of the cause, not a proof of it.

It takes a lot of work to establish causal relationship even in simple situations where factors can be isolated and conditions controlled in experiments. Developing the Salk polio vaccine illustrates the rigorous investigation of causation. Though an immense amount of work had to be done, still the effects of that

---

[1] Account of Fra Jacopino del Torchio related to Lorenzo Ghiberti (1378–1455) as published in Elizabeth G. Hold, ed., *A Documentary History of Art*, Vol. 1 (Garden City, N.Y.: Doubleday, 1957), pp. 165–66.

vaccine together with the effects of alternate vaccines all were eventually determined satisfactorily enough.

To assume a cause is a fallacy. Neither the fact that the cause assumed seems plausible nor that it would be difficult to produce satisfactory evidence permits one to announce a cause merely by making a likely choice among prior events. Where it is hard to do what we want, at least we can know what we are doing. The fallacy of *post hoc* reasoning can be avoided by asserting that *we assume* so and so is the cause. We do not say it *is* the cause. Indicating uncertainty is a favor all around, for everybody benefits by recognizing a shaky foundation.

19. MISUSE OF HYPOTHESIS CONTRARY TO FACT

A misuse of hypothesis contrary to fact occurs when one represents as sure to happen an outcome of what is in truth a mere speculation.

When discussion waxes hot over some event in history or politics or our personal lives, claims are apt to be made about what would have happened if something had been done differently in the past. "If the incumbent senator had voted for the treaty, then he would have been re-elected" is the kind of statement we have in mind. We shall never know for sure whether this assessment is correct, for it is a hypothetical situation. We may speculate to our heart's content and possibly with profit in such matters—providing a word like "might" or "in my opinion" accompanies the speculation. These are terribly feeble words to use in argument, however. Perhaps this is why "would" creeps in instead. It is a fallacy to assert as sure to occur something that rests on a tissue of uncertainty.

What about statements for which the computations are mechanical and there is no real doubt? Are we to suppose that the engineers who compute the force needed to return a spaceship from the moon should look up from their labors to say modestly, "If we succeed in producing this amount of thrust, the spaceship might get back"? Should the mother who wants to be ethical in warning Johnny not to play on the railroad tracks say, "If the Red Ball Express runs over you, you might get killed"? In mechanical or lead-pipe-cinch situations in which natural laws apply, it would be insufferable quibbling to argue against "would" being applied to the prediction.

It is well to have a harness for speculations all the same. The use of the word "alleged" to indicate that responsibility is not assumed for the truth of a statement is similar to what we are trying to avoid here, for confusing speculation with certainty is the essence of a *misuse of hypothesis contrary to fact*. "Would" is an illegitimate claim wherever the hypothetical situation is anything but mechanical and obvious, while "might" insulates against the fallacy by conceding that the point is a matter of conjecture.

20. FALLACIOUS EXTENSION

Fallacious extension is exaggerating an opponent's argument with an unjustified implication that the opponent's position entails a defense of the exaggerated position also.

It's a handy thing, when your opponent will let you do it, to drag him off the subject to some more extreme and less defensible position and annihilate him there. If the extended position is absurd, all the better, provided debate can be shifted over to this ground and your opponent be made to defend it. This book is being written for ethical people, however, and not as a manual for persuading an audience by unfair means. We will concentrate on what a fallacious extension is and how to rebut one when it appears in argument.

Taking account of precedents has to be distinguished from fallacious extension. Good judgment requires one to notice where an action sets a precedent for other claims falling under the same principle. Fallacious extensions, however, differ at precisely this point, for they do *not* fall under the same principle; rather they distort the original argument by claiming that it covers matters that it does not necessarily include. Some examples will illustrate the difference between unwarranted extension and a legitimate precedent:

Example 1

> A: The United States should withdraw a part of its forces from Europe. This commitment is a tremendous expense, a drain on the balance of payments, and a reduction of the commitment might stimulate European states to assume more of the burden of their own defense.
>
> B: Nothing would encourage Communist aggression more than for the United States to withdraw from Europe or to maintain only a token force there.

This kind of case, in which the original position is misstated, is a common sort of fallacious extension. "A" advocated neither complete withdrawal nor reduction to a token force and, of course, he should point this out. If "A" is unskillful enough to allow "B's" extension to go unchallenged, then he will be out on a limb far from his original proposal.

Example 2

> A: We should adopt city refuse collection in this town. The change should provide a more regular service and end the temptation to dispose of refuse improperly or to accumulate it in homes.
>
> B: Well, if the city takes on refuse collection, next it will be hauling leaves in the fall and plowing driveways in winter. It isn't wise for the town to keep finding more and more things for the government to do.

The red-road-to-socialism argument is a familiar—and typical—extension. Although "B" can make a legitimate point of the proper sphere for government activity, usually it is best to resolve problems on their own merits. Certainly "A" need not agree to the spectre of undertaking a list of activities which he has not proposed. Though "hauling leaves" is at least a type of refuse disposal, "plowing driveways" is far afield and can only confuse orderly discussion. "A" can readily distinguish the extraneous matters or, better, simply state that they are not necessary consequences of the proposal and return to the special situation he is trying to solve.

Example 3

> A: Mr. Mayor, our department store has been operating in this city for 55 years and we now have 204 people on our payroll. As you know, the company is in a most serious financial state, and we simply have to get some tax relief if we are to avoid bankruptcy. So I am forced to ask you to support our request for a 40% tax rebate until the company ceases to operate at a loss.
>
> B: Yes, as mayor I am much concerned about the trouble your business is in. It's trouble for me, too. But I cannot support special tax relief for you. I couldn't justify helping one business and not another, and the city could not afford the practice to become a rule.

No fallacy here. The mayor must be careful of the precedents he sets, and likelihood of other requests for tax relief on the same ground does not distort the situation as did the extensions in Examples 1 and 2.

21. FALSE ANALOGY

A false analogy is an argument resting on a comparison of two situations that are essentially different.

Drawing analogies is one of the commonest ways of thinking about new problems. Unfortunately, it is also one of the most abused ways. To avoid false analogies, one must begin by understanding when two situations are comparable in a logical sense. A sound literal analogy exists when—and only when—two situations are compared which have:

1. A number of essential similarities within the area of comparison, and
2. An absence of essential differences within the area of comparison

A great deal of thinking is analogical. The mechanic may work on one machine by applying his knowledge of similar machines with which he is familiar; the medical researcher experiments with animals with a view to applying what he discovers to humans; the lawyer argues that his case should be decided according to a rule which was applied to a similar case in the past. The analogies in these situations range from strong to weak according to how well they fulfill the requirements of (1) possessing essential similarities within the area of comparison and of (2) not having essential differences within the area of comparison.

Very different is a *figurative* analogy, in which resemblances are merely figurative. Life, for instance, may be compared to a river, for life moves inexorably through time as a river flows unceasingly to its destination. Life begins small and with bounding energy; characteristically, it creeps sluggishly to its end after a long course, as rivers frequently do. To assert that life is like a river may be a colorful way to convey one's feelings, but since the resemblances are merely figurative, we cannot reason that some feature we know about rivers—say, annual floods—will be found correspondingly in life.

Three kinds of mistakes—two common and one rare—are made through failure to observe the requirements for sound use of analogy. The *first* is taking figurative resemblances which do not satisfy the requirement of "essential similarities within the respect compared" and treating such a comparison as a basis for argument. A *second* mistake is to reason on the basis of "essential similarities within the respect compared" without noticing that the particular situation involves essential differences also. A *third* and rather rare fault is proposing that an analogy establishes a conclusion with a high degree of reliability, whereas a further correspondence on the basis even of the best analogy is only reasonably probable.

The practical importance of analogy makes it desirable to consider analogical reasoning at some length. This is done in Chapter 16.

EXERCISES FOR THE FIRST HALF OF CHAPTER 3
pages 36–43

I.   Answer **T** for "true" or **F** for "false":

_____ **1.** The saying "That is only a generalization" correctly reflects the fact that generalizations are weak.

_____ **2.** The "inductive leap" involves forming a conclusion about *all cases* on the basis of observing some of the cases only.

_____ **3.** Since the process of forming a generalization involves the "inductive leap," logic holds no generalization to be certainly true.

_____ **4.** Some generalizations are reliable.

_____ **5.** Where a generalization rests upon the examination of a great many cases it is sure to be reliable.

_____ **6.** No matter how many cases are examined, it is always possible for the next case to be different from the group examined. Consequently, no generalization is reliable.

_____ **7.** No fallacy of *post hoc* reasoning is committed where the cause assumed is in fact the true cause.

_____ **8.** A cause always precedes its effect.

_____ **9.** *Post hoc* reasoning asserts a causal relationship merely on the basis that the alleged cause did precede the effect.

_____ **10.** Logic holds it to be a fallacy to advance a hypothesis contrary to fact.

_____ **11.** To test a policy by extending it to another situation to which the same principle applies is not a fallacious extension.

_____ **12.** One may reason by analogy whenever one finds two situations that have a number of essential similarities in the respects compared.

_____ **13.** Within the area of eugenics—i.e., the laws of heredity—a mouse and a human being are too different to support a strong literal analogy.

_____ **14.** A figurative analogy may be a colorful way to illustrate a point but it is not support for any conclusion.

_____ **15.** It is always possible for even a strong literal analogy to break down through failure of the expected further correspondence to occur.

II.   Provide short answers for these questions:

1. What are the two types of faulty generalization?

2. Why does logic hold no generalization to be certainly true?

3. Explain the difference between asserting that something is "true" and asserting that it is "reliable."

4. How can the fallacy of *post hoc* reasoning be committed when the conclusion asserted is in fact correct?

5. How can one present a hypothesis contrary to fact without being vulnerable to a charge of fallacy?

6. Explain the difference between a fallacious extension and an extension that is justifiable.

7. What conditions must exist between two things or situations in order for them to be literally analogous within the respect compared?

8. What is the difference between a literal analogy and a figurative analogy?

9. What legitimate use can be made of a figurative analogy?

III.   Each of the following passages contains a clear instance of one of the fallacies discussed on pages 36–43. Some passages contain an additional fallacy as well. Spot the fallacy or fallacies in each case and fill in the blank from memory.

1. We wouldn't have gotten so deeply involved in Vietnam if President Kennedy had lived.

_____   _____

2. Before Alfred Stoss became company president, the firm had 100 employees and annual gross sales of $5,000,000. In four years those figures have more than doubled. Stoss certainly has done great things for the business.

_____   _____

3. Safer cars! Why some people want us to build veritable Sherman tanks so you can play dodge-'em on the highways and not get hurt.

_____   _____

4. You say you would fight if somebody attacked your mother? I can agree with that, all right. But just don't bother claiming to me that you have conscientious objections to war.

_____   _____

5. *Idle Moment* is an insipid play. In fact, but for the notoriety of the leading actor's private life it would be playing before half-empty houses instead of the shamefully full ones that it is getting.

_____   _____

6. A state is like a person in many ways. It owns property, it carries on business, it protects its own interests when the need arises. Indeed, states are similar to people in using both peaceful means and violence to attain their ends. Since the individual who resorts to violence is punished for breaking the law, we ought to punish states when they wage aggressive wars.

_____   _____

7. During his two-week trip to Japan, our Consul-General enjoyed an official welcome from the Japanese government, and in the course of his stay he took the opportunity to visit officials in practically every level of the administration. He has come home with a keen realization that the Japanese people hold the most cordial feelings toward Americans.

_____   _____

8. It is unwise to change horses in the middle of a stream. I suggest we look at the crisis in our symphony orchestra with this lesson in mind. With all the public criticism both of the programs and of the personal conflict between the conductor and many of the players, it strikes me that this is no time to set about changing the leadership.

_____   _____

9. Most of the people of this town are against locating the new firehouse on the site proposed on Chapel Street. Letters are three to one against it in the local paper, and the neighborhood is up in arms.

_____   _____

10. If you favor stopping people from getting their fix with drugs, then you ought to stop people from drinking hard liquor—and from smoking, too, for that matter.

_____   _____

11. Our sewing-machine sales are down. If the company had spent as much money advertising this year as it did last, that wouldn't have happened.

_____   _____

12. When my car acted the way yours is acting now, it needed a new coil. So I'm positive that's your problem.

_____   _____

22. COMPOSITION and DIVISION

Composition is reasoning that the characteristics possessed by the various parts will be found also in an organized whole.

Division is reasoning that the characteristics found in an organized whole will be possessed by the various parts.

Composition and division are like Tweedledum and Tweedledee. It's easy to get mixed up as to which is which. The important thing is to recognize that it is a mistake to reason either way—that because some parts have a certain quality, a resulting whole will have the same quality; or that because a whole has some characteristic, the individual parts will share it also.

Let's take a clear case of composition. A new house is being built on the edge of town and the local lumberyard is delighted with the business. The best wood, the best roofing material, the best pipe, the best of everything. "That must be a wonderful house they're building out there," exclaims the lumberman. Next day he drives by with his wife. "Gosh, I wouldn't live in the place!" he remarks. Here the parts are excellent. But, of course, a house isn't boards, pipe, concrete, etc., piled up in the yard. It's how these things are put together that makes the entity—that is, the house. Obviously, if the design is poor or the workmanship sloppy, then the good-quality materials will not produce a good-quality house.

Let's look at some more important cases. Consider the cardinal assumption of Adam Smith's *laissez faire*—namely, that if each individual is free to seek his own greatest individual gain, then the total productivity of society will be at a maximum. Does a multitude of individually oriented productions necessarily add up to the greatest total production possible? Or, if a tariff on meat benefits the ranchers, a tariff on coal benefits the coal miners, a tariff on toys benefits the toy manufacturers, etc., does it follow that a tariff on everything benefits everybody? *Why* not?

Division is easily illustrated. If a university is distinguished as a whole, one can't assume that every department in it has a strong faculty. An expensive car may not possess parts of the highest quality at every point. So we see, it does not follow either way: a whole does not necessarily share the quality of its parts, nor does it follow that each part possesses the quality of the whole.

23. FALSE DILEMMA

Creating a false dilemma is representing the situation as offering only undesirable alternatives when the facts do not warrant this.

True dilemmas, in which one must choose between undesirable alternatives, are all too common. To have this operation is dangerous; not to have it is to risk illness or even death. To study tonight is to give up the party; not to study is to risk flunking the test. To go to the party *and* study is to give up all sleep. As long as it is true that one must accept a disadvantage whichever way one turns, there is a true dilemma.

Debaters love the chance to corner someone in a dilemma. But before being overwhelmed by the apparent disadvantages, one has to look around for a way of escape, and where an escape can be found then a false dilemma has been created. The most common escape is to show that there is another alternative which is not a disadvantage and, because of this, no dilemma exists. The legendary Ulysses contrived such an alternative to deal with the sirens who, with irresistably beautiful singing, lured sailors to their death. Ulysses had his crew plug their ears so that the crew avoided the fatal seduction, but incurred the disadvantage of the dilemma by missing the wondrous singing. Ulysses escaped the dilemma by ordering himself bound to the mast so that he could enjoy the singing and yet not be lured to his death.

Sometimes a dilemma can be dealt with by showing that one of the alternatives is beneficial rather than undesirable. Abbé Sieyès, a leader in the French Revolution, posed this famous dilemma concerning a bicameral legislature: "If the second chamber agrees with the first, it is superfluous; if it disagrees, it is pernicious." A moment's thought shows the falseness of this dilemma since disagreement of the second chamber is not necessarily "pernicious." Far from being a disadvantage, the device of a bicameral legislature is in widespread use for its merit in providing a check against ill-considered action or the tyranny of a temporary majority. One should always question the assumptions of a dilemma—namely, that the alternatives are exhausted or that all the alternatives are undesirable.

Occasionally one encounters a pleasant dilemma, in which the choices are competing delights. From the standpoint of argument, pleasant dilemmas are so unimportant that we have concentrated upon the more common type.

24. BLACK-OR-WHITE FALLACY: the great either . . . or

The black-or-white fallacy is assuming that only two choices exist when more than two are available.

Sometimes truth is a matter of black or white; sometimes it ranges through a whole spectrum of colors. One catches the ferryboat or fails to catch it; an electric light is "on" or it is "off." There is no middle ground. On the other hand, a government is never simply "good" or "bad," for here the range of possibilities is infinite. When a situation requires a relative judgment, it is a fallacy to wrap it up into a single bundle hastily labeled Black or White, All or Nothing, Good or Bad. This kind of thinking peoples the mind with simple heros and villains instead of characters that are true to life.

Black-or-white thinking asserts a naked dichotomy where no such simplification is warranted. Mr. Justice Frankfurter called this "the great either... or." The assumption that there is no middle ground is a favorite weapon of persons who want to force others to take sides in black-or-white terms even though the problem is not simple and its fair solution requires an evaluation of several possibilities. Fanaticism is not the child of doubt. Hitler takes shrewd account of this in discussing propaganda:

> The task of propaganda is, for example, not a weighing of the various rights, but the exclusive emphasis of the one advocated by it. It has not to inquire objectively into the truth, so far as it favors the other sides, in order to represent it to the masses in doctrinary honesty, but it has to serve its own side continuously. . . .

> This feeling [i.e., the thinking of the masses] is not complicated, but very simple and conclusive. There are not many differentiations, but a positive or a negative, love or hate, right or wrong, truth or lie, but never half so and half so, partially, etc.[2]

It would be wrong to think of black-or-white thinking as a problem confined to propaganda situations. No one can wholly avoid this fallacy of treating complex things as if they could be divided into simple extremes. The usual shortness of time and the desire not to clutter thinking with all possible qualifications presses everybody to sharpen evaluations into "good" or "bad," which is not entirely defensible.

Perhaps the most trying aspect of this fallacy comes where an unambiguous decision must be made even though a twofold classification is unrealistic. Doctors squirm when the lawyer demands whether or not a certain individual is sane or insane. Medicine is more complicated than the gates of an asylum, yet someone must know whether he is to swing those gates open or shut. The voter must choose between candidates though he agrees with no one of them entirely; the legislator will answer "aye" or "nay" to bills whose details seem full of flaws. These trying situations do not exemplify black-or-white thinking in the sense of mistaken reasoning, for the instances cited here presuppose a recognition of the difficulties, of the shades along the spectrum. Not to understand that there are shades is the true mark of an all-or-nothing mentality.

A couple of examples will show this fallacy at work. In considering what motivation, if any, is induced by prizes I once suggested to a prize committee that honor often is a more important motivation than money. "You mean that the money doesn't matter?" queried a committee member.

The Communist Manifesto ends with a ringing use of black-or-white thinking:

[2]Adolf Hitler, *Mein Kampf* (Munich: Franz Eher Nachfolger, 1934), pp. 200–201. English translation by W. Ward Fearnside.

The proletarians have nothing to lose but their chains. They have a world to win.

Workers of the world, unite!

One is tempted to reply:

Proletarians! Lives, property, freedom may be lost. The world may be less than "won."

The reply is reasonable. But let no one underestimate the power of a slogan.

25. ARGUMENT OF THE BEARD: one more doesn't matter

The argument of the beard is contending that "one more doesn't matter" in a situation where a line has to be drawn on a continuum.

The word "continuum" refers to situations where there is a continuous gradation of small steps from one condition to another. Hair by hair, one moves from clean-shaven to bearded, and, so long as nothing of consequence is at stake, the selection of a dividing point will stir no more than an amiable smile. But woe unto he who must make an important decision that turns upon the difference of a hair! What separates the reasonable from the unreasonable in disputes over the dividing point on a continuum?

Through all the vast difference between one end of a spectrum and the other, the difference between its various shadings remains infinitesimal. We grow old day by day, temperatures rise in a continuous sequence, pound by pound the ship loads cargo from empty to overloaded, day shades into night. The practical affairs of life absolutely require breaking into such sequences. The child must begin school at a certain age, he can marry at another, join the army at another, vote at another, run for U.S. Senator at another, get Social Security at another, and so on. These are only some of the lines drawn across the continuum of our lives. They have one thing in common: all are arbitrary. Now, "arbitrary" in this sense means that the rules are matters of human convenience, not that they are unfair. There is no principle involved in whether the line 16, 17, 17 1/2, or whatever is taken as the age required in order to become a licensed driver. The line is arbitrary; it has to be. If it turns out to be a poor choice then some other arbitrary point along the age continuum can be selected instead.

Whether the point at which a continuum is broken into is a wise choice for the distinction made is always open for debate before a proper authority. It's hardly fair to debate the point with some enforcement agent who can't change matters. If the enforcement agent happens to be a burly cop—well, tact as well as logic counts in this world. Besides, logic may demand that the line be enforced. Let's see.

The essence of the *argument of the beard* fallacy is the contention that *one more doesn't matter*. The most extreme form of the fallacy occurs where there is a suggestion that the fact of a continuum situation makes *any* distinction at some definite point along the line unreasonable. To take a consequential example, racial discrimination has a long and sorry history. Sometimes opponents of discrimination adopt the tactic of ridiculing the hair-splitting distinctions that arise concerning the products of mixed marriages for, as everybody knows, races shade into one another as people intermarry.[3] No race is "pure" and, I suspect, no person on earth, in the unlikely case he knew his complete genealogy, would find only a single racial stock in his ancestry. Still, races do exist. The sound attack against racial discrimination is not questioning the existence of races by ridiculing borderline situations, for hairline instances on either side of the chosen point will exist whenever a continuum is broken into, to make some distinction. The sound attack here is that *no point* of discrimination on a racial basis is justifiable.

There are many situations where a single point along a continuum *must* be chosen and rigidly kept. No one a day under the specified age can expect to be registered as a voter. Here a line has to be drawn and held absolutely. In other cases, say in the case of the number of students who may enroll in a class, complete rigidity may not be necessary. Though it may seem pedantic, the proper argument is not that one more does not matter. The argument properly is whether or not, under the circumstances, the line of division is to be kept. *Somewhere* one will have to hold the line. The biblical account of the destruction of Sodom is a fine example of this problem.

When Jehovah determines to destroy Sodom for the sinfulness of its inhabitants, Abraham proposes that the city be spared if fifty righteous inhabitants can be found therein. Jehovah agrees. Evidently Abraham reflects that this may be a difficult mark, so he proposes:

> Peradvanture there shall lack five of the fifty righteous: wilt thou destroy all the city for the lack of five? And He said, if I find there forty and five, I will not destroy it.

---

[3]The bare outline of Nazi anti-Semitic distinctions provides an enlightening-depressing illustration of the problem. When the Nazi regime embarked upon its notorious discriminations against Jews, it had to answer the question, "Who is a Jew?" The famous Nuremberg Laws provided a definition. Under these laws Jewishness was determined according to the race of the four grandparents and *each grandparent was counted either as a Jew or a non-Jew*. This fiction ruled out noticing whatever mixed ancestry a grandparent might have; genealogical research would establish according to apparent Hebrew descent and adherence to the Jewish religious community that a grandparent was to count as Jew or non-Jew. Accordingly, every individual could be classified as full Jew, three-quarter Jew, half Jew, one-quarter Jew, or non-Jew. Different legal discriminations applied to each of these classes. Again, the fault lies not in defining borderline cases but in the baselessness of discrimination in any case.

But the dickering goes on. Abraham proposes forty, then thirty, then twenty, finally ten. To all this Jehovah assents. At ten the final line is firmly drawn. Unhappily, there are not ten, and Sodom is razed with fire and brimstone.

26. LEADING QUESTIONS

A leading question seeks to influence the answer, usually by making it easier to respond in one way than in another.

Leading questions are of several types, and fallacy results whenever the leading character of such a question influences the answer. In a way this influence is akin to the deflection of thought by emotive language. But not wholly so. Some leading questions rely upon the desire to agree by doing what seems expected, while others are pitfalls to tumble into before the implications of the answer are perceived. Understanding how such questions work helps in resisting them. Here, most briefly, are four types:

1. The phrasing of the question may suggest the answer: "You wouldn't go to Waterman Park, would you?" "Say, it's thirty days before you can order a postal tracer, isn't it?" Such questions lull the person questioned into not doing his own thinking. "Would you go to Waterman Park?" "When can one order a postal tracer?" In this form the questions offer no cues to the answer and are not leading.
2. The question may assume a fact not yet established: "Where did you take your date before you went home?" is leading unless the assumption that the date was not taken directly home already has been determined. Questions that assume certain states of affairs trap the unwary into admissions or tempt the questioned party to commit a small lie in line with what is assumed.
3. A question may be phrased to raise an unintended implication unless it is skillfully answered: "Have you stopped your heavy betting?" is an old cracker of this sort where either a "yes" or a "no" answer carries an unfavorable implication. Nobody is obligated to answer questions in a single word. "I never have been a heavy better" refutes the unwelcome implication.[4]
4. It is leading for the questioner to supply all the details needed in the answer so that the party questioned need only ratify the description already given. As a witness to a will I was once asked "Is it true that the testator acknowl-

---

[4]The popular impression that courts unreasonably confine witnesses to respond with "yes" or "no" is largely unfounded. Any unreasonableness is more apt to be the other way around, for witnesses who are evasive, excited, or merely dull tend to produce a fog of explanation instead of responding with an unequivocal answer. To save time and to prevent obfuscation a court occasionally may order a witness to answer "yes" or "no" to a particular question where the question asked calls for no more.

edged to you that this was his will, that he signed it first, and after that you and all the other witnesses signed without anybody leaving the room until the signing was completed?" Here the examining lawyer, rather than myself as witness, was supplying the details for a validly executed will.

Sometimes a statement that is not a question can be leading—for example, "Don't let the court coddle criminals" leads one to suppose that the court has been doing so and directs effort toward deciding whether to let the practice continue, rather than to questioning the supposition. This example and the others that have been given are fairly strong and therefore objectionable. On the other hand, one need not be a stickler who is aroused by the slightest leading influence, for any dialogue is apt to contain material that is technically leading. For example, the innocent query, "What would you like for dessert?" leads in the way set forth in (2) above, because it assumes what has not been established—that is, that you want to have a dessert.

27. BEGGING THE QUESTION

Begging the question is assuming what should be proved. The question may be begged by a definition, by circular reasoning, by assuming the conclusion, or by certain words such as "too" or "reasonable."

Question begging is a slippery fallacy. It has various forms, like several kinds of fish in a pond: some are harder to catch than others, but all are slippery.

Begging the question by definition is one common sort. No use talking about a question if a definition already contains the answer. Suppose Mr. A asserts, "A good team does not rely upon one or two stars." Mr. B, who has doubts about this being a satisfactory criterion, counters, "Maybe what you say is usually so, but Ned Battleman is credited with being the player resonsible for the Ranger's undefeated record this year." "Well," replies A, "I don't call that a really good team then." Here the contrary case is being ruled out by A's definition, so nothing remains to be discussed.

Circular reasoning is a much more difficult fish to land. A tight circle swinging right back to the beginning point is obvious—and not likely to happen. Here is a sample: " 'Good' is what a person of good will approves, and such a person seeks socially constructive action. Actions are socially constructive when they serve the general welfare, which is, of course, to benefit all. That all of society is served is the best indication of what is good." The full circle here may be too abrupt to deceive. Scatter the assertions through a paragraph or more, and the circularity becomes hard to trace.

"I oppose excessive penalties for drug abuse," declares Judge Grass. "So do I," agrees Mr. Pot, "but the question is *what* is 'excessive'? No one can defend a position stated as "too much," "inordinate," "outrageous," "undesirable," and so on. Nor can one challenge a position favoring what is "reasonable," "sound," "desirable," or the like. Transparently question-begging words like these, however, will harm discussion only where they are passed over, for each one offers a good springboard for getting at the issue: "What is excessive?" "What is reasonable?" and so on.

28. OVERSIMPLIFICATION: tabloid thinking

Oversimplification refers to reducing discussion of a complicated situation to simple descriptions that are inaccurate.

As one wit remarked, there always is one simple solution that is wrong! Would that oversimplification were as simple as this!

"Tabloid thinking," "capsule thinking," "headline thinking" are other names applied to this fallacy. I suspect that any long discussion of the fallacy itself would be unwarranted; the difficulty is largely in knowing enough about particular situations to reject oversimplifications where they occur. And tolerance is needed for the simplifier if not the oversimplifier. Let's see what is meant by this.

The error of oversimplification is hard to avoid. In the first place, time generally makes it impractical to elaborate all qualifications. Moreover, in many discussions full exposition of detail would obscure matters rather than clarify them. For example, textbook writers habitually wrestle with the dilemma of whether to make statements that are, though not wholly accurate, yet clear and serviceable enough for students, or whether to incorporate all the qualifications necessary to fend against possible criticism from professional colleagues. Students shouldn't be drowned in details, nor should they be fed a sort of false clarity. Its a nice balance.

In the second place, when one does not possess a detailed knowledge, the very lack of familiarity with the complexity of the subject is apt to increase confidence in what are mere "tabloid" thoughts about it. Thus, a superficial knowledge can make a complicated situation appear quite simple, as the adage "A little learning is a dangerous thing" reminds us. Finally, even when one is aware of the existence of complexities, there is the temptation in "the human quest for certainty," as John Dewey argues, to try to cut through them and to set up an oversimplified system with everything tidy and neat.

Illustrate oversimplifications? They flourish in daily speech. "Freud teaches that everything is sex," "Hard work is the key to success," and so on. Slogans and headlines almost invariably are oversimplifications—they *have* to be by their very brevity. The pairs of conflicting adages found in the language are interesting illustrations: "Look before you leap" and "He who hesitates is lost"; "Out of sight, out of mind" and "Absence makes the heart grow fonder"; "Two's company, three's a crowd" and "The more the merrier"; "Never leave until tomorrow what you can do today" and "Act in haste and repent at leisure." What goes on here? Each of these is a pithy sentence summing up some common human experience, and each has its appropriate applications. That old saws of this sort are not truths in themselves is clear from the fact that the adages contradict one another. Consequently, citing an adage is not persuasive until it is clear that the saying applies to the situation.

29. WORD MAGIC

Word Magic is the assumption that the existence of a word or phrase assures the existence of the thing the word describes.

This fallacy is called *Word Magic* because if one needed but coin a word and, lo, *the thing it names would exist*, then words would have a magical power. Words are not like Aladdin's lamp, alas. Just by creating the word we cannot be sure the genie will appear. We have words for "potato" and "mermaid" and "luck." Which ones are Word Magic and which are not?

Word Magic is a fun fallacy and more of a challenge than most. Of all the material fallacies, this one is the biggest joke—the handing out of an empty package or, more puzzling, handing out a package that defies investigation as to whether it is empty or not. Of course, when you think of it, it's pretty evident that some words do not designate things that exist. We've been all over the world without finding any unicorns, for instance. There are no purple cows. Granted, it was natural enough for unsophisticated and little-traveled people of the past to believe in the strange creatures of myth and imagination. The medieval copyist who believed in the existence of the fanciful animals he illustrated in a bestiary can be reproached at most for carelessness in his acceptance of authority. One reads with bemusement of Jason seeking the Golden Fleece—and finding it; the Knights of the Round Table going on a quest for the Holy Grail, and Ponce de Leon slogging through the swamps of Florida in pursuit of the Fountain of Youth. My bemusement turns into amazement when I read of a modern expedition searching high on the slopes of Mt. Ararat for remnants of Noah's Ark.[5] Assumed correspondence of word and thing in these tangible instances is more a matter of ignorance than of the Word Magic we are interested in.

Witchcraft has gone out of Salem. Marvelous though the notions are, we need not give serious thought to enchantment, sorcery, omens, ghosts, clairvoyance, hexes, voodoo, exorcising spirits, Black Magic, and the whole rubric of the powers of darkness. *It is not for the logician to announce that any one of the above*

---

[5]Mt. Ararat's 16,946 feet make its extension above the waters understandable.

does not exist. What we are noting here is that words or phrases do not *guarantee* existence to what they designate. No Word Magic occurs in a discussion about centaurs or hexes when everyone is clear on the point that the names for these phenomena are no evidence that the phenonena ever occur.

Physical objects such as a "unicorn" are fundamentally different from alleged magical states like "bewitched." However unlikely, if ever I meet a unicorn I shall know it. But if the old hag or beautiful damsel behaves strangely, is she bewitched? If a comet appears and something happens on earth, is this proof of the comet's being an omen? So you see, the unicorn and the witch stand in different circles: one is verifiable in principle while the other is not.

Now it is time to move to things in which many people still believe. Take the sentence, "The Jews are achieving their destiny in Palestine." That the state of Israel exists is undeniable. Is that fact a matter of *destiny*? What does it mean to attribute the quality of "destiny" to an event? The word evidently has a magical use, for people speak of a destiny being unfulfilled. When a thing happens or fails to happen in this world, how is one to recognize that the event was touched by destiny? No conceivable experience would verify the reality of this claim. Where language conjures up notions that elude confirmation by their very nature, then we have stepped into the true domain of Word Magic. Maybe there is destiny in the Scheme of Things. We shall never know.

"Fate" is in the same category as destiny. So strong is this notion for some people, particularly throughout the Islamic world, that it inhibits action to combat the evils of this life. Whatever happens has been fated by the will of God, so why mount a puny human struggle against the inevitable? Lines from Matthew Arnold's *Sohrab and Rustum* proclaim the belief:

> For some are born to do great deeds and live,
> And some are born to be obscured and die.

Next we come to "luck" who gathers around the gaming tables. If this reference merely is a way of saying, "Player A is benefiting by a greater number of favorable throws of the dice than normal expectancy promises," then the reference to "luck" is a shorthand way of saying a rather complicated though readily understandable thing. For instance, to sit down and roll double six on three consecutive castings is not a common experience. On the other hand, *any* series of rolls may contain three rolls of double six even though the odds are 46,656 to 1 against its happening. No mystical explanation is needed for the occurrence of long odds. So if by "luck" the gambler means only that events favorable to his interest have been happening, there is no magical use of the term. Future rollings remain free and there is no reason to continue the game because "luck" is around, or discontinue it on a belief that "bad luck" has taken over. But those who believe in luck as a sort of force mysteriously helping or hindering the players are believers in *Word Magic*. One can only tap on wood and cast a counterspell.

Familiarity with Word Magic suggests that since words present questionable concepts as well as true ones, one should maintain a certain skepticism. Some mighty ideas may be no more than Word Magic. Among them I would include Hitler's master race and the inevitable progression suggested by Marx's dialectic. I may be right or wrong. In any case, one has to pick and choose unswayed by the magic of words.

BARE ASSERTION vs. FALLACY

A bare assertion is a statement offered without evidence to support its truth.

The study of fallacy directs attention to whether what passes as support for a conclusion actually does so. This focus makes it natural to look upon bare assertions which offer no evidence at all in support of a conclusion as somehow fallacious. A little thought will show that this is not so.

A fallacy is a mistake in reasoning. A bare assertion cannot be a mistake in reasoning since the assertion is "bare"—no reasoning is offered. Suppose someone declares, "The recent wage increases are adding to inflation." This is a bare assertion. The person making it may have an enormous amount of evidence he could produce to support it, or he may have some evidence, or he may have none at all. We don't know his reasons because, whatever they are, he has not taken time to state them. And so long as we don't know what his argument is, we cannot complain that it is fallacious.

A bare assertion has one thing in common with a fallacy, however. In either case the conclusion rests unsupported. Where fallacy exists one has to resist the temptation to let the mind form the link *fallacy* and *false conclusion*. When one notices a fallacy, then one knows that the conclusion urged is not supported by *that argument*. Also, to notice that an assertion is bare is to notice that the conclusion has not been supported. In either case, one who decides to accept the conclusion will have to find his own reasons for doing so.

Everyone makes many bare assertions for the good reason that many things are obvious and, in any case, no one has time to produce evidence in support of everything he says. As audience members we are, so to speak, consumers of bare assertions. Often we can understand in a flash that *we* have reasons of our own to accept such an assertion. Or, we may accept a bare assertion because we trust the speaker as an authority. If so, we let the matter pass. But what if we *don't* know anything to support a bare assertion and we are unwilling to accept it merely on the speaker's say-so? Then, obviously, we must ask what support there is for the notion or, if we cannot inquire, then we will make a mental note that we find no reason for believing it.

EXERCISES FOR THE SECOND HALF OF CHAPTER 3
pages 48–58

I.   Answer **T** for "true" or **F** for "false":

_____   **1.** The fallacy of composition means that a whole does not possess the quality of its parts.

_____   **2.** If a proposed dilemma does not acknowledge some alternative that is available, then it is a false dilemma.

_____   **3.** A bare assertion offers no evidence and, therefore, is a fallacy.

_____   **4.** One may argue properly that an arbitrary line in a continuum is poorly chosen.

_____   **5.** Hairline instances on either side of the point chosen for breaking into a continuum situation necessarily exist.

_____   **6.** Sometimes, but not always, it is a practical necessity to strictly follow the arbitrary "cutoff" point along a continuum without exception.

_____   **7.** A black-or-white fallacy occurs when only two extremes are recognized, although other possibilities exist.

_____   **8.** Whenever an individual—or a whole society—lacks knowledge of the many ramifications of a problem, the result is apt to be an oversimplified view of the situation.

_____   **9.** When a word designates a notion that cannot be confirmed in principle, then we know that the notion may be mere *word magic*.

_____   **10.** Where a word or phrase is identified as word magic, then one can be sure that the notion it stands for does not exist.

_____   **11.** There is no fallacy of word magic when all parties to the discussion understand that the word or phrase being employed creates no implication that the notion it stands for exists.

_____   **12.** The term "flying saucers" is Word Magic.

II.   Provide short answers to these questions:

1. State two ways for rebutting a false dilemma.

2. Why is there a common tendency to think in black-or-white terms?

3. Question #2 above is a leading question. What makes it so?

4. Cite instances to illustrate each of the following situations:

    a. An instance for which it would not be necessary to apply without exception a distinction or cutoff point along the line of a continuum.

    b. An instance for which it would be a practical necessity to apply rigidly and without exception whatever cutoff point was chosen along the line of a continuum.

5. State as many types of leading questions as you can. (The text lists four types, pp. 53–54.)

6. Circular reasoning often is hard to detect. Why so?

7. "A little learning is a dangerous thing" points to the danger of oversimplification. Explain the link between "little learning" and oversimplification.

8. Illustrate each of the following:

    a. A situation that is confirmable in principle but not in practice.

    b. A situation that is not confirmable even in principle.

III.   Each of the following passages contains a clear instance of one of the fallacies discussed on pages 48–58. Some passages contain an additional fallacy as well. Spot the fallacy or fallacies in each case and fill in the blank from memory. If you cannot recall the name applied to the fallacy in this book, make up an appropriate name of your own.

1. A company is as good as the people who run it.

_____   _____

2. They cracked down on our truck for being 288 lbs overweight. That's the most unreasonable thing I ever heard of. Why, in the trucking business, 288 lbs doesn't amount to anything at all.

_____   _____

3. The Boston Museum of Fine Arts is one of the great museums of the world. So if it's jade you're interested in, you should go there. The Museum is sure to have an exceptional collection.

_____   _____

4. Though the road be long and hard, it is a way all of us should travel. It is our sacred duty to ourselves.

_____   _____

5. I believe the government should take all reasonable steps to assure a sound currency.

_____   _____

6. You wouldn't allow a child of that age to climb one of your trees, would you?

_____   _____

7. A suit by Lamberaux is specially crafted from the very best cloth. This policy assures our customers that a Lamberaux suit is a suit of distinction.

_____   _____

8. I have an inalienable right to do what I want with my own land.

_____   _____

9. I tell you that we will have to either beat out that competition or go down before it. In this life one is either the hammer or the anvil.

_____   _____

10. If an individual is thrifty, he will prosper. So if everybody would be thrifty we would have a prosperous society.

_____   _____

11. Our mail-order catalog has models for clothing and every other sort of thing. The result is an attractive catalog, I know, but the cost is enormous. So I'm ordering all the models dropped. (The year that Mr. Avery of Montgomery Ward gave this order, I lost all hope as I turned the pages.)

12. Iyawo Okan says, "Blacks are a piscean race. This means they cannot compete with the technological white Americans (a people of Aries) because the strong suit of the piscean people is spirituality" (*New Republic*, May 27, 1978, p. 17). (This is a wild one. Please exonerate the *New Republic*, for it merely reports the statement.)

REVIEW EXERCISE

This exercise affords a chance to spot fallacies from the whole list of those discussed since the beginning of the book.

1. If you don't like the way we do things here, why don't you go back to Russia?

2. I'm dead against a government requirement to register firearms. After all, lots of things are dangerous—explosives, poisons, axes, and knives. When guns are outlawed, then only outlaws will have guns.

3. If you know what's good for you, you'll keep out of the school committee fight. The townspeople are all embroiled in it and you don't want your business to suffer.

4. John Thomasaro, M.D., is the best-known surgeon in this area. So when he speaks out against changing elegibility for Social Security, I'd follow his

advice any day rather than take recommendations from these know-it-alls who want to tinker with the law. (Look for three fallacies.)

_____   _____

_____

5. No one in his right mind would favor expanding credit now.

_____   _____

6. I can't take seriously your argument that I spend too much on clothes. Look what you spend on clothes yourself, to say nothing of what it cost you to go to Tahiti.

_____   _____

7. Mrs. Newhouse recommends that we allow 20,000 refugees from South America to enter the USA. We can't do that. Next there'll be 40,000 from Africa or 100,000 from Asia. There's simply no end to the refugee problem.

_____   _____

8. The University of California is one of our most distinguished universities. It must offer exceptional training in art.

_____   _____

9. Since Frank can't prove that he was not involved in the crime, it's fair to assume that he was involved in it.

_____   _____

10. If elected, I pledge to serve all the people. There will be no forgotten citizens in my district. There will be no special favors for special people.

_____   _____

11. If only our quarterback hadn't been injured in running back the kickoff, we'd have won the game all right. It was close even with Feldman out of the game.

_____   _____

12. I'm selling magazine subscriptions so that I can go to college. My quota is 250 subscriptions and I have nearly 200 already. I get a scholarship if I fill the quota. So I hope you will buy a magazine from me.

_____   _____

13. No one of common decency could oppose this increase of the pension benefits.

_____   _____

14. Every malcontent in the county is after our chemical company to cut down pollution. It doesn't seem to occur to them that their rosy dreams cost money or that we're the biggest employer in the area. Where would they all be without our payroll? (Three clear cases here.)

_____   _____

_____

15. Our fathers' struggle for this land has made it hallowed ground for us. Honor bids us not to break faith with them. Honor bids that we preserve what they created.

_____   _____

16. There's been altogether too much regulation of the trucking industry. The only thing to do is to get rid of the regulations and let the industry regulate itself.

_____   _____

17. Those who contend that our state is corrupt should be ashamed of themselves. No one of public spirit would make such a charge. And the harm that is done is seen every time the state's reputation deters a business from settling here.

_____   _____

18. The present administration's policies have been a success because, as everyone can see, business is good and employment is high. The administration must be given the credit.

_____   _____

19. I can't see dismissing Sergeant Scott from the police force for accepting a small bribe. After all, last year when Captain Turner was found guilty in an equally serious case, he was only demoted.

_____   _____

20. After the election, over a hundred voters were asked why they voted the way they did. Only two mentioned that the scandal in the private life of the incumbent influenced their choice. So it's clear that few voters put any stress on that.

_____   _____

21. Examiner taking a statement from a witness: "Isn't it true that you first noticed the Chevrolet when it entered the intersection just as the light changed?"

_____   _____

22. A state is like a ship with a captain, officers, and crew. When a ship faces a storm, it is for the captain to command and the officers and crew to carry out his orders. Thus when our country faces the storms of war, our president should command and the rest of us should carry out his decisions.

_____   _____

23. If I am elected to the school committee, I will oppose excessive frills in the school curriculum.

_____   _____

24. Either we close our branch in this city or we spend a lot of money renovating what is essentially an old store in an old part of town. Either way, it's a painful choice.

_____   _____

25. Those who are well informed recognize the need for the urban renewal project. Some real estate interests are howling against the proposal, but those interests have a well-earned reputation for unpatriotic shortsightedness. (Three clear cases here.)

_____   _____

_____

Logical Fallacies

At the outset, you may recall, we divided fallacies into three general kinds: psychological, material, and logical. So far we have discussed psychological and material fallacies. So you should be asking, "What about the logical ones?"

The practical way to understand the logical fallacies is to learn the rules for deduction first. Any violation of a rule for proper deduction will be a fallacy, a mistake in reasoning. You will find the *logical fallacies* treated in PART II. Also, they are described briefly in the *Appendix: Checklist of Fallacies*, which provides an orderly list of all the fallacies treated in this book. Unless you are already familiar with the rules for formal logic, it will not be useful to consider the logical fallacies until you have read Part II.

part two

Deduction

chapter 4

Classes, Propositions, and Quantifiers

I enjoy a remark by Alfred North Whitehead:

There is a tradition of opposition between adherents of induction and deduction. In my view, it would be just as sensible for the two ends of a worm to quarrel.

Presumably the readers of this book aren't signed up in either of these opposing camps. Indeed, it *is* a pointless quarrel. But what is the quarrel about?

Logic divides reasoning into two basic types—inductive and deductive. You will notice the division is followed in this book: Part II, *Deduction* and Part III, *Induction*. It may be a good idea to consider the basic difference between the two before becoming involved with either one.

Inductive reasoning notes particular facts and draws a conclusion therefrom.

Remember the hat with the white beans? When you had had enough of drawing beans out one at a time, you formed a general conclusion covering the entire contents of the hat. On the basis of examining *some* of the contents you took the "inductive leap" to conclude that "All the objects in the hat are white beans" or "Most of the objects in the hat must be beans" or some such conclusion fitting the evidence you had. In doing so you were reasoning inductively from observed particulars to a general conclusion. The white bean problem involved one kind of induction—namely, generalization. Another kind of inductive reasoning is forming a theory or hypothesis. Here one notices particular facts of *different kinds* and then advances a theory that will explain all of them, much as the detective story ends with a solution fitting all the clues. Still another kind of induction is reasoning by analogy, which has been touched upon already. Here a number of particular resemblances between two things or situations are noticed and the conclusion is advanced that one may expect some further similarity. Now, no generalization and no hypothesis and no analogy can establish a conclusion as certainly true. We may examine a million cases and still the next one may not bear out our expectations; a hypothesis may fit ever so many facts and yet some other hypothesis-that-hasn't-been-thought-of may fit all those facts too; analogies are notoriously unreliable and the best of them can break down.

Uncertainty troubles logicians. Though it's wholesome to remember that a conclusion arrived at by induction is not beyond question, still, many things established inductively do approach certainty. To cite an extreme case, that all people die is established by induction. Clearly, so far at least as *some* inductive conclusions are concerned, discussion of the uncertainty of inductive procedures relates to a philosophical problem rather than to actual doubt. Finally, induction is indispensable, for it allows us to acquaint ourselves with our world and universe. All of us are born without knowledge and we encounter the things that we encounter. We are on our own to observe facts and from them draw conclusions inductively, since, as Buckminster Fuller put it, "Spaceship Earth did not come with an instruction book." Now let's look at the other end of the worm—deduction.

Deductive reasoning starts with one or more statements called premises *and investigates what conclusions necessarily follow from these premises.*

So you see, deductive reasoning runs the other way round from induction: instead of examining facts to reach a conclusion, deduction accepts the material as given and examines the implications to be drawn from this material. And deduction contrasts with induction in another way. While inductive processes cannot establish anything as certainly true, the process of deduction results in the elegant certainty of knowing just what does—or does not—follow from a given set of premises. No question about it. Grant the premises and the conclusion inescapably follows: Look here:

Premise 1   All teachers have two heads.
Premise 2   Ichabod Crane is a teacher.
Conclusion   Therefore, Ichabod Crane has two heads.

Now one doesn't have to be a logician to see intuitively that if one simply accepts the two premises, then the conclusion follows. Though the first premise is nonsense, its truth or falsity is not our present concern. In fact, one can investigate what premises imply by using symbols rather than meaningful ideas, just as mathematics employs symbols in its formulas. For example, our two heads argument can be restated in this form:

Premise 1	All A is B.
Premise 2	C is A.
Conclusion	C is B.

The form of the argument makes the conclusion inescapable. Formal logic! In deduction the form of the argument determines whether it is valid—that is, whether the conclusion follows inescapably. Hence deductive processes are called *formal logic*.

When deduction is applied in reasoning about factual problems where one wishes to determine the truth, then the security of its conclusions being inescapable consequences of the premises turns out to be a mirage. Sure, the conclusion follows from the premises, but it is no more reliable than the premises are, and if we trace back to the justification for the premises we will find ultimately that they are the result of induction or, at worst, a mere assumption or philosophical commitment. Whoops! I'm on the brink of the quarrel between induction and deduction. Better get on with the business of this chapter, which is to investigate some notions needed as a foundation for deduction.

CLASSES

A class is a group of things or situations which share one or more characteristics prescribed to determine membership in the class.

Examples of the notion of classes come in torrents. For instance, "vertebrates" is the group of animals distinguished by the single common characteristic of possessing a backbone composed of vertebrae; "students at Bowdoin College" is just that—all those who are both students and enrolled at Bowdoin College. The number of classes is infinite, literally infinite. Quite naturally, every language generates single words for those notions which are most important and frequently referred to by users of the language. Probably there is no language without its special word for "mother," "rock," "swim," "heavy," and so on through many universally common situations. The need to designate classes of things soon outruns any possibility of creating a special word for each. Nouns can be modified by adjectives to produce a host of classes—e.g., "large dog," "fast runner." This possibility gives way to phrases to describe the class. So we have "champions in doubles tennis," "women veterans of the Vietnam War," etc. The various characteristics that are laid down to determine class membership may require a longish phrase. "Those who lost a relative on the ship Portland," is a class. (A club was formed by people of this macabre tie.) "Single taxpayers who do not qualify for rates in Schedules II and III, and married persons filing separate returns" is a class under U.S. Income Tax law. (You may have the privilege of belonging to this one.) And so on *ad infinitum*.

We haven't gotten to the end of possible classes—by no means. In discussing *Word Magic* we touched on the delightful ideas of mermaids, the Fountain of Youth, Jack in the Beanstalk, and all sorts of nonexistent beings. These are all class groups even though the terms designate classes that don't happen to have any members. We can conjure up longer or more sophisticated exhibits: Hegel's "World Spirit" or "ceremonies that ward off the Evil Eye" are classes devoid of members as far as I am concerned. Empty or "null" classes do not necessarily concern farfetched situations—for example, "lifeguards now on duty at Jones Beach" may be an empty class. Later on we will find that there are some difficulties when one feeds a null class into the machine of deductive reasoning, for sometimes the effect is like an air bubble in the gasline which stalls the engine.

It is possible for a class to be composed of a single member. "Ted Kennedy" designates a unique individual and one would not ordinarily think of him as a "class." "The first man to run the 4-minute mile" is another instance. Though single-member classes do raise some problems in logic, they are not problems that need concern us here. Without introducing an inaccuracy, we will simply treat a class with one member as any other class. "Oscar was jilted" means "All Oscar was jilted."

The more the characteristics added to the requirements for membership, the smaller the number of members in the class tends to be. "Living people" is a very large class, "living people who have competed in the Olympics" is a much smaller class, while "living winners of three or more Olympic medals" reduces membership to a roomful. The characteristics set down to determine a class usually are positive traits like "living," "competing in the Olympics," and so on in the examples just given. Occasionally the absence of some fact or condition is made a determining characteristic, as in "those who have not had a turn before" or "plywood that has not been finished on either side." One consequence of studying deduction is to become more conscious of *exactly* what groups are being dealt with and how these groups—which is to say "classes"—are related to one another.

PROPOSITIONS

A proposition is any assertion capable of being true or false.

It does not matter whether a statement is true or false as far as its being a proposition is concerned. Every declarative sentence contains one or more propositions. Here are some propositions:

> The mongoose always wins.
> Lazarus was raised from the dead.
> Inflation injures some investors while benefiting others.

All these sentences make assertions that are capable of being true or false, so all of them are propositions. The inflation example contains two propositions, either of which could be true or false. Some types of sentences, however, are not designed for making propositions. These include questions, imperatives, and exclamations, for none of these assert anything, directly at least, and hence they do not ordinarily contain propositions. It would not make sense to say "true" or "false" after any of these:

> Is Mary at home?
> Forward, MARCH.
> Hooray for our side!

Once in a while a question may be rhetorical and then it may be construed as having an assertion as its intended meaning, in which case it implies a proposition. To take one famous example, when Shylock observes, "If you prick me, do I not bleed?" he is in reality referring to his common humanity by reminding his audience, "If you prick me, I do bleed." With this interpretation there is an assertion and, hence a proposition. In the vast majority of cases, however, questions, commands, and exclamations are not being used as indirect means of implying some proposition.

A proposition is not the same as the words in which it is expressed. For example, these statements all express the same idea and, therefore, are but different ways of stating the same proposition:

> The mongoose always wins.
> In all cases the mongoose is victorious.
> Der Sieg geht immer zum Mungo.
> नेज का ई मे शा जीतना ऐ

Since a proposition is a meaning apart from the words in which it is stated, it follows that any idea can be reworded to suit the convenience of analysis *so long as the meaning remains the same.* Furthermore, determining the meaning of a proposition is not strictly speaking the concern of a logician. In practical fact, however, language must be dealt with in order to understand what relationships are asserted.

So far we have been developing a greater awareness of classes, and we have seen that a proposition is any assertion capable of being true or false. All assertions—that is, propositions—claim that one class is related in some way to some other class. When a class is taken up and used in a proposition it is called a "term," so a proposition consists of two terms related together. The words "class" and "term" present a sort of chameleon situation—by itself the group that shares the class characteristics is called a "class"; move it over to its place in a proposition and it is referred to as a "term." For instance, the proposition:

> Term 1   Term 2
> <u>Bicycles</u> are <u>fun to ride.</u>

relates the two classes bicycles and (things that are) fun to ride.

Almost all propositions can be analyzed into a subject term and a predicate term joined together by some form of verb "to be." In this use the verb "to be" is called the "connective" or "copula." Since language affords numerous ways to express relationships between terms, many sentences that state propositions do not have an expressed connective. However, there is very rarely any difficulty in restating an assertion so that some form of "to be" is used as the connective. Here are some examples:

| Penguins do not fly | *becomes* | <u>Penguins</u> are not <u>(birds that) fly.</u> |
| Nobody knows my troubles | *becomes* | <u>My troubles</u> are <u>(troubles) nobody knows.</u> |

The relationship between two terms can be made even more evident by stating "are included in" or "are excluded from" instead of simply saying "are" or "are not." The presentation is further sharpened and time is saved by using two symbols:

> $<$ = are included in
> $\not<$ = are excluded from

You may think of these like the = symbol in mathematics. Imagine writing "equals" every time! It would be neither as convenient nor as clear. So, for practice, I will restate the illustrations used above to show the connectives used in this stilted expression which is called *standard form*.

> $\not<$
> <u>Penguins</u> are excluded from <u>(birds that) fly.</u>

> $<$
> <u>My troubles</u> are included in <u>(troubles) nobody knows.</u>

Though an English teacher would be unhappy with a composition made up of sentences like these, he couldn't complain that it was unintelligible. Nobody wants to talk this way, of course, but if one has learned how to contort ordinary sentences correctly into standard form, then there can be no mistaking what the terms are or how they are related. This makes a solid, readily understandable foundation for analysis.

QUANTIFIERS

The next thing to notice is that we have to indicate *how much* of the first term is related to the second term. For example, one might say:

All employees work from 9:00 to 5:00.
Some employees have interesting jobs.
No employees are over 70.

These words *all, some, no* are called quantifiers because they indicate the quantity of the first term that is included in the second. The proper word is *quantifier,* which is easily remembered by associating it with *quantity.* Language offers several ways to designate *all* or *no,* while a whole host of words indicate degrees between *all* and *no.* Thus, "each" and "every" are alternate ways for asserting *all;* "most," "many," "a majority," "62%," "half," "a small number," "a few" are all equivalent to *some;* "none," "not," "never" are available to express the quantifier *no.* The quantifiers *all* and *no* refer, so to speak, to total situations one way or the other—that is, *all* totally includes one class in another while *no* totally excludes one class from the other. Everything in between is partial and can be boiled down to *some.* Since *all* and *no* refer to every member of whatever class they are applied to, they proclaim a total relationship commonly referred to as *universal.* On the other hand, *some* or any other word claiming something about a part of a class only designates a relationship that is partial and is referred to as *particular.*

How should one deal with instances in which no quantifier is expressed, as in the sentence, "Employees must follow safety procedures"? Should it be all employees or some employees? Where no quantifier is stated, in logic the presumption is made that *all* is intended. Like any presumption, this is a handy way to cut a Gordian knot so that one may go on with a set meaning for the assertion. After all, if a user of the language wants to indicate less than *all,* he can easily do so and it is reasonable to insist he indicate that his assertion is only of a partial relationship if this is what he means it to be. Also, in fact, the presumption of *all* produces good sense in a majority of cases.

SUMMARY

Deduction is concerned with the relationship between the premise or premises and the conclusion. The premises imply the conclusion inescapably even though they may be without content—mere symbols such as A < B. Since the form of the assertion implies the conclusion, deduction is known as "formal logic."

A *class* is a group of things or situations which share one or more characteristics prescribed to determine membership in the class. "One-armed paperhangers" is a class. Sometimes a class is composed of only one member, or it may be an empty class with no existing members.

A *proposition* is an assertion capable of being true or false. Any declarative sentence will contain one or more propositions. Exclamations, imperative sentences, and questions that are not rhetorical do not make assertions and, therefore, do not contain propositions. Since a proposition is a meaning distinct from the language that expresses it, two ways of saying the same thing are statements of the same proposition.

A *term* simply designates a class. One speaks of a "term" rather than a "class" when referring to a class that appears in a proposition.

The *connective* relates one term to another in a proposition. The connective is not always expressly stated, but with very rare exceptions an unstated connective can be expressed as a form of the verb "to be." The auxiliary "have" is not a connective.

A *quantifier* is a word designating how much of one class is related in some way to another. Quantifiers can be reduced to three basic types: *all, some,* and *no.* Since *all* and *no* cover every case, propositions employing them or any equivalent of them are called universal propositions; propositions quantified by *some,* or any word that is partial, are called particular propositions. Where no quantifier is expressed, *all* is presumed.

EXERCISES FOR CHAPTER 4
pages 69–76

I.   Answer by writing **T** for "true" or **F** for "false." These T/F questions are just to test whether you were awake when you read the chapter. You ought to make a high score.

_T_   **1.** The terms of a proposition are classes/that are the subject matter of the proposition.

_T_   **2.** Some classes have only one member.

_T_   **3.** A class may be defined as "a group of things or situations which share one or more characteristics prescribed to determine membership in the class."

_F_ ✓ **4.** One cannot alter the language in which a proposition is expressed without creating a new proposition.

_T_   **5.** Empty classes always are ridiculous things like "purple cows."

_T_   **6.** If something is not capable of being true or false, then it cannot be a proposition.

_T_ ✓**7.** A proposition is a meaning, so if the same meaning is expressed in different ways the statements are of the same proposition.

_F_   **8.** In logic, a quantifier indicating a large majority like 97% cannot be rendered merely "some."

_T_   **9.** "Some" stands for any quantifier that refers to a part only.

_F_   **10.** When a statement is made without expressing the quantifier, then the quantifier "no" is assumed to be intended.

_T_   **11.** If an argument is valid, then the conclusion has to be true.

_T_   **12.** An argument may be constructed from a false premise.

II.   Some of the sentences below are propositions and some are not. In the blanks provided, write **P** if the sentence is a proposition, and **No** if it is not a proposition.

_T_   **1.** Children learn by exploring their environment.

_T_   **2.** The *id* refers to the subconscious.

_F_   **3.** What do you plan to do this summer?

_F_   **4.** Thou shalt not steal.

_F_   **5.** Look how that man drives!

_T_   **6.** The Carthaginians may have sailed around Africa.

_T_   **7.** Gremlins cause engine trouble.

_T_   **8.** The New York Yankees will win.

_T_   **9.** No man is a hero to his valet.

_F_   **10.** Why are you going to marry him/her?

III.   Each sentence of this exercise set is a proposition with an expressly stated quantifier, a connective, and two terms. Perform the following steps as a basic drill:

1. Underline the two terms *exactly*.

2. Express the connective by using the symbols

     $<$ = is included in
     $\not<$ = is excluded from

3. Express the quantifier by **all**, **no**, or **some**.

4. Write **Q** over the quantifier and **T-1** and **T-2** over the two terms.

Here is an example of the steps you are asked to perform:

Example:

Most wisdom is the product of experience.

   Q   T-1   T-2
Some <u>wisdom</u> $<$ <u>the product of experience</u>

or

   Q   T-1   T-2
Some <u>wisdom</u> $<$ <u>(things that are) the product of experience</u>

Note: The alternate solution inserting "things that are" is redundant and not necessary. At the very beginning, however, it helps to give a feeling for the classes involved.

$Q \quad T_1 \quad ∠ \quad T_2$

1. All radiation is harmful to human beings.

$Q \quad T_1 \quad ∠ \quad T_2$

2. All very small children are self-centered.

$Q \quad T_1 \quad ∠ \quad T_2$

3. Some cultures are extremely oppressive to women.

$Q \quad T_1 \quad 4 \quad T_2$

4. Many great people were not respected in their own time.

Same $Q \quad T_1 \quad ∠ \quad T_2$

5. Some people are successful in spite of their environment.

6. All whales are unable to escape modern equipment.

7. A few of our team members are seasoned players.

8. Every society is constantly changing.

9. About 50% of the prisoners are paroled.

10. Some of the greatest artists were exploited in their lifetime.

11. Anyone who suffers injustice is apt to react.

12. Every superstition is a bar to understanding the world.

13. Some needed reforms are not likely to be undertaken this year.

14. All good historians are aware of the limitations of history.

15. Nearly all issues are forgotten in the long run.

Quantifiers are not expressed in the next five sentences. Supply the quantifier and solve the problems.

16. Orangutangs are on the list of endangered species.

17. Conversation about politics is not enjoyed by small children.

18. Honoré Daumier was buried in a pauper's grave.

19. Our senator is in favor of promoting solar energy.

20. Nobody wins.

The connective "to be" does not appear in the next twenty sentences. Quantifiers are expressed in some and not in other instances. Express the connective in each case by either "are included in" < or by "are excluded from" ≮. Then solve the problems as before.

21. Most athletes practice faithfully.

22. Some people do not have enough courage.

23. Investments require reappraisals.

24. Absence makes the heart grow fonder.

25. The Greeks never held gladiatorial contests.

26. Our prisons do not have good results.

27. Out of sight, out of mind.

28. A man cannot serve two masters.

29. Nearly everybody likes a good melody.

30. Help did not arrive in time.

31. Civil liberties ought to be upheld.

32. Happiness does not require great possessions.

33. Slavery existed for thousands of years.

34. Every human being has weaknesses.

35. Any responsible parent teaches his children to be honest.

36. A corporation continues to exist indefinitely.

37. He who is ignorant of history stands condemned to repeat it.

38. Some knowledge contributes to happiness.

39. Education opens doors to appreciation.

40. He who increaseth knowledge addeth unto sorrow.*

*No. 40 is a biblical quotation that refers to the sorrow of realizing how ignorance and greed prevent people from reaching their potential.

chapter 5

Class Relationships

In the last chapter we had, so to speak, a look at some of the foundation stones of deductive reasoning. First we were engaged in getting a clear notion of a class and in identifying propositions. Then we investigated some propositions which we found could be analyzed as two classes related by either inclusion or exclusion, and the extent of this relationship was reduced to one or other of three stark quantifiers: *all, no,* or *some.* All of this procedure has the purpose of enabling any statement to be put into a standard form, making the relationship between the terms unmistakable. The goal of this chapter will be to examine the relationship between terms by presenting a convenient terminology and by explaining the use of circle diagrams which show each of the four possible relationships visually.

A *categorical proposition* asserts something unconditionally or, as we say, categorically. "Dancing is fun," " 'Nova' is an excellent program," "Many UFOs are reported"—all these are categorical propositions. There are four and only four ways in which the two classes of a categorical proposition can be related. These ways are:

1. All <u>tigers</u> are <u>dangerous</u>.   Total inclusion or A-form

2. No <u>rabbits</u> are <u>dangerous</u>.   Total exclusion or E-form

3. Some <u>elephants</u> are <u>dangerous</u>.   Partial inclusion or I-form

4. Some <u>snakes</u> are not <u>dangerous</u>.   Partial exclusion or O-form

These four relationships are fundamental to deduction. The phrases "total inclusion," "total exclusion," "partial inclusion," and "partial exclusion" are easily learned as a quick mental response. It takes more time to develop an automatic response to the A-, E-, I-, or O-form terminology.[1] You will find, however, that the brevity of the A, E, I, O terminology makes it worth using, so here is a scheme to aid as a ready reference:

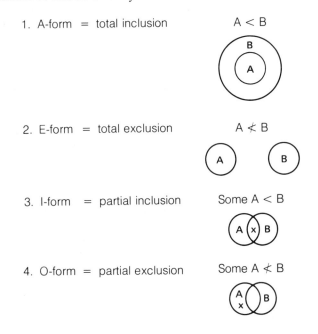

1. A-form = total inclusion   A < B

2. E-form = total exclusion   A ≮ B

3. I-form = partial inclusion   Some A < B

4. O-form = partial exclusion   Some A ≮ B

The circles exhibit the relationships visually. The first two are clear from inspection. The "x" found in numbers 3 and 4 indicates that at least one case will be found in the area where the "x" appears. Partial inclusion promises that some A (at least one) is a B, while partial exclusion promises that some A (at least one) is not a B. Now we are ready to take a more careful look at each of these relationships.

The circle diagrams that we are using are called "Euler diagrams" after Leonhard Euler, a Swiss mathematician who devised them in the eighteenth century. Each term is represented by a circle and is placed in relation to other circles as the language *compels* it to be. It doesn't matter how large the circles are drawn or how much they overlap if they do overlap. All that is necessary is for the circles to conform to the language exactly.

---

[1]The A=E=I=O terminology was derived from the first vowels found in two Latin words. *AffIrmo*, meaning *affirm*, gives the A and I letters to designate total and partial inclusion, while *nEgO*, meaning *negate*, gives the E and O letters for total and partial exclusion. The association of "affirm" with "include" and "negate" with "exclude" makes sense.

A-FORM or TOTAL INCLUSION

Innumerable things are included in something else. "All snow is included in things that are cold." "All zebras are herbivores." "All residents of Dallas are residents of Texas." Here is the Euler diagram for this latter statement.

All *Dallas residents* < *Texas residents.*

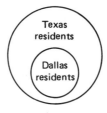

The circles make plain that if a person is a Dallas resident, he must also be a Texas resident. Nothing could be more simple.

E-FORM or TOTAL EXCLUSION

All sorts of things are totally excluded from one another. "Bicycles are not permitted here." "No British judges are elected officials." We can be as silly as we please: "No baboons are marshmallows." Let's use the British judges to illustrate total exclusion.

British judges ≮ elected officials.

The diagram shows immediately that if someone is a British judge, he is not an elected official. If someone is an elected official, he is not a British judge. Before going on, we will stop to notice that sentences expressing total exclusion may begin with the word "no" or they may use "are not" as the connective. For example, these two sentences are exact equivalents and thus express the same proposition:

No parking is allowed here.
Parking is not allowed here.

"No <u>parking</u> is <u>allowed here</u>" is the same as "<u>Parking</u> is not <u>allowed here</u>" is the same as "All parking is not allowed here." So you see, the "no" goes into an exclusion and the first term becomes quantified by "all." Accordingly, an analysis of a sentence beginning with "no" runs like this:

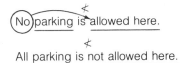

All parking is not allowed here.

The form "All... are not..." is not actually ambiguous or, at least, so it seems to me. But since failing to distinguish correctly between "All... are not..." and "Not all... are..." is common among English speakers, the recommended standard form for a relationship of total exclusion is "No... are..." for this is never mistaken.

I-FORM or PARTIAL INCLUSION

Frequently one knows that a part of one class is included in some other class. "Some marriages are happy." "Some businesses are profitable." "Some student council members were at the game." Here is the diagram for a partial inclusion:

Some *student council members* < *those at the game.*

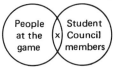

The overlapping circles show partial inclusion of one class in the other. The part common to both circles has a "x" to indicate that there definitely is at least one case in that location, for we have been told "Some student council members were at the game." Now notice the area labeled "student council members" that is outside the area for "people at the game." The statement given does not tell us whether there were student council members who did not attend the game: all we are told is that some did attend. There may be student council members who did not attend the game or it may be that they all attended. Further, maybe it was a tiddlywinks game and there were no "people at the game" except for one or more student council members. All we really know is that at least one student council member was at the game.

Many people have a habit of assuming that an assertion that something is included in something else implies that other cases are not. For instance, many would believe that the statement "Some drivers are considerate" implies that

"Some drivers are not considerate." Otherwise, one would have said "All drivers are considerate," would one not? The answer is *yes* and *no*. Part of the trouble is that we already know too much about the classes of "drivers" and "considerate people," and this, as was mentioned earlier, tends to distract us from examining the inference by itself. We might do better with As and Bs. Does the statement "Some A is B" imply that "Some A is not B"?

Probably in the majority of times when the quantifier "some" is used, the situation is one in which some members of the first class are related to the second class in the way asserted while other members are not. For instance, if I say, "Some men like military life," everybody knows from his experience with the real world that it is also true that "Some men do not like military life." And so it turns out to be in statement after statement. "Some government bureaus are highly efficient." "Some birds migrate to South America." "Some people are generous." Yet if we add the idea "others are not" for any of these, we do it out of knowledge of the world and not out of anything in the original assertion. There are situations, however, where the speaker is NOT using "some" because he knows of other instances contrary to the relationship he is asserting. In the example "Some student council members were at the game" it is likely that the speaker here observed one or more student council members but not all of them at the game. Though his evidence is not sufficient to bear an "all" statement, in saying "Some members were at the game" he does not necessarily mean to imply that others were not there. It is quite possible that all the student council members attended the game, but the speaker did not see everybody and recognizes that he does not know.

You may imagine logic as a severe goddess, but a just one. Logic holds everyone strictly to support his assertions; on the other hand, assertions are narrowly interpreted so a speaker is held only to support the minimum that he *must* have asserted. Overtones and assumptions that go beyond what was stated will not be taken as the meaning for which the speaker is responsible.

O-FORM or PARTIAL EXCLUSION

Any number of assertions tell us that part of one class is excluded from some other class. "Some roads are not open." "Some policemen are not jovial." "Some famous alumni did not attend the dinner." Here is a diagram for this kind of relationship:

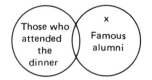

Again, the "x" indicates that at least one of the "famous alumni" is outside the area for those who "attended the dinner." The statement does not tell us whether any famous alumni did attend the dinner or, for that matter, we do not know whether anybody showed up for the dinner. Just as the partial inclusion "Some student council members were at the game" told us only that at least one student council member was at the game, so also the partial exclusion "Some famous alumni did not attend the dinner" tells us only that at least one of the famous alumni was not at the dinner.

Now we come to the notion of "distribution." I'm sorry to say that this notion, which is crucial to deduction, turns out to be hard to explain. For a start, we may note that the significance of whether a term is distributed or not is like the difference between:

distributed term   <
<u>All snakes in this region</u> are <u>harmless</u>.

undistributed term   <
<u>Some snakes in this region</u> are <u>harmless</u>.

Distributed terms yield a solid basis for knowing which undistributed terms do not. In line with this idea, some logic texts assert: "A term is distributed if one knows the relationship for every member of its class to the other class." This description works beautifully for the A-, E-, and I-forms; it gets into trouble when applied to the O-form. So we will not use this rule. We will use instead a set of rules that work easily for every case. Master this set and your reward will be sure, for these rules are both much used and easily applied.

Distribution of the First Term

The quantifier determines whether the first term is distributed.

(a) "All" and "no" or their equivalents distribute.
(b) "Some," "15%," "most," or any other quantifier referring to a part only does not distribute.

Distribution of the Second Term

The relationship determines whether the second term is distributed.

(a) When the relationship is exclusion, the second term is distributed.
(b) When the relationship is inclusion, the second term is undistributed.

These rules save a lot of time. With a little practice, you will be able to identify a term as "distributed" or "undistributed" in a flash. Follow through with the rules and notice how they tell the distribution immediately for every term of the A-, E-, I-, and O-forms. It's neat.

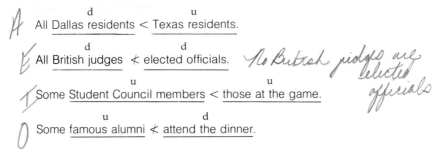

$$\overset{d}{\underline{\text{All Dallas residents}}} < \overset{u}{\underline{\text{Texas residents.}}}$$

$$\overset{d}{\underline{\text{All British judges}}} \not< \overset{d}{\underline{\text{elected officials.}}} \quad \textit{No British judges are elected officials}$$

$$\text{Some } \overset{u}{\underline{\text{Student Council members}}} < \overset{u}{\underline{\text{those at the game.}}}$$

$$\text{Some } \overset{u}{\underline{\text{famous alumni}}} \not< \overset{d}{\underline{\text{attend the dinner.}}}$$

As you see from the rules, the quantifier "all" distributes the first term, and the quantifier "some" makes the first term undistributed. You will soon find that when you have posted a "d" or a "u" over a first term to show its distribution, it isn't necessary to write the quantifier, because a "d" implies "all" and a "u" implies "some."

$$\overset{d}{\underline{\text{Vases found here}}} < \overset{u}{\underline{\text{Etruscan}}} \quad \textit{means} \quad \text{All } \overset{d}{\underline{\text{vases found here}}} \text{ are } \overset{u}{\underline{\text{Etruscan.}}}$$

$$\overset{u}{\underline{\text{Vases found here}}} < \overset{u}{\underline{\text{Etruscan}}} \quad \textit{means} \quad \text{Some } \overset{u}{\underline{\text{vases found here}}} \text{ are } \overset{u}{\underline{\text{Etruscan.}}}$$

As in mathematics, to gain a feel for the subject one has to take time out to work problems as well as reading explanations. There are three pitfalls in the exercises for this chapter, and I might as well warn you of them:

1. Underline terms exactly and do not discard words that belong in the term—e.g., good tennis players and tennis players are different groups, so "good" or comparable words cannot be discarded. In your analysis, account for all the words.
2. Do not underline quantifiers. A quantifier is not a part of a term. Some good advice is not followed.
3. Before beginning the exercises, sit down and learn the rules for distribution which are given on p. 87.

Deduction cannot be unraveled without determining distribution correctly in every instance. Knowing the rules is indispensable to the game.

SUMMARY

The four possible relationships between terms in a categorical proposition are defined and diagramed on pages 82–83.

Use of a partial inclusion introduced by "some" does not imply in logic that other cases exist outside the area of the inclusion. For instance, "Some members of the orchestra are outstanding" does not imply that others are not. Though experience with the outside world often tells us that "others are not" is true in a particular situation, where we do happen to know this we know it from experience and not as a matter of logic.

The relationship of partial exclusion expressed by "some are not" does not imply that other cases exist inside the excluded area. For instance, "Some employees are not loyal to this company" does not imply that other employees are loyal.

The distribution of terms must be determined accurately in order to check the validity of deduction. Rules for quickly determining the distribution of any term are given on p. 87.

EXERCISES FOR CHAPTER 5
pages 82–89

I.   Answer **T** for "true" or **F** for "false":

_____ **1.** There are only four ways in which the two classes of a categorical proposition can be related.

_____ **2.** In the absence of a quantifier, "all" is presumed.

_____ **3.** All propositions are also statements.

_____ **4.** A categorical proposition asserts something unconditionally.

_____ **5.** An assertion is not always a proposition.

_____ **6.** The statement "Some readers have understood this chapter" implies that other readers have not understood it.

_____ **7.** The size of the circle or how much circles overlap if they do overlap makes no difference in a Euler diagram.

_____ **8.** The quantifier determines the distribution of the first term.

_____ **9.** The quantifier "some" does not distribute.

_____ **10.** Where a "u" for "undistributed" is found over the first term, this implies a quantifier of "some" even though this quantifier may not be expressed.

II.   Write **d** or **u** over each term to indicate whether it is distributed or undistributed. Fill in the blanks by writing **A, E, I,** or **O** followed by **total incl., total excl.,** etc. as appropriate.

_____ **1.** All trucks < subject to inspection.

_____ **2.** All artists < need freedom to express themselves.

_____ **3.** All people < have need of a balanced diet.

_____ **4.** Some chemical wastes ≮ harmful.

_____ **5.** Some luxuries < beyond my means.

_____ **6.** Most people < want to be self-supporting.

—————————— 7. Almost all <u>skindivers</u> < <u>very careful</u>.

—————————— 8. All <u>thoughtful people</u> < <u>apprehensive about man's future</u>.

—————————— 9. No <u>credit</u> ≮ <u>given here</u>.

—————————— 10. Many <u>discoveries</u> < <u>remain to be made</u>.

—————————— 11. Ten percent of <u>my customers</u> < <u>have lost money</u>.

—————————— 12. Every <u>lie</u> < <u>breaks confidence in communication</u>.

—————————— 13. No one's <u>character</u> ≮ <u>formed suddenly</u>.

—————————— 14. Some <u>water</u> < <u>runs uphill</u>.

—————————— 15. Many <u>beliefs</u> < <u>have consequences to others</u>.

—————————— 16. All <u>water</u> < <u>runs downhill</u>.

—————————— 17. A few <u>people</u> < <u>liked the play</u>.

—————————— 18. Most <u>people</u> < <u>gave nothing at all</u>.

—————————— 19. All <u>people</u> < <u>can bear the troubles of others</u>.

—————————— 20. No <u>man</u> ≮ <u>an island</u>.

III.   Underline the terms in the sentences below. Put in the symbols for inclusion or exclusion as appropriate, and place a "d" or a "u" over each term to indicate whether it is distributed or undistributed. To complete the exercise, draw circles to indicate the relationship each sentence asserts. Identify this relationship by writing **A-form**, etc. or **total inclusion**, etc. as you choose.

—————————— 1. All elephant herds are cramped for space.

—————————— 2. No prisoners will escape.

—————————— 3. Some jobs are pleasant.

—————————— 4. Some businesses are not profitable.

—————————— 5. All giant sequoias have fire scars.

—————————— 6. Cro-Magnon man is extinct.

—————————— 7. Nobody is immune to radiation.

—————————— 8. Some deserts are not advancing.

—————————— 9. Nearly all modern states have trouble with inflation.

—————————— 10. Those who abuse their health pay later.

_____ **11.** Seventy percent of the people voted.

_____ **12.** Every tree was infected.

_____ **13.** She never goes there.

_____ **14.** Many tugdabs were found.

_____ **15.** Some jaybells are not snickerbars.

chapter 6

The Categorical Syllogism

No one goes about his daily living for an hour without using syllogisms many times over. College graduates and illiterate people alike employ this kind of reasoning constantly, even though only a tiny fraction could explain what a syllogism is, much less unearth one from the tangle of daily conversation. Perhaps your reaction to these introductory remarks is, "Well, knowledge of syllogisms seems to be something that people get along pretty well without!" Perhaps so, by and large, most of the time. I'll try to explain by comparing the situation to the practice of an unskillful doctor.

The worst general practitioner in town will find that the great majority of his patients get well. After all, most people do not suffer from obscure diseases; the obvious, routine cases will be the majority and these the poor practitioner can hardly miss. It is the difficult cases which test the abilities of a physician. So it is with logical problems. The untrained thinker reasons correctly most of the time; it is situations which are not obvious that test his competence. Understanding syllogisms puts one on the way to becoming a skilled practitioner with ability to solve some of the more difficult problems which are flubbed by bungling practitioners.

Basic to an understanding of deduction is observing sharply the distinction between "valid" and "true." To say that something is "valid" means that the inference made is a necessary consequence of the premises given. To say that something is "true" means that it corresponds to fact. I will demonstrate the point with a fanciful syllogism:

Premise 1	All angels are immaterial beings.
Premise 2	All immaterial beings are weightless.
Conclusion	All angels are weightless.

Now this syllogism is *valid* for, as you can see intuitively, grant the premises and the conclusion is inescapable. Its *truth*, however, is a matter of conjecture. It is worth noting also that "valid" or "invalid" relate to arguments, while "true" or "false" relate to statements.

We are now ready to investigate categorical syllogisms. A model with all parts labeled will be a start in finding out how they work:

	Quantifier	Term 1	Connective	Term 2
Major premise	All	leaders	are	apt to make mistakes.
	Quantifier	Term 3	Connective	Term 1
Minor premise	All	presidents	are	leaders.
	Quantifier	Term 3	Connective	Term 2
Conclusion	All	presidents	are	apt to make mistakes.

The model shows the conventional arrangement of a categorical syllogism with the major premise stated first, then the minor premise, and, last, the conclusion. No harm is done if the major and minor premises are switched around. Further, the correct identification of the major as distinguished from the minor premise is a technical matter that makes no difference to the validity of a syllogism. So we have given definitions for "major" and "minor" premises in a note below[1] and will not place any emphasis upon this distinction either in the text or in the exercises. A practical suggestion for arranging a syllogism is to take the broadest generalization for the major premise and to designate as the minor premise the more limited situation that falls under the broad generalization.

Notice that the quantifiers and the connectives are not underlined in the model because they are not part of the terms. *Everything else belongs in the terms.* Resist the temptation to casually leave a few words unaccounted for in an analysis of a syllogism. Later on, we will take up the occasional instances in which words can be dropped. For the present, we will present no such problems.

Now we will take the relationships stated in the model syllogism and represent each with a circle diagram. The major premise "All leaders are apt to make mistakes" is represented:

The second assertion is that "All presidents are leaders," which diagrams thus:

Placing these two diagrams together, one gets a diagram showing that the conclusion, "All presidents are apt to make mistakes," is inescapable.

One may look upon drawing circle diagrams as a sort of game in which one seeks to embarrass the syllogism. If the syllogism is valid, the language will compel you to draw circles in a way that shows that the conclusion is an inescapable consequence of the premises. Whenever there is a choice about where a circle is to go, put it in a place (if you can) that will escape the conclusion of the syllogism. If there is such a place, then the diagram shows that the premises do not necessarily imply the conclusion announced and, therefore, the syllogism is invalid. Here is a diagram for an invalid syllogism:

All liberals want to regulate nuclear power plants.
All conservationists want to regulate nuclear power plants.
So, all conservationists are liberals.

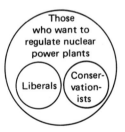

The conclusion here is shown to be invalid, for the language did not force the conservationists to be diagramed within the area of the liberals.

Intuitive perception of validity works only in obvious situations and circle diagrams, though effective in illustrating relationships, take time. We need a set of rules that will test whether a conclusion follows from the premises given. Four rules will do this job of testing any categorical syllogism. If any of the four is not satisfied, then it is a fallacy—a mistake of reasoning—to claim that the conclusion is a consequence of the premises.[2]

Rule 1 *A syllogism must have exactly three terms, each used exactly twice.*

Note: *Breaking this rule is "the fallacy of four terms."*

Look over the model again and notice that there are three terms with each term being used twice. So the model satisfies this requirement. It isn't too hard to see why there must be three terms and why each must be used twice. Let the assertion be:

> T-1 d   <   T-2 u
> All steel construction is erected by union workers.

> T-3 d   <   T-4 u
> That building is of wood construction.

> No conclusion possible

One can't go on because there are four terms in these two premises. In other words, the two premises are statements about different things, so it isn't possible to conclude anything. Maybe the wooden building was erected by union workers, but there is nothing in these premises that tells us that it has to be. Let's try again.

> T-1 d   <   T-2 u
> All steel construction is erected by union workers.

> T-3 d   <   T-1 u
> That building is of steel construction.

> T-3 d   <   T-4 u
> So, that building is erected by highly skilled workers.

Here a fourth term turns up in the conclusion. Since nothing has been said about "highly skilled workers" in the premises, it is not possible to have a conclusion about this group, which was not previously mentioned. Though it may seem startling at first, conclusions from premises only tell us what.is already *in the premises.* All of the theorems of geometry, for instance, rest upon the axioms: given the axioms, each theorem follows inescapably. As Laplace observed, if we had God-like minds, we would realize at once the implications of any set of premises that were given. Since we don't have such intelligence we realize implication more slowly, and may have a feeling of surprise when we find what the premises imply. Nevertheless, nothing *new* does appear in the conclusion. Go back to the model syllogism or to any valid syllogism given so far and you

---

[2]Winston W. Little, W. Harold Wilson, and W. Edgar Moore, *Applied Logic* (Boston: Houghton Mifflin, 1955) provided this model for testing the categorical syllogism with four rules. Other logic texts commonly present six or even eight rules to cover the same ground. The difference is in part accounted for by presenting as separate rules matters that can be combined.

will discover that the conclusion is made up of two terms, both of which have appeared already in the premises.

Now that we have just shown that a syllogism must have exactly three terms, each used exactly twice, we have to acknowledge a situation that looks like four terms but operates with three terms only. In identifying terms, we have insisted that different groups must be realized to be different terms—which they are. For example, "children" and "happy children" are different groups. All "happy children" are also "children," so anything true of all children will be true of happy children also. It doesn't work the other way around, though, for what may be true of the smaller group "happy children" may not hold for the larger group of all "children." This situation occasionally comes up in a syllogism. Let's suppose:

> T-1 d   <   T-2 u
> All children   like to ride on the ferryboat.
>
> T-3 d < T-1 u (a subgroup of "children")
> John is a happy child.
>
> T-3 d <   T-2 u
> John   likes to ride on the ferryboat.

Here John qualifies for the group that the major premise declares likes to ride on the ferryboat, and the conclusion follows inescapably. But if we put the more limited term into the major premise, then it won't work. Thus:

> T-1 d   <   T-2 u
> All happy children   like to ride the ferryboat.
>
> T-3 d < T-4 u (not a subgroup of "happy children")
> John is a child.
>
> T-3 d <   T-2 u
> John   likes to ride the ferryboat.

Here the major premise asserts only that the group "happy children" enjoy riding the ferryboat. Since we are not told that John is a happy child but only that he is a child, we cannot be sure that he is in the group that likes to ride the ferryboat.

This same possibility of having a fourth term which is a subgroup of one of the three terms already introduced may occur in the conclusion. Take, for instance:

> T-1 d   ≮   T-2 d
> All fish from polluted water are not safe to eat.
>
> T-3 d   <   T-1 d
> The fish in Mercury Bay   live in polluted water.
>
> T-3 d (a subgroup of
> "fish in Mercury Bay")   ≮   T-2 d
> Swordfish from Mercury Bay are not safe to eat.

According to these premises, all kinds of fish from Mercury Bay are not safe to eat. Though by mentioning swordfish alone, the conclusion states less than it could have claimed, still it inescapably follows that these swordfish are not safe to eat. When one class is wholly included in another class, we need to take a second look to see whether the situation comes under one of the possibilities we have just discussed.

Rule 2   *A syllogism must have either no exclusion or two exclusions, one of which must appear in the conclusion.*

Note: *Breaking this rule is "the fallacy of faulty exclusions."*

So far we have been dealing with syllogisms in which all the relationships were inclusions, and under these conditions there can be no trouble with exclusions. Now it is time to look at a syllogism with exclusions:

$$\text{T-1 d} \qquad \nless \qquad \text{T-2 d}$$
<u>Bagpipe players</u> are not <u>members of the band.</u>

$$\text{T-3 d} \qquad < \qquad \text{T-1 u}$$
<u>The MacGregor brothers</u> are <u>bagpipe players.</u>

$$\text{T-3 d} \qquad \nless \qquad \text{T-2 d}$$
<u>The MacGregor brothers</u> are not <u>members of the band.</u>

Here the rule is satisfied, for there are two exclusions and one of them is in the conclusion.

Let's take a moment to figure out why this rule exists. First, two exclusions in the premises can't produce a conclusion. For instance:

$$\text{T-1 d} \qquad \nless \qquad \text{T-2 d}$$
<u>State employees</u> are excluded from <u>this insurance plan.</u>

$$\text{T-3 d} \; \nless \qquad \text{T-1 d}$$
<u>We</u> are not <u>state employees.</u>

No conclusion possible

Where do we go from here? Two exclusions in the premises do not tell us where anything is to be included, so no conclusion is possible.

Now, why is it that when one premise has an exclusion then there must be an exclusion in the conclusion also? Though this demonstration is longer, it is not complicated. Suppose:

$$\text{T-1 d} \qquad \nless \qquad \text{T-2 d}$$
<u>A gambling contract</u> is not <u>enforceable in court.</u>

$$\text{T-3 d} \; < \qquad \text{T-2 u}$$
<u>This claim</u> is <u>a gambling contract.</u>

The conclusion must have an exclusion

First, one knows that a syllogism must have three terms, each of which is used twice. The term <u>gambling contract</u> is used in both premises and two uses are exhausted. So the conclusion must be made up of a second use of the terms <u>this claim</u> and <u>enforceable in court</u>. The minor premise identifies <u>this claim</u> as a <u>gambling contract</u>. If we drew the positive conclusion "This claim is enforceable in court" we would have a contradiction, since we know already from the minor premise that "This claim is a gambling contract" and that "A gambling contract is not enforceable in court." Therefore the relationships must be one of exclusion, so using the two terms that we know make up the conclusion, the result is "<u>This claim</u> is not <u>enforceable in court</u>." Hence, in working out a valid syllogism we end up with a second exclusion as the rule requires. The complete syllogism is:

$$\text{T-1 d} \quad \not< \quad \text{T-2 d}$$
<u>A gambling contract</u> is not <u>enforceable in court</u>.

$$\text{T-3 d} \quad < \quad \text{T-1 u}$$
<u>This claim</u> is a <u>gambling contract</u>.

$$\text{T-3 d} \quad \not< \quad \text{T-2 d}$$
<u>This claim</u> is not <u>enforceable in court</u>.

Rule 3   *The middle term must be distributed at least once.*

Note: *Breaking this rule is called "the fallacy of the undistributed middle term."*

The middle term is the term in common between the two premises. It is the connecting link between the premises, and if there were no such link the argument would simply fall apart for lack of any idea in common. Further, the requirement that a syllogism have *three* terms, each of which is used exactly twice, necessarily results in a middle term. After all, each premise has two terms, so it follows that one of the terms must be repeated in the premises in order to avoid introducing four terms. It's as simple as $2 + 2 = 4$.

Chapter 4 gave rules for quickly determining distribution. So we recall that quantifiers of "all" or "no" distribute the first term, while "some" makes the first term undistributed. Where the second term follows a relationship of exclusion it is distributed, and where it follows an inclusion it is undistributed. Here we must apply this knowledge to determine whether the middle term is distributed at least once. The following example shows a case in which the middle term is undistributed in both of its uses so that the syllogism is invalid:

$$\text{T-1 d} \quad < \quad \text{T-2 u}$$
All <u>police chiefs</u> <u>favor gun control</u>.

$$\text{T-3 d} \quad < \quad \text{T-2 u}$$
All <u>sheriffs</u> <u>favor gun control</u>.

$$\text{T-3 d} \quad < \quad \text{T-1 u}$$
So, all <u>sheriffs</u> are <u>police chiefs</u>.

Term 2 is the term in common between the two premises and, hence, it is the middle term. Since it is not distributed at least once, the syllogism is invalid. Circle diagrams will show that the conclusion is not forced.

Rule 4   *Any term distributed in the conclusion must be distributed in the premise where it appears.*

Note: *Breaking this rule is "the fallacy of illicit distribution."*

A conclusion may have no distributed term, or it may have one distributed and one undistributed term, or both terms may be distributed. This rule is concerned only with terms that *are* distributed in the conclusion, so if there are no such terms, all is well for the rule could not be violated. If one term is distributed, then that term has to be distributed in the premises. When a conclusion happens to have two distributed terms, then both must be distributed in the premises.

A syllogism that does not satisfy this rule will illustrate why a conclusion does not inescapably follow in such a case. Say:

$$\begin{array}{cc} \text{T-1 d} \quad < & \text{T-2 u} \\ \text{All \underline{pesticides} are \underline{damaging to the ecology}.} \end{array}$$

$$\begin{array}{cc} \text{T-3 u} \quad \not< & \text{T-1 d} \\ \text{Some \underline{poisons} are not \underline{pesticides}.} \end{array}$$

$$\begin{array}{cc} \text{T-3 u} \quad \not< & \text{T-2 d} \\ \text{So, some \underline{poisons} are not \underline{damaging to the ecology}.} \end{array}$$

The minor premise places some poisons outside the class "pesticides" without telling us whether they are inside or outside the larger class "things damaging to the ecology." So poisons outside the class "pesticides" may all be damaging to the ecology, or none may be damaging, or some may while others may not damage the ecology. The conclusion claims that some poisons are not damaging to the ecology, a claim inconsistent with the possibility just cited of all poisons being damaging. Hence the conclusion is not forced by the premises and we can win the game of embarrassing the syllogism with a circle diagram that conforms to the premises and fails to produce the conclusion.

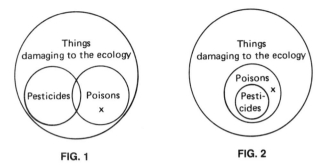

FIG. 1   **FIG. 2**

Check Fig. 1 against the assertions of the two premises and you will find that it conforms to the premises without producing the conclusion "Some poisons are not damaging to the ecology" which is asserted. The syllogism is, therefore, invalid. The invalidity is traceable to the fact that the term "damaging to the ecology" is undistributed in the first premise. Fig. 2 showing "pesticides" wholly included in "poisons" is an alternate way of drawing the circles in conformity with the premises, and this situation demonstrates invalidity also.[3]

Now we have seen how each of the rules for the syllogism is necessary to fasten the conclusion inescapably to the premises. If any one of the rules is not fulfilled, then the argument is invalid. What if two rules are broken? This can happen but it makes no difference since, so to speak, nothing can be deader than dead. A logician takes no further interest in a syllogism as soon as he notes a single ground making it invalid. Now I'm going to add a pedantic thought. Though speech seems to indicate the contrary at every turn, there is no such thing as a *syllogism* with four terms, or an undistributed middle term, or any other defect. A syllogism is a pattern of reasoning which meets certain conditions, and whatever doesn't conform to the conditions really isn't an "invalid syllogism" but no syllogism at all. We will go right on using the expression

---

[3]Completeness and interest require mention of a possible difficulty in the rare situation in which both premises are universals and the conclusion is particular. The problem arises because universal or "all" statements do not guarantee existence, whereas a particular or "some" statement is taken in logic to assure the existence of at least one case.

Example 1	*Example 2*
All dragon meat is green.	All dragon meat is green.
No green meat is tasty.	No green meat is tasty.
Some dragon meat is not tasty.	*All* dragon meat is not tasty.
Invalid because "some" asserts existence	Valid because "all" does not assert existence

It takes a fifth rule to meet the situation of Example 1. The rule is:

Two universal premises may not be followed by a particular conclusion unless the classes appearing in the premises are known to exist.

I suggest that the four rules given in the text will satisfactorily solve the usual situations encountered in deductive reasoning. For further discussion of the question of existence, see p. 113.

"invalid syllogism" with the understanding that it refers to arguments *claiming* to be syllogistic which turn out not to satisfy the rules.

Deductive reasoning is an instrument of intellectual power where conclusions follow inescapably from premises and where conclusions are authoritatively stamped "valid" or "invalid" according to whether they comply with the rules. Logicians are understandably fascinated by the elegant certainty with which validity is determined. I hope you will feel the tug of fascination, too. I like to think of deduction as a formal garden where everything is neat and orderly; he who learns the form will never lose his way. Yet if one is interested in the *truth* of the conclusion then, alas, we find that it is not deduction, ultimately at least, that tells us what is true. All deduction can ever tell is that a conclusion is *valid*, that it follows inescapably from the premises given. And if the premises are true, then a valid conclusion will be true also. This last idea is the kernel in the chaff: *true premises coupled with valid argument always yield a true conclusion.*

How do we know that the premises are true? Maybe a premise is the conclusion of some other deduction. If so, what about its premises? Pressing the question "How do we know?" must end either in a truth established by observation or by induction or by a mere assumption. In other words, the truth of a conclusion of a syllogism is not better established than the premises upon which it rests and, ultimately, the premises can be traced back to some origin not involving deduction.

Suppose a syllogism flunks the test, fails to fulfill one of the rules for valid inference from premises to conclusion? What do we know in this situation? A violation of a rule is a mistake in reasoning which is a fallacy, and we named the various fallacies for the categorical syllogism as we went along: "The four terms fallacy," "The fallacy of faulty exclusions," and so on. When a fallacy is discovered, there is a powerful temptation to believe that the conclusion reached by the fallacious argument is false, as indeed it may be. But the detection of a fallacy justifies only the realization that the conclusion has not been supported by the argument given: it remains possible for the conclusion to be true for other reasons. Further, even though an argument complies with all rules and is valid, if the premise material is false, then the conclusion may be false—or it may just happen to be true. I think these situations are worth illustrating.

Example 1

All presidents are wealthy men.	(False)
Abraham Lincoln was a president.	(True)
So, Abraham Lincoln was a wealthy man.	(Valid. Happens to be false.)

Example 2

All generals become president.	(False)
Abraham Lincoln was a general.	(False)
So, Abraham Lincoln became president.	(Valid. Happens to be true.)

Example 3

> All presidents are citizens of the USA.   (True)
> Abraham Lincoln was a president.   (True)
> So, Abraham Lincoln was a citizen of the USA. (Valid. MUST BE TRUE.)

Example 3 is the important situation. *Where the premises are true and the argument valid, then the conclusion must be true.*

It is now time to practice solving syllogisms that are in standard form—that is, syllogisms stated in an orderly way with premises first, conclusion last, and all terms repeating with little variation in wording. Actual speech rarely is so orderly and neat. After this formal garden is mastered, we can take up the challenge of how to pick a way through language presenting the infinite variety of a natural forest.

SUMMARY

> *Valid* means an inescapable consequence of the premises.
> *True* means that which corresponds to fact.

The conclusion of a syllogism may be valid without being true. But wherever the premises are true and the argument valid, then the conclusion will be true. See examples on pages 102–103.

The rules for the categorical syllogism are:

1. *There must be exactly three terms, each used exactly twice.*
   (Violation of this rule is the fallacy of *four terms.*)
2. *There must be either no exclusion or two exclusions, one of which must appear in the conclusion.*
   (Violation of this rule is the fallacy of *faulty exclusions.*)
3. *The middle term must be distributed at least once.*
   (Violation of this rule is the fallacy of the *undistributed middle.*)
4. *Any term distributed in the conclusion must be distributed in the premise where it appears.*
   (Violation of this rule is the fallacy of *illicit distribution.*)

With a little practice, the four rules given above can be applied mechanically in a few seconds. And it is simply not possible to analyze any syllogism until one knows the rules a syllogism must fulfill. Though "memorize" is a dirty word to some, time is saved by doing just that.

EXERCISES FOR CHAPTER 6
pages 93–103

I.   Answer **T** for "true" or **F** for "false":

_____ **1.** If a syllogism is valid, its conclusion must be true.

_____ **2.** One definition of "truth" is "That which corresponds to fact is true."

_____ **3.** Valid means only that the rules of logic have been met.

_____ **4.** If the material in the premises is true and the argument is valid, then the conclusion must be true.

_____ **5.** To check validity with circle diagrams, one tries to "embarrass the syllogism" by placing the circles to show the conclusion is not a necessary consequence of the premises.

_____ **6.** The conclusion of a syllogism is a new truth going beyond the material found in the premises.

_____ **7.** All valid syllogisms have either no exclusions or two exclusions, one of which appears in the conclusion.

_____ **8.** The middle term is the term in common between the two premises.

_____ **9.** If an argument is invalid, then the conclusion cannot be true.

_____ **10.** The conclusion of a syllogism is no more reliable than its premises.

_____ **11.** Where one of the rules for the syllogism is not satisfied, then a fallacy has been committed.

_____ **12.** When a fallacy is discovered, it remains uncertain whether the conclusion reached is true or false.

_____ **13.** Where there is fallacy committed, it's dead certain that the premises do not imply the conclusion given.

_____ **14.** A conclusion reached as a result of deduction is not always more likely to be true than a conclusion reached by any other kind of reasoning.

_____ **15.** Putting an argument into standard form makes an argument easier to analyze.

II.   The following syllogisms all illustrate the *four terms* fallacy. Underline the terms and number them in the order in which they occur. Write the fourth term in the blank provided in each case.

1. All people at Marsh Bay are bitten by insects.

The Jones family visited Marsh Bay.

The Jones family were bitten by mosquitos.

Fourth term: _____

2. Last Chance Mine stock is going up.

This security is a Last Chance Mine bond.

This security is going up.

Fourth term: _____

3. An expert marksman could hit that target.

Rufus Cramer is a marksman.

Rufus could hit that target.

Fourth term: _____

The next three syllogisms have *faulty exclusions.* Underline the terms and number them in order of their appearance. Then put in inclusion < and exclusion ≮ symbols as appropriate and check the blank with the explanation of how the faulty exclusion is committed.

4. A good electrician would not make that mistake.

George is not a good electrician.

So, George would make that mistake.

Only one exclusion _____   *Two exclusions in the premises* _____

5. No careful person takes that risk.

Pamela isn't a careful person.

Pamela will take the risk.

Only one exclusion _____   *Two exclusions in the premises* _____

6. Those who pick fights aren't wise.

But Charlie isn't wise.

So, Charlie is sure to pick a fight.

Only one exclusion _____   *Two exclusions in the premises* _____

The next three syllogisms have *undistributed middle terms*. Make a complete analysis by underlining the terms and numbering them in order of their appearance. Enter **d** or **u** over each term according to whether it is distributed or undistributed. Write the middle term in the blank provided, and be sure that your analysis shows it is undistributed both times.

7. Some talented people are eccentric.

   Randolf of Roanoke was talented indeed.

   Randolf of Roanoke was eccentric.

   Middle term: _____

8. All Van Gogh's later paintings have brilliant color.

   "The Vision after the Sermon" has brilliant color.

   So, "The Vision after the Sermon" is a late painting by Van Gogh.

   Middle term: _____

9. Every psychiatrist knows that diet may influence mental illness.

   Dr. Ruth Viau understands that diet may be connected with mental illness.

   Dr. Viau is a psychiatrist.

   Middle term: _____

Each of the next three syllogisms is afflicted with *illicit distribution*. Make a complete analysis for each—i.e., underline and number the terms, put in < or ≮ symbols, and place **d** or **u** over each term as appropriate. Write in the blanks the term or terms that are distributed in the conclusion without being distributed in the premises.

10. All those sent to county jails are apt to be abused.

    Some prisoners are not sent to county jails.

    So, some prisoners are not apt to be abused.

    _____

11. All who suffer neglect are apt to react.

Many musicians were neglected in their lifetimes.

All musicians are apt to react.

_____

12. Some of the assets are not easily sold.

Most of the stocks are easily sold.

So, some of the assets are not stocks.

_____

III.   Analyze the following syllogisms and rate each one **valid** or **invalid.**

1. Heaven is a perfect place.

A perfect place is a place without imperfection.

Heaven is a place without imperfection.

_____

2. Heaven is a place without imperfection.

Places without imperfection are places without dust.

Heaven is a place without dust.

_____

3. Heaven is a place without dust.

Places without dust are places having no raindrops.

Heaven is a place having no raindrops.

_____

4. Heaven is a place having no raindrops.

Places having no raindrops are not perfect places.

Heaven is not a perfect place!

_____

For heaven's sake, what's wrong? Give a one sentence explanation of how such a contradiction could come about.

_____

_____

_____

chapter 7

Immediate Inference

Whenever one asserts something—anything at all—then other things can be derived from what has been asserted. These "other things" are a kind of deduction called *immediate inference*. To give an example, if we allow that "Some geniuses are peculiar people" then it follows as the night the day that "Some peculiar people are geniuses." The second sentence is an immediate inference from the first, since, as the term *immediate inference* suggests, the inference is made directly from the first statement to the second without any additional information being used. So, to give a definition, we can say:

Immediate inference is deriving a conclusion from a single premise.

Investigating the additional information to be derived from a single statement presents a sort of paradox. Your first impression is apt to be that immediate inferences are self-evident, and you may react, "Why trouble to elaborate such obvious things?" After you are convinced that you are being bored and underwhelmed, then you may run into trouble and discover that the subject can become confusing. Let me put in a plea to become familiar with the *rules* for immediate inference so that you will develop the ability to unravel what inferences follow from any statement, obvious or not.

SHIFTING PROPOSITIONAL FORMS

Any statement in any form can be shifted into the other three forms and the resulting assertions can then be rated as "true," "false," or, if the resulting statement could be either true or false, then "doubtful." For example, let us accept the total inclusion "All motorboats are taxed" as true. Acceptance of this truth implies:

Total inclusion	A	All motorboats are taxed.	*true*
total excl.	E	No motorboats are taxed.	*false*
partial incl.	I	Some motorboats are taxed.	*true*
partial excl.	O	Some motorboats are not taxed.	*false*

Where a total inclusion is true, it is easy enough to shift through the other three forms and see which also must be true and which false. First, the shift into a relation of total exclusion is a contradiction of what is true and, therefore, is false. If it is true that "All motorboats are taxed," then "No motorboats are taxed" can't be true at the same time. Next, the partial inclusion is evidently true, for if "All motorboats are taxed," then some of them must be taxed. Indeed, they all are. The partial inclusion states less than might be asserted, but it is certainly true as far as it goes. Finally, if "All motorboats are taxed," there is no room for "Some motorboats are not taxed." This is clearly false. So you see, beginning with a total inclusion one may make three other statements and rate each "true" or "false."

The "additional information" produced by immediate inference is not new information; it is merely the necessary implications of the material found in the original statement. Just as with syllogisms, had we Laplace's famous God-like mind, we would realize at once all the implications of any statement and there would be no feeling of surprise in discovering them. It is as stumbling mortals that we feel surprise and even make mistakes in working out immediate inferences.

Suppose we are given a total exclusion, say, "No sailboats are taxed." Then we get this pattern:

Total exclusion	E	No sailboats are taxed.	*true*
total incl.	A	All sailboats are taxed.	*false*
partial incl.	I	Some sailboats are taxed.	*false*
partial excl.	O	Some sailboats are not taxed.	*true*

Any discussion would merely repeat explanations just given for inferences from total inclusion. You may follow through the cases, checking the inferences for yourself.

Now let's investigate what happens when a partial inclusion is taken to be true, say, "Some ferryboats are taxed."

Partial inclusion	I	Some ferryboats are taxed.	*true*
total incl.	A	All ferryboats are taxed.	*doubtful*
total excl.	E	No ferryboats are taxed.	*false*
partial excl.	O	Some ferryboats are not taxed.	*doubtful*

This series, though different, is not hard to follow. You recall that on p. 85 we explained how "Some student council members were at the game" does not have as a necessary implication that others were not there. Here we have the same sort of situation. You may imagine that you have taken a ferryboat in France and find a certificate displayed: *"Cet bac a payé la taxe annuelle."* (This ferryboat has paid the annual tax.) Now you know this ferryboat has paid a tax, but you really don't know much about French taxes and you can't be sure that every ferryboat in France pays a tax. Maybe all are taxed or it could be that some are exempt. So you don't know. Therefore the statement "All ferryboats are taxed" is doubtful, and so is "Some ferryboats are not taxed."

The last form to consider is partial exclusion. Suppose, for example, "Some barges are not taxed" is known to be true.

Partial exclusion	**O**	Some barges are not taxed.	*true*
total incl.	**A**	All barges are taxed.	*false*
total excl.	**E**	No barges are taxed.	*doubtful*
partial incl.	**I**	Some barges are taxed.	*doubtful*

These results follow the explanation given for partial inclusion above.

The shifts for all four propositional forms may be brought together in a single tabulation:

If a total inclusion is true, then a
    total exclusion = F
    partial inclusion = T
    partial exclusion = F
	If a partial inclusion is true, then a
	    total inclusion = D
	    total exclusion = F
	    partial exclusion = D

If a total exclusion is true, then a
    total inclusion = F
    partial inclusion = F
    partial exclusion = T
	If a partial exclusion is true, then a
	    total inclusion = F
	    total exclusion = D
	    partial inclusion = D

Stating the same shifts for all four propositional forms in the more economical A-, E-, I-, and O-form terminology, we have:

A-form true, then	E-form true, then	I-form true, then	O-form true, then
E-form F	A-form F	A-form D	A-form F
I-form T	I-form F	E-form F	E-form D
O-form F	O-form T	O-form D	I-form D

Nobody walks around with this tabulation so impressed in his mind that he checks shifts of propositional forms against it. However, one *can* check any proposed shift of propositional form against this chart and read off the answer. It may be useful to refer back to it until you get the hang of how this type of immediate inference works. Shifting propositional forms correctly is useful even in those cases where the shifted form is "doubtful" rather than "true" or "false," for to know what has not been established is a signpost also in the search for truth.

INFERENCE FROM THE KNOWLEDGE THAT A PROPOSITION IS FALSE

It can be a lot of help to know that something is false. "The rumor 'Well 84 has struck oil' is false." "The claim 'Some cancers cure themselves' is not true." Clearly, to know that something is false is to know something. But just what? This "just what" is our concern here.

Whenever a statement is known to be false, then by immediate inference certain other statements must be true. Given a false statement, what can be validly inferred is the *minimum* that must be true to sustain the falseness of the original statement. An example will make this meaningful. Assume the total inclusion "All the windows in this house are locked" is false. Then at least one window must exist that is not locked, for otherwise the given statement would not be false. Maybe three, five, or all the windows in the house are unlocked— no telling about these possibilities. We can be sure, however, that at least one window is unlocked, or, in other words, that the partial inclusion "Some window is not locked" is true.

Now take the total exclusion "No door of this house is green" to be false. Then there must be at least one green door, or, in other words, the partial inclusion "Some door in the house is green" must be true. Again, there might be two green doors or they could all be green. We don't know about these possibilities. What we know is that there must be at least one green door, because if this were not the case then the statement "No door of this house is green" would be true.

Partial inclusion and partial exclusion are equally easy. If we take "Some rooms of this house are freshly painted" to be false, then we know for sure that no room in the house can be freshly painted. After all, if there were a freshly painted room, the statement "Some rooms of this house are freshly painted" would be true. To conclude with a partial exclusion, assume that "Some rooms in this house are not heated" is false. We know at once that all rooms of the house must be heated, for this is the minimum situation that will sustain the falsity of the assertion "Some rooms in this house are not heated."

One can arrange into a neat pattern this series of valid inferences following from the knowledge that a proposition is false:

> Where a **total inclusion** is false, then a **partial exclusion** is true.
> Where a **total exclusion** is false, then a **partial inclusion** is true.
> Where a **partial inclusion** is false, then a **total exclusion** is true.
> Where a **partial exclusion** is false, then a **total inclusion** is true.

Applying the A-, E-, I-, and O-form terminology brings out the pattern:

> **A**-form false, then **O**-form true
> **E**-form false, then **I**-form true
> **I**-form false, then **E**-form true
> **O**-form false, then **A**-form true

Notice that the left column runs in the usual order in which the four relationships are presented, while the right column runs the opposite way. They sing do, re, me, fa and fa, me, re, do! But I must come down to earth and take up the legitimate question, "What use is this?"

Inferences drawn from the knowledge that something is false are not difficult. Winston Churchill's famous remark, "I have not always been wrong" is an arresting proposal of a false proposition, yet clear enough for anybody to draw the proper inference. Though the basic pattern for implying truths from statements known to be false is not hard to remember, one can always work out the valid inference from some simple example such as the ones used above. The basic fact is to realize that any statement known to be false will also imply *one* other statement that must be true.

CONVERSION

In conversion we have a common kind of immediate inference; many occasions call for quick and correct recognition of converted forms. So, what is a conversion?

A conversion is the interchanging of the subject term and the predicate term of a proposition.

For example, if "All elephants are heavy" can we say "All heavy things are elephants"? No one is likely to make this mistake, though many would scratch their heads if the conversion involved kinds of things that were unfamiliar. Many people would not know readily whether "All A is B" does or does not justify saying that "All B is A." Pity such people, for they will surely be fooled as argument gallops along.

It just happens that with the conversion of a total inclusion like "All elephants are heavy" we have stumbled into a point debated among logicians. Though one may find differing views in logic texts, I think we can deal with the problem in a way that forestalls any practical difficulty. The source of the difficulty, too, is sort of an interesting one and we'll venture to look at it even at this very beginning of conversion. If "All elephants are heavy," then it must be that "Some heavy things are elephants" right enough. But if "All dragons are dangerous" is it proper to say that "Some dangerous things are dragons"? We have come to a case of an empty class, that air bubble that can stall the machine of formal logic once in a while. The crux of the problem is that an *all* statement does not guarantee existence, whereas a *some* statement in logic is taken to guarantee the existence of at least one case. "All violators are towed to ABC Garage" is not a statement that any violators exist, but a declaration that violators, if there are any, will be towed. So you see, "all" does not promise existence of the class. The quantifier "some," however, does promise that at least one case exists. Thus, the conversion of a total inclusion from *all* to *some* gets caught up in this difficulty. Logicians are a strange lot. They'll let you go around all day declaring, "All unicorns have a single horn," and they will only nod amiably, but the moment you opine that "Some unicorns are bad-tempered" they'll get up and shout, "Now you must show me a unicorn!" And if you produce one they won't be satisfied unless he/she has a bad temper to boot. I propose to sidestep this problem of existence by setting up a rather obvious condition. A statement making a total inclusion can be converted—have its subject and predicate term swapped around—provided no term is empty. To put it in another way, don't convert a total inclusion unless you know that what you are talking about actually exists. Only the most imaginative souls will chaff under this restraint.

Conversions are common. "All passport applicants present papers at Window A." Now let's see, can I reason that everybody in the line for Window A should be a passport applicant? What we need to do now is to examine how conversion works in each of the four relationships, and in doing this we will find that circle diagrams are a handy way of showing what converts and what does not. Here are some simple illustrations:

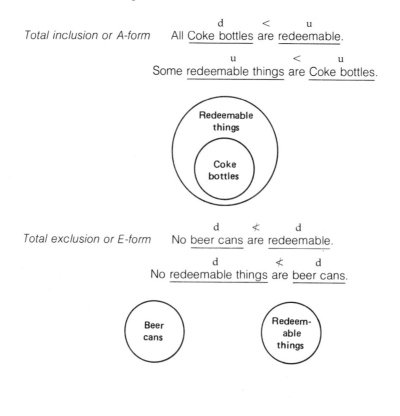

Total inclusion or A-form   All Coke bottles are redeemable.
　　　　　　　　　　　　　　　　　d　　<　　u

Some redeemable things are Coke bottles.
　　u　　　<　　u

Total exclusion or E-form   No beer cans are redeemable.
　　　　　　　　　　　　　　d　　≮　　d

No redeemable things are beer cans.
　d　　≮　　d

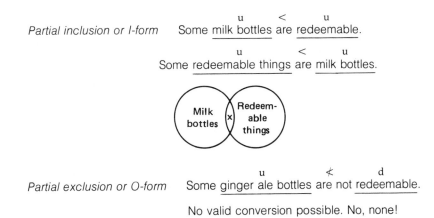

Partial inclusion or I-form   Some milk bottles are redeemable.

Some redeemable things are milk bottles.

Partial exclusion or O-form   Some ginger ale bottles are not redeemable.

No valid conversion possible. No, none!

The relationships shown by the circle diagrams demonstrate how conversion works for the A-, E-, and I-forms. A-form conversions require that the classes concerned be not empty, and *all* becomes *some* in the converted form. E- and I-forms always convert without a hitch. So let's concentrate on why the O-form, partial exclusion, simply won't convert. This causes lots of trouble. We will start by looking at the circle diagrams for an O-form situation:

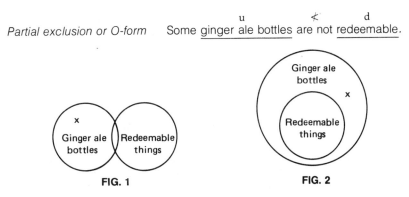

Partial exclusion or O-form   Some ginger ale bottles are not redeemable.

FIG. 1   FIG. 2

The statement "Some ginger ale bottles are not redeemable" definitely asserts that there are ginger ale bottles outside of the class of redeemable things. As you may recall, the statement does not tell us whether any ginger ale bottles are redeemable.

Further, for all we know from the assertion, there may be no redeemable things that are not ginger ale bottles. Fig. 2 depicts this situation where redeemable things are limited to ginger ale bottles and even some ginger ale bottles can't be redeemed. It could even be that nothing is redeemable, for we actually have not been told anything about the class "redeemable things." If Fig. 2 strikes you as a preposterous situation, your feeling comes from knowledge of the outside world and not from anything given in the original assertion. Maybe I can demonstrate that your reaction really is unjustified if we change the class a bit. Suppose instead of talking about "redeemable things" which your worldly experience has taught you is an enormously variable class, we make the statement "Some ginger ale bottles are not redeemable at Dan's Refreshment Stand." Could it not be that this refreshment stand redeems nothing but ginger ale bottles and not all brands of these? Could it not easily be that Dan's Refreshment Stand redeems no bottles at all? If you answer these questions "Yes," then you are envisioning the situations of Figs. 1 and 2. So we see (I like to assume my efforts to persuade are successful), knowledge of the real world is an influence deflecting thought from purely logical considerations, otherwise a change of class from "redeemable things" to "redeemable at Dan's Refreshment Stand" would make no difference in one's feelings. As remarked before, symbols do have an advantage in removing the distraction of meaning from influencing a logical analysis.

One way to show that conversion won't work for a statement of partial exclusion is to go ahead and make such a conversion and then point out its invalidity. Might as well stick to the example already begun

Partial exclusion or O-form   Some ginger ale bottles are not redeemable.

*This is **invalid***   Some redeemable things are not ginger ale bottles.

This invalid conversion runs smack into the Fig. 2 situation just discussed. The fact that common knowledge tells us that in fact "Some redeemable things are not ginger ale bottles" makes the error converting partial exclusions all the more seductive. Deductive reasoning approves as valid only those inferences which follow 100% of the time, not usually, or 95% of the time, or anything less than always.

Probably the best way to handle conversion is to remember how conversion works out for each of the four forms individually. It isn't much to remember:

Total inclusion	(A-form)	Converts with *some* as the quantifier
		Converts only where the classes are not empty
Total exclusion	(E-form)	Always converts
Partial inclusion	(I-form)	Always converts
Partial exclusion	(O-form)	Never converts

Another way to handle conversion is to know the rules a valid conversion must meet. The rules are:

1. The converse must retain the same quality as the original assertion—i.e., both must be affirmative or both be negative.
2. No term may be distributed in the converse unless it was distributed in the original.

It will do no harm to look over these rules regardless of whether or not they appeal to you as the easiest way to deal with conversions. The first rule declares that relationships of inclusion must be kept as inclusions, and exclusions must remain exclusions. Actually, there is little temptation to break this requirement. The second rule requires that when a term is distributed in the converse it also must be distributed in the original. This requirement resembles the rule against illicit distribution. If you reread the examples with these two requirements in mind, you will see how the examples conform to them in every case. You will find that the rules neatly require a quantifier of *some* in converting a total inclusion, for without this quantifier the distribution requirement for terms distributed in the converse would be violated. Also, examination will show that it is impossible to convert a partial exclusion and comply with the rules. We will take final leave of the ginger ale bottles by noticing in the sentence

u   ⊀   d
Some <u>ginger ale bottles</u> are not <u>redeemable</u>.

the term "ginger ale bottles" is undistributed. If this sentence were converted to place ginger ale bottles as the second term following an exclusion, it would become a distributed term and Rule 2 would be violated. Were one to change the relationship of exclusion into the inclusion that is needed to keep the second term undistributed, then a violation of Rule 1 would be committed.

To make any conversion that the rules do not permit is to commit the fallacy of *false conversion.*

OBVERSION

The last kind of immediate inference we will consider is obversion. What sort of an animal is this? I'll show you with a bit of imaginary conversation.

Original   <u>John</u> is not <u>short</u>.
Valid obversion   <u>John</u> is <u>non-short</u>.

"Look here. This logic bit is getting out of hand. Whoever, I ask you, would go around saying that 'John is non-short'? Anyone who speaks English knows the way to say this—'John is tall.'"

"I'm sorry. The logician must have it as 'non-short.' Let's try again."

Original   Those who have a ticket can go in.
False obversion   Those who do not have a ticket cannot go in.

"Now come on. If those who have a ticket can go in, I'm sure that those who don't have one can't go in."

"Sorry again. A logician can't approve of this obversion because things don't *have* to work out that way. So it is not a valid inference. At the famous Woodstock Festival thousands of young people came back bemoaning the fact that they had bought tickets and everybody who arrived simply walked right in. And the tickets weren't cheap, either."

"I've always wondered about the Woodstock Affair. You say the tickets were expensive...?"

"I'm sorry, but I've got to interrupt. I didn't say the tickets were 'expensive.' I said only that they were 'not cheap.' You keep making mistakes with obversion. Really, we must get down to business and see how obversions work."

A valid obversion is made by changing a relationship of inclusion into exclusion, or vice-versa, and by placing the negative "not" (or non-) before the second term of the assertion.

You will soon find this rule is an easy one, and any statement can be obverted according to it. Whatever the relationship between the terms—inclusion or exclusion—the relationship is changed to its opposite; that is, an inclusion is made into an exclusion, or an exclusion is changed into an inclusion. Then an offsetting change is made by placing "not" or "non-" before the second term. If the second term already has a negative before it, the double negative can be canceled out to make a positive. The result of this procedure will be no change of meaning, though there may be a change in tone. The result of an obversion may always be obverted back to its original form—indeed, any immediate inference can be transformed back into the assertion that one started with. Here are a few valid obversions:

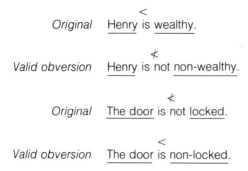

Original   Henry is wealthy.

Valid obversion   Henry is not non-wealthy.

Original   The door is not locked.

Valid obversion   The door is non-locked.

<
Original   Spending time together is part of successful marriage.

⟨
Valid obversion   Spending time together is not a non-part of successful marriage.

In every case the rule has been followed rigidly, slavishly. Each result is valid. But the English! No one is going to talk this way no matter what. Agreed. We will have to understand strictly carried out obversions first and then take up the problem of euphonious English.

Everything in the world can be divided sharply into two classes by placing "not" or "non-" before class names. All situations are covered if we talk about old and not old, rich and not rich, strong and not strong, virtuous and not virtuous. When my daughter was a small child she once sat on the edge of the pottie, rocking back and forth singing, "Some do—some don't. Some do—some don't. Some dooo—some dooonn't. (pause) I don't fall in the pottie!" She was right. All the world can be divided into those who do and those who don't fall in the pottie.

A twofold division allows for no intermediate cases. Sometimes this works well enough—a door may be described as "locked" or "not locked" without raising a problem of intermediate cases. Often the price for the sharp clarity of simply placing "not" before a term is the acceptance of an arbitrary dividing line—using "arbitrary" in the sense of a dividing point chosen for convenience. Thus a single day of age divides "eligible" from "not eligible" to receive Social Security. Unless some compelling reason makes it necessary to apply a clear standard, it may be whimsical to break into a continuum with a twofold division: one speaks of people as babies, toddlers, children, teenagers, young adults, middle-aged, octogenarians. Generally it is needless to divide people crisply into "old" or "not old," while "old" or "young" is even worse, because it leaves out the middle-aged.

A mechanical performance of obversion—that is, simply changing the inclusion relationship into an exclusion, or vice-versa, and placing "not" before the second term—always yields a valid result though the expression may be awkward. If the expression is unacceptable, at least it will mark out the limits of what the valid inference is. Then, if necessary, one may seek to express the valid result in a more normal, euphonious way. Sometimes an expression that is not awkward can be found; at other times an acceptable-sounding result for obversion is not available. Here are two examples:

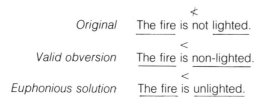

⟨
Original   The fire is not lighted.

<
Valid obversion   The fire is non-lighted.

<
Euphonious solution   The fire is unlighted.

Original	David is tall.
Valid obversion	David is not non-tall.
Euphonious solution	None. *"David is not short" is tempting, but this fails to exclude David's being of ordinary stature.*

Difficulty in finding euphonious words to express the outcome of obversion is no great problem because wherever obversion produces an awkward phrase one may always go back to the original to express the meaning.

The other common mistake made with obversion is obverting the first term. Only the *second* term is negated in an obversion. "The good die young" asserts just that: The good < die young. Nothing is said about the fate of "those who are not good." It is a common fallacy—and an easily spotted one—to assume that an assertion about one group implies that a contrasting situation exists for a contrasting group. A contrasting group may, of course, have a contrasting outcome, but where this is so it just happens to be so; there is no necessary inference whereby anything said about one class implies the opposite for a contrasting class. "A good businessman pays his bills promptly" does not imply that one "not a good businessman" never does. "A slow reader can follow this paragraph" does not inevitably mean that a reader who is not slow cannot follow it. In short, the first term does not obvert.

It is a fallacy known as *false obversion* to make a mistake in obversion, either by obverting the first term or by introducing words that are not equivalent to a negation of the second term.

Though there are other kinds of immediate inference, the four we have presented are a good base to work with and will handle the most common problems. Putting immediate inference to work in one's thinking requires practice. Sometimes the drills dreamed up to give practice in working out immediate inferences may seem like pointless mental gymnastics. They aren't. Do not regard intuitively perceived answers as solutions, for what is sought is using the *process* that produces the answer, or, shall we say, grinds out a valid inference. Finally, and with a confessed echo of inconsistency, I realize that the tables and rules given in this chapter are not a body of material through which the mind always operates in dealing with immediate inferences: they are ways for making a rigorous check whenever one wants to test this kind of inference. And with practice one can better sense where the pitfalls lie, better realize where care is needed. The useful outcome is this feel for the subject that helps to avoid errors.

SUMMARY

An immediate inference is an inference drawn from one premise. Four kinds of immediate inference have been presented:

1. *Shifting propositional forms* takes the original assertion as true and rates the remaining three forms as true, false, or doubtful according to whether the shifted form is necessarily consistent with the original statement (true), or is inconsistent with it (false), or could be either consistent or inconsistent (doubtful). The shifts for all propositional forms are given on p. 111.

2. *Inference from the knowledge that a proposition is false* is the minimum that must be true in order for the original statement to be false. The pattern of valid inferences resulting from the knowledge that a proposition is false is given on p. 112.

3. *Conversion* is interchanging the subject term and the predicate term. One should know the convertibility or lack of convertibility for each of the four propositional forms. It runs this way:

   Total inclusion   (A-form)   Converts with *some* as the quantifier
                                    Converts only where terms are not empty
   Total exclusion   (E-form)   Always converts
   Partial inclusion   (I-form)   Always converts
   Partial exclusion (O-form)   Never converts

4. *Obversion* is made by changing the relationship of inclusion to exclusion, or vice-versa, and by placing the negative "not" or its equivalent before the *second* term of the assertion. Any proposition can be obverted, and no change in meaning takes place. One common mistake in obversion arises from substituting a euphonious term that is not equivalent to a negative before the original term: thus "non-hot" cannot be changed to "cold." Another error comes from obverting the first term: only the *second* term can be obverted.

EXERCISES FOR CHAPTER 7
pages 109–121

I. Answer **T** for "true" or **F** for "false":

_____ 1. Any conclusion that can be derived from one premise is an immediate inference.

_____ 2. If one is given the statement that "Some tom-toms are extremely loud," then one knows by immediate inference that "Some tom-toms are not extremely loud."

_____ 3. Given the knowledge that a statement is false, one may infer by immediate inference the minimum that must be true in view of the falseness of the original statement.

_____ 4. The knowledge that a statement is false always implies one other statement which will be, not doubtful, but true.

_____ 5. In logic, the quantifier "all" does not guarantee that there are any members of the class designated, while the quantifier "some" is taken to indicate that at least one member exists.

_____ 6. There is no valid conversion for any statement that is a partial exclusion or O-form.

_____ 7. When a valid obversion has been carried out, it may be carried out a second time with the result that one comes back to the original statement.

_____ 8. "Not heavy" is equivalent to "light."

_____ 9. There is no necessary inference whereby a thing said to be true for one class implies the opposite for a contrasting class.

_____ 10. Since those who have not studied obversion are apt to make mistakes when carrying out obversions, it follows that those who have studied obversion are not apt to make such mistakes.

II. Shift each statement into the other three propositional forms, writing the shifted forms in the blanks provided. Accepting the original statement as true, rate each of the others as **T**, **F**, or **D**.

1. *Total incl.*   **A**   All profits are reinvested.   ___T___

    Total excl.   **E**   _____   _____

Partial incl.	**I**	_____	_____
Partial excl.	**O**	_____	_____
2. *Total excl.*	**E**	No books are stored here.	T
Total incl.	**A**	_____	_____
Partial incl.	**I**	_____	_____
Partial excl.	**O**	_____	_____
3. *Partial incl.*	**I**	Some poems are short.	T
Total incl.	**A**	_____	_____
Total excl.	**E**	_____	_____
Partial excl.	**O**	_____	_____
4. *Partial excl.*	**O**	Some people are not patient.	T
Total incl.	**A**	_____	_____
Total excl.	**E**	_____	_____
Partial incl.	**I**	_____	_____
5. *Total excl.*	**E**	No X is Y.	T
Total incl.	**A**	_____	_____
Partial incl.	**I**	_____	_____
Partial excl.	**O**	_____	_____
6. *Partial excl.*	**O**	Some Dungos are not prolific.	T
Total incl.	**A**	_____	_____
Total excl.	**E**	_____	_____
Partial incl.	**I**	_____	_____

III.   Consider each of the given statements is known to be false. Fill in each blank with a true statement derived by immediate inference.

1. *False:*   All immediate inference is difficult.

True: _____

2. *False:*   No one can be forced to accept beliefs.

True: _____

3. *False:*   Some high-speed typists have poor fingering.

True: _____

4. *False:*   Some glaciers are not moving.

True: _____

IV.   For each of the following, underline the terms exactly, insert the appropriate connective symbol and identify each of the terms as distributed (d) or undistributed (u). In the blank provided to the left of each number state the form of each proposition as A, E, I, or O.

After completing the steps given above, convert the statement in the space provided. If it is not possible to make a proper conversion, point out why this is so.

_____   **1.** No musicians are acrobats.

_____

_____   **2.** Some drivers are careless.

_____

_____   **3.** Every loss is painful.

_____

_____   **4.** Some mountains are snowcapped.

_____

_____ **5.** Some temples are not pagodas.

_____

_____ **6.** No liquor is sold after midnight.

_____

_____ **7.** All witches are people.

_____

_____ **8.** All former employees will be rehired.

_____

_____ **9.** Some mining practices are not wise.

_____

_____ **10.** Some beliefs are threats to peace.

_____

_____ **11.** Some advertising is not truthful.

_____

_____ **12.** Many works of art are poorly displayed.

_____

_____ **13.** No guests allowed here.

_____

_____ **14.** Revolutions produce unintended results.

_____

_____ **15.** Most metals are not combustible.

_____

_____ **16.** Some brands of paint can't be bought there.

_____

_____ **17.** All griffins are mythical beings.

_____

V.   For each of the following, underline the terms exactly and insert the appropriate connective symbol. Then obvert the statement in the space provided. Carry out the obversion by following the procedure for proper obversion mechanically—do not alter wording at any point for the sake of euphony.

   1. Kangaroos are interesting animals.

   _____

   2. Athletic awards are not won by all.

   _____

   3. Success in business requires courage.

   _____

   4. Ignorance is not a helpful thing.

   _____

   5. Recklessness never is good judgment.

   _____

   6. Sharks are an ancient form of life.

   _____

7. Love is forgiving.

_____

8. Some history books are not reliable.

_____

VI.   In this exercise shifts of form, conversions, and obversions are mixed together. A few of the immediate inferences proposed are not valid. Although intuitive thinking will produce many correct answers, eventually it leads to becoming not non-confused. So, to get the right answer in each case, identify the type of immediate inference involved and then apply the proper rule. Here is a box to aid in doing this:

> 1. Is there a **shift in propositional form** whereby the new statement has the same subject and predicate as the given statement, only the new statement differs as to A, E, I, or O-form?
> 2. Is there a **conversion** whereby subject and predicate of the given statement have been interchanged?
> 3. Is there an **obversion** whereby the *second* term of the given statement has been changed from positive to negative, or vice versa, and the relationship between the terms changed from < to ≮, or vice versa?
> 4. Is the new statement to be derived from the given statement by any two of the above possibilities?

Remember that where the given statement is true, validly carried out conversions or obversions will be **T** while false conversions or obversions will be **D**. Shifts in propositional form will be **T, F,** or **D** according to the table on page 111. Now, examine the model below and fill in the blanks according to the same pattern. Rate your solutions as **T, F,** or **D**.

Model:

All logic problems are mental exercises. (Given as T)

A-form (total incl.) _____   T

   a. No logic problems are mental exercises.

Shifted to E-form (total excl.) _____   F

b. Some logic problems are mental exercises.

Shifted to I-form (partial incl.) _____   T

c. Some logic problems are not mental exercises.

Shifted to O-form (partial excl.) _____   F

d. Some mental exercises are logic problems.   T
if classes
Conversion of A-form _____   not empty

e. All logic problems are not non-mental exercises.

Obversion of A-form _____   T

1. No skills are learned immediately.

_E_ _____   T

    a. Some skills are not learned immediately.

Partial exclusion O form   T

    b. Some skills are learned immediately.

Contradictory   I form   F

    c. All things learned immediately are excluded from skills.

Converted   T

    d. Some things learned immediately are not skills.

Convert + shift in propos.   T

    e. All skills are not learned immediately.

_____   _____

2. Some laws are easy to enforce.

_____   T

    a. Some laws are not easy to enforce.

_____   _____

    b. Some laws are not not easy to enforce.

_____   _____

    c. Some non-laws are not easy to enforce.

_____   _____

    d. No laws are easy to enforce.

_____   _____

3. Some customs are not beneficial.

_____   _T____

    a. All customs are not beneficial.

_____   _____

    b. Some customs are beneficial.

_____   _____

    c. Some beneficial things are not customs.

_____   _____

    d. Some customs are non-beneficial.

_____   _____

    e. Some customs are highly undesirable.

_____   _____

4. All A is B.

_____   _T____

    a. All B is A.

_____   _____

    b. A is not non-B.

_____   _____

    c. Some B is A.

_____   _____

    d. Some A is B.

_____   _____

e. Some B is not A.

_____   _____

5. Some inferences are confusing.

_____   __T__

a. Some inferences are not confusing.

_____   _____

b. Some confusing things are not inferences.

_____   _____

c. All inferences are confusing.

_____   _____

d. Some inferences are not non-confusing.

_____   _____

e. Some inferences are not very simple.

_____   _____

VII.   Assume that each of the four following propositions is false. From each draw the necessarily true inference, then convert and/or obvert the resulting true inference as directed below. Write your answers in the blanks provided.

1. It is false that "No species of man has become extinct."

    a. Inference from false prop. _____

    b. Conversion of (a) _____

    c. Obversion of (b) _____

2. It is false that "All wars are great population checks."

    a. Inference from false prop. _____

    b. Obversion of (a) _____

3. It is false that "Some DDT does not harm the ecology."

    a. Inference from false prop. _____

    b. Conversion of (a) _____

    c. Obversion of (b) _____

4. It is false that "Some human societies achieve justice."

    a. Inference from false prop. _____

    b. Conversion of (a) _____

    c. Obversion of (b) _____

chapter 8

The Hypothetical Syllogism

The categorical syllogism is a ponderous machine for reasoning. You are familiar with the process it entails: consider the exact meaning for each term, be sure each is used exactly twice, observe the number of negatives used, check the distribution of the middle term and of any term distributed in the conclusion—when and only when all these conditions are met will the conclusion be valid. As we continue with other types of syllogisms, you will find the rules no less rigorous, and conclusions are stamped "valid" or "invalid" with the same finality. But to your relief you will discover that all the other syllogistic forms are simpler, have fewer rules, and often may be grasped and checked without resort to pencil and paper.

The hypothetical syllogism describes what will happen under certain conditions. Its major premise does not say that the conditions do exist; it is hypothetical, saying only what will happen *if* they do exist. For example:

If it rains, then the river will rise.

Here we have a hypothetical statement expressed in standard form for easy use as the major premise of a hypothetical syllogism. One does not have to tax the mind to see that a conclusion will follow as soon as we add "it is raining" to this hypothetical statement.

<pre>
       A   C
If it rains, then the river will rise.
It is raining.
Therefore, the river will rise.
</pre>

The condition is called the *antecedent* or "A," while the state of affairs asserted to ensue if the antecedent occurs is called the *consequent* or "C." Notice in the example that the minor premise affirms that the antecedent occurred and, therefore, the consequent must occur too. So the assertion of the consequent appears as the conclusion.

Now let us look at another possibility in this hypothetical situation.

> A   C
> If it rains, then the river will rise.
> The river will not rise.
> Therefore, it will not rain.

Here the minor premise denies the consequent. Since the major premise promises that the consequent will occur if the antecedent occurs, it must be that the antecedent will not occur. Hence, a conclusion asserting the antecedent will not occur is valid.

From these two examples one can derive the rule for solving hypothetical syllogisms. Though we have yet to discuss some minor points, still the one really important rule for a valid hypothetical syllogism boils down to seven key words. Here it is:

For a valid hypothetical syllogism one must AFFIRM THE ANTECEDENT OR DENY THE CONSEQUENT.

Brand the seven capitalized words into your mind! Your effort will be rewarded, since this short rule will answer most of the problems that arise with hypothetical syllogisms. The terminology "antecedent" and "consequent" makes it clear that the rule applies to the hypothetical syllogism, for these words do not apply to any other kind of syllogism. All rules set down in this book are for valid forms; no need to remember whether the rule concerns the valid form.

Now two errors are commonly made by those unacquainted with how a hypothetical syllogism is supposed to work. The first is the fallacy of denying the antecedent.

> A   C
> If it rains, then the river will rise.
> It will not rain.

Lots of people would draw a conclusion from these two premises. To do so is a mistake, a fallacy, as those seven key words of the rule will tell you. Why doesn't a conclusion, "The river will not rise," follow in this case? Nothing in the information given tells us that rain is the only condition under which this river rises.

Maybe melting snow in the mountains will make it rise; maybe a dam is opened on occasion and the water rises. We do not know about these possibilities. To be valid, the antecedent must be affirmed and here it is not.

The second possibility is the fallacy of affirming the consequent.

<pre>
        A   C
If it rains, then the river will rise.
The river is rising.
</pre>

Here again one cannot conclude that it rained. Nothing in the material given tells us that rain is the only condition that makes this river rise; indeed, we just pointed to snow melting and a dam opening as other possibilities. To be valid the consequent must be denied, and this is not done here.

It is confusing and unnecessary to remember the conditions producing an invalid result. It takes but seven words to deal with *all* possible situations: *Affirm the antecedent or deny the consequent.* That's valid. Anything else is invalid. And, of course, anything else is a fallacy.

The points remaining for discussion are neither troublesome nor frequent sources of error. The first is that the minor premise must clearly affirm the antecedent or clearly deny the consequent. For example:

<pre>
        A   C
If it rains, then the river will rise.
The weather forecast is for rain.
</pre>

This won't do. The rise of the river is promised only if it does rain; a forecast of rain is not rain. Likewise, an unequivocal denial must be made for the consequent. For instance, "John didn't notice any rise of the river" is not a firm commitment that the river did not rise. Lack of a clear commitment by the minor premise invalidates the syllogism for uncertain relationship between the premises.

The conclusion has to fit the material of the premises. Let's change examples, just to avoid becoming mesmerized.

<pre>
        A   C
If the bell rings, then it will be Jane's date.
The bell is ringing.
So, Jane will have a wonderful time.
</pre>

Though we wish Jane well, one would hardly make such a gross error as to suppose that this conclusion fits the material in the premises. It is like introducing a fourth term, and we shall call this error an *unauthorized conclusion.* Where the minor premise affirms the antecedent, the conclusion is limited to declaring that the consequent will occur—that it will be Jane's date.

Now for the other valid case, denying the consequent. Suppose the hypothetical syllogism is:

          A   C
If the key fits, then he can open the door.
He cannot open the door.
So, the key does not fit.

Where the consequent is denied, the conclusion is a denial of the condition of the antecedent. This is not a likely point for confusion, however, because usually the conclusion appropriate to the premises is manifest. If a wrong conclusion were drawn, say, "So the key won't go into the lock," we call this an *unauthorized conclusion* to indicate that the premises imply a conclusion but not the conclusion drawn.

Affirming an antecedent does not always mean an affirmative sentence, nor is denying the consequent necessarily negative. The idea of affirming means to confirm or agree with, and thus a negative assertion will agree with a negative in an antecedent. The following two examples both fulfill the rule and are valid.

          A   C
If Henry is not home, then he is at the store.
Henry is not home.
So, he is at the store.

Valid: affirms the antecedent

          A   C
If Sarah is living downtown, then she does not need a car.
Sarah does need a car.
So, she is not living downtown.

Valid: denies the consequent

Occasionally one encounters the words "if and only if," always an expression bespeaking some care in the use of language. The word "only" is a trouble-causing word. "Only those with normal vision are taken into the army" does not mean "All those with normal vision are taken." The meaning is "All those taken are people having normal vision" or, by obverting and then converting one arrives at the equivalent statement: "Those not having normal vision are not taken." Mindful of this meaning, one can see that the words "if and only if" serve to coalesce two hypothetical syllogisms into one. Suppose:

If and only if the weather improves will we sail today.

This statement in effect declares:

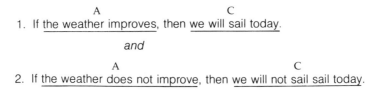

          A   C
1. If the weather improves, then we will sail today.

                    and

          A   C
2. If the weather does not improve, then we will not sail sail today.

Since the (1) and (2) statements cover all possible situations, a valid conclusion results regardless of what the minor premise asserts, provided, of course, that it clearly affirms or denies one or other of the antecedents or consequents. Fully spelled out, the situation is:

A   C

1. If the <u>weather improves</u>, then <u>we will sail today</u>.
   The weather improves.
   So, we will sail today.
   Valid: affirms the antecedent

A   C

If the <u>weather improves</u>, then <u>we will sail today</u>.
We will not sail today.
So, the weather does not improve.
Valid: denies the consequent

A   C

2. If the <u>weather does not improve</u>, then <u>we will not sail today</u>.
   The weather does not improve.
   So, we will not sail today.
   Valid: affirms the antecedent

A   C

If the <u>weather does not improve</u>, then <u>we will not sail today</u>.
We will sail today.
So, the weather does improve.
Valid: denies the consequent

So we see, a hypothetical syllogism conditioned by "if and only if" gives no trouble, for the resulting conclusions all are valid.

All the examples given so far have been couched in standard hypothetical form—that is, the antecedents introduced by "if" have stood first, and consequents have stood second with "then" expressed to introduce them. If we always designated our hypotheticals this clearly, then the structure of our argument would be obvious. Of course, we don't always designate our hypotheticals clearly. Oops—a hypothetical with a denied antecedent just got loose in the text here! Invalid! It's easy to do. "If we always designated our hypotheticals clearly, then the structure of our argument would be obvious." "But the structure of our argument is not always obvious"—now we're on the valid track with a denied consequent, so there is no escaping the conclusion that "hypotheticals are not always designated this clearly." But you won't let me con you into accepting a conclusion as true as well as valid until I show that the premises are true. Well, here are just a few ways for expressing the idea of this particular hypothetical, and I must leave it to you to decide whether the structure of the argument is obvious in every case.

If the weather improves, then we will go sailing. (standard form)
We will go sailing if the weather improves.
We'll go sailing when the weather improves.
Given improved weather, then we will be sailing.
We certainly will be sailing as soon as the weather improves.
I sure am impatient to have some better weather in this God-forsaken summer because, assuming there's going to be a break sometime, we'll get in some sailing.

Even though there are innumerable ways for expressing conditional relationships, still the word "if" remains the great badge of the hypothetical. My guess is that "if" introduces about 80 percent of hypothetical relationships in English. Practice, certainly no rule, will increase ability to pick out conditional propositions and arrange them in standard form with the antecedent introduced by "if" and the consequent by "then." The attached box lists some indicators helpful in picking out antecedents and consequents. Though the material in the box isn't worth committing to memory, a little dwelling on these words may whet the imagination in recognizing conditional propositions.

These words indicate Antecedents	*These words indicate Consequents*
if	then
when	as a result
where	as a consequence
in the event	
given that	
had . . . occurred	

SUMMARY

The conditions for a valid hypothetical syllogism are the following:

1. The minor premise must **affirm the antecedent or deny the consequent.**
2. The affirmation of antecedent or consequent must be unequivocal.
3. The conclusion must follow the declaration of the major premise. Though there is little danger of mistaking what conclusion accords with the premises, the valid conclusions are as follows:
   a. Where the antecedent is affirmed, the conclusion declares that the consequent must occur.
   b. Where the consequent is denied, the conclusion declares that the antecedent did not take place.

Failure to follow the rules results in fallacies corresponding to the rule violated:

1. Fallacy of denying the antecedent
2. Fallacy of affirming the consequent
3. Fallacy of uncertain relationship between the premises
4. Fallacy of an unauthorized conclusion

EXERCISES FOR CHAPTER 8
pages 132–138

I.   Answer by entering **T** for "true" or **F** for "false":

_____   **1.** The condition of a hypothetical syllogism is called the antecedent.

_____   **2.** The consequent is the state of affairs promised to ensue if the antecedent occurs.

_____   **3.** Among other requirements, in a valid hypothetical syllogism one must *affirm the antecedent or deny the consequent.*

_____   **4.** So long as the antecedent is clearly affirmed or the consequent is clearly denied, a hypothetical syllogism can't miss being valid.

_____   **5.** The idea of affirming an antecedent means to "agree with."

_____   **6.** A negative word never appears in a sentence that is affirming an antecedent.

_____   **7.** "If and only if" is an emphatic way of asserting what is normally asserted by "if."

_____   **8.** Standard form for a hypothetical syllogism means that the major premise is expressed with "If . . . , then . . . ," and that the minor premise and conclusion appropriately follow the wording used in the major premise.

_____   **9.** Sometimes the structure of an English sentence is such that the consequent is stated before the antecedent.

_____   **10.** The words "if and only if" introduce two different conditional assertions which together cover all cases.

II.   For each of the following hypothetical syllogisms, underline the antecedent and write **A** above it; underline the consequent and write **C** above it. Then fill in the blanks by writing **valid** or **invalid**. When your answer is **invalid**, indicate the ground upon which you find the argument invalid by supplying the appropriate number from the following list:

    1. Invalid: antecedent denied
    2. Invalid: consequent affirmed
    3. Invalid: relationship between premises is uncertain
    4. Invalid: conclusion given is unauthorized by premises

Example:

A   C

<u>If Mr. Bourse keeps the stock</u>, then <u>he will make a lot of money</u>.

Mr. Bourse will not keep the stock.

Therefore, he will not make a lot of money.   <u>   Invalid-1   </u>

1. If everybody works hard, we'll finish the job.

   John won't work hard.

   So, we won't finish.   _____

2. If the cut heals well, then it cannot be infected.

   The cut is not healing well.

   Therefore, it is infected.   _____

3. If the burglar got in through the window, it would be unlocked.

   The window is unlocked.

   Therefore, the burglar got in through the window.   _____

4. If it is after 10:00, then the Cavallos will be home.

   It is 10:30.

   So, the Cavallos will be home.   _____

5. If no apparent problem arises, then people see no need to change their ways.

   For a long time pollution was not an apparent problem.

   So, for a long time people saw no need to change their ways. _____

6. When change is needed, vested interests always oppose.

   Vested interests oppose regulation of strip mining.

   It follows that change is needed.   _____

7. If his alibi is true, then he could not take part in the crime.

His alibi is confirmed by two witnesses.

So, he could not take part in the crime.   _____

8. If the witness made a mistake, this does not mean all his testimony is false.

This witness is clearly shown to have been wrong.

So, not all his testimony is false.   _____

9. If the medicine is effective, then the patient will get well.

The patient has recovered.

So, the medicine is effective.   _____

10. If nations are not compelled to settle disputes by law, then they will settle important matters by force.

Nations are not compelled to settle disputes by law.

Therefore, they will continue to settle important matters by force. _____

III.   Restate each of the following hypothetical syllogisms in clear If..., then... form. Then indicate the following:

   a. If the syllogism is valid, indicate one of the following:

   valid: affirms the antecedent
   valid: denies the consequent

   b. If the syllogism is invalid, indicate the ground on which you hold it invalid:

   invalid: antecedent denied
   invalid: consequent affirmed
   invalid: relationship between the premises uncertain
   invalid: conclusion given unauthorized by premises

Example:

He would have gone, if he's been able. He didn't go. So I'm sure he wasn't able.

If he had been able to go, then he would have gone.

He did not go.

So, he was not able to go.

Valid: denies consequent

1. She would have taken the job if she'd been ready. But she turned it down, so she must not have been ready.

2. Had the fishing been good, they would have stayed. But the fishing can't have been too great because I know they've left already.

3. When interest rates rise, bond prices fall. The bond market has gone way down, which means interest is up.

4. Given a dishonest government administration, then the supplies will not reach the people. Nobody in that country dares talk about dishonesty in the government, so we can see the supplies won't reach the people.

_____

_____

_____

_____

5. The dogs are barking. They always bark when there is a tiger around the village. So there must be a tiger nearby.

_____

_____

_____

_____

6. If and only if the expedition were starving would the reserve rations be used. Evidently the expedition wasn't starving, because the reserves were untouched.

_____

_____

_____

_____

7. There must be some difficulty because had everything gone well the party would have reached the summit by 2:00 P.M, and it hasn't arrived there yet. Why, it's nearly 4:00 o'clock.

_____

_____

_____

_____

8. When our oil is nearly exhausted, it will be too late to save it effectively. But it still isn't too late, so the oil isn't exhausted yet.

_____

_____

_____

_____

chapter 9

Disjunctive and Alternative Syllogisms

Though disjunctive and alternative syllogisms are less common than the categorical or hypothetical forms, still they are not rare. Happily, they are easy to handle. We will begin with the disjunctive.

DISJUNCTIVE SYLLOGISMS[1]

In a disjunctive situation it is asserted that two conditions cannot both be true. "You can't have your cake and eat it too" is an example. The standard form for disjunction is "not both . . . and. . . ." "Not both <u>eat your cake</u> and <u>have it too</u>." "Not both <u>neglect practice</u> and <u>play the cello well</u>." The world is all too full of such uncomfortable choices.

By examining a simple disjunction, we can determine for ourselves how to reason validly in this form. Suppose Mr. Jones is sitting at the breakfast table and announces firmly, "I will not both go hunting and go to the circus." Now this is pretty clear and everyone should know exactly where matters stand. Let's suppose that later in the day we learn that Jones has gone hunting. Obviously, we can conclude that he will not go to the circus, for he is not to do both. (If he should change his mind and in fact go to the circus after going hunting, then we should blame the premise that turned out to be false. No use criticizing our reasoning because, given the premise, he was not to do both.) I'll state the full syllogism for absolute clarity:

	Disj. 1	Disj. 2
Major premise	Not both <u>Jones goes hunting</u> and <u>Jones goes to the circus.</u>	
Minor premise	Jones goes hunting.	
Conclusion	Jones does not go to the circus.	

[1]"Disjunction" refers to any total division that leaves nothing over. The division into "disjunctive" and "alternative" syllogisms is made here to distinguish two syllogistic forms governed by different rules.

Here the minor premise is affirming the first disjunct and the conclusion denies that the second disjunct will take place. If we had affirmed the second disjunct, then we would know that the first was not to take place. Stop to note this. So we see, to affirm a disjunct yields an inescapable—that is, valid—conclusion.

What about the other way around? Consider:

	Disj. 1	Disj. 2
Major premise	Not both <u>Jones goes hunting</u> and <u>Jones goes to the circus.</u>	
Minor premise	Jones is not going hunting.	
Conclusion	?	

Now when Jones announced he would not both go hunting and go to the circus, he did not promise to do either one. You may have felt that since he brought up these two possibilities he would do one or the other. Still, if Jones in his capricious way decides to spend the day at a marionette show, you really can't accuse him of doing anything inconsistent with his promise. All that was promised was that he would not *both* go hunting and go to the circus. Logic, you recall, construes assertions narrowly to what they *must* mean and does not rely on overtones.

We are now in a position to derive the rule for a valid disjunctive syllogism. When one disjunct is affirmed, the other cannot take place, for the "not both" forces this conclusion. On the other hand, if one denies a disjunct, there is no saying that the other must occur. Accordingly, the rule is:

For a valid disjunctive syllogism, one must AFFIRM ONE DISJUNCT.

Three words do the trick. The word "disjunct" indicates that the rule applies to disjunctive syllogisms, and all the rules describe conditions that produce valid syllogisms. So brand these three words "affirm one disjunct" into your mind. Wait a bit! It may be better to defer whatever you use as a branding procedure until the end of this chapter, where you will find a pattern that makes the process easier.

Discussion of the remaining problems of the disjunctive syllogism is similar to the not-so-common difficulties that can occur with the hypothetical. The minor premise of a disjunctive must clearly affirm one of the disjuncts; otherwise there is uncertain relationship between the premises. For example:

Not both <u>fail to take care of the injury</u> and <u>make a good recovery.</u>
John is walking without crutches.

This won't do, because one cannot say whether "walking without crutches" fulfills the requirement of "fail to take care of the injury." So we can't say that John will not make a good recovery.

In a disjunctive syllogism, the conclusion is limited to asserting the other disjunct cannot occur:

Not both pay low wages and retain employee good will.
Hartfaust, Inc. pays low wages.
Hartfaust, Inc. is bitterly resented.

Here the conclusion goes beyond the premises: "Hartfaust, Inc. does not retain employee good will" is all that the premises support. Though it is possible to make the mistake of wandering from the material presented in the disjuncts, this kind of blunder is not common. Where such a mistake is made, the error is much like introducing a fourth term in a categorical form.

ALTERNATIVE SYLLOGISMS

Some assertions promise that either one thing or another is true. "Either have the operation or die." "Either a dog or a raccoon has been in our garbage can." The use of the words "either . . . or . . ." is the standard form for alternative syllogisms and is by far the most common way for expressing them. The claim in an alternative situation is that only two possibilities exist and that one or the other of these possibilities will happen. So, if one of the possibilities is excluded, then the other must occur. For example:

	Alt. 1	Alt. 2
Major premise	Either the light bulb is broken or	the current is off.
Minor premise	The current is not off.	
Conclusion	The light bulb is broken.	

Since the major premise promised that at least one of the alternates was true, a denial of one requires the other to be true.

What will happen if one of the alternates is affirmed—say, if the minor premise is changed to "The current is off"? This will not guarantee any conclusion, for the bulb may be broken as well as the current being off. Of course, the bulb may not be broken: there simply is no saying from the material we have been given. Though "either . . . or . . ." definitely promises one alternate must occur, it does not promise that the other will not happen also.

Now we have arrived at the rule for alternative syllogisms, and again, three words will do the trick.

For a valid alternative syllogism, one must DENY ONE ALTERNATE.

The words "deny one alternate" are enough to overcome those errors most apt to be made in handling this type of syllogism, for the word "alternate" shows that the rule refers to alternative syllogisms, and all the rules of this book describe conditions for valid reasoning. So, to *deny one alternate* is the valid form.

Although we have presented in summary fashion the meanings for disjunctive (not both... and...) and alternative (either... or...) statements, I know there is a temptation, a strong magnetic pull as it were, to believe that alternative and disjunctive statements promise more than the limited meanings that have been given above. Perhaps we can avoid errors by stopping to understand why we feel this magnetic pull to interpret the promises as wider than they are.

When it is stated that "not both" of two things will happen, the practical situation usually is that one of the two disjuncts does occur. The person who discusses his plans in terms of hunting and circus going usually ends up by taking one of these choices even though, strictly speaking, the promise is merely not to do both. And since one's feeling for the meaning of words derives from the situations which the words usually describe, one comes to associate a "not both" assertion with the happening of one of the possibilities mentioned. Since deduction is a matter of inescapable inferences, not just likelihoods, any feeling about statements developed from how things usually turn out is not good enough. So disjunction does not promise that any one thing will happen; it promises merely that *not both* will.

The feeling that the alternative "either... or..." promises more than it does has the same explanation. Usually the outcome of a situation in which alternates are presented is that only one of them happens. Indeed, many times the laws of physics make it impossible for both alternates to occur—for example, the statement "David will spend all day Sunday either in Cincinnati or Memphis" does not admit a possibility of doing both. Not all alternatives are this way, as we have seen. Yet, whether through impossibility of both occurring or just the way things usually turn out, experience with "either... or..." assertions commonly ends with one alternate only taking place. So we develop an unsound feeling that this is always the outcome.

Now it is possible to spell things out so that the scope of an alternative or disjunctive cannot be misunderstood. This is accomplished by combining the two forms, which, as we shall see, is easily done. For instance, one may assert:

> I cannot both buy a new Toyota and travel to Japan this summer, but I will do either one or the other.

or

> Either I will buy a new Toyota or I will travel to Japan this summer, but I will not do both.

These two assertions are exact equivalents. Each statement separates into two syllogisms, a disjunctive and an alternative, which between them cover all cases as with the "if and only if" hypothetical. Again, all four forms are valid.

CONNECTION BETWEEN VARIOUS FORMS OF SYLLOGISMS

The material stated in one form of syllogism can be shifted into all the other types without any change of content. If the argument is valid in one form of syllogism, it will be valid when arranged in any other type and conversely, invalidity never is cured by recasting the material in some other type of syllogism. A moment of reflection shows that this is what one should expect. After all, deduction is concerned with uncovering the inferences that follow from some given relationship. Whether the language is English or Spanish, whether the relationship is expressed in one type of sentence or another, will make no difference as long as the relationship is the same. Since the type of syllogism into which material is cast is merely a matter of form, the validity of the conclusion cannot be changed by shifting from one form to another. Consequently, one is free to restate an argument in *any* form of syllogism, with common sense suggesting that usually it will be easiest to restate it in the form closest to the wording originally used. At this point, it may be useful to show identical material shifted through all four types of syllogisms.

Categorical Syllogism

1-d   2-u
All good businessmen < make decisions with care.

3-d   ≮   2-d
Paul does not make decisions with care.

3-d   ≮   1-d
Paul is not a good businessman.

Valid: all rules of categorical syllogism fulfilled

Hypothetical Syllogism

A   C
If a man is a good businessman, then he makes decisions with care.
Paul does not make decisions with care.
Paul is not a good businessman.

Valid: consequent denied

Disjunctive Syllogism

Disj. 1   Disj. 2
One may not both be a good businessman and not make decisions with care.
Paul does not make decisions with care.
Paul is not a good businessman.

Valid: disjunct affirmed

149

Alternative Syllogism

Alt. 1   Alt. 2
Either <u>a man is not a good businessman</u> or <u>he makes decisions with care.</u>
Paul does not make decisions with care.
Paul is not a good businessman.

Valid: alternate denied

SUMMARY

It is impossible to solve any type of syllogism without knowing the rules govern-
ing its validity. Unfortunately, it's easy to get confused as to whether a valid
result requires affirming or denying some particular part of a hypothetical, disjunctive, or alternative syllogism. So I have stated the rules in the order that
makes them easiest to remember:

Valid hypothetical: Affirm the antecedent or deny the consequent.
Valid disjunctive: Affirm a disjunct.
Valid alternative: Deny an alternate.

The scheme above reduces to two rules, both starting with *affirm* and both
running *Affirm–Deny.*

Affirm the antecedent or deny the consequent.
Affirm a disjunct or deny an alternate.

The words "antecedent" or "consequent" and "disjunct" or "alternate" indicate
the kind of syllogism the requirement applies to. One needs to learn these rules
to the point where they are instant responses. To accomplish the needed quick
response is a lot harder than it looks.

Failure to follow a rule of logic results in a logical fallacy. Accordingly, we have
the fallacies of *failing to affirm a disjunct* and *failing to deny an alternate.*

EXERCISES FOR CHAPTER 9
pages 145–150

I. Answer by entering **T** for "true" or **F** for "false":

_____ 1. A statement that two things will not both occur implies that one of the two will occur.

_____ 2. Where a premise declares that two things will not both occur but in fact both events take place, then the trouble is that the premise is false.

_____ 3. When one starts with a valid disjunctive syllogism and restates it in the form of a categorical syllogism, sometimes it will be invalid in the categorical form.

_____ 4. Every rule in this book refers to valid forms. This is because the author regards rules about what is invalid to be both confusing and unnecessary.

_____ 5. DENY ONE ALTERNATE is the main thing to know to determine the validity of an alternative syllogism.

_____ 6. If one disjunct is affirmed, then one must accept whatever conclusion is given.

_____ 7. When you discover that an alternative syllogism is invalid, you know its conclusion is untrue.

_____ 8. Wherever "either... or" appear in a statement it is physically impossible for both alternates to occur. ·

_____ 9. When the words of the minor premise which purport to deny one alternate are not clearcut and unambiguous in their denial, no conclusion is justified.

_____ 10. Experience with assertions containing "not both" or "either ... or" usually ends with one and only one of the two possibilities taking place. This builds up a feeling these words require that one and only one possibility will take place. Logic does not accord with this feeling.

II. 1. Write the seven key words necessary to solve a hypothetical syllogism.

_____

_____

2. a. Write the rule of three key words that applies to valid disjunctive syllogisms.

_____

b. Write the rule of three key words that applies to valid alternative syllogisms.

_____

III.   The syllogisms given below are disjunctive. Perform the following operations:

a. Underline the two disjuncts.

b. Write **Valid** or **Invalid** in the blank.

c. If invalid, write the number indicating the ground for invalidity:

1. Invalid: neither disjunct affirmed
2. Invalid: unclear whether a disjunct is affirmed or not
3. Invalid: conclusion is unauthorized

1. Not both train a lion and never crack the whip.

Horatio sure trained that lion.

Horatio cracked the whip.   _____

2. One cannot think objectively and give way to emotional responses at the same time.

Arthur is reacting with an emotional response.

Arthur is not thinking objectively.   _____

3. It's impossible to both be happy and have paranoid fears.

Martha isn't happy.

So, she has paranoid fears.   _____

4. Nobody is at the same time a kindly person and never helps anybody.

Mary never does anything for anybody.

So, Mary isn't kindly.   _____

5. No one can neglect training and be a good marathon runner.

John Longstride has signed up for the marathon.

So, he has not neglected training.   _____

6. Not both be a great actress and not give up many things.

Veronica Traverso is a very great actress.

So, Veronica has had to give up family life.   _____

7. One can't lead troops well and set a poor example.

Lieutenant Sturmer never set a poor example.

Sturmer led his troops well.   _____

8. A musical can't lack a catchy song and be a popular hit. Well, the new musical

has a very catchy song, so it will be a hit.   _____

IV.   The syllogisms given below are alternative. Perform the following operations:

   a. Underline the two alternates.
   b. Write "valid" or "invalid" in the blank.
   c. If invalid, enter number indicating ground for invalidity:

   1. Invalid: neither alternate is denied
   2. Invalid: unclear whether an alternate is denied or not
   3. Invalid: conclusion is unauthorized

1. Either Alice will call at your house or she will phone.

Well, she has already phoned.

So, she will not call. _____

2. Albert will either do the job or get fired.

Albert says he won't do the job.

He'll be fired. _____

3. It's clear we have to increase our offer or forget about the deal.

I've thought long and hard; we simply can't increase the offer.

So, we will pass up this deal. _____

4. We must either turn back here or risk being overtaken by dark.

I'm not turning back.

I risk being overtaken by dark. _____

5. One must choose between learning the business or making costly errors.

Perez has learned the business thoroughly.

So, he won't make costly errors. _____

6. Either the candidate will be confirmed on Monday or his name will be withdrawn.

The candidate won't be confirmed on Monday.

So, his name will be withdrawn. _____

7. The new judge will either be well qualified or there will be opposition to the appointment.

But the new judge has splendid qualifications.

So there'll be no opposition to the appointment.   _____

8. Either the ore vein has run out or Deep Dig Mine is making money.

The ore vein has not run out.

So, Deep Dig Mine is making money.   _____

chapter 10

Enthymemes

In all the speeches, writings, and conversations that one encounters, practically none contain fully expressed syllogisms of the types we have been describing! There will be many fragments of syllogisms; rarely a perfect specimen. The situation isn't as hopeless as it may sound, however, because a part of a syllogism can be expanded into a completely stated one. Though one might assume it would be difficult to do this, actually in many instances, so obvious is the unstated part that one performs quite unconsciously the process of "discovering" it. Suppose, for instance, a boy undertaking a carpentry project picks out an oak board from the woodpile. His older brother notices the board and remarks: "That board will be hard to work because it's oak." Neither boy has sawed, planed, or driven a nail into the board—it merely has been identified as an oak board. What is the reasoning? One can see intuitively that the older boy has a generalization in mind, a major premise that he expects his younger brother to understand as a part of a deduction running:

> All oak is hard to work.
> That board is oak.
> Therefore, that board will be hard to work.

This sort of statement of a part of a syllogism, leaving the rest to be implied, is called an enthymeme. The omitted part may be a premise or it may be the conclusion; more often than not it is a major premise considered too obvious to require statement. Consider another example. A father notices that his teenage daughter is taking up smoking. Knowing of many smokers who regret the habit and have tried hard to break it, the father remarks: "Those who start smoking are likely to wish they hadn't, and you're starting." The daughter won't need much acumen to get the point. The father has stated two premises, leaving the conclusion to be drawn as a matter of course. The enthymeme expands into this syllogism:

> Those who start smoking are likely to wish they hadn't.
> You are starting to smoke.
> You are likely to wish you hadn't.

It wouldn't be at all farfetched to imagine the father saying merely: "Those who start smoking are likely to wish they hadn't." The daughter could decide whether the shoe fits or not. She doesn't have to be told she is beginning the habit.

Such easily expanded enthymemes occur by the hundred every day of our lives, and supplying the missing premise or unstated conclusion by intuition usually serves well enough. To deal with a not-so-obvious case, however, one has to be able to analyze the argument.

A first step in understanding any argument is to locate the conclusion. After all, if you don't know what the conclusion is, you really can't fathom what the argument is all about. The other half of figuring out an argument is to identify the material alleged to support the conclusion, that is, the premises. How can one do this? Though there is no mechanical rule, you will find that language offers considerable aid.

Since stating premises and drawing conclusions plays a large part in communication, it is natural for any language to evolve a number of words whose function is to point out premises or indicate conclusions. Below are two boxes of these words that serve to make argument followable:

Some common conclusion indicators	
so	for this reason
therefore	it must be
consequently	evidently
accordingly	it seems that
evidently	it follows that
apparently	implies that
then	infers that
thus	suggests that
hence	demonstrates that
so we see	in conclusion

Some common premise indicators

because	granting that
for	assuming that
since	supposing that
inasmuch as	seeing that
it follows from	in view of the fact that
it is evident from	on the ground that
we know from	on the premise that

Any writer or speaker who has a knack for keeping his meanings clear makes generous use of both conclusion and premise indicators. They're handy words. But, you may ask, what about the times when no conclusion indicator is used? Well, then find a premise indicator and the premise will point to the conclusion. "You're dodging!" I can hear you shout, "What I want to know is how to handle this problem when there isn't a nice little word in a box to tell me the answer. Besides, I might forget this box, if ever I learn it!" Yes, we'll have to face up. Where there is no conclusion or premise indicator, one has to step back, mentally speaking, and decide what the passage is driving at. What the speaker wants us to accept will be his conclusion, while the material he uses to support this conclusion is premise material. And, as we said, it's crucial to identify the conclusion correctly. After all, if you mistakenly select a premise as the conclusion, then any analysis made will be analyzing a *different* argument from the one the speaker proposed. In homely English, you will be barking up the wrong tree.

After finding the conclusion, the next thing is to look for premises. If you are in luck, a premise indicator will have been used; if not, you may be able to utilize a conclusion indicator as a link to the premise material. If no indicators are to be found, then you will have to fall back on the overall view. What about deciding what may be a major premise and what a minor premise? Identifying material as belonging to a major or a minor premise won't affect the validity of the argument. It is well to remember, nonetheless, that major premises tend to be general rules while minor premises usually are particular applications. Also, enthymemes with unstated major premises are far more common than those with missing minor premises.

Now we will examine a step-by-step method for determining the missing part of an enthymeme. Suppose we take the assertion:

Our merchant marine is important in war so it ought to be subsidized.

The first step is to look for the conclusion. Is the speaker trying to convince us that "our merchant marine is important in war" or that "it ought to be subsidized"? In this case the word "so" is a clue since this word is a common conclusion indicator: after citing one or more facts, *so* often appears to indicate the conclusion reached. This is the case here, so we have:

Conclusion   It (our merchant marine) ought to be subsidized.

The remaining portion of the enthymeme—that is, the statement "Our merchant marine is important in war"—is a particular application of things that are important in war. So it is best put down as the second or minor premise. We now have:

Major premise

Minor premise   <u>Our merchant marine</u> is <u>important in war</u>.

Conclusion   <u>It (our merchant marine)</u> <u>ought to be subsidized</u>.

Having identified the conclusion and one premise, the next step is to number the terms of what we have, put in the appropriate $<$ and $\nless$ symbols, and place "d" or "u" above each to indicate its distribution. So now we have:

Major premise

	1-d	$<$	2-u
Minor premise	<u>Our merchant marine</u> is		<u>important in war</u>.
	1-d	$<$	3-u
Conclusion	<u>It (our merchant marine)</u>		<u>ought to be subsidized</u>.

Recalling that a categorical syllogism has three terms, each of which appears twice, one of the terms in the part we have will necessarily appear twice. In this case you will observe the term "our merchant marine" already has two usages. Since the terms "important in war" and "ought to be subsidized" have been used only once each, the missing part must be made up of a second use for each of these terms.

Now that we have put a finger on the terms in the missing part, the next step is to construct an assertion using this material in a way that produces a valid syllogism. In other words, the statement we will construct must satisfy the rule against faulty exclusions, must have the middle term distributed at least once, and must have no illicit distribution. Meeting all these requirements sounds complicated. It isn't. It is like a game of solitaire where one can move the cards around a bit to make it come out. But unlike solitaire, he who plays with enthymemes always wins. (If the game won't come out, then the player may declare the argument invalid and demand a new deal.)

The game is to arrange the terms "important in war" and "ought to be subsidized" into a sentence that completes a valid syllogism. Here's how to go about it. Notice that "important in war" is the middle term, so it must be distributed at least once. Since it was not distributed in the minor premise which we have, we must make it distributed in the major premise which we are creating. It can be made distributed by being used as the first term following "all" or "no," or by being used as the second term following an exclusion. To choose "no" as quantifier results in the second term following an exclusion, which produces faulty exclusions in this case and would be invalid. Consequently, "important in war" must be the first term following "all" as quantifier. Only this solution makes the middle term distributed as it needs to be without running into faulty exclusions. "Ought to be subsidized" becomes the second term following an inclusion, so it is not distributed. A check of the conclusion for illicit distribution reveals that "ought to be subsidized" is not distributed in the conclusion, so there is no need to have that term distributed in the premise where it appears. Accordingly, "ought to be subsidized" can properly follow an inclusion and the syllogism will be valid.

		2-d	<	3-u
Major premise		All merchant marines important in war		ought to be subsidized.

		1-d	<	2-u
Minor Premise		Our merchant marine is (a merchant marine) important in war.		

		1-d	<	3-u
Conclusion		It (our merchant marine)		ought to be subsidized.

One wrinkle remains to iron out. You will notice that the minor premise was stated with the words "a merchant marine" slipped in like this:

Minor premise   Our merchant marine is (a merchant marine) important in war.

Well, our merchant marine could hardly be an elephant important in war, so the addition may have struck you as the sort of super-obvious locution that logicians seem to relish. Actually, the words were added to help avoid a possible error, and to understand this error we'll have to take another look at the expanded enthymeme. The point is that in expanding an enthymeme a rule of fairness requires that the missing part should not be broader than is needed to make the argument valid. Now there are two major premises that will produce a valid syllogism from the material given:

Major premise	1. *All things important in war ought to be subsidized.*
	2. *All merchant marines important in war ought to be subsidized.*
Minor premise	Our merchant marine is (a merchant marine) important in war.
Conclusion	It (our merchant marine) ought to be subsidized.

Since the narrower claim of the two major premises given above is all that is needed to support the conclusion, it is unfair to expand the enthymeme as if the broader claim were required.

What about expanding an enthymeme into a syllogism in one of the other forms—hypothetical, disjunctive, or alternative? This is done by the same method of working backward from the given material. When one of the premises is missing, determine the conclusion first and then find the stated premise in the remaining material. If the conclusion is the missing part, put down the two premises and then supply the conclusion which they validly imply. Enthymemes that readily expand as hypothetical syllogisms are common; material that expands naturally into a disjunctive or alternative form is encountered much less often.

We can easily expand the merchant marine case in the hypothetical form. First, set down the conclusion and minor premise as before:

		A		C
Major premise	If	_____	then	_____

Minor premise   Our merchant marine is important in war.

Conclusion   It (our merchant marine) ought to be subsidized.

Next, look at the minor premise, keeping in mind the "if . . . then . . ." form of the hypothetical and remembering that a valid hypothetical must *affirm the antecedent or deny the consequent.* Is this minor premise affirming an antecedent or denying a consequent? Though the fact that it is an affirmative statement does not necessarily mean that it is affirming (agreeing with) an antecedent, still we might as well begin with the assumption that it does affirm an antecedent. If this doesn't work out, then we can investigate it as a denial of the consequent. Taking the minor premise "Our merchant marine is important in war" and placing it in the antecedent position of a clearly stated "if . . . then . . ." hypothetical, we will have the conclusion "It ought to be subsidized" for the consequent.

Major premise   If *a merchant marine is important in war* then *it ought to be subsidized.*

Minor premise   Our merchant marine is important in war.

Conclusion   It (our merchant marine) ought to be subsidized.

Since this produces a valid syllogism, it is the proper expansion of the enthymeme and there is no need to look further.

Expansion of an enthymeme into a disjunctive or alternative form of syllogism is performed by the same method of determining the parts you have in the enthymeme and working backward to discover the material needed to form a valid syllogism. Disjunctive and alternative forms are apt to work out with the contorted language of double negatives, and I will not add to the detail of this chapter by discussing the solutions here. Using the merchant marine material given here, it will tax your ingenuity and be a good test of your command of the rules to work out the missing premise in the disjunctive and alternative forms. For those undertaking these riddles, solutions are at the bottom of the page.[1]

Of what practical use is this game of expanding enthymemes? One use is to locate invalid argument when it is offered to us, and a second use is to decide for ourselves whether the hidden assumptions contained in unstated premises are true or, more accurately, reasonably reliable. Let's take a look first at the possibility of invalid argument.

Once in a while someone plays a conscious trick by citing material that the audience is expected to expand to reach an invalid conclusion. Richard Nixon played this trick in his campaign for senator—years before he became a president. Nixon listed various bills for which his opponent, incumbent Senator Helen Douglas, had voted and for which the lone Communist congressman of the day also had voted. Clearly, the voters were invited to reason incorrectly that if a Communist voted for measures A, B, and C and Douglas voted for A, B, and C then Douglas must be a Communist or a radical or in some way connected with Communism. The premises offered contain an undistributed middle term, so the conclusion they were designed to imply is invalid.

> T-1 d   <   T-2 u
> <u>Marcantonio (the Communist congressman)   voted for A, B, and C.</u>
>
> T-3 d   <   T-2 u
> <u>Douglas   voted for A, B, and C.</u>

<u>*Undistributed middle term. No valid conclusion possible.*</u>

Resisting being taken in by invalid argument is, however, not at all the chief usefulness of expanding enthymemes. It matters little that an argument is valid if its premises are unreliable. *In critical thinking, the most common product of expanding enthymemes into fully expressed syllogisms is not discussion about validity but making a decision about whether there is evidence to justify the premises.*

Unstated assumptions often come crashing down when they are exposed. "You won't find him friendly, he's from Boston." A person from Boston never is friendly? "That business is doing well. You should see the modern office building it has leased." All businesses leasing modern offices are doing well? "Our merchant marine is important in war so it ought to be subsidized." A merchant marine important in war should be subsidized without a determination of whether it is profitable enough to pay its own way? Now and again in discussion you may have noticed people who seem to have an ability to point out unstated assumptions. Maybe you have done so yourself. In any case, it is mastery of the enthymeme that gives this ability.

[1]The solutions are upside down:

Disjunctive   Not both our merchant marine is important in war and it should not be subsidized.

Alternative   Either our merchant marine is not important in war or it should be subsidized.

SUMMARY

An enthymeme states part of a valid syllogism, leaving the rest to be implied. Though the unstated part may be either a premise or a conclusion, the major premise is the part most commonly left unstated. The major premise usually states a general rule.

All enthymemes expand into valid syllogisms. If it is not possible to expand the apparent enthymeme into a valid syllogism, then one has demonstrated that any inference from the material would be invalid.

The most important benefit from expanding an enthymeme into its fully stated syllogism is the opportunity this gives to decide whether or not the unstated premise is reliable. Manifestly, it is impossible to evaluate an assumption until one can formulate what the assumption is.

When an enthymeme is being expanded into a syllogism, no statement should be introduced that is broader than need be to support the conclusion given.

The English language has a variety of common words whose function is to identify conclusion material and premise material (see boxes at pages 157-158). When no word or phrase clearly identifies whether material is to be taken as a premise or a conclusion, then it is necessary to determine the argument being made from the general context.

EXERCISES FOR CHAPTER 10
pages 156–163

I.   Answer **T** for "true" or **F** for "false":

_____   **1.** All enthymemes expand into valid syllogisms.

_____   **2.** The chief practical benefit from expanding enthymemes is to discover those which turn out to be invalid.

_____   **3.** When expanding an enthymeme into a categorical syllogism, it is best to make the major premise as broad as possible.

_____   **4.** If there isn't a conclusion indicator, then one is sure to find a premise indicator.

_____   **5.** Any writer who is careful to keep his argument clear makes generous use of both conclusion and premise indicators.

_____   **6.** "Because" is a conclusion indicator.

_____   **7.** It is possible to expand any enthymeme into all four forms of the syllogism.

_____   **8.** The most important benefit from developing an ability to expand enthymemes into syllogisms is to place oneself in a position to evaluate the reliability of the argument.

_____   **9.** If one never perceives an unstated premise in the course of conversation or reading, then one has not learned how to expand enthymemes.

_____   **10.** Enthymemes aren't as common in discussion as fully expressed syllogisms.

_____   **11.** If material that appears to be an enthymeme cannot be expanded into a valid syllogism, then in fact the material is not an enthymeme.

_____   **12.** "So" is much used as a conclusion indicator.

II.   Expand the following enthymemes into valid categorical syllogisms. These enthymemes are simple so that you may be able to solve some of them intuitively without going through an analysis of the terms, distribution, and quantifiers. However, for practice in each case, write down the given material first. Then determine the unstated part of the syllogism by a full analysis as is done in the following model:

Model:

John must be an expert rock climber because he climbed El Capitan.

Major premise	T-2 d < T-3 u All *those who climb El Capitan* are *expert rock climbers*.
Minor premise	T-1 d T-2 u John < climbed El Capitan.
Conclusion	T-1 d < T-3 u John is an expert rock climber.

First practice group.   All the following enthymemes are of the common type in which the material for the conclusion and the minor premise is given.

1. I conclude it isn't a land turtle. It has flippers.

2. That is not a star because it gives steady light.

3. He's a musician. Hence, he won't understand business.

4. The bank must be preserving cash. It won't make any new loans.

5. Johnson was well liked in India for he learned to speak Hindi.

6. The bristlecone pine grows slowly because it is a timberline tree.

7. We should avoid further population increase, for it places a strain on all kinds of resources.

8. Lots of people will see the match since it's a championship match.

9. Racial discrimination is intolerable because it is morally wrong.

10. These mandibars are cantankerous, so they should be fed lots of honey.

Second practice group.   The following enthymemes are of the type in which the two premises are given and the conclusion is left unstated. Analyze each fully as in the group above.

1. Happy people are contented, and many primitive people are happy.

2. He's lazy, and lazy people don't last long here.

3. Everybody likes an exciting game, and that is what we're having.

4. Those who buy stock on margin lose their money eventually. Yet that is what Peter is doing.

5. Ruth Cavallo is a good portrait painter. Nobody achieves that without years of practice.

6. Shutting down this inefficient plant will save money, and saving money is something this company always does.

Third practice group. The following examples cannot be expanded into valid syllogisms, though many people would feel that each contains a sound argument. In other words, the material in each example seems to be an enthymeme but is not. Analyze these examples and for each one show a rule of the syllogism that is violated when the attempt to construct a syllogism is undertaken.

Model:

Heavy cars never get good mileage, but this isn't a heavy car.

> *Premise*   Heavy cars ⊄ good mileage.
>
> *Premise*   This car ⊄ heavy cars.
>
> *Faulty exclusions*

1. Many radicals signed the petition and just as one would expect, Henry signed it.

2. Careless driving eventually brings about an accident, but Jane is very careful.

3. People who travel in the tropics can't expect to be comfortable. But we're *not* in the tropics.

4. Good executives do not make themselves unapproachable, and nobody can say that our company president is unapproachable.

5. To decide not to buy the land next to the plant would be an obvious mistake, and the company management doesn't make obvious mistakes. (At first sight, faulty exclusions may seem to bar drawing a valid conclusion in the above example. But this is an enthymeme that expands validly. Can you see how?)

Fourth practice group.   The following are all enthymemes of the common type in which the material given is a conclusion and a minor premise. On the line provided, write the unstated major premise in hypothetical form. Then, as an exercise in critical thinking, check in the blanks provided whether you **accept**, **reject**, or have **no opinion** about the truth of this major premise.

1. That bird flies, so it isn't an ostrich.

_____

accept _____   reject _____   no opinion _____

2. He's a politician, so he's looking out for himself.

_____

accept _____   reject _____   no opinion _____

3. That is a natural food, so it will be good for you.

_____

accept _____   reject _____   no opinion _____

4. There will be more inflation because the budget is unbalanced.

_____

accept _____   reject _____   no opinion _____

5. He has no respect for the environment since he represents industry.

_____

accept _____   reject _____   no opinion _____

6. She was a Phi Beta Kappa. She must have studied all the time.

_____

accept _____   reject _____   no opinion _____

7. We never asked her to go snowshoeing because she's a prominent surgeon and that activity would have seemed too simple.

_____

accept _____   reject _____   no opinion _____

8. Since the company won't do as well this year as last, you shouldn't buy the stock.

_____

accept _____   reject _____   no opinion _____

9. Proposition 13 will force a cut in the government budget with the result that wasteful spending will be cut.

_____

accept _____   reject _____   no opinion _____

10. Atomic missiles won't be used, because for any nation to resort to such missiles would bring more devastation upon the user than any possible gain.

_____

accept _____   reject _____   no opinion _____

Further practice in hypotheticals may be obtained by expanding the first and second practice groups in hypothetical form.

chapter 11

Standard Form

Language has astonishing flexibility; any idea can be expressed in numerous ways. Although this is fine from the standpoint of avoiding monotony and conveying overtones through nuances of expression, the price for this variety and richness is the obscuring of the simple, direct expression preferred for logical analysis. So, in order to exhibit with unmistakable clarity what is asserted, the first step in analysis is to restate material in standard form if it is not in that form already.

The following nine statements show the same idea stated in a number of ways. Though their constructions differ and though they may suggest different overtones, each of the nine is equivalent to all the others:

1. Obtaining a knowledge of logic requires thought about the subject.
2. If one is to have a knowledge of logic, then one must think about it.
3. One can't both not think about logic and get to know the subject.
4. Either one thinks about logic or one won't acquire knowledge of it.
5. Only those who think about the subject learn logic.
6. Nobody masters logic unless he thinks about it.
7. Thought about logic alone leads to understanding of it.
8. None but people who mull logic over in their minds will master it.
9. It is false that one may learn logic without thinking about it.

Each of these statements is equivalent to the total inclusion:

All <u>obtaining a knowledge of logic</u> < <u>things requiring thought</u>.

Now you probably noticed that Nos. 1–4 are statements in standard form for categorical, hypothetical, disjunctive, and alternative propositions. That all four statements have the same meaning comes as no surprise, since we have already seen at p. 149 how any syllogism can be cast into all the other forms. Statements No. 5–9 are not in standard form, and you may have had the feeling that it wasn't immediately apparent that each was equivalent to Statement No. 1. In fact, Nos. 5–8 illustrate some common trouble-causing words in English which, odd as it may seem, those who speak the language as a mother tongue frequently are unable to interpret correctly. No. 9 is a false proposition which translates by immediate inference into the total inclusion of No. 1. Now we will take a closer look at some of the trouble-causing words in English. Were this book written in French or Japanese, not these difficulties but, presumably, others would need attention.

1.   The position of the word "not" in a sentence is a source of misunderstanding in English. It was for this reason that we recommended that a relationship of total exclusion be stated "No . . . are . . ." rather than "All . . . are not . . . ." Although these two forms are the same in the absence of some special tonal emphasis, the first can never be confused, while the second may be. For example:

a. No oil stocks are good buys today.

Meaning: This is standard form and unmistakable.

"All <u>oil stocks</u> ⋠ <u>good buys today</u>."

b. All oil stocks are not good buys today.

Meaning: Less clear than (a). Still the grammatical meaning seems to make sense and is acceptable.

"All <u>oil stocks</u> ⋠ <u>good buys today</u>."

c. All doctors in New York are not skillful.

Meaning: Though this follows the pattern of (b) above, it does not make a sensible assertion when so interpreted. Evidently, the speaker intends to assert: "Not all doctors in New York are skillful."

This later assertion is not in standard form. For its meaning see (d).

d. Not all doctors in New York are skillful.

Meaning: This instance, in which the "not" is properly placed, produces by immediate inference the assertion in standard form:

"Some <u>doctors in New York</u> ⋠ <u>skillful</u>."

2.   The word "only" is a reef upon which many a linguistic ship is wrecked. "Only" does not, as many English speakers suppose, imply "all," and it does not necessarily promise that any cases will be found. What it asserts, strictly speaking, is that those things not falling within the group it designates are excluded from the other term. The same is true for various equivalents for only—none but, no one except, alone. For example:

> *Only* an expert canoeist could shoot those rapids successfully.
> *None but* an expert canoeist could shoot those rapids successfully.
> *No one except* an expert canoeist could shoot those rapids successfully.
> An expert canoeist *alone* could shoot those rapids successfully.

None of these statements promise that all expert canoeists could shoot the rapids or even that any could. What they assert is:

> All <u>non-expert canoeists</u> ⊄ <u>shoot those rapids successfully</u>.

However, with conversion and obversion as tools, one may investigate equivalent statements to what may have seemed to some readers a most limited interpretation of "only" as given above. By conversion we know:

> All <u>those who can shoot those rapids successfully</u> ⊄ <u>non-expert canoeists</u>.

By obversion, we come to:

> All <u>those who can shoot those rapids successfully</u> < <u>expert canoeists</u>.

You may recall statements such as "All mermaids are beautiful to behold" do not, alas, promise there are any members of the classes concerned. In the same way, the statement "All those who can shoot those rapids successfully are expert canoeists" does not guarantee any canoeist can shoot the rapids successfully. We'll concede, however, that anybody who can is an expert.

It is well to keep the limited meaning of "only" and its equivalents in mind; any lawyer or businessperson who wants his terms to stick will not rest content that "only" has done a job broader than the meaning described above. On the other hand, context often suggests a wider scope as the intended meaning, and this may not be ignored if one seeks to interpret an assertion. "Only those with reservations are admitted" informs that those without reservations are excluded. Most would rely upon knowledge of the function of reservations to conclude that reservation holders would be admitted. "Employees only" will inform the public that non-employees are excluded. If the sign were on a door in a small photography shop, one would generously suppose that all employees could pass the door. Were the sign on Building D of a dynamite factory, one might not conclude that every secretary employed by the company was authorized to enter the building. Whatever one divines to be the meaning, at least the fact that interpretation is running beyond what has been unambiguously asserted needs to be recognized.

3.   The words "all but" and "all except" give trouble.

> All but those who study will fail.
> All except those who study will fail.

Neither of these is a promise that study will remove one from the class of those who fail. The assertion is that those who do *not* study will get into the class of failing. The clear form is:

> All those who do not study < will fail.

4.   "Unless" poses a similar problem and produces a negative term similar to the solution above. For example, the statement "All patients must register here unless it is an emergency" should be stated in clear form:

> All patients who are not emergency patients < must register here.

Where "unless" is used with a singular subject, putting it into categorical form is awkward, although it makes perfect sense.

> I will go unless I am needed here.
> (All) not-needed-I < those who will go

Hypothetical form would be an easier and more natural form to use in this case.

> If I am not needed, then I will go.

5.   The distinction between "a few" and "few" is tricky. "A few" asserts that there will be some cases, while "few" used alone does not guarantee that any cases exist. Thus, an announcement that "A few people will be admitted to the gallery when the legislature reconvenes" would be not fulfilled if the legislature reconvened and no one was admitted, for the clear form assertion was:

> Some people < people admitted to the gallery, etc.

On the other hand, suppose we take the statement "Few people in this room are heros." This is not a guarantee that there are any heros in the room, but a statement that most people in the room are not heros. Since we translate *most* into *some*, we get:

> Some people in the room ≮ heros.

Perhaps these lines will serve as a warning against using "few" as a quantifier. "Few, possibly none . . ." will keep meaning straight, if that is the situation intended.

6.   As we have said before, negatives generally indicate exclusions and negative terms should be avoided where possible. The possibility that a negative belongs in the term was left open, however, for cases such as "Those not holding a license are not real estate brokers." The same caution has to be added to the discussion of "only," "except," "unless," and other words that give difficulty, for these words too may be embedded in the term. So one has to approach them with care rather than with any fixed rule about their interpretation. Here are some instances where the trouble-causing words belong in the term.

> Sandra expects interest to decline only slightly.
> Sandra < those expecting interest to decline only slightly.

> Alfred likes to work alone.
> Alfred < those who like to work alone.

7.   Sometimes terms are split and must be gathered together to make a statement in standard form:

> In case of emergency, all passengers will report to A deck. *becomes*
> All passengers < those who will report to A deck in case of emergency.

8.   Although language usually presents terms in the order of their logical relationship, this is not always the case. When the subject is not placed first in a sentence, the order will be reversed when translating to standard form.

> Happy is he who has peace of mind. *becomes*
> All he who has (or, those who have) peace of mind < happy.

9.   Though singular terms cause some problems at advanced levels of logic, we are not apt to run into any practical difficulties by treating them as classes that happen to have only one member. Thus:

> Giotto was a fourteenth-century painter. *becomes*
> (All) Giotto < those who were fourteenth-century painters.

10.   In handling tense, one needs to remember that the relationships between terms are tenseless. References to time belong in the term, not in the relationship. Accordingly:

> The plane from Miami will not be on time. *becomes*
> (All) the plane from Miami < planes that will not be on time.

Or, one may express the same idea in an obverted form:

> (All) the plane from Miami ≮ planes that will be on time.

11.   Modal expressions such as "should," "might be," "I believe," "I assume," etc. ordinarily are not part of the statement in which they occur. Their use is rather to show the manner in which the statement is viewed. Since deduction is concerned with the validity of argument and not the truth or falsity of the material, modal terms are dropped. This allows us to concentrate on what is asserted. For instance:

> I believe Congress will prescribe some new pollution requirements. *becomes*
> (Some) <u>new pollution requirements</u> < <u>requirements Congress will prescribe.</u>

Occasionally the substance of a discussion is concerned with an attitude toward a statement rather than the assertion itself. In such a case, the modal expression is retained.

A few words are meaningless and, therefore, can be dropped from analysis without loss. *Actually, really, however, moreover, yet, on the other hand,* and like expressions used for emphasis or to suggest connections and contrasts between statements are not ordinarily a part of the assertion made.

Only practice can develop a feeling for how sentences in their unending variety are reduced to assertions in standard form. We have looked at a few problems and noted that recasting into standard form is apt to produce stilted language. Stilted or not, when one wishes to examine an argument rigorously, getting the meaning expressed in standard form is the essential first step for dealing with it.

SUMMARY

Language is extremely flexible, offering many ways for expressing the same meaning. Desirable though this is from the viewpoint of elegance in style, it is useful to reduce statements to standard form in order to make the terms and their relationship to one another unmistakably clear.

As far as deduction is concerned, it is generally best to state an argument in standard form for a categorical, hypothetical, disjunctive, or alternative syllogism according to whichever is closest to the original language used.

A term is the same whether singular or plural. Tense does not affect the relationship expressed, for relationships are tenseless. References to time belong in the term, not in the relationship. Generally, negatives indicate a relationship of exclusion, but occasionally a negative is an integral part of a term, as in "members who are not charter members."

Every language has constructions not easily translated into standard form. Some problems that arise in English concern the position of "not" in a sentence, cases where the predicate is placed before the subject, split terms, and certain frequently misunderstood words such as *only, alone, none but, all but, except, unless, few,* and *a few*.

EXERCISES FOR CHAPTER 11
pages 171–177

I.   Answer **T** for "true" or **F** for "false":

_____ **1.** The purpose of standard form is to make an assertion unmistakably clear.

_____ **2.** Material expressed in standard form for a hypothetical syllogism may not be re-expressed in standard form for a categorical syllogism.

_____ **3.** Changing from singular to plural does not create a new term.

_____ **4.** The relationship between two terms is tenseless.

_____ **5.** The word "only" is equivalent to "all."

_____ **6.** "None but residents can dig clams" must mean that "Residents can dig clams."

_____ **7.** "Only well-informed investors make money in the long run" means "Well-informed investors make money in the long run."

_____ **8.** "All except those with experience will be rejected" assures us that "Those with experience will not be rejected."

_____ **9.** "A few traders in futures will make money in this market" commits the speaker to the position that "Some traders in futures will make money in this market."

_____ **10.** Some words and structures in English give difficulty to many speakers of the language. Any other language, one may safely assume, would have different words and structures giving problems of meaning to users of that language.

II.   Each of the following sentences contains a trouble-causing word discussed in this chapter. Restate each as a single statement in standard form.

Example:

Only the strong can be free.

      a. All <u>those who are not strong</u> $\not<$ <u>free.</u>

               _or_

      b. All <u>the free</u> $<$ <u>strong.</u>

Note that solutions (a) and (b) are equivalent. Statement (b) is obtained by converting and then obverting (a).

1. Good swimmers alone will be accepted.

_____

2. A few people can climb Ship Rock.

_____

3. All except those under 30 will be excluded from flying.

_____

4. None but the best speakers are invited.

_____

5. One is promoted here only after years of experience.

_____

6. The factory always operates unless the power goes off.

_____

7. Few members of the club are poets.

_____

8. Everyone but the school staff was amused.

_____

9. Only a skilled craftsman could make such a casting.

_____

10. We will work tomorrow unless it rains. (State this in hypothetical form as well as in the categorical.)

_____

_____

III.   The following sentences contain split terms, negatives embedded in the term, and assertions with terms reversed from the order of standard form. Restate each in standard form.

Example:

It does not pay to be dishonest in the long run.

Being dishonest ⊀ things that pay in the long run.

1. Worth mentioning is the fact that the driver was overtired.

_____

2. Many people who never take chances remain in little jobs.

_____

3. Not to be loved is not to be happy.

_____

4. Fortunate are those who have steady nerves.

_____

5. At this time the housing shortage is severe.

_____

6. Slowly, the earth's climate will change.

_____

7. Welcome is the conversationist who talks not only of himself.

_____

8. That was a never-to-be-forgotten date.

_____

9. Actually, the storm abated in time.

_____

10. There was more than one cause for the decline of Rome.

_____

11. One may not receive Social Security payments before the age of 62.

_____

12. For the Revolution, the Battle of Valmy was politically important.

_____

13. Not to have peace of mind is unenjoyable.

_____

14. In case of fire, all alarms will ring.

_____

15. It takes courage to stand against popular opinion.

_____

16. Some Americans are malnourished who have never missed a meal.

_____

IV.   The following require that immediate inference be applied to arrive at standard form. Put them in standard form.

1. Not every mine is a bonanza.

_____

2. It isn't true that Tracy saw the game.

_____

3. I don't believe every economy is wise.

_____

4. Not all that glistens is gold.

_____

5. Some people are not unrewarded here.

_____

6. Homicides aren't all murders.

_____

7. Not only food prices have been rising.

_____

8. It is false that no forest fires are beneficial.

_____

chapter 12

Argument in Ordinary Language

One of the troubles with textbook explanations is that the illustrations and exercises are too orderly. Though clear cases separated from extraneous material are necessary to make early explanations effective, still at some point one ought to grapple with argument as it comes embedded in ordinary language. Instead of finding that everything given is relevant and fits into the final solution, more advanced exercises need to include some verbose expression, obscurely stated terms, and plain irrelevancies—for such is the nature of communication. Moreover, evidence in support of premises will be mingled with statements of premises and conclusions. Again, in order to avoid monotony, the choice of words varies constantly as if speakers were possessed of a compulsion not to repeat any phrase that has just been used. Although shifting expression contributes to style, it obscures argument grievously. One has to perceive where the intention is to express identical meanings and to generously refrain from crying "fourth term" when the wording, though not identical, is intended as a statement of the same idea.

Ordinary discussion has some helpful characteristics, too. At p. 157-8 we listed conclusion indicators and premise indicators. These words are much used precisely because they help to make argument followable. Further, though the conclusion may be stated at any point in the exposition of argument, it is more likely to appear at the beginning or end than toward the middle. This is because a conclusion placed in the middle of an explanation is apt to interfere with the flow of thought, and most people avoid this either consciously or by intuition. Finally, the ability to expand enthymemes helps in figuring out deductive argument as it occurs in ordinary language.

The first step in analyzing an argument is to spot the conclusion. Placing the conclusion first aids by orienting the audience at once to what the speaker seeks to establish—often an effective strategy. Or, premises and facts in support of the premises may be produced first in order to prepare the audience to accept the conclusion when it is stated later on. We know also from studying enthymemes that unstated premises are more common than unstated conclusions. So the sensible approach is to realize that the conclusion may be found at any point and that probably it appears either early or late in the argument. If the conclusion isn't evident, then we will have to start looking for premises. Now, let's begin by picking out conclusion and premises in a few lines of ordinary speech. I've numbered the sentences for ready reference.

> (1) It is not easy to find good investments for a modest family since they should combine safety for the principal with a lack of vulnerability to inflation. (2) Most long-term bonds offer safety for the principal, but all of them are vulnerable to inflation. (3) It is of little comfort to receive a fixed amount of money back if its purchasing power has shrunk seriously. (4) When there is rapid inflation, then interest rates rise and the capital value of low-yield bonds declines because their fixed income is unattractive. (5) Unless inflation is controlled, investors should avoid this type of security.

Looking over this passage fails to turn up a conclusion indicator. However, there are two premise indicators: "since" in (1) and "because" in (4). In (1) "since" introduces the idea, "... they (good investments for a modest family) should combine safety for the principal with a lack of vulnerability to inflation," which is a general rule and, hence, likely to be a major premise. The "because" in (4) introduces wholly different material: "... fixed income at a generally low yield is unattractive." Evidently these two premises won't go together in the same syllogism since they have no terms in common and therefore lack a middle term. In other words, these premises belong to different arguments. Since there was no conclusion indicator and since locating premises did not put us clearly on the track, we'll have to take an overall view to discover the argument. Reading the passage as a whole makes it pretty evident that the speaker wants to convince us that long-term bonds are not good investments in times of inflation. We can rephrase (5) as:

	T-1		T-2
Conclusion	Long-term bonds in times that inflation is not controlled	$\not\subset$	good investments

Now, if the premise material that we identified uses either of these terms, then it will fit into an argument leading to this conclusion. We find that (1) is about "good investments for a modest family" while (4) refers to neither term of this conclusion. But premise indicators, though handy, are not always used and we will have to look over the other sentences in the passage in a search for premise material. We notice that (2) has something to say about "long-term bonds" which resembles term-1 of the conclusion, though it does not correspond exactly. Might as well try (2) as a premise:

T-1?   T-3

Premise   <u>Long-term bonds</u> < <u>vulnerable to inflation</u>

We identified the term "long-term bonds" as "T-1?" to indicate uncertainty about whether it is intended as equivalent to "long-term bonds in times that inflation is not controlled." Now, applying the technique for expanding an enthymeme to the *conclusion* and *premise* set down above, we find that the missing premise should be about the ideas "good investments" and "vulnerable to inflation." Looking at the passage, we find that (1) contains these ideas along with some other material.

T-2?   T-3?

Premise   <u>Good investments for a modest family</u> < <u>combine safety of principal and lack of vulnerability to inflation</u>

So far we have a faulty exclusion staring us in the face and three terms are marked with a ? because their wording is not the same as the terms they should match. Can these defects be remedied? We have to expect to reword terms, since ordinary speech rarely repeats ideas exactly. The apparent trouble with exclusions isn't so common: let's see what is wrong. Looking over the terms, one is "vulnerable to inflation" while another is "lack of vulnerability to inflation." "Lack" is a negative idea which can be put into an exclusion. So the premise can be restated as in Premise 1:

T-2   T-3

Premise 1   <u>Good investments for a modest family</u> ⊀ <u>vulnerable to inflation</u>

T-1   T-3

Premise 2   <u>Long-term bonds *in times that inflation is not controlled*</u> < <u>vulnerable to inflation</u>

T-1   T-2

Conclusion   <u>Long-term bonds in times that inflation is not controlled</u> ⊀ <u>good investments *for a modest family*</u>

With the faulty exclusions eliminated, can we reword the terms to repeat each other without changing the meaning of the argument as stated originally? Premise 1 speaks of "Good investments for a modest family," while the conclusion refers to the wider class "good investments." To be sure, the investment standards "for a modest family" and investment standards in general may differ, so we can chide the author of the passage for having reasoned sloppily—and invalidly—in stating a conclusion that is broader than its premises. There is a presumption that a valid argument is intended, and by cutting down the claim of the conclusion to "good investments for a modest family" we will have a valid result. So we will limit term-1 in the conclusion by adding the words "for a modest family." In correcting this invalidity we presume we are correcting an unintended change in terms through shifting expression. Of course, if we want to we can dig in our heels and say, " 'Invalid' as originally stated." It will make no difference as long as we understand what we are doing.

Premise 2 is about "long-term bonds" while the conclusion speaks of "long-term bonds in times that inflation is not controlled." "Long-term bonds" always are potentially vulnerable to inflation and when "inflation is not controlled" they become actually vulnerable. So, adding "in times that inflation is not controlled" to term-2 in Premise 2 would not violate the speaker's intent. Finally, in the statement of the syllogism you may have noticed that the idea "combine safety of principal" was dropped from term-3. This is justified because the original assertion "Good investments for a modest family combine safety of principal and lack of vulnerability to inflation" contains two propositions and only the proposition "Good investments for a modest family lack vulnerability to inflation" was used in the argument.

Now it's understandable if you're getting impatient with the convolutions of analyzing the argument hiding in, after all, only a few lines. More than one argument found, trouble with exclusions, rewording the cumbersomely expressed terms—a saint's patience would be tried. It's time to look for a simpler way. As this analysis demonstrates, casting arguments into categorical form can be an awkward process requiring much changing of wording and with four rules to check in testing validity. The hypothetical form generally is easier to formulate, requires less rewording of terms, and its most common ailment checks out with a seven-word rule. Look how simply we can get to the heart of the last example that we labored over:

>   A   C
> If <u>it is a good investment</u>, then <u>safety and no vulnerability</u>
>
> Long-term bonds are vulnerable in times of inflation.
> (This denies C as to vulnerability in times of inflation.)
>
> Therefore long-term bonds are not a good investment in times of inflation.
>
> Valid: consequent denied

There is another way to simplify matters. You may remember that we suggested at first that one should not shorten terms by dropping words. By now we have worked with terms enough to start shortening them to bare references which, though technically inaccurate, are enough to allow one to keep them in mind. In fact, clarity may be gained by expressing argument briefly rather than in the clumsy wording of fully stated terms. We shortened terms in the hypothetical syllogism above. Even though making use of the hypothetical syllogism is helpful, still it takes practice to expand enthymemes or find syllogisms in the weed-choked garden of ordinary expression. Let's look at one more case.

> (1) The U.N. can't deal effectively with the problem of peace, and this is not surprising. (2) In fact, within weeks after the U.N. Charter was completed in

1945, a group of political scientists and others interested in peace met to study and discuss it; their conclusion was that the Charter was unworkable. (3) So the many years of experience with the U.N. Charter which have demonstrated its shortcomings all too well have been an unnecessary tragedy, intellectually at least, since fundamental defects in the organization and its lack of essential powers made its weakness foreseeable. (4) The provision for veto by any great power in the Security Council and the unrealistic overrepresentation of tiny states in the General Assembly are but the most widely known weaknesses. (5) The organization is without independent finances, it lacks so much as a token force over which it has full control, it cannot even send its officials to make an investigation without permission—frequently refused—of the state in which the investigation is to take place, there is no court to which international disputes must be referred, for submitting a case to the World Court is optional and occurs only where all parties agree in advance which rarely happens. (6) The list of weaknesses goes on and on. (7) Yet the paragraphs that set up an organization and provide for the powers which it can exercise are but half of the reality of any political institution. (8) The other half lies in the support the organization receives from whatever people are subject to its control. (9) Here, again, the U.N. is a pitiful Cinderella. (10) States disregarding U.N. resolutions find that in doing so they enjoy the full support of their people, governments bypass the U.N. in matters concerning peace and their peoples remain unconcerned, little protest is heard from the citizens of states that undertake to gain their ends by withholding financial support from the U.N. or its affiliated organizations. (11) Though there are good reasons for public disillusionment and indifference, this is not the issue. (12) The point is that lack of popular support is itself a fact contributing to the weakness of the U.N. (13) And the consequence of an ill-structured, inadequately powered and neglected world organization is enormous: repeated wars, huge armaments, and reliance upon force as the necessary arbiter of international affairs.

We have found already that real paragraphs are apt to have more than a single argument, but before things get too far out of hand let's try to locate the main argument. To do this it is best to take an overall view. Rather clearly, the speaker sets out to show that the U.N. is ineffective as a preserver of peace. Sentences (1) and (13) both express this conclusion while the material in between has the purpose of persuading the audience that the claim is true. This time we will put the argument in hypothetical form.

Hypothetical

                              A   C
If <u>a governmental organization is to be effective</u>, then <u>it must have a workable structure, adequate power, and popular support</u> (expressed in sentences 3, 7, 8, and summarized in 13).

The U.N. does not have a workable structure, adequate powers, and popular support (expressed in 4, 5, 6, 9, 10, 12).

Therefore, the U.N. is not an effective governmental organization (expressed in 1, 13).

Valid: consequent denied

It is possible, as you know, to cast the analysis in any of the other forms of syllogism. Here's how the other forms work out:

Categorical

T-1 d		T-2 u
Effective organization	$<$	having workable structure, adequate powers, and popular support

T-3 d		T-2 d
U.N.	$\not<$	having workable structure, adequate powers, and popular support

T-3 d		T-1 d
U.N.	$\not<$	effective organization

Valid: all four rules satisfied

Disjunctive

Disj. 1   Disj. 2
Not both be an effective organization and not have a workable structure, adequate powers, and popular support

The U.N. does not have a workable structure, adequate powers and popular support.

Therefore, the U.N. is not an effective organization.

Valid: second disjunct affirmed

Alternative

Alt. 1
Either an organization has a workable structure, adequate powers,

Alt. 2
and popular support or it is not an effective organization.

The U.N. does not have a workable structure, adequate powers, and popular support.

Therefore, the U.N. is not an effective organization.

Valid: first alternate denied

We started this chapter by declaring bravely, "One of the troubles with textbook explanations is that the illustrations and exercises are too orderly." Now that we have unraveled some deductive arguments as they come embedded in a longer passage, the care and thought required makes one wonder how often, in practice, one is likely to comply with such a demanding procedure. The difficulty is intrinsic. It is simply true that deductive arguments are harder to analyze than are fallacies to identify or, fortunately, than are the inductive arguments which we are about to take up. Yet a major part of all argument is deductive, and there is no escaping the necessity of locating conclusions and tracking down premises when one desires to examine such an argument and assess its support.

SUMMARY

Since this chapter concerns deduction, only deductive arguments are analyzed here.

Conclusion indicators and premise indicators are a substantial aid in sorting out material (see lists on p. 157-8). However, these helpful words are not always used, and where such a word does appear one still has to decide whether it relates to the principal argument being made or merely to some incidental inference.

No analysis can be right unless the conclusion is identified correctly. Though it is best to determine the conclusion first, if this proves difficult one may turn to seek premises.

Remember that enthymemes are a very common form of deduction with unexpressed premises being more frequent than unexpressed conclusions.

One is free to change language without altering the meaning. Since ordinary speech seeks to avoid monotony by not repeating terms exactly, one should expect shifts in expression and not be overzealous in insisting on technical fourth terms. There is a presumption in favor of interpreting meaning in a way that results in a valid argument.

Hypothetical form is easy to check and many arguments are more easily dealt with if they are recast in this form.

Expressing an argument in standard form permits a check of its validity and enquiry into whether the premises, now sharply stated, are reliable. Though logic is not concerned with whether or not the premise material is true, one should realize that the application of logic to everyday reasoning uncovers questionable premises more often than it discovers invalid argument.

EXERCISES FOR CHAPTER 12
pages 183–189

I.   Answer with **T** for "true" or **F** for "false":

_____ **1.** Words or phrases to distinguish premises and conclusions always are present in an argument.

_____ **2.** If one is unable to spot a conclusion indicator, then at least there will be premise indicators to fall back on.

_____ **3.** Undeniably, premise and conclusion indicators are in common use.

_____ **4.** Reasonable use of premise and conclusion indicators is part of the art of clarity in argument.

_____ **5.** "For" is a premise indicator.

_____ **6.** If an argument is well organized, then the conclusion will appear at the end.

_____ **7.** One may always change the wording of an argument provided the meaning remains unaltered.

_____ **8.** The chief use one can claim for reducing a complicated argument into syllogistic form is to decide whether the argument is valid.

_____ **9.** Though there is no rule about the matter, it is generally best to express an argument in the particular type of syllogism which involves the least change in the wording of the original argument.

_____ **10.** Though premise and conclusion indicators help to identify the structure of deduction expressed in a sentence or a paragraph, an argument expressed in several paragraphs or in a whole essay probably can be determined only by taking an overall view.

II.   All the following arguments are valid. In the first set of exercises, premise and conclusion indicators identify every part of the argument; later these props are reduced in frequency and the argument is obscured to a degree by more verbose expression, inclusion of some irrelevant statements and statements of evidence. Use a separate sheet of paper to analyze each argument in whatever form of syllogism you choose.

1. Since hunting an endangered species is forbidden and the leopard is an endangered species, it follows that hunting leopards is prohibited.

2. Evidently tariffs alone cannot explain economic prosperity, since some nations have prospered without significant tariffs and this would not be possible if tariffs were necessary.

3. It is a fact that a preservative that increases shelf life may not be good for the human body. Yet increased shelf life is a factor in some manufacturing decisions, so it follows that some decisions concerning food are not beneficial to the body of the consumer.

4. The president of the United States is expected to perform many ceremonial duties which take time and energy away from important decisions. Ceremonial duties never are important to the nation, therefore some presidential activity is not important.

5. Since some charges are not substantiated and all unsubstantiated charges should be avoided, consequently some charges should not be made.

6. No trout are found in badly polluted water and this water is indeed polluted badly. Consequently, there can be no trout here.

7. All the trails have water, so if you use the Blueberry Ledge Trail you will find water along it.

8. If you are going into the cave you are required to carry three independent sources of light, and I see you have only two, so you cannot go into the cave.

9. We have not reached 14,000 feet because at that elevation I always have trouble with the thin air and I am not having any trouble yet.

10. Cumulus clouds are a sign of stable weather and these are cumulus clouds. We can expect stable weather today.

III. Some of the arguments in this set are valid while others are invalid. Analyze each as a categorical syllogism. Then check whether each argument is **valid** or **invalid**. Where the argument is invalid, write in the blank provided **four terms**, **faulty exclusions**, **undistributed middle**, or **illicit distribution** as the case may be.

1. There is no safe climbing without proper equipment, and the Carmargo party hasn't got good equipment. Why, their gear is pathetic! It won't be a safe trip for them.

    Valid _____   *Invalid* _____   _____

2. The Belottis are happy because happy people find time to relax and enjoy themselves and everyone can see that the Belottis live this way.

Valid _____   *Invalid* _____   _____

3. Most outstanding atheletes train very hard, but Johnson never does, so he can't be very good.

Valid _____   *Invalid* _____   _____

4. Fossils are found only in sedimentary rock. Since Mt. Baldy is a great granite dome and granite is an igneous rock, we would be wasting our time looking for fossils there.

Valid _____   *Invalid* _____   _____

5. One who wants a successful marriage will have to give up some things for the sake of the family. I know that Albert will do that, so it is evident that he'll have a successful marriage.

Valid _____   *Invalid* _____   _____

6. The colonists were not satisfied at home because people who are content as things are do not leave for the uncertainties and hardships of a new world, which is what the early settlers did.

Valid _____   *Invalid* _____   _____

7. This statue does not represent a leader of Republican Rome because the Roman leaders of that period were clean-shaven and this sculpture shows a man with a beard.

Valid _____   *Invalid* _____   _____

8. It must be a serious fire because there have been three alarms, and only when things are out of control is this action taken.

Valid _____   *Invalid* _____   _____

9. Those who invest after hearing rumors aren't good investors, but this is the last thing that Mr. Farrell would do. So you see, he's competent in handling investments.

Valid _____   *Invalid* _____   _____

10. Those who work hard and have good judgment are apt to succeed in business. Since George has these qualities, I expect him to succeed as an actor.

    Valid _____   *Invalid* _____   _____

IV.   Analyze the arguments in this set as hypothetical syllogisms. Then check whether the argument is **valid** or **invalid**. Where you find an invalid argument, fill in the blank with the reason for its invalidity—i.e., **denied antecedent, affirmed consequent, uncertain relation between the premises,** or **unauthorized conclusion.** Be prepared for shifting expression of terms. It will be for you to decide whether changes in wording amount to the introduction of a new idea.

1. If one saves enough money to keep a good balance on hand in the bank, then one can always deal with minor financial problems. That's what we always do, so we don't have that "too much month for money" problem that can be a real headache.

   Valid _____   *Invalid* _____   _____

2. If the Red Sox win tonight, they'll get the pennant. They have a strong team this year, so everybody expects them to win. That means they'll get the pennant, all right.

   Valid _____   *Invalid* _____   _____

3. What an upset! The Red Sox lost. If they'd won, they would have gotten the pennant. So now they won't get it.

   Valid _____   *Invalid* _____   _____

4. The mounds of the Ohio Valley would not appear in so many fanciful shapes if they had been made for a practical purpose. Therefore they must have served a religious or ceremonial purpose rather than a practical one.

   Valid _____   *Invalid* _____   _____

5. A government will not be workable if its key officials do not cooperate to make it a success. Unfortunately, Louis XVI as constitutional monarch of the first government established in the French Revolution regarded the new political arrangement as a scandalous usurping of his power. His unwillingness to try to make the government work assured its failure.

   Valid _____   *Invalid* _____   _____

6. A government will not be workable if the key officials of that government do not cooperate to make it a success. Fortunately, George Washington did cooperate fully to make the new U.S. Constitution serve as a workable government. Clearly, then, Washington's support assured success to the new government.

Valid _____   *Invalid* _____   _____

7. Since we know that the criminal would have to be small to have gotten through the broken grate that was used to gain access, we have a valuable clue. We can dismiss Thompson, for he is a large man.

Valid _____   *Invalid* _____   _____

8. Had Hitler invaded Russia in the early spring of 1941, very likely his army would have captured Moscow. But Hitler ordered an invasion of the Balkans, and this occupied his armies in the spring, thus delaying the invasion until June 22. So there was no possibility of taking Moscow.

Valid _____   *Invalid* _____   _____

Numbers 9 and 10 contain enthymemes, and each passage will expand into two or more "valid" syllogisms. Take a piece of paper and see if you can discover a chain of syllogisms that end with the conclusion for the passage. Use whatever form of syllogism you find most convenient.

9. Because they lack extra clothing it would be dangerous for that party to get caught in a storm, and sudden storms are common above timberline. So that party should not venture above the shelter of the trees.

10. Birds of prey stand at the top of the food chain, and thus they concentrate in their bodies whatever poisons are found in their food supply. Many birds and rodents accumulate pesticides from the insect and plant life upon which they feed. This is why the peregrine falcon (a bird of prey) is approaching extinction.

V. Analyze the following arguments in whatever form is closest to the language of the particular passage. Then fill in the blanks as you did for sections III and IV.

1. This boiler must have been leaking for some time, since it is deeply pitted with rust and only water over a period of time would produce so much rust.

Valid _____   *Invalid* _____   _____

2. A poor manager wouldn't get that business out of the red. But George is not a poor manager, so he'll be able to put it into the black OK.

Valid _____   *Invalid* _____   _____

3. The Schneiders cannot live beyond their means and save money to buy a house at the same time. Since spending everything that comes their way is a way of life with the Schneiders, they can't buy a house.

Valid _____   *Invalid* _____   _____

4. Either we get the grant or we can't proceed with the project. June Levine is well acquainted with the foundation that we applied to and she is confident we'll get the grant all right, so we will be able to carry on the project.

Valid _____   *Invalid* _____   _____

5. It is not possible for our society to have large numbers of people living in poverty and not have street crime. Well, there is no immediate prospect of ending poverty, for that is a most difficult undertaking even if there were great public support for such a change, which there isn't. It follows that we will continue to be plagued with street crime.

Valid _____   *Invalid* _____   _____

6. When the public is poorly educated, the government is apt to be corrupt. Many underdeveloped countries illustrate this sad fact—sad because those who are already poor suffer most where there is corruption. But no country has a higher level of education than our country, so our country is not apt to be corrupt.

Valid _____   *Invalid* _____   _____

7. Scuba diving isn't safe unless one has a responsible associate. Franklin's associate is very responsible. Why, he's considered the best diver in the area. They will be safe.

Valid _____   *Invalid* _____   _____

8. One can't be a good manager without demanding hard work and real effort from employees at every level. After all, taking things easy doesn't add up to an efficient operation. I never saw anybody more exacting, one might even say more ruthless, in requiring the best efforts of everybody connected with the company than our new manager, Mr. Billideau. He'll be a good manager all right.

Valid _____   *Invalid* _____   _____

Numbers 9–12 contain material requiring an immediate inference to put the argument into standard form. Take a piece of paper and see if you can work out the inference necessary to arrange the argument in standard form. Use whatever form of syllogism you find most convenient.

9. Not all the green apples are unripe. That's good. If some of the apples are ripe, we will have enough fruit for today.

   Valid _____   Invalid _____   _____

10. It is false that only some of our mail was delivered. And if our mail was delivered, then any letter Jane wrote last week would be in that mail. Evidently, she didn't write.

    Valid _____   Invalid _____   _____

11. Although not every architect is a good engineer, at least every architect knows something about construction. This leaves me with a conclusion that sounds strange, I admit: some who know something about construction aren't good engineers.

    Valid _____   Invalid _____   _____

12. Everybody knows that no patent claim can be unoriginal. Since the process for making nylon was extremely valuable when it was patented, one can be sure that it was indeed an original idea.

    Valid _____   Invalid _____   _____

VI.   In the following longer passages, some of the reasoning is expressed in enthymemes and there may be more than one argument in a passage. Each passage, however, can be reduced to a main argument that is expressed in a single valid syllogism. On the other hand, in a number of cases the reliability of the premises is questionable.

Reduce the principal argument of each passage to a single syllogism of any type you choose. Write this syllogism on a sheet of paper. Then check the blanks below to indicate your opinion of the reliability of the premises. Be prepared to defend your opinion.

1. It is important to preserve free speech. No institution is more basic to democracy than that which protects the free expression of ideas to the end that the public will be informed both of the strengths and the weaknesses, both of the accomplishments and the scandals, of our society. Without this knowledge

the public cannot intelligently choose between alternatives and without being able to make an intelligent choice there cannot be successful direction in a democratic process. A restriction of free speech is more than a mere infringement of the rights of some individual; it is a denial of the right of all of us to hear and judge for ourselves.

Premises reliable _____ *Premises not reliable* _____ *No opinion* _____

2. The Charitable Fund has the worthy cause of feeding the hungry, and this is the most basic sort of human need. There can be little doubt in the mind of a humane person that efforts to meet basic needs deserve support ahead of the many things which, though desirable, are not so essential to human survival. Therefore, if you possibly can, you should give to the Charitable Fund.

Premises reliable _____ *Premises not reliable* _____ *No opinion* _____

3. Any sort of understanding may open a door to pleasure and a fuller life. For example, to look at a cathedral or hear a symphony or witness the grandeur of the Grand Canyon may give *some* pleasure without special knowledge; it may also confront one with one's own ignorance. With an understanding of architecture or music or geology or whatever is appropriate to the experience, then appreciation and enjoyment is heightened. So I'm delighted to hear that Irene has a good knowledge of botany, and I am sure that this knowledge will be a source of pleasure to her.

Premises reliable _____ *Premises not reliable* _____ *No opinion* _____

4. Taxation does more than provide necessary income for the state; it reflects the social policy of the society of which it is a product. To tax one group of people more heavily than another, to tax one type of product and exempt another, or to tax one kind of transaction and not another—all these distinctions encourage one thing or discourage something else, or, in other words, all give effect to some sort of social policy. Consequently, the system of taxation that prevails in a nation is an index to the values which dominate that society.

Premises reliable _____ *Premises not reliable* _____ *No opinion* _____

5. If Patricia Hearst were not guilty of voluntarily participating in the bank robbery and other criminal activities of her alleged "captors," then she would not have claimed the Fifth Amendment forty-two times in the course of her trial. The Fifth Amendment, you will recall, is the privilege of a witness not to testify on the ground that the evidence called for by the question might be incriminating to him/her. And we all know that in our society one charged with crime is not to be compelled to testify against oneself. One may indeed not testify—but at one's peril, so to speak. For there is no avoiding the conclusion that refusal to testify bespeaks of something to hide, and in the case of Miss Hearst that something to hide was that she did voluntarily participate in the criminal activities of her associates.

Premises reliable _____ *Premises not reliable* _____ *No opinion* _____

6. Every college student wants a job after graduation and, moreover, wants a better job than he or she could have secured without having gone to college. If this desire is accepted as reasonable, then one cannot escape questioning the time devoted to liberal arts, which occupies so large a place in today's college curriculum. Everyone should notice the importance of being able to do something in demand by society—whether it be keeping accounts, developing a new synthetic material, or playing in a rock band. After all, it is those who are ready to fill specific jobs who can and will fill the jobs for which they are prepared. The liberal arts graduate who lacks a particular applicable skill may struggle to find a suitable job and, all too often, not find it. There can be no escaping the conclusion that the emphasis on liberal arts in our colleges ought to be reduced.

Premises reliable _____ *Premises not reliable* _____ *No opinion* _____ *part three*

Induction

chapter 13

Generalization

Deduction has neat rules. It has a machinelike quality, and to pass on the validity of deductions can be fun when one knows the rules well enough. It is nice to be right, and the game of deduction offers chances for being just that. The whole scene changes when one comes to induction, for in this half of logic nothing follows with certainty, and worse, the whole process of induction can be charged with invalidity! It's an embarrassing charge. Let us look at the framing of a generalization to see how it can be attacked as invalid and why it can never enter the Promised Land of Certainty.

One way to form a conclusion about the characteristics of a lot of particular facts is to examine them all. For instance, suppose I examine the books on my shelf and I observe, "Book 1 is about business. Book 2 is about business. Book 3 is about business." And so on through all the books on the shelf, all of which turn out to be about business. Then I can say solemnly, "All the books on my shelf are about business." This is an enumeration. It is a report based on all the facts. It would make no difference if it turned out that only three-quarters of the books were about business, for the statement "Three-quarters of the books on my shelf are about business" is equivalent to "Of *all* the books on my shelf, three-quarters are about business." It is a statement about all the books. When such a statement rests upon an examination of all the cases covered, and not on a sample, then it is an enumeration.

When the total number of cases is accessible and not very great, then the best procedure is to investigate them all and report the result. A city council, for example, is too small to sample accurately; if you want to forecast its opinion, every member should be contacted. Enumeration is not an important problem in reasoning, however, and I shall say no more about it.

Far more significant is the situation in which not all cases can be observed.

Those forecasting a national election will not find it practicable to interview all the voters. It would be utterly impossible for anybody to examine every past, present, and future armadillo in order to come to definitive conclusions about this intriguing animal. No, if we had to reach conclusions this way we should never reach them at all. Characteristically, our general conclusions about what goes on in the world are founded upon some minute fraction of all the cases there are.

A generalization is formed by taking the "inductive leap"—that is, on the basis of examining some cases only, a conclusion is formed which covers all the cases there are.

In order to "make sense" of the world around us, we have to notice the similarities between one situation and another. We must form classes. Noticing the similarities of this animal to that one convinces us that both are armadillos, a class that strikes us as an evident "natural" class. One who has more interest and opportunity to observe armadillos will notice that there are regular variations between them, and he will form subgroups or subspecies and relate his observations to these more refined groups. Having the class "armadillo" in mind with whatever refinements we have formed, we begin to notice other things about them: how they behave when caught, or their visual ability at night, for instance. We begin to have all sorts of convictions about their nature and behavior, and these convictions all are generalizations.

We have seen that generalization is a process of examining particular cases and forming a general conclusion concerning them. It starts with particulars and leaps to the general. On the basis of *some* cases only, the inductive leap reaches a conclusion covering *all* cases. Now this causes a difficulty which logicians have investigated at length without locating a really satisfying solution; the problem prompted my remark about induction being charged with invalidity. What is this invalidity? It's plain. As a matter of immediate inference, if we accept "Some A is B"; then "All A is B" is *doubtful*. The inductive leap brazenly violates this rule and it has to pay the penalty, which is foregoing a claim that the conclusion is valid. What better place to remind ourselves that "invalid" is not equivalent to "false" but only to the chiding "*that* conclusion is not a necessary consequence of the premises." Though it is well to note the logical difficulty, there is no need for alarm once we admit the different claims made for deduction and induction. Deduction claims, rightly, that its valid conclusions are inescapable consequences of the premises and, further, that if the premises are true then the conclusion must be true. Deduction claims *certainty for the operation of its process.* On the other hand, induction cannot and does not make such a claim. The immediate inference from *some* to *all* is logically *doubtful* (see p. 110), so there always is a logical possibility of a case turning up which does not conform to the induction made.

All the forms of induction—generalization, hypothesis, analogy—are to be judged for their *reliability*, which is their purpose. None of them are valid, nor claim validity. So our next question is, *What is necessary for generalizing reliably?* Though a great deal has to be said in taking up even the elementary ramifications of this question, the essential requirements are easy to state.

The requirements for a reliable generalization are:

1. The generalization must be based upon a *sufficient number of cases*
2. The generalization must be based upon *cases that are fairly representative* of the group that the generalization covers

These requirements are old friends, encountered before in the discussion of the fallacy of *faulty generalization.* Here we will not stress the rules, which are simple, so much as the practical difficulties that are met in satisfying the rules.

In the first place, what is a "case"? Each example of the subject generalized about is a case. For the generalization "All fossils occur in sedimentary deposits," each fossil in the world is a case. For the generalization "Revolutions evolve new goals as they proceed," every revolution is a case. Further, *each case is an instance of the truth of the generalization made.* If one should find a revolution that did not evolve new goals, then the unquantified generalization "Revolutions evolve new goals as they proceed" would have to be modified to "Most revolutions, etc." or whatever was appropriate to fit the evidence. Then the majority of revolutions that do evolve new goals are instances of the truth of the generalization and the lesser number of revolutions that do not evolve new goals are instances of the correctness of the quantifier "most."

To continue with the cases in the examples just discussed, paleontologists usually would agree on whether an object were a fossil or not, but "revolution" refers to a whole complex of events; it is a vague notion fraught with borderline cases. A decision about whether a revolution had "evolved new goals" would also encounter marginal areas leaving much to the interpreter. Manifestly, some cases are clearcut while others are not. Wherever it is difficult to distinguish the cases or to decide about their application, it becomes hard to generalize reliably. The problem resembles the celebrated croquet game in *Alice in Wonderland* in which the mallet was a live flamingo and the ball a perambulating hedgehog. Reliable generalization needs accurately identified and measured material upon which to rest, and material that resists clear classification and measurement will provide only shaky ground for generalizing.

Now we come to the question, *What is a sufficient number of cases for reliable generalization?* It would be absurd to set down any particular number, since what is needed varies enormously. Even so, some rather definite things can be said about what is "sufficient." We will start by taking a look at the notion of the *uniformity of nature,* one of man's key realizations that has evolved to general acceptance over the past three centuries. According to the uniformity of nature, there is order in the universe and that order prevails without exceptions. This conception of natural phenomena, always operating in the same way under the same conditions, is borne out by trillions of observations and is subject to no exceptions that are well authenticated. There is no stronger generalization in human experience. Further, the conception of an orderly universe is necessary to enable man to deal successfully with the physical world. A world that has order is understandable and is predictable to the extent that it is understood; a world without order would be a chaos beyond fathoming. Now we must not fall into the ancient error of believing that truth is determined by human convenience or interest. What makes the uniformity of nature a tenable belief is not its convenience but that it is confirmed and reconfirmed in constant human experience. Further, it is those who have accepted the notion of an orderly world who have patiently built the accomplishments of modern science, while those who have pursued the occult have gone down a blind alley that has not led to impressive additions of knowledge. Ready though science must be to reconsider its theories in the light of reliable new evidence, this open posture does not mean that science could readily give up the notion of an orderly universe. To admit phenomena as capricious is to make the world *un*understandable; thus the whole structure of science requires profound resistance to admitting miracles defying the order of nature. Where a phenomenon cannot be fitted into what is known of the natural order, the scientist declares the phenomena not understood and he does not receive it as an exception to natural laws.[1]

A moment ago we raised the question of how many cases are needed for reliable generalization. The answer depends in large measure upon the nature of the cases. First, some situations are *homogeneous*—that is, all the cases have identical characteristics relating to the generalization. Perfectly homogeneous situations occur now and then, and when they do one may generalize from a single case without chiding himself for doing so. One sip of milk will convince us whether the whole quart is sour. If the judgment that all cases are the same is correct, then there is no need for further sampling, since any case will be representative of the whole group. The real problem lies in establishing that the cases are homogenous in some respect. Once this is established, it becomes a major premise, permitting the characteristics of a single case to be cited as a minor premise and leading on by deduction to a conclusion.

Physics and chemistry deal with homogeneous materials where one instance has the same characteristics as any other instance. For example, the expansion of pure iron under the same conditions through the same range of temperature would not vary. Since, as we know, any particular piece of iron will contain impurities and further, measurement never can be entirely accurate, the scientist will investigate a number of instances, not so much because he needs more cases as such but rather to average out his own errors of observation in identifying and measuring the material.

---

[1]Realization of the uniformity of nature was at the core of the ideas of the Enlightenment in the eighteenth century and was elaborated by John Stuart Mill, a nineteenth-century logician and political philosopher. Though it is an undeniably useful concept, some logicians raise objections, not to its truth, but to its theoretical justification. For a statement of these objections, see Morris R. Cohen and Ernest Nagel, *An Introduction to Logic and the Scientific Method* (New York: Harcourt Brace Jovanovich, 1934), pp. 267–69.

The uniformity of nature and homogeneous situations are well and good where they apply. Quite different is the number of cases needed when the situation is *heterogeneous*—that is, when the cases exhibit differences between one another. The cases may have a few differences or many indeed, and as a rule the more differences they exhibit that may bear on the generalization, the greater the number of cases needed for reliable generalization. Much of the generalizing we do concerns heterogeneous situations that are not tied to the uniformity of nature.

Now we are off to Chile, visiting thirty towns. In each town we notice red fire engines. When we have seen 30 of them, or 300 of them, do we conclude, "All Chilean fire engines are red"? Certainly not. We don't need any great perception to understand that the color of fire engines is set by the whim of man, and the very next town may turn up a white one or a blue one. So we will hesitate to be so positive in a situation where the uniformity of nature does not apply and countercases are plainly possible. Only after adequate sampling, which will be discussed later, could a reliable generalization be made, and even though the sample turned up nothing but red engines, one might still prefer to quantify the generalization as "Almost all Chilean fire engines are red" to leave room for the possible exception.

"All swans are white." The older logic books were fond of this one until the disturbing black swans of Australia came along. What happened here? The uniformity of nature certainly didn't break down—rather, logicians but slightly acquainted with ornithology got a surprise. Color in birds is a superficial characteristic that may vary according to locality or even within the same locality. Had the illustration taken some fundamental characteristic such as "All swans have livers," then the uniformity of nature as it pertains to the structure of birds would have applied. One can rescue the textbooks, partly at least, by pointing out that the swans-are-white generalization would have held had it been confined to Europe, as it should have been in view of the limited location of all the supporting cases. One can question also whether the black swans were within the intended generalization, for they constituted a new subspecies of swan, distinct from the European variety the logicians were talking about. The lesson learned from the incident, however, is that generalizations are less secure if they do not relate to a fundamental characteristic of the subject being generalized about. Now how to decide what a "fundamental characteristic" may be is a skunk I'd rather not skin. Though common sense can distinguish fundamental and superficial characteristics on many occasions, the difference is not always self-evident and I know no useful principle that will demark the fundamental for every situation.

How far does the uniformity of nature extend in supporting generalizations? With the materials of physics and chemistry it works well, as everybody knows. Here situations are identical, or, admitting the impossibility of obtaining pure substances and the random movement of particles of which scientists speak, any lack of identity is not great enough to hinder reliable generalization. Soon, however, one encounters situations which cannot be reduced to identical cases as, for example, the fact that each human being is the product of a unique genetic code so that in some instances a treatment effective in curing one may set up an allergic reaction in another. Consequently, in medicine although many generalizations are so fundamental that they apply to all humans, in other matters individual variations in the cases result in generalizations which are quantified, making the effect of the treatment in some cases unknowable without trial. The more narrowly human beings can be classified so as to make the cases more homogeneous with respect to some particular feature, the better the chance for a universal reaction knowable in advance. That is why soldiers wear "dog tags," stamped with the blood type. That is why colleges have admission standards.

We have just seen that the uniformity of nature is a sort of ultimate generalization greatly increasing the reliability of any induction that can be related to it. Noticing that some generalizations are *empirical* while others are *explained* is another approach useful in evaluating reliability. An empirical or practical generalization is simply a rule implied from observed cases without an understanding of why the phenomenon occurs, or, in other words, without our being able to connect the generalization to anything else within human knowledge. We never can be satisfied with mere empirical knowledge, for even though the support of a great deal of experience may make it quite reliable, still it always will be more reliable if it can be supported theoretically too.

Empirical generalizations may be the best we have, and, if so, we should follow those with adequate support. There are many examples. Though the ancients did not know what made the tide rise and fall, they took it into account in sailing. Though no one in the Middle Ages could explain how land left fallow could regain some productive power, the three-field system was developed and used. Though the members of the British Parliament did not understand why lime juice helped prevent scurvy, they decided to require that it be served to British seamen. All these empirical generalizations can now be supported theoretically. They have taken their places as explained generalizations that are borne out by theories systemizing large areas of experience. Empirical generalizations still hold sway in other fields, and we do well to heed them where this is the best we have. For instance, aspirin sometimes helps arthritis, although no one yet knows how. Doctors prescribe it, though they would welcome an explanation of how it works, or, preferably, a more adequate treatment.

Generalizing in the social sciences runs into obstacles we have noted before. Often the cases are diffuse events differing considerably from one another so that there is no hope for classifying them into groups whose members approach identity, and, further, control over the material for the purpose of experiment commonly is out of the question. Still, something can be accomplished: social scientists both generalize carefully and conduct experiments where they can. Let's look at two examples of generalizations in social science fields. First, consider Alfred T. Mahan's *The Influence of Sea Power upon History, 1660–1783*, a book written to demonstrate how sea power was the deciding factor in the wars between England, Holland, France, and Spain during the period, and, as Mahan intended, to cultivate a belief in the decisiveness of navies in future wars as well. How reliable was Mahan's idea? He did an admirable job of surveying all the conflicts between the four nations with which he dealt, omitting no embarrassing cases and attributing with some justice the dominance of England to her successful sea power. I say "attributing with some justice" to indicate that the procedure could not be definitive as with a tape measure; it was, at best, an evaluation of different conflicts the outcome of which can hardly be viewed as a consequence of one factor alone. Nor, if we accept the generalization as applying to the particular states upon which it was so largely based, can we apply it willy-nilly to other powers with different geographical characteristics, say Russia, or to different historical periods, say to our own age of air power and atomic capability. When the differences are acknowledged, as they must be, then clearly, Mahan's celebrated thesis about the decisiveness of sea power does not attain a reliability in any way matching the reliability possible when cases are clearcut and their measurement indisputable. In fact, supporting generalizations in history is so difficult that historians do not offer many of them, while historical analogy—also plagued with difficulty—sometimes is used as a basis for argument in the absence of satisfactory generalizations.[2]

We will conclude with a more hopeful note. Amid the array of situations discussed, can one find any unifying idea about what a "sufficient number" of cases may be? *The need is for enough cases to turn up any differences there are likely to be.* When one deals with a homogeneous group, the focus is upon care in correctly identifying the conditions and ensuring accurate measurement. The number of cases is secondary. When the group is heterogeneous, then numerous cases have to be examined in order to provide reliable support for a generalization. Moreover, generalizing will not be satisfactory when the total number of cases is small or when an insignificant number of counterinstances exists amid large numbers. One needs an enumeration to determine the opinion of a committee, and no size of sample will give reliable information about how many pearls exist in an oyster bed when the fact is that there is one pearl amid a thousand oysters.

Now we turn to the second requirement for reliable generalization: *The cases must be fairly representative of the generalization made.* Since the inductive leap involves moving from *some* cases to *all* cases, it is easy to see that there will be error in the conclusion if the cases used are not a group typical of the situation. Yet daily conversation often ignores this fact, offering selected examples as proof of some general condition. For instance, one person talks about the extent of

[2]Incidentally, Mahan's generalization holding sea power decisive in national conflicts was influential, for Kaiser William II was impressed, ordered the book kept upon every German ship, and lent his influence to increasing the German navy, a move arousing British hostility. With the 20–20 vision of hindsight one can now see that Germany's second-best navy remained bottled up in port throughout World War I (bearing Mahan out, in a way) while the German army fought a desperate land war lacking that extra bit of support that could have been available to it had not effort been deflected in building a navy.

inflation by citing as evidence a few of the greatest price rises he knows, while another contends that the situation isn't so bad and bases his counterargument upon a few items that have lagged behind the general trend. Granted that a fair selection of the cases may be hard to come by, at least one can be aware of such biased proofs. "You can prove anything by examples" protests justly against argument using selected instances to reach distorted conclusions. On the other hand, if a typical group can be identified successfully, then there will be great economy in giving reliable support to a generalization. In fact, if a completely representative group of cases is obtained, then the generalization will be true—though because of the passage from *some* to *all* we will never know it to be more than reliable. How does one obtain representative cases—that is, a sample forming a group typical of the whole situation?

We will begin with a trivial example to make the point. Suppose we have an urn containing 1,000 balls—200 red, 300 white, and 500 blue. The balls are all the same except for the color, and you do not know whether they have been mixed or not. Yes, you've guessed it, we want to get a sample that will be fairly representative of the group. The problem is so easy that you may be impatient with me. "Why, draw out 100 balls at random and that sample should be close enough," you say. "Oh, yes, you can get a random sample by stirring the balls thoroughly between draws or by reaching down and taking out balls from each strata in the urn in the same proportion that the number of balls in the different levels bears to the total number of balls." This artificial case samples well: 100 out of 1,000 is an adequate sample and the numbers of red, white, and blue balls is substantial enough in relation to the total number to reasonably assure inclusion in the sample of an approximately proper proportion of each color of ball. There is no one-in-a-thousand oyster problem here. The vital requirement for a fair sample is satisfied by any procedure that gives each case as much chance of being selected as every other case. Sampling is a large subject which we will not take up here. It may be interesting to note that mathematical procedures exist for determining the range of expectable error in a sample.

We have spent some time delving into the two requirements for reliable generalization: enough cases and typical cases. Before leaving the subject, I want to stress a rule which, though it is not properly analyzed as a separate requirement for sound generalization, is nevertheless a practical test. *No case may conflict with a generalization.* The widely used statement "The exception *proves* the rule" refers to this process when it is taken, as it should be, to mean "The exception *tests* the rule." After all, a proving ground is a testing ground. The citing of "The exception proves the rule" as if it were a sort of excuse for generalizations that break down errs seriously; it misses the function of quantifying, which is to keep generalization in line with the facts. Being alert for cases in conflict with a proposed generalization is an *intellectual habit* indispensable for deflating faulty generalizations. A critical mind matches what is asserted against what it knows. "If it's natural, it's good for you." What about poison mushrooms? "Arms assure peace." Think of a few wars you know about and decide if those involved were little armed. Looking for counterinstances screens out loose talk.

What about the conflicting case that is a freak—the white blackbird, or the reputedly vegetarian lion that was somebody's pet in Seattle a few years ago? Should generalizations recognize blackbirds as sometimes white and lions as occasionally vegetarians? Well, yes and no. There's a bit of ambiguity here. If one intends to assert that each individual blackbird in the world is black or that every last lion eats only meat, then the generalization has to be quantified to recognize the freakish situations. More likely a generalization such as "Blackbirds are black" means that *characteristically*, blackbirds are black, in which case the atypical white blackbird need not be recognized. Man is a biped even though everyone knows of individuals who have lost their legs or who have been born without legs through a genetic disaster.

Correct quantifying is necessary for reliable generalization because, otherwise, the statement made will be out of line with the cases that should support it. So this book has harped upon care in quantifying, praised it, and castigated careless quantifying as a badge of sloppy thinking. Well, what *is* a quantifier? Back on p. 75 we said, "These words *all, some, no* are called quantifiers because they indicate the quantity. . . ." Our statement served well for deduction as far as we followed the subject. And you may recall that deduction seemed to be fond of *some*, insisting that any quantifier that was not a commitment to *all* or *no* could be reduced to *some*. Generalization won't stand for this telescoping of quantifiers. Not in the least. *Some* won't even make a generalization at all! The reason is that one can apply *some* to any number from one instance up to and including all the instances there are. Suppose, for example, a teacher says, "Some of the class passed the test," and proceeds to hand out the papers. If only one student passed, the class probably would be angry but no one could say that the teacher had been guilty of falsehood. If every student passed, it is likely that the class would be annoyed at the teacher for being so needlessly inexact but, again, there would be no saying that the statement was false. This breadth of application bars *some* from being a sufficient commitment to make a generalization, for it does not refer even vaguely to a particular portion of all the cases. Nevertheless, *some* remains a useful quantifier for times when one does not want to make a commitment about the proportions involved. For instance, a doctor who has prescribed for a patient and is pleased with the recovery might say to a fellow practitioner, "Some patients respond well to that prescription" without wanting to generalize about the extent the treatment is successful. For a generalization to exist, there must be at least a vague commitment to quantity. Examples are "most," "less than a third," "on rare occasions" and so on.

We have seen that the reliability of generalizations varies enormously according to kind of material to which the generalization applies and the number and representative quality of the cases available. Where the support of a generalization is less than one would wish, then it is best advanced tentatively.

SUMMARY

An enumeration is based upon an investigation of all the cases there are. An enumeration is a report, not a generalization.

A generalization involves taking the "inductive leap"—that is, on the basis of examining *some cases only* a conclusion is formed which covers *all* the cases there are.

Each case that falls under a generalization is an instance of the truth of the generalization. A generalization quantified by "all" or "no" can have no exceptions and is falsified by a single counterinstance; where a generalization is quantified by "90%," "most," etc., then counterinstances are in conformity with the generalization up to the point where they show some different quantifier to be appropriate. Searching for a conflicting case is an intellectual habit for puncturing faulty generalizations.

Generalization and other forms of induction do not claim to be valid; their aim is to achieve a reasonable degree of reliability. No generalization is certainly true, although as a practical matter some generalizations are so well supported as to be beyond actual doubt.

The requirements for a reliable generalization are:

1. A sufficient number of cases
2. Cases that are fairly representative

Though no set number or formula can settle the problem of "enough" cases, the need is for a sufficient number of cases to turn up—in their proper proportion—all the characteristics covered by the generalization.

Though the practical task of obtaining "representative" cases calls for both ingenuity and understanding of the particular subject matter involved, the goal is to devise a method whereby each case has as much chance of being selected as every other case.

The concept of the "uniformity of nature" is universally used as a sort of master generalization serving as the major premise for a large part of all reasoning. The idea is simply that natural laws operate uniformly and without exceptions.

Generalizations concerning natural phenomena—the fields of physics and chemistry are outstanding examples—do not need the support of large numbers of cases since they are supported by the uniformity of nature. Generalizations about matters reflecting the choice of man require support by many cases, since they do not follow the uniformity of nature, at least in any discernible way.

A close similarity between the cases used to support a generalization is crucial. Here again, natural sciences have the advantage of virtually identical and measurable cases while social sciences often struggle with situations where the cases are not numerous, or where they are not virtually identical or accurately measurable.

A group is *homogeneous* when the cases are identical with respect to the quality being examined. If a group were known to be perfectly homogeneous, then one could base a reliable generalization upon a single case. Sour milk is an example. Even when a group is homogeneous, an examination of several cases may be needed to reduce the effect of errors in observation and measurement.

A group is *heterogeneous* when the cases exhibit differences with respect to the quality being examined. In general, the more heterogeneous the group, the larger the number of cases needed to assure representation of all types within the situation.

An *empirical generalization* is founded upon observed cases without an understanding of why the phenomenon occurs. It is the result of experience alone. Such a generalization, if well supported, may be so strong that there is no actual doubt about it being correct.

An *explained generalization* is found true in experience and also can be explained in terms of other areas of knowledge. Explained generalizations are most satisfactory, since they are doubly secured by experience and by consistency with other knowledge.

When a generalization is not supported to a degree that makes it reliable, then it should be kept tentative.

EXERCISES FOR CHAPTER 13
pages 201–211

I. Answer **T** for "true" or **F** for "false":

_____ 1. No generalization has exceptions.

_____ 2. It is logically possible for water to run uphill.

_____ 3. A well-supported generalization is reliable.

_____ 4. It is always possible to get an adequate sample.

_____ 5. The inductive leap involves going from "some" to "all."

_____ 6. Starting with "Some A is B," the immediate inference "All A is B" is doubtful.

_____ 7. Induction is doubtful and therefore one never can trust conclusions resting upon induction.

_____ 8. When a generalization is being made about a homogeneous group, it is necessary to seek a large number of cases.

_____ 9. By and large, it is safer to generalize about narrow classes than about wide ones.

_____ 10. Generalizations about matters subject to human choice are not as reliable as those about situations not subject to human will.

_____ 11. Atypical cases can be ignored in some generalizations.

_____ 12. Ignoring any case that is not an atypical case would violate the requirement that a generalization may have no exceptions.

_____ 13. "The exception proves the rule" shows that generalizations do in fact have exceptions.

_____ 14. Homogeneous groups are the most easy to generalize about accurately.

_____ 15. An "empirical generalization" never is as satisfactory as an "explained generalization" concerning the same problem would be.

_____ 16. An "empirical generalization" cannot be highly reliable.

_____ 17. An "empirical generalization" means a generalization without very much evidence to support it.

_____ 18. An enumeration is not a generalization since there is no "inductive leap."

_____ 19. Any procedure that gives assurance of an equal chance to every instance of every type to be selected is a satisfactory sampling procedure for constructing a generalization.

_____ 20. A statement using "some" as a quantifier cannot be a generalization.

_____ 21. An assertion that something is true of 80% of the cases is an assertion about all cases there are.

_____ 22. Searching for conflicting cases is always hard to do.

_____ 23. If the uniformity of nature is true, then no miracle is true.

_____ 24. The uniformity of nature cannot be proven true.

_____ 25. The factor of human will is the chief obstacle to reliable generalization in the social sciences. (This was not discussed in the text. Give it a try.)

II.   Each of the following statements gives some evidence for a generalization. In the blanks provided, rate each generalization advanced according to the following scale:

   1. Extremely reliable (error highly unlikely)
   2. Well supported (convincing for ordinary purposes)
   3. Not reliable (not convincing enough to be accepted)

Be prepared to justify whatever ratings you give.

_____ 1. The type of service one can expect doctors to give under socialized medicine is shown by the English physician who boasted of examining eighty patients in three hours. Yes, this was after England adopted a socialized medicine plan.

_____ 2. A mixture of equal parts of sulphur and saltpeter will explode if placed upon a cement floor and struck with a hammer. I know this, because I tried it once.

_____ 3. I didn't realize what the most popular soft drinks in this locality were until my son began collecting bottletops in the park last Sunday. He got a good supply from the refreshment stand, and he arranged them in rows on the rug when we got home. The rows turned out this way:

Fizzo	58
Pinkpop	40
Steinola	16
Miscellaneous	5 or fewer for each

Fizzo and Pinkpop lead in this area.

4. We made a poll on the main street in town on the question of a 5% tax raise to improve the school system. The replies of the first hundred people we asked are pretty conclusive: yes—56, no—14, don't know—30. It is obvious that a good majority of citizens are willing to pay for better schools.

5. Now that over a generation has passed since the last grizzly bear was shot in California, it seems safe to assume that the grizzly is extinct in that state.

6. I have been riding up and down in that elevator every day for the past ten years. Now they come around to inspect it. Hasn't it proved safe already?

7. As a Congressman, I feel obliged to vote according to the clear will of my constituency. My mail in the past weeks has proved to me that my duty is to vote against the budget proposed by the Administration in its present form. My constituents are 2–1 against the foreign aid sections.

8. While shopping on the Via Veneto in Rome I never encountered a clerk who did not speak very good English. It is not necessary to speak Italian to shop in Italy.

9. Ever since 1881 the Grange has kept records of hail damage suffered by its members in this area. The losses have averaged about 2%. So I consider this a fair statement of the danger of hail loss for corn in this area.

10. We sent out a questionnaire to 1,000 of the residents of this town with the single question: "Do you favor permitting more saloons in Bloomingdale?" We used every sixth name on the voting lists, which have 6,042 names. The 329 replies that came back to us in the postage-paid envelopes we supplied indicated that only 41% of the voters want more saloons, 4% marked "don't know," and a clear majority of 55% opposed saloons. So if there were an election now, saloons would be voted out of town. This is just one project of our "Better Bloomingdale Committee."

III.   Try puncturing each of the following assertions by citing some conflicting instance that you happen to know.

1. This world is arranged for the benefit of man.

2. Nobody can be forced to believe or not to believe something, so repression
   of an idea is futile.

3. An industrial state can't prosper without high tariffs.

4. The best movies are love stories.

5. All men are created equal. (Consider ambiguity. Better yet, what, in good
   sense, must this mean?)

6. Without intellectual freedom there can be no scientific progress.

7. It doesn't matter what a person's religion is as long as he has a religion.

8. The reason that there are wars is that it is human nature to like to fight.

chapter 14

Causal Relationship

Human beings do not control nature; they conform to it. People have learned in many fields how to arrange causes so that the effects they desire will take place. Sometimes we succeed in dealing with problems empirically without understanding the cause; for example, many practical remedies were evolved before medical science attained any real understanding of the causes for disease. Consider the appalling errors that flourished also. No need to belabor the point that identifying the cause gives a much better chance to solve a problem.

The cause of a particular event is the total of all the factors that made it happen, or, as John Stuart Mill pointed out, a cause may be traced back as a sort of "infinite regress" of events leading up to it. Obviously, this view of a limitless interconnection of causal factors has to be brought under control if we are to get on with the solution of practical problems. The notion is useful as a reminder that the mention of one or a few factors on which we ordinarily focus in a discussion of cause is in fact but part of the whole causal situation.

Sometimes the causal problem is to find out what made a particular event happen. Why did the American effort in Vietnam fail? At other times cause is studied to establish a general understanding of the conditions for some type of event. What causes a sonic boom? When interest is in unraveling the factors underlying a particular event, one is concerned with Mill's "infinite regress" and will have to cut off consideration when the contributing causal factors become too insignificant or remote to be dealt with profitably. The understanding of a causal situation removed from any particular event in time is a different problem. This brings us to the notions of *sufficient* and *necessary* conditions.

The *sufficient* conditions for a certain effect is *one way* which will produce the effect. Thus, Mrs. O'Leary's cow kicking over a lantern was a sufficient condition for the great Chicago fire. The *necessary* conditions for bringing about a certain effect is a statement of the causal factors in general terms. Fuel, kindling temperature, and oxygen are the necessary conditions for fire. The goal of science is, as far as possible, to describe in general terms those conditions which are necessary to the existence of a phenomenon.

This chapter describes the procedure to confirm whether or not there is a causal relationship for any problem in which the causal factors can be isolated and measured. The rules for establishing causes are known as Mill's Canons or Mill's Methods after John Stuart Mill, who gave them a classic formulation. Unfortunately, Mill claimed more for the Methods than they can deliver, and this sparked vehement criticism which, it seems to me, sometimes has obscured the value which they have. Though we will have to confess their limitations as we go along, the Methods are indispensable tools for checking whether a supposed causal circumstance actually is the cause. What the Methods will not do is to provide the flash of insight as to what the cause may be. For instance, once one suspects the mosquito may be associated with the cause of yellow fever, the Methods will quickly confirm the connection. If the hunch were wrong, the Methods would determine this, too. But the Methods will not point out the causal factor in the first place.

THE METHOD OF AGREEMENT

By definition, when the cause is present the effect must take place, so if only one circumstance is always present when the effect occurs, then that circumstance must be the cause or at least one factor of the cause. To look at the matter from another direction, a circumstance not present on every occasion when the effect occurs cannot be the cause since the effect may occur without it. The pattern of the **Method of Agreement** can best be seen abstractly:

Supposed relevant causal circumstances					*Effect*
A	B	C	D		E occurs
A	B	F	G	H	E occurs
A	C	I	J		E occurs
A	C	I	J	K	E occurs
A	B	F	G	H	E occurs
A	B	C	D	F	E occurs

Here A is the only common circumstance present whenever the effect occurs; hence, A is either the whole cause or at least a factor in the cause. So, to employ the Method of Agreement one looks among the relevant circumstances preceding the event to see if there is one and only one that always appears. The Method deserves an italicized statement:

Method of Agreement   *If one and only one relevant circumstance is common to all cases in which the effect occurs, then this circumstance is the cause or is associated with the cause.*

The term "Method of Agreement" indicates that the cases *agree* in having a common factor. It will pay to note the agreement of Circumstance A in the abstract model above as well as to get the definition for the method in mind. Although the five Methods to be discussed are not difficult, the patterns of the abstract models will prevent confusing one Method with another.

Now let's look at a concrete example. Suppose Mrs. Smith is troubled with an annoying stomachache every morning after breakfast. She decides to see if the Method of Agreement will help locate the cause of her difficulty, and she recalls that she must find one and only one relevant circumstance common to all cases in which the effect occurs. But what circumstances are the "relevant" ones? There are innumerable common circumstances such as the sun rising each morning before the stomachache. Being a sensible person, she dismisses this thought as ridiculous since it is not the kind of thing that she considers could be a cause of her problem. All the same, deciding what sorts of things may be relevant is a crucial decision and not a self-evident one. As Cohen and Nagel suggest, circumstances are not a neat group of factors, each distinct from everything else and each labeled with a tag saying, "I am a circumstance."[1] It takes knowledge outside the Methods to identify the circumstances. Hence Mills' Methods are not self-starting: they do not tell what is relevant and what is not, and the flash of insight into what may be a cause usually is the most difficult step in solving a causal problem.

Since Mrs. Smith views food as a likely sort of cause for a stomachache, she decides to see if the cause can be found among any of the foods she eats for breakfast. This decision is a working hypothesis declaring foods at breakfast to be the relevant circumstances. So she makes a list:

Monday	A banana, coffee, sugar, scrambled eggs, toast, butter
Tuesday	A banana, milk, French toast, maple syrup
Wednesday	A banana, coffee, sugar, kippered herring, toast
Thursday	A banana, oatmeal, sugar, milk, poached egg
Friday	A banana, milk, pancakes, maple syrup

The stomachache makes life miserable after each of these breakfasts, so we look over the list and at once pick out banana as the one food in which all the

---

[1]Morris R. Cohen and Ernest Nagel, *An Introduction to Logic and The Scientific Method* (New York: Harcourt Brace Jovanovich, 1934).

breakfasts agree. So banana appears to be the culprit. We have used the Method of Agreement with apparent success, but do things really work out as easily as this? No—unfortunately, there are three ways in which Mrs. Smith's investigation may be derailed even though the Method of Agreement seems to apply. First, her hypothesis that her stomachache is caused by some type of food may be wrong; her trouble could be caused by an ulcer, or some other condition unrelated to food. Nothing in the Method of Agreement has screened out these other possibilities. Second, if the cause is a food it could be that the trouble lies in a food that Mrs. Smith ate a day or two before she began her investigation and that she was wrong in assuming that the cause could not be so far removed in time from its effect. Third, the list of foods may not have been properly analyzed. For instance, maple syrup is equivalent to sugar, making sugar as well as banana a circumstance common to all the meals. Maybe sugar is the cause and she failed to notice it as a common factor. A joke takes its point from the feebleness of the Method of Agreement when the circumstances are wrongly analyzed:

Monday	Scotch & soda	Drunk
Tuesday	Irish whiskey & soda	Drunk
Wednesday	Bourbon & soda	Drunk

The soda does it!

The joke stirs a guffaw from the absurdity of overlooking the relevant component here. But in real situations where neither the ingredients of the materials nor the relevance of those ingredients are known, then it is quite possible to be misled by the Method of Agreement to identify the wrong circumstances as cause while some common element goes unobserved because it is removed in time or is hidden among other components. So we see, merely taking a look at the crude food units suggested by language may not be enough to locate what it is that disagrees with Mrs. Smith. If so, a lot of painstaking work will be needed to analyze the foods into their component parts. It will take a chemist to analyze all the ingredients. Though all this is discouraging, there is no way to make the determination of cause simple where it happens to be subtle and difficult. When a case yields to rough classifications, one is in luck. Where it does not, the problem will require one able and willing to do thorough research.

The example covered only five breakfasts and this number, like hasty generalization, leaves room for coincidence to account for the result. If bananas were eaten every day for a month along with a wide variation of the other foods, the reliability of the conclusion identifying bananas as the only common factor would increase. If enough cases are examined, then, whatever else, coincidence will become an unlikely explanation for the persistent presence of the common circumstance.

What if more than one factor is common to all the cases? Say, for instance, that both banana and sugar were present in all the breakfasts? Then Mrs. Smith should have another breakfast omitting one of the two and see how she feels. Where it is possible to vary the circumstances, this procedure usually will be effective in eliminating one factor as irrelevant. Yet occasionally, matters do not work out here, for it is possible that eliminating either the banana or the sugar will be followed by a nonoccurrence of the stomachache effect. If so, then the cause may lie in an interaction of the two rather than in either one alone. Again, suppose Mrs. Smith discovers to her dismay that she suffers a stomachache if she eats either banana or sugar. This third possibility is one in which the Method of Agreement seems to confirm two sufficient causes for Mrs. Smith's discomfort, and in this eventuality we are stuck, temporarily at least. The explanation could be that banana and sugar have a component in common which would make the Method of Agreement apply after all, or it could be that each of these different foods disagrees with Mrs. Smith. Though the point may seem technical, if two different foods each are capable of producing a stomachache, then the stomachache response is not identical. Small comfort to Mrs. Smith, and the difference may be slight and hard to trace.

Sometimes when one sets out to apply the Method of Agreement, no circumstance is found common to all the cases. When this happens either the circumstances are not being properly analyzed so that what they have in common goes unnoticed, or a wrong assumption has been made about what kind of circumstances are relevant. Should Mrs. Smith's problem not be related to the foods she eats, then a working hypothesis seeking to locate the cause among foods will fail.

We have seen that the Method of Agreement requires a working hypothesis directing attention to those circumstances that include the cause, and that applying the Method may involve considerable difficulty in analyzing crudely expressed circumstances into component parts which will reveal any significant points of agreement. It is time to acknowledge the virtues of the Method. First, the Method of Agreement will quickly show that many circumstances are *not* the cause, for wherever the effect occurs without the presence of a particular circumstance then that circumstance cannot be the cause. Again, over the long run the Method tends to correct its own errors, since the surveying of a large number of instances with varied circumstances both renders the chance for coincidence minimal and provides much evidence to review in search of the common factor. Most of all, the Method of Agreement does not stand by itself; it is a tool reinforced by the other Methods.

THE METHOD OF DIFFERENCE

By definition, where the effect does not take place, then the cause must be absent. Hence, if it is possible to obtain two cases that are alike in all relevant circumstances with one exception, and if the effect follows when this one circumstance is present and does not follow when the circumstance is absent, then this circumstance will be either the cause or associated with the cause. This procedure is called the **Method of Difference.** Its pattern can be shown abstractly:

Supposed relevant causal circumstances	*Effect*
A B C D F	E occurs
B C D F	E does not occur

As you can see, all the relevant circumstances are constant except A, and where A is present the effect occurs while it does not occur when A is absent. Hence, A is the cause or, at least, contains the cause. Here is the Method, briefly stated:

Method of Difference   *If two situations are alike in all relevant respects but one, and if the effect occurs in one instance but not in the other, then the one difference is the cause or is associated with the cause.*

Note exactly how "Method of Difference" refers to a single crucial *difference* which is taken to be the cause. Let us apply the Method to Mrs. Smith's case. Her Friday breakfast consisted of a banana, milk, pancakes, and maple syrup and was followed by the stomachache. So she decides to eat the same meal on Saturday, taking care that the foods and quantities eaten will be exactly the same, except on Saturday she omits banana. Happily, Saturday morning passes without the stomachache, so banana was the cause, or at least, so the Method of Difference tells us. Can we be sure? Though banana may indeed be the cause, we need to recognize how easy it is for the Method of Difference to be wrong and deceptively convincing at the same time.

   The Method says to take "two situations alike in all relevant respects but one," and this prescription is practically impossible to follow. We say that Mrs. Smith ate the "same" breakfast on Saturday that she had had on Friday. Disregarding minute variations in measurement and composition of the ingredients, what about Mrs. Smith? She is part of the situation. Is she the same? Not only is she one day older, but more importantly her body chemistry and mental outlook vary from day to day. To apply the Method of Difference to two situations which are *not* alike in all relevant respects but one may misidentify the cause. And where the two situations seem to be the same, it will be a most convincing error. Think of all the testimonials given in good faith to support useless patent medicines by people who have experienced a headache or whatever, taken the medicine, and gotten better. The body is assumed to have remained in the same state except for the medicine when, in fact, the body is not the same from day to day; it constantly generates its own defenses, usually curing itself with time. The assumption of similarity underlying the Method of Difference is crucial; an error at this point can be just as destructive as a wrong assumption about what sorts of circumstances are relevant is destructive to the Method of Agreement.

When one cannot obtain exact similarity "in all relevant respects save one" which the Method of Difference requires, still the possibility of some difference other than the one observed being the causal factor can be reduced by using a large number of closely similar pairs. This may be hard to do. So one has to acknowledge that the Method of Difference cannot be applied satisfactorily whenever the requirement of exact similarity cannot be met. On the other hand, the Method does lend itself to laboratory conditions which allow closely identical situations to be constructed by careful control of the materials, heat, noise, psychological expectations, or whatever else may be involved. Testing a light bulb is a simple application of the Method of Difference in daily living. One unscrews a lighted bulb to be sure the socket is functioning, and screws in the bulb to be tested. Current, switch, and contact with the socket are assumed the same, so if the bulb being tested fails to light the trouble must be in the bulb and it is thrown away.

The definitions for the Methods speak of locating the cause or something "associated with the cause." This phrase recognizes that the presence of any factor which is sufficient to produce the effect in connection with other circumstances will be identified as causal by the Methods. Take, for example, the statement "Everything was all right until John was unable to get into journalism school, and this brought about his nervous breakdown." Obviously, a lot of things besides the disappointment over studying journalism may have contributed to the breakdown; the journalism school incident may have operated as a last straw in connection with other frustrations. Perhaps no one will miss this possibility here; it is well to be on the watch for other factors operating together with whatever circumstance the Method of Difference may single out as causally connected.

Where the Method of Difference is limited, as it is in the case of John's nervous breakdown, to a single occurrence of the effect following the introduction of the supposed cause, there is a high risk of unobserved circumstances accounting for the effect, while coincidence may account for the effect taking place at an appropriate time after the supposed cause. The nervous breakdown situation could not be repeated; a situation like Mrs. Smith's breakfasts could be repeated under conditions exact enough to give a good chance for extraneous influences to show their irrelevance by varying over the long run. Hence, the probability that the Method of Difference has correctly identified the cause will increase when it is applied several times before concluding that the causal connection has been located.

JOINT METHOD OF AGREEMENT AND DIFFERENCE

Perhaps you have been impressed with the amount of space devoted to weaknesses and difficulties in the use of Mill's Methods. The warnings are necessary; unluckily there is no easy way to establish causation reliably. Combining the Method of Agreement and the Method of Difference, however, offers a way to reduce the chance of error in either Method alone. Here is the pattern for the **Joint Method:**

	Supposed relevant causal circumstances	*Effect*
Agreement	A B C D	E occurs
	A B F G H	E occurs
	A C I J	E occurs
	A C I J K	E occurs
	A B F G H	E occurs
Difference	A B C D F	E occurs
	B C D F	E does not occur

The scheme provides a double check by using the Method of Agreement to identify A as the cause since it is the only common circumstance, and using the Method of Difference to show that other circumstances without A do not produce the effect. A full statement of the Joint Method makes difficult reading, but it isn't so hard to follow the abstract scheme given above and to remember this shortened rule:

Joint Method   *A relevant circumstance that is present in all instances in which the effect occurs and absent whenever the effect does not occur is the cause or is associated with the cause.*

The Joint Method offers a considerable chance for correcting any mistake about the cause which the Method of Agreement or the Method of Difference might ratify when used alone. Consider the joke based upon the Method of Agreement:

Monday	Scotch & soda	Drunk
Tuesday	Irish whiskey & soda	Drunk
Wednesday	Bourbon & soda	Drunk

The soda does it!

But

Thursday	Scotch & soda	Drunk
Friday	Soda	Sober

No, it isn't the soda.

What does this outcome tell us besides that the trouble is not the soda? Obtusely assuming that our inebriate doesn't know, he can try some Scotch without soda; the expected result will show him that the cause is not a combination of Scotch and soda. In a fairyland ending, he may now avoid the crude circumstances of Scotch, Irish whiskey, and bourbon; should he seek a better understanding of the causal situation, the occurring of the effect following each liquor suggests a search for some component common to all.

We can be brief in illustrating how Mrs. Smith could apply the joint method to her irksome stomachache. First, she eats a number of meals, having only the supposed cause, banana, common to all of them. Persistence of the stomachache throughout this series points to banana as the "cause or associated with the cause" according to the Method of Agreement. Now Mrs. Smith eats a meal identical with one of the meals that she consumed in the series used for the Method of Agreement, only this time she does not eat any banana. This action provides the conditions for the Method of Difference. Now if Mrs. Smith experiences no stomachache following the meal without banana, she has again secured an indication that banana is the "cause or associated with the cause." Notice that the Joint Method is simply an application of the Method of Agreement followed by an application of the Method of Difference. If, however, Mrs. Smith is wrong in believing that food is the cause of her problem, then the Joint Method will confirm the lack of an unvarying association between any particular food and her discomfort. This result will tell her to think again about what kinds of things might be relevant to her condition. It will still be possible for the Joint Method not to work even though food is the cause of the stomachaches if the various foods are treated as units while significant ingredients common to different foods are overlooked. Also, in causal investigations one has to consider any assumptions being made about time. In the soda example above, we indicated that the inebriate was sober on Friday. But what if he were still drunk from his binge on Thursday?

THE METHOD OF COVARIATION

We have been considering causal problems as if causal circumstances were present or absent, and effects simply occurred or did not occur. Now it is time to consider differences in degree. One drink of Scotch, thank heaven, does not make a person "drunk"; raising prices penny by penny will, generally, reduce demand; the deeper the diver goes, the greater the pressure becomes. Differences in degree are all about us.

Where two or more things vary together persistently and beyond the limits of anything accountable by coincidence, then there must be some sort of causal connection between them. Mill called this approach to causation the "Method of Concomitant Variation," a term for which the word "covariation" is often substituted.

Method of Covariation   *When one circumstance varies in a regular manner whenever some other circumstance varies, then there must be some sort of causal connection between the two.*

It does not matter which way the variation runs—that is, an increase in the first circumstance may lead to an increase or to a decrease in the second. Another telltale sign of covariation is that when one circumstance is kept the same, then the second circumstance will not continue to vary—a result required by the causal axiom holding that the same causal circumstances always produce identical effects.

An example of the Covariation Method is more helpful than an abstract scheme. Suppose I want to find out how a certain fertilizer affects the growth of azalea plants, so I plant several rows, giving Row 1 no fertilizer. Row 2 receives unit A of the fertilizer, Row 3 receives 2A, Row 4 receives 3A, and so on. If I am a fanatic, I can go on to the extent of planting a row in pure fertilizer. All other relevant circumstances such as type of soil, amount of sunlight, water, cultivation, etc., are kept the same for all rows. Now several things are quite obvious. Assuming that fertilizer has a beneficial effect, adding fertilizer would add to plant growth up to a point. The variation would be a curve rather than a straight line, for adding fertilizer wouldn't be beneficial indefinitely. Evidently covariation holds only within limits.

Another wrinkle needs mention. A certain amount of poison—say, rattlesnake venom—will make a person sick *up to the point* when the dose becomes lethal. At that point the difference in degree changes to a difference in kind. More poison will not make the person any more dead though, it may be worth noticing, the deaths will not be the same. So, there may be a point along the path of covariation where a difference in degree turns into a difference in kind or, as the adage reminds us, there is the straw-that-breaks-the-camel's-back phenomenon.

Our definition of covariation speaks of the variation taking place "in a regular manner." Must it be completely regular? Ideally, yes. Supposing all other factors remain constant, the causal factor underlying a covariation would be entirely regular. For example, Boyle's law applied within a certain range of pressure to a gas kept at a constant temperature will show an exact variation of volume in relation to pressure. Many important applications of the Method of Covariation, however, show less than complete regularity because the causal situation contains a multitude of circumstances which vary in degree from case to case. One thinks immediately of the response to medical treatment. No two human beings are alike, and their response to drugs or foods or any sort of medical treatment is not uniform; the best medical science may be able to do is to note a rate of success for one treatment that exceeds the rate for no treatment or for some alternative treatment. If the groups compared are large enough to average out the effect of individual differences, then the pattern of covariation will be regular enough to indicate causal connection.

The Method of Covariation is most useful when it is impossible to remove a circumstance entirely or when the effect is always present in some degree. If a person has hay fever persistently through the summer, the Method of Agreement won't work because there is one long case and not several occurrences neatly in step with each introduction of the common circumstance; nor will the Method of Difference work, since there is no period free from hay fever to match the removal of the causal circumstance. The Method of Covariation will work in this situation if some circumstance that varies along with the effect can be found as, for instance, if increasing the amount of pollen in the air increases the severity of the hay fever while diminishing the pollen diminishes the symptoms. The allergist will have to break "pollen" into its numerous components and will try to refine the circumstances to identify the disturbing varieties. Hence, covariation is useful whenever an effect is a matter of degree or when causal circumstances cannot be isolated one from another. Sometimes we only partially understand the cause and yet the method may afford statistical correlations indicating an area where the cause is located. Such is the situation today concerning the health hazards associated with smoking.

Smoking is not the whole causal explanation for lung cancer, coronary heart disease, or any other health condition it may influence. If it were the whole cause for lung cancer, for example, then every incident of smoking some particular amount would be followed in a certain time by lung cancer, while nonsmokers would not contract the disease. Smoking, then, is at most associated with the cause of lung cancer and certain other health hazards. All the same, if the Method of Covariation shows a persistent and regular variation too extensive to be attributed to coincidence, then there is evidence of a causal connection. We will review the evidence, or, I should say, a tiny part of the evidence since many studies have been made.

If smoking has a positive association with lung cancer, then the greater the number of cigarettes smoked per day, the greater the incidence of lung cancer; the greater the number of years smoked, the more lung cancer; ceasing to smoke should bring a decline in lung cancer. Here are the figures for 440,000 male and 560,000 female subjects in twenty-five states followed for a four-year period:

Mortality from Lung Cancer

Males		Females	
No. of Cigarettes Smoked per Day	Mortality Ratio	No. of Cigarettes Smoked per Day	Mortality Ratio
None	1.0	None	1.0
1–9	4.8		
10–19	6.4	1–19	2.1
20–39	11.6		
Over 40	12.6	Over 20	4.4

Source: Harold J. Diehl, *Tobacco and Your Health: The Smoking Controversy* New York: McGraw-Hill, 1969, p. 63.

One needs to examine the term "mortality ratio" in order to interpret the covariation exhibited here. A mortality ratio is obtained by first analyzing the age distribution of the members of the group so that actuarial experience can be weighted appropriately. Then the number of expected deaths for nonsmokers is computed, and this number is divided into whatever number of deaths occur among smokers. Thus, a mortality ratio of 1 for smokers signifies a death rate for smokers equal to nonsmokers, a mortality ratio of 2 signifies a rate of death for smokers twice that for nonsmokers, and so on.[2]

Though the columns for both males and females exhibit a clear covariation between the amount of cigarettes smoked and the incidence of lung cancer, this survey shows a remarkable difference in degree between the results for males and females. Why? Though the different classes used in tabulating the material relating to females is regrettable, this does not explain the apparent lesser vulnerability of females than males. Possibly there is a sex difference in response. On the other hand, this cannot be assumed without considering the extent to which differences in smoking habits between males and females may exist: Do female smokers inhale to the same degree as males? Do they start as young? Is the average number of years smoked for the female group the same as for the male group?

We will continue the problem by examining another possible covariation. If smoking is causally related to lung cancer, then the greater the number of years smoked, the greater the incidence of lung cancer. Constructing groups according to the age of commencing smoking produced the following results for males:

Mortality from Lung Cancer

Age when Smoking was Commenced	Mortality Ratios		
	Age 35–54	Age 55–69	Age 70–84
Under 15	12.80	15.81	16.76
15–19	8.71	13.06	19.37
20–24	5.83	11.11	12.11
25 and over	2.77	3.39	3.38
Nonsmokers	1.00	1.00	1.00

Source: E. Cuyler Hammond, "Smoking in Relation to Mortality and Morbidity," Journal of the National Cancer Institute, 32, no. 5 (May, 1964), 1161–68.

These results need to be surveyed both vertically and horizontally. The covariations show that the earlier smoking is started and the longer it is continued, the greater the incidence of lung cancer compared to the experience of nonsmokers of corresponding age groups. But there are two discrepancies: reading horizontally, in the column for ages 70–84, the 3.38 figure is less than the 3.39 figure for the 55–69 group; reading vertically, again in the column for ages 70–84, the 19.37 figure exceeds the 16.76 figure above it. What are we to do about these discrepancies? The wording of Mill's Methods tells us that covariation applies

[2]For a detailed explanation of "mortality ratio," see U.S. Department of Health, Education & Welfare, Smoking and Health, Public Health Service Publication No. 1103 (Washington D.C.: U.S. Government Printing Office, 1964), pp. 82–84. Further references to this source will be by its popular name, "The Surgeon General's Report."

where "one circumstance varies in a regular manner" and here, undeniably, there is some irregularity. Have we come to a dead end? Hardly. As mentioned before, a covariation reflecting the variation of a single causative agent with all other causative factors held constant is an ideal situation. The response of a scale to additional weights would be an instance of this sort. No investigation involving human beings can attain comparable regularity, since there are variations within any group of human subjects. Considering the unavoidable variations within human groups, one will have to be content with covariations that are marked enough to be significant and not explainable by chance. No sensible person would claim that the covariation between cigarette smoking and lung cancer is meaningless, nor that complete accuracy was possible in measuring the degree of variation. One has to look at statistical tabulations without demanding more precision than the nature of the materials permits.

There are other covariations to look for. If cigarette smoking is associated with the cause of lung cancer, then abandoning smoking should be coupled with a decline in lung cancer as the period without smoking increases. A study of 20,000 British physicians[3] confirmed this covariation when the incidence of lung cancer among those who stopped smoking was compared with the incidence among those who continued to smoke:

Length of Time Smoking Discontinued	Percentage of Lung Cancer Compared to Those Continuing to Smoke
Less than 5 years	52%
5 to 10 years	38%
Over 10 years	14%

THE METHOD OF RESIDUES

Sometimes the causal circumstances for a part of the effect is known while the remainder of the effect must be attributed to other circumstances. Determining the weight of a load of sand illustrates this situation most simply. First, the truck is weighed empty, then filled and weighed again. By deducting the weight accounted for by the truck, one obtains the amount for the other "circumstance" depressing the scales—namely, the sand. Another favorite example of application of this Method is the discovery of the planet Neptune. When the motions of Uranus were found not to correspond to the then known gravitational forces, a planet that would exert an additional gravitational force to make up the discre-

[3]U.S. Department of Health, Education, & Welfare, *The Health Consequences of Smoking*, Public Health Service Publication No. 1696 (Washington, D.C.: U.S. Government Printing Office, 1967), p. 139.

pancy was assumed to exist. Observation soon discovered the planet Neptune close to the point its presence had been calculated to be. Though it was nice to pull this rabbit out of the hat so handily, the matter might not have been so simple. Had two additional planets rather than one been the source of the discrepancy, the search would have been harder. Unlike the load of sand, it may take an assumption and real work to determine the residual part of the cause. Yet the method is not as full of pitfalls as the others and its definition is easy:

Method of Residues   *Where part of an effect remains unexplained by known causal circumstances, then an additional circumstance or circumstances must be sought to account for the unexplained portion of the effect.*

The Method of Residues was applied substantially in the Surgeon General's Report in assessing the effects of smoking. As we have already noted, smoking is not a necessary causative factor for cancer since nonsmokers also are subject to the disease. However, because significantly higher rates of several types of cancer occur among smokers than nonsmokers, the question arises as to how much, if any, of this residue is attributable to smoking. By making the assumption—an assumption we'll examine in a moment—that the mortality rate for any particular disease experienced by nonsmokers is the product of all causal factors other than smoking, then whatever significant difference exists in the mortality rate that smokers experience from that disease is the residue accounted for by smoking.

From the Surgeon General's Report we have selected comparative mortality rates in five areas to illustrate a few problems in interpreting causal influence by the Method of Residues. Item 6, "Deaths from all causes," is a total including Items 1–5 as well as other sources of excess deaths of smokers as compared to nonsmokers.

Underlying Cause of Death	Expected Deaths	Smoker Deaths	Mortality Ratio	Nonsmoker Deaths
1. Cancer of the lung	170	1,833	10.8	123
2. Bronchitis & emphysema	89	546	6.1	59
3. Cancer of larynx	14	75	5.4	8
4. Coronary artery disease	6,430	11,177	1.7	4,731
5. Cancer of the intestines	422	395	.9	307
6. Deaths from all causes	15,653	26,223	1.68	11,168

Source: The Surgeon General's Report, Table 26, pp. 109–10. Table 26 combines the results from seven studies totaling 1,123,000 males who provided usable histories of their smoking habits.

The first three items on the list show a mortality ratio for the smokers running five to ten times the rate for nonsmokers. Item 3, however, is a rare condition, so that the small number of cases reported does not make an adequate base for a reliable mortality ratio. The fourth item, coronary artery disease, shows the smokers' mortality ratio to be 1.7 times that of nonsmokers, a ratio considerably less than for the first three diseases of this summary. The number of cases, however, is by far the largest, so this particular mortality ratio probably is the most accurate in the group. In fact, all studies show a residue of excess deaths from coronary artery disease exceeding by about two to one the volume of excess deaths from the more publicized lung cancer. Item 5 shows a mortality ratio of .9, thus indicating smoker deaths slightly below the level expected for nonsmokers. The variation is not statistically significant in the sense of establishing smoking to inhibit the occurrence of this disease, but the result does provide fairly strong evidence that smoking is not a causal factor here. Finally, Item 6 shows an interesting residue of excess deaths among smokers from "all causes" in comparison to the nonsmoker group. Although this is the most significant figure from the point of view of assessing risks, it is not helpful in determining *how* smoking affects health. It takes linking the excess deaths to specific diseases to spur investigation into how the causal factor operates.

The causal effects of smoking have been the subject of much probing, both honest and dishonest. Since causal generalization is an inductive procedure and induction does not claim certainty for its proofs, it always will be possible to contend that the results are not established. On the other hand, the possibility that other than smoking factors underlie at least some part of the residues of excess deaths is real. What can we say about this possibility? Does smoking attract a group differently oriented toward health and with different habits in other respects than nonsmokers as a group? Could the different mortality rates be a reflection of something in the genes of smokers which makes them as a group more susceptible than nonsmokers to disease? More questions can be raised. Our purpose, however, is to show how to check whether an alleged influence exists once it is raised. We will start with the suggestion that smokers as a group may have somewhat different health habits than nonsmokers as a group. To make this suggestion concrete, it is conceivable that smokers as a group consume more alcohol than nonsmokers as a group and that the excess deaths are accounted for by alcohol consumption rather than smoking, or by alcohol consumption in connection with smoking. I am not suggesting that smokers actually do vary from nonsmokers in their consumption of alcohol. The first thing would be to determine with a study whether the alleged difference exists. Should the drinking habits of smokers as a group turn out to be significantly different from the habits of nonsmokers, then the Method of Agreement could be applied by comparing the mortality record of a group of smokers who also consumed alcohol with the record of a group of nondrinking smokers. This way of proceeding is sound, but it is also an immense amount of labor. And an indefinite number of alleged differences between the smoking and nonsmoking group can be urged as possible biasing influences, so that proceeding to investigate each possibility by the Method of Agreement could require more research than could be financed for the study of even such an important problem as smoking and health.

The Method of Difference, if it could be applied, would eliminate suggestions that the smoking and nonsmoking groups were not comparable. Can the Method of Difference be applied? Not exactly, to be sure, for the Method prescribes "two situations alike in all relevant respects but one" and no two human beings, not even identical twins, are alike in all relevant respects except for smoking. All the same, the force of the Method of Difference in eliminating noncausal factors is so great that an attempt to apply it to the smoking situation was made in a study of 36,975 matched pairs of smokers and nonsmokers. Though the matching must be acknowledged to be imperfect, the numbers of pairs matched would tend to reduce the affect of imperfect matching. The characteristics matched were:

> race (white, Negro, Mexican, Indian, or Oriental); height; nativity (native-born or foreign-born); residence (rural or urban); urban occupational exposure to dusts, fumes, vapors, chemicals, radioactivity, etc.; religion (Protestant, Catholic, Jewish, or none); education; marital state; consumption of alcoholic beverages; amount of sleep per night; usual amount of exercise; nervous tension; use of tranquilizers; current state of health; history of cancer other than skin cancer; and history of heart disease, stroke, or high blood pressure.[4]

All subjects were men, aged 40–79, and the study was continued for 34 months during which 2,047 deaths occurred within the two groups. When broken down into the particular causes of death, the numbers involved are too small to yield reliable mortality ratios, especially for the less common diseases. Yet the results were closely similar to those obtained by other surveys. Here are the figures:

	Death of Smokers	Death of Nonsmokers	Mortality Ratios	
			Matched Pairs	Seven Studies
1. Cancer of the lung	110	12	9.2	10.8
2. Emphysema	15	1	insufficient cases	
3. Cancer of larynx	3	0	insufficient cases	
4. Heart and circulatory system—coronary	654	304	2.1	1.7
5. Cancer of colon and rectum	25	20	insufficient cases	
6. Deaths from all causes	1,385	662	2.09	1.68

So we see, the correlations of smoking with various diseases among matched pairs are not greatly different from the correlations observed in other studies. The slightly higher mortality ratios for the matched pairs at most points is itself a covariation in tune with the fact that the "Seven studies" column

[4]E. Cuyler Hammond, "Smoking in Relation to Mortality and Morbidity," *Journal of the National Cancer Institute*, 32, no. 5 (May, 1964), 1161–68.

includes smokers of under 20 cigarettes per day as well as smokers of over 20, while in the "Matched pairs" study all smokers consumed at least 20 per day. Insofar as the matched pairs as a group conform to the Method of Difference, causal factors other than smoking are eliminated.

SUMMARY

The cause is all the factors that make an event occur. This notion is so unmanageable that one or more factors usually are singled out and spoken of as "the cause."

A sufficient cause is one way in which the effect may be brought about. Leaving oily rags in a basket is a sufficient cause for fire.

A necessary cause is the cause expressed in general conditions that must exist for the effect to occur. Fuel, oxygen, and kindling temperature are the necessary cause of fire.

Method of Agreement.   If one and only one relevant circumstance is common to all cases in which the effect occurs, then this circumstance is the cause or associated with the cause.

Method of Difference.   If two situations are alike in all relevant respects but one, and if the effect occurs in one instance and not in the other, then the difference is the cause or is associated with the cause.

Joint Method of Agreement and Difference.   A circumstance present in all instances in which the effect occurs and invariably absent when the effect does not occur is the cause or is associated with the cause.

Method of Covariation.   When one circumstance varies in a regular manner whenever some other circumstance varies, then there must be some sort of causal connection between the two.

Method of Residues.   When part of an effect remains unexplained by known causal circumstances, then an additional circumstance or circumstances must be sought to account for the unexplained portion of the effect.

The word "relevant" as it appears in Mill's Methods is justly accused of being question-begging. Since what is relevant has to be perceived apart from the Methods, the Methods are not a procedure for automatically solving causal problems. Nevertheless, wherever enough is known about what kinds of circumstances are relevant, then the Methods will identify the cause if data is available. Also, familiarity with the Methods is background knowledge that helps in perceiving the possible causal significance of evidence.

Establishing a cause requires the supporting of a causal generalization. The requirement of enough cases and representative cases applies to all generalizations including those concerned with causes.

EXERCISES FOR CHAPTER 14
pages 216–233

I.   **Answer T** for "true" or **F** for "false":

_____   **1.** When investigating a causal problem, what is relevant is pretty obvious.

_____   **2.** Mill's Methods automatically lead to the discovery of the cause.

_____   **3.** Knowledge of Mill's Methods helps one to notice the causal significance of data.

_____   **4.** All sufficient causes embody the requirements of the necessary cause for the phenomena.

_____   **5.** A sufficient cause is one way in which the phenomena may be brought about.

_____   **6.** Causal generalizations are supported in the same way as any other generalization.

_____   **7.** Understanding the cause is necessary to deal successfully with any problem.

_____   **8.** An attempt to reveal the entire cause of a particular event is both futile and unnecessary.

_____   **9.** The cause is all the factors that make an event occur.

_____   **10.** In many social science problems the cause is notoriously hard to establish. This is because Mill's Methods do not apply to such problems.

_____   **11.** Before they can be applied, Mill's Methods require an assumption about what may be the relevant circumstances.

_____   **12.** No event can occur without the existence of its necessary cause.

II.   Using letters to indicate the supposed relevant causal circumstances, see if you can make up brief schemes like those used in the text to show the operation of the Method of Agreement, the Method of Difference, and the Joint Method.

III.   When there are differences in degree instead of a simple occurring or nonoccurring of an event, the Method of Covariation may permit a causal factor to be identified. Yet, characteristically, covariations are not completely regular. Why is this so? Explain how much irregularity may exist before the point is reached at which the covariation becomes too weak to be taken as indicating a causal relation.

IV.   *In 1886 a young Dutch physician, Dr. Christian Eijkman, was sent to the East Indies with specific instructions to find the microbe responsible for beriberi, a disease widespread in Southeast Asia.*

> After several years of little progress, he [Eijkman] noticed, in a fortuitous accident now famous in the history of nutritional research, that a mysterious occurrence had taken place among the chickens in the laboratory compound.
>   For a time the chickens had also been stricken with a strange fatal paralysis similar to beriberi, which then just as suddenly ceased to affect them. An inquiry showed that some months earlier, the chickens had been placed on a diet of polished rice, the more expensive grains from which the outer husk is removed. This took place before the onset of the malady. Then a new cook, wishing to economize, switched back to the cheaper, unpolished rice, whereupon the disease promptly disappeared.[5]

1. Which one of Mill's Methods applies to the chance experiment that seemed to show a causal link between the disease prevalent among the chickens and the presence or absence of the husks on the rice they consumed?

Since the disease affecting the chickens produced symptoms similar to beriberi in humans, Dr. Eijkman put to himself the question whether populations suffering a widespread incidence of beriberi were also populations in which polished rice was the staple food. He noted that India, South China, Indonesia, the Philippines, and parts of South America and Japan were the areas where polished rice was the staple food and these areas were the areas in which beriberi was common. Other areas of the world where polished rice was not the staple food were little troubled with beriberi.

2. Which of Mill's Methods seems to apply to this situation?

3. Imagining yourself to be in Dr. Eijkman's position, how would you go about gathering further evidence to establish whether or not the consumption of polished rice was causally related to beriberi?

V.   *Rocky Mountain Spotted Fever in the remote Bitterroot Valley of western Montana was no more than a sideshow:*

> The fever itself did not exist as a public health problem, according to some opinion. Hardly a dozen people a year died of it, and they were usually obscure

[5]Harold Rosenberg and A.N. Feldzamen, *The Doctor's Book of Vitamin Therapy* (New York: G.P. Putnam's Sons, 1974), p. 82.

shepherds, trappers, fishermen, hunters, cowhands or marginal farmers whose departure left no immediately obvious mark on the society to which they belonged.[6]

Yet investigation seemed reasonable in view of the inadequacy of local belief attributing the disease, which occurred only in the spring, to be an effect of drinking water from melting snow.

It was known that Texas cattle fever was carried from steer to steer by ticks transmitting a single-celled protozoan in the red blood cells. Could ticks also carry spotted fever from other animals to man? Dr. Ricketts demonstrated that guinea pigs were susceptible to Rocky Mountain Spotted Fever and that the disease could indeed be transmitted from animal to animal by the bite of a tick. Then, unfortunately, Dr. Ricketts died of typhus. His work languished. Understandably, fifteen years later when a Montana State Senator and his wife, she the president of the State Federation of Women's Clubs, both died of the fever after a visit to the Bitterroot Valley, the public was aroused. Something would have to be done! Dr. Spencer was assigned to investigate.

Ticks lay eggs in the ground which hatch in the spring. The young ticks climb the nearest green plant, waving their hooked legs. When an animal brushes by, the "seed ticks" grab hold and go after a blood meal. There are two practical ways of obtaining ticks for investigation: one may shoot an animal and remove the ticks, or one may drag flannel over the bushes at the right season and pick off the ticks that adhere to it.

Dr. Spencer secured "drag ticks" on flannel, made several lots of "tick juice" by grinding up ticks, and injected 101 guinea pigs with the juice. None of the guinea pigs got spotted fever. Next, a goat was shot and over 1,000 ticks obtained from the goat. Five lots of "tick juice" made from "goat ticks" were injected into five guinea pigs. All five guinea pigs got spotted fever. So, "drag ticks" were harmless and "goat ticks" were deadly.

1. What possibly relevant difference occurs to you between the "drag ticks" and the "goat ticks"?

2. Apply Mill's Methods to secure further evidence about whether the "possibly relevant difference" you chose for (1) above actually is a relevant difference.

3. I will use Dr. Spencer's words for the final question.

> Dr. Ricketts . . . had tried in vain to make a spotted fever vaccine. . . . But a Czechoslovakian investigator, Frederick Breinl, had found that he could protect guinea pigs against typhus fever with the ground bodies of infected lice treated with phenol. I therefore saw good reason to believe that phenolized infected tick suspension might act likewise in spotted fever.

> My next experiment was obvious.

What would you suggest as a next experiment?

[6]Roscoe Spencer, "The Fleas, the Ticks, Spotted Fever and Me," *Saturday Review*, November 2, 1963, pp. 47–48. The material and quotations of this exercise all come from Spencer's witty article.

chapter 15

Hypothesis

In 1897 the Swedish explorer Andrée and two companions sailed off in a balloon to explore the Arctic. The rest was silence—until thirty years later, when a tent containing the well-preserved body of Andrée and one of his men was found far in the North on bleak White Island. The third explorer evidently had died first, for his body had been buried nearby. Andrée and his companion were in their underwear and they were not in their sleeping bags. Why did they die? Perhaps they starved? No, there was plenty of food around the camp. Possibly they froze to death? No, with a tent, warm sleeping bags, and fuel still in the stove, that seems improbable. Also, had freezing been a problem, one would expect to find the bodies in the sleeping bags, though to cite a diverging possibility, it would be possible for both men to have crawled out of their bags in the irrational stage of death by freezing. Still, the good quality of the equipment and the availability of heat makes trouble with cold unlikely. Maybe they died of contagious disease such as cholera or pneumonia? Well, disease would kill neither immediately nor simultaneously, and the last entry in the journal made no mention of any problem with illness. Could there have been foul play? Again, the facts fail to support this theory, for the bodies showed no signs of violence and the expedition's equipment was lying about unpilfered and undisturbed.

It took Vilhjalmur Steffansson, an experienced Arctic explorer, to produce a theory in harmony with all the facts: the men were killed in the tent by carbon monoxide poisoning from the stove. Though there is no knowing for sure what befell the expedition, still this theory seems likely to be true, because it fits all the facts while the other explanations do not. Steffansson's explanation is a special theory, which means that its conclusion explains a particular set of facts and has no general application beyond that single situation. Unlike the process of generalization, in which all the facts are members of the same class, a theory is supported by different sorts of facts which have the common link of all being explained by the conclusion drawn.

This chapter is entitled "Hypothesis," but in the discussion so far we have used only the word "theory." Though writers occasionally set up some distinction between "hypothesis" and "theory," there is no distinction that is generally followed, and the terms will be used interchangeably in this book. The word "law" is adopted only for general theories—that is, theories having a general application, like Ohm's law, in contrast with special theories that explain a particular set of facts only. Nothing is called a "law" unless it is viewed as having overwhelming support, and even then custom may not sanction applying this description; for instance, we speak of "Mendel's law" but of the "theory of evolution." In fact, as Copi points out, the use of "law" is unfortunate since it obscures the important fact that *all* the general propositions of science are regarded as hypotheses open to revision, never as dogmas.

Logic does not countenance the popular use of the word "theory" as one finds it in the claim, "That's all right in theory, but it won't work in practice." A theory in logic is something that does work in practice, and if it doesn't work in practice then it isn't a sound theory. It's as simple as that. What sense then can be made of the popular notion of things being all right in theory but not in practice? Well, the saying seems to point to the difficulty of executing *plans* that look good on paper. Often there is a hitch. Again, some people attach to the word "theory" a connotation of "impractical": such individuals like to declare that they want the facts and are not impressed by "mere theories." Although this prejudice is a crude one, yet if it is a poorly expressed protest against unsubstantiated speculation, then we can sympathize. So far as our discussion here is concerned, "hypothesis" and "theory" are words referring to an important type of induction which, if sufficient facts are available, will lead to a reliable conclusion.

REQUIREMENTS FOR A RELIABLE THEORY

1. The theory must fit all the facts
2. The theory must be supported by a number and variety of facts
3. No reasonably possible rival theory may exist

The Theory Must Fit All the Facts

The facts that support a theory are consistent with it, and when a true explanation has been advanced, then characteristically all sorts of facts will fall in line. Already we have seen how Steffansson's faulty-stove theory fit the facts while other explanations were more or less inconsistent with them. The reliability of a theory is weakened by a diverging fact, and the theory will collapse upon the appearance of a contradictory fact.

A *divergent fact* is one not in accord with a theory even though it is possible for the theory to be true despite the diverging fact. In the loss of Andrée in the Arctic, absence of any signs of struggle or of missing property diverge from any theory of foul play but do not rule it out entirely.

A *contradictory fact* is physically inconsistent with the theory it contradicts so that the contradictory fact and the theory cannot both be true. The alibi is the classic illustration of a contradictory fact. An alibi alleges that a person was physically elsewhere than at the scene of an act so that it sets up a physical impossibility of that person's taking part in the act. This is why the alibi is such an effective defense to a charge of crime, for no matter how many facts may seem to indicate guilt, if the accused can establish that he was somewhere else when the crime was committed then he cannot be guilty. (Though alibis have a bad smell because sometimes they are falsified, consider your first thought of defense if you were accused of, say, malicious mischief (vandalism) by painting names on a downtown sidewalk at 11:00 P.M. last night.) Finally, natural laws are continuously operating facts; nobody who seeks to approach a problem rationally will accept explanations that presume the suspension of a natural law. Consequently, any theory must be in harmony with the physical facts of nature, and, so far as it is not, the natural law is a contradiction.

What are the "facts" which a theory must fit? All facts must fit any theory because *every fact in the world is consistent with every other fact*. To declare that something is "false" is merely a way of declaring it inconsistent with something regarded as true. Since there are innumerable facts in the world, when one speaks of a theory as "fitting all the facts," one means all the known relevant facts. And what are the relevant facts? Well, though the answer has to be vague and isn't satisfying, the relevant facts are the facts which the theory should explain. Whatever caused Andrée and his companions to die, the explanation should be consistent with the condition of the bodies and of the camp. Other facts beyond this narrow scene may be relevant, too, and a satisfactory theory will have to fit any such facts as there are. We have a two-way relationship here: the theory explains all the facts, and the facts—the more the better—support the theory. There will be many other facts in the world which simply are unrelated, and give no support to the theory though they are not inconsistent with it either, as, for instance, "Andrée's wife lived for many years." The idea of a theory being supported where it fits all known relevant facts brings up an inherent weakness in theory building: a diverging or a contradictory fact may not be known or the relevance of a fact may not be recognized. In either case, the theory may seem in harmony with all the events when this is not so.

The Theory Must Be Supported by a Number and Variety of Facts

Though in general the more facts supporting a theory the greater the confidence in it, sheer number is not everything, for some facts are more distinctive than others. To say that a fact is "distinctive" or even "highly distinctive" simply means that an inference drawn from such a fact is unlikely to be mistaken. For instance, if you observe snowshoe tracks, this circumstance alone would give you a lot of confidence in a theory that somebody had been snowshoeing. But if your evidence were not of the tracks, but instead you knew that a hiking club had announced a snowshoe walk at that place, the snow was deep, and you had seen a party with snowshoes in the neighborhood, your confidence that snowshoeing had taken place would be much less than if you had seen the tracks. Common sense based upon life experience has to be the guide in assessing the distinctiveness and directness of facts supporting a theory. Without de-emphasizing the contribution that numbers of facts have in building a reliable theory, it's obvious that distinctiveness counts as well.

A theory is supported by a variety of facts when the evidence for it converges from various directions, and any explanation showing a connection between facts which otherwise seem unrelated gains strength from the variety of facts supporting it. The theory that the Minoan civilization of Crete was destroyed by a volcanic eruption on the island of Santorini about 1500 b.c. is an example of a variety of facts all converging on an explanation of catastrophic damage from the eruption.[1] In the first place, houses of the Minoan civilization buried by a huge layer of volcanic ash laid down at a time when the houses were occupied have been found on the island of Santorini itself. Further, at the same time a large amount of volcanic ash was distributed over Crete in a deposit that would ruin crops and make the land unusable for several years. A contemporary Egyptian chronicle refers to dust in the air which obscured the sun for several days. Geologists concur that the Egyptian report is credible since the condition of dust obscuring the sun is quite possible after a major eruption. The chronicle goes on to bemoan the fact that ships no longer came from Keftiu (Crete) asking, with true Egyptian concern, "What shall we do for the cedar for our mummies... ?" Geologists calculate that the northern shore of Crete would suffer from an enormous tidal wave as a result of the eruption. Finally, there is no evidence of the continuance of the Minoan civilization with vigor after that time. All these various facts converge in support of the theory that the Minoan civilization of Crete disappeared suddenly as a result of a catastrophic eruption on Santorini. One would like to have more facts, and if more should be discovered that are consistent with the theory, then the theory will become better supported. The more the facts and the greater their variety, the stronger any theory that they support will become. It may be that no single fact taken alone is very impressive, and yet a number of facts taken in conjunction with one another will operate to establish a theory reliably.

A general theory of physical science gains strength also from the numbers of facts which it can explain and, as a further possibility, a theory in science may receive added support when it is consistent with other theories. For this reason, a general theory in science becomes better established whenever the range of phenomena that it accounts for can be increased.

---

[1]John Lear, "The Volcano that Shaped the Western World," *Saturday Review*, November 5, 1966, pp. 57–66.

No Reasonably Possible Rival Theory May Exist

No theory can be reliable so long as some other reasonable hypothesis gives an alternate explanation for all the facts. Holding the rival theory to be "reasonable" cuts out foolish explanations such as attributing actions to an escaped gorilla, which, though physically possible, is not believable or, worse, claiming supernatural intervention which cannot even be tested. On the other hand, a rival theory need not be as well supported as the main theory in order to render the main theory unreliable. This situation occurs in many criminal cases when the defense produces witnesses who testify to a theory of the facts which leaves the defendant innocent while the prosecution presents its case, possibly an impressive one, showing that the accused is guilty. It may be that the jury is much more impressed with the prosecution's case than with the testimony produced by the defense and, say, the jurors would be willing to bet ten-to-one odds that the theory of guilt is true. Still, the defendant should and we hope would be acquitted in these circumstances because the rival theory is clearly strong enough to raise a reasonable doubt about the correctness of the case for the state. The necessity of disposing of rival theories before any guilt can be established beyond reasonable doubt is the reason the state ordinarily will not start a prosecution without proof of the *corpus delicti*—that is, without evidence demonstrating that the fact essential to the crime did occur, as the body to support a charge of murder, or charred remains of a building for a charge of arson. Until the body is found, for example, rival theories accounting for the disappearance of a human being will be many: amnesia, suicide, accident into water or at a remote place, fleeing from one's former life to live under an assumed name, and so on. Production of the body decisively cuts off these possibilities which otherwise could provide rival theories with enough strength to raise at least some doubt about the situation.

When only a few facts are known, usually it is easy to think of several theories which will explain them all. As more facts come to light, some of the explanations can be discarded as they encounter contradictory or strongly diverging facts. For example, we began this chapter by posing several possible explanations for the death of the Andrée party; each of the questions raised was a tentative or "working" hypothesis and each contributed to the investigation by suggesting a look at the evidence from its point of view. Each was rather quickly put aside as it ran afoul of one or more strong diverging facts. All of the first-blush explanations crumbled, leaving no tenable explanation until Steffansson came along with knowledge of what malfunctioning stoves can do. If the true theory is proposed, it can be discredited only by a mistake of some kind—by accepting a false statement or a misobservation as a fact or by misinterpreting a fact to signify something that it does not signify. Everything that has ever happened—that is, all the actual facts of the world—are consistent with one another so the truth never will be embarrassed by anything else that is true. And it is common, when the right hypothesis has been found, for fact after fact to fall in place so that what started out with the support of only a few events may acquire the support of many additional facts—including testimony of witnesses, results of physical tests, time sequences, motives, etc. There may be some diverging facts which do not help the theory but fall short of contradicting it. With luck, one reaches the point at which support becomes overwhelming and the theory is reliable.

If people had God-like knowledge and wisdom, we can imagine them as always able to pick out the correct theory and to see how other explanations ran afoul of some fact, as must invariably happen at some point to any explanation that is not true. Being human, we make mistakes, bark up the wrong tree, hold to explanations after the evidence begins to tell us to consider other possibilities. So we need to make a conscious effort to think of rival theories and not to allow them to be smothered through neglect or emotional attachment to a preferred explanation. Every lawyer senses this phenomenon when enough evidence has been presented so that the jury—or judge, if the case is tried without a jury—begins to "take a slant" on the case. From that time on there is a temptation to view further evidence with a resolution to fit it into the theory that has become favored as the solution, and *to disregard evidence that counters the slant*. It may take strong facts supported by good argument to turn the case around and reopen minds to an alternate interpretation. Nor is the tendency to adopt a view too soon and to maintain it against further evidence confined to law. In a much-quoted passage, Darwin notes that he made a practice of writing down any facts contrary to his tentative hypotheses since otherwise he had a tendency to forget them. As Darwin's action shows, consciously searching for facts counter to a hypothesis and looking for alternate explanations of the evidence is a healthy intellectual habit for testing a theory before accepting it as reliable. It performs the same service as searching for a conflicting case before adopting a generalization.

PRINCIPLES OF THEORY BUILDING

Simplicity

Three principles need to be included in any discussion of theory building. One is the principle of *simplicity*. Given two theories, either of which will account for a situation, the theory affording the simpler explanation is more likely to be true. It isn't easy to explain just what simplicity is in this connection. Certainly the notion does not imply that all theories should be simple in the sense of being easily grasped or being bereft of details. Simplicity in a special theory of the kind that has been discussed so far refers to a preference for viewing facts in their usual light rather than construing them in the light of special assumptions that are somewhat unusual. For example, it is more simple to believe that a man who opens an office door and enters does so because he intends to enter than to believe that his entering was by mistake. It may be a mistake, of course. Yet a theory that required several such less probable assumptions soon would lose all credibility. In fact, without the principle of simplicity, one could indulge all sorts of fanciful explanations because it frequently is possible to propose some complex set of facts that also is consistent with what can be simply explained.

In science the ideal of economy is kindred in spirit to simplicity. This ideal moves the scientist to seek to explain phenomena with the smallest number of broadly inclusive laws. Accordingly, in science a general theory will have preference over multiple explanations if it can explain as one system what formerly was explained by two or more unconnected theories. Special *ad hoc* (for this purpose alone) assumptions are frowned upon in science. One factor leading Copernicus to seek an alternative explanation to the Ptolemaic theory of the solar system was the excessive complexity that it entailed with its nine concentric, crystalline spheres in which eight spheres served to imbed the sun, the moon, the five known planets, and the fixed stars, while the outermost ninth sphere served as the prime mover to spin the entire system around the earth from east to west every 24 hours. Since the planets, as seen from the earth, do not move continuously from east to west, some eighty epicycles—circles within circles—were postulated to account for their erratic courses. By assuming the sun to be the center of the solar system, Copernicus was able to produce a simpler explanation, but he was not able to dispense with epicycles entirely because he assumed the planetary orbits to be circular instead of elliptical.

Capacity to Predict Further Facts

A theory will receive added strength—very convincing added strength—if it can be used to predict further facts. Yet the conviction attending a successful prediction is largely psychological, for had the predicted fact been known as part of the original data it would have given equal support to the theory while seeming, psychologically, less striking. To adopt an example from *The Rhyme of Reason*, a witty work of Roger W. Holmes,[2] suppose I suspect my daughter Frieda plans to elope; I have the evidence of inordinate numbers of love letters, dates, a scene with the family, a secretly packed suitcase, and her beloved's imminent departure for a distant place. Naturally, the moon is full. Knowing the strategic placement of the living room in relation to the staircase, I theorize that her clandestine departure will have to be by a ladder to her window. So I look out the front door and there is the ladder! I'm impressed. But suppose I had noticed the ladder when I came home from work and before I began to construct

---

[2]Roger W. Holmes, *The Rhyme of Reason* (New York: Appleton-Century-Crofts, 1939), p. 161. Paraphrase by permission of Roger W. Holmes.

the elopement theory on the basis of the other facts—packed suitcase, etc. My theory would be supported by the same facts, but it would lack the psychological impact of having been used to predict one of them. It would be equally well supported, all the same. The fact added by prediction should be recognized for what it is—*an added fact*. Of course, it may be a highly significant fact, and every fact in connection with others becomes a strand, as it were, in a cable of evidence.

Theories are used to predict in physical science also, and with a similar result in building confidence. For example, Mendeleyev's periodic classification of the elements enabled him to predict the existence and some of the properties of certain unknown elements appearing as gaps in his periodic table. Three of the predicted elements were discovered within twenty years, and modern science has added further elements together with a redetermination of atomic weights in accord with the sequences of the table, so that elements 1 to over 100 are now known. Also, the theory of evolution is confirmed by numerous instances of successful prediction, for the theory creates an expectation of the discovery of intermediate forms between existing known species. Such intermediate forms are regularly discovered, the best known example being, possibly, the horse, which now happens to be traceable through an unusually complete sequence of prototypes.

Testability

The final principle to consider in evaluating reliability of a theory is *testability*. One of the weaknesses of medieval thought was a willingness to accept theories which not only were untested but, more, were untestable in principle. The sky is the limit for such speculation. By waving aside the operation of natural laws and assuming the interference of unobservable phenomena, one can claim to explain anything at all without possibility of refutation. If events are attributed to stars or spirits or bewitchment, then *whatever happens* is allegedly what was ordained to happen. Either to confirm or to refute such claims is impossible. Maybe spirits do run the world—as people long believed—but to proceed with this assumption means the world cannot be understood rationally on an examinable basis. Hence the requirement that a theory must be testable *in principle* is a necessary barrier against the occult.

Requiring a theory to be testable in principle is not a requirement that it must be practically testable. This may seem strange. It is only superficially strange, however, because the point is explained easily. A theory about the rings of Saturn, for instance, which would require a human being to go there for a close inspection, could not be tested at this time. Or, we might like to know more about why Rome fell, but we are limited to the evidence we happen to have. Whether a theory concerns Saturn or Rome, in either case we know the kind of evidence that would tend to confirm or refute our theories. Entertaining theories which cannot be tested practically, or which are supported only by limited and inadequate evidence, does not break down a dike to permit a tidal sweep of speculation. After all, until a practical test is achieved or adequate evidence is found, the untested theory will be classed as unreliable.

The progress of science consists in framing theories that will account for the facts of experience. When a scientific theory is regarded as having overwhelming support, it may be termed a "law," but in principle science always is open to revision so that even a scientific law may be modified or abandoned in the light of new knowledge. In fact, it is a goal of science wherever possible to combine its theories into fewer and wider theories which will then express the interconnection between events to a greater extent. Just as confidence in the reliability of a special theory increases as the number of facts that it explains is increased, so also a general theory of science gains strength according to the number and variety of phenomena for which it can account.

Whenever a new theory is advanced in science as an alternate explanation for something already covered by an existing theory, an attempt is made to set up conditions which it will not be possible for both theories to accommodate. This is called a "crucial experiment." The crucial experiment takes the form of a hypothetical syllogism: "If theory so and so is true, then such and such will occur." If the predicted result does *not* occur, then there is a valid form, a denied consequent, and we will know that the theory is not true since its predicted result does not occur. But suppose the predicted result does occur. Then there is an affirmed consequent which is invalid, so even though the theory has predicted successfully, it has not been proved true. We can see, then, that a crucial experiment may eliminate an alternate theory as untrue but it does not establish any theory to be true. A theory subjected to a crucial experiment is in the position of "Tails you lose, but heads you don't win." Paradoxical though this may seem, reflection shows it is the result to be expected. When a theory predicts a result that does not occur, then the facts do not bear out the theory and the theory is false. But if the predicted result does occur, one simply has an additional fact to support the theory. Though an additional fact increases the reliability of a theory, it never can be final proof that the theory is true.

DEVELOPING A THEORY OR HYPOTHESIS

So far we have presented a sort of checklist of elements to be satisfied by all reliable theories. This is well and good when the problem is to evaluate a theory, to assess its reliability. But what about constructing a theory in the first place? Granting that there is no pat procedure for gaining the flash of insight by which the mind suggests an explanation, still some things can be said about how to go about developing a theory. We will discuss six steps.

1. Stating the Problem

Without a statement of the problem, there is no getting off the ground. And we pass up this step constantly—indeed, we have to, because one can hardly pursue a theory for everything he encounters. John spells abominably, but we don't bother to wonder why; a whip cracks and we aren't spurred to ask how the sound occurs. But to develop a theory, our very first step is to realize that an explanation is needed and to want to find out.

Assuming that there is a decision to take up a problem and resolve it, then we need to be clear about *what* problem should be solved. Though many texts in logic, English, and science warn of the need for care in defining the problem, it is not so easy to give practical advice about how to do this. Yet defining the problem is vital, and a story told of World War II, though possibly apocryphal, certainly makes this point. The story goes that during the planning stage for the invasion of North Africa, the mission was described as "to land at the ports of Casablanca, Oran, and Algiers and to occupy the ports and surrounding country as quickly as possible." After a time some new brass was added to the planning staff. One of the new officers took a look at the plan and remarked, "That is not the mission." "What is it, then?" the original staff asked. "The mission is, 'to land at the ports of Casablanca, Oran, and Algiers and to occupy the ports and surrounding country as quickly as possible *without arousing French opposition.'*" Though, as remarked before, a plan is not a theory, choosing what problem to solve is the first step that each must take.

A theory is an answer to a question, so it helps to begin by putting the problem to be solved in the form of a question. Take this seriously and be sure the sentence framed has a question mark at the end. The more specific the question can be made, the more productive it is apt to be. The notion that a problem may be more than half solved if one can ask the right question is true, because the right question focuses attention upon what is relevant for the answer, and this may indeed be more than half the problem. Questions can be revised as one learns more about the problem. To take a simple case, a mechanic does not find it helpful to ask, "Why doesn't the car run?" This is too general. Rather, he poses a number of specific questions: "Is the engine getting gas?" "Is there gas in the tank?" "Is the carburetor flooded?" And so on. The questions direct his search for evidence, and when he hits upon the right question he will be on his way to making the repair.

Important problems are apt to be far more complex than a mechanical situation like getting a car to run. "What is the effect of the Common Market?" is an enormously broad question, a question that will be manageable only if it is broken up into questions about how the Market has affected its various member states—or nonmember states—in particular respects. The answers to such questions often are so intertwined with conflicting evidence and value judgments that their reliability is debatable. Despite the difficulties, it will be better to seek explanations within the requirements for a sound theory than to proceed with hunches and unchecked speculation.

Finally, some questions deal with problems not answerable in the space–time world, and these questions cannot be answered by hypotheses supported by evidence of the kind dealt with in this chapter. The answers to philosophical problems such as "Is this conduct acceptable to God?" "What is virtue?" "What is justice?"—though they may be the questions about which we should care most—are not reducible to theories supported by facts justifying the claim of at least a roughly assessed degree of reliability. Conclusions about problems of this type are more a matter of philosophical commitment than of evidence.

2 & 3. Gathering Evidence *and* Forming Tentative Hypotheses

These two steps are combined here to emphasize their "chicken and egg" nature. Neither comes sharply first, since it is impossible to gather evidence without anything in mind and it is impossible to form a tentative hypothesis without some evidence or, at least, without some notion of what sort of explanation might apply. Perhaps you have been sick and the symptoms gave you no clue to what was wrong. Very likely your physician was able to apply his special knowledge to observe symptoms and to diagnose the problem—that is, to arrive at a theory concerning it. He then prescribed a treatment. Thus it requires adequate background knowledge to get started along the process of gathering evidence and forming tentative hypotheses.

While it is true that at least some ideas about the problem are needed if one is to gather evidence that will support a hypothesis, yet the solution may not—indeed, generally, it will not—be known in the early stages of evidence gathering. An agent's report of the facts bearing on the death of the first husband of Mary, Queen of Scots provides an unusual illustration of the division between evidence gathering and hypothesis. The king met his death on the night of February 10, 1567, in the course of a plot involving a tremendous gunpowder explosion in the basement of a house in which he was staying in Edinburgh. But how? Contemporaries found the situation most mystifying, and an investigating agent made an accurate drawing of the scene at the time. The agent's drawing has come down to us. It shows the body of the king, apparently unharmed, as it was found together with that of his valet in a nearby garden. The king's body is nearly nude and his clothing is scattered in a line toward the demolished house. Both men are lying on the ground with their heads toward the house, and a small chair lies beside them tipped over in the direction of the house. Contemporaries could see that apparently the king had suspected trouble by fire or plot immediately before the explosion, and had fled to the garden to dress. But why had the men not survived? The mystery was solved in 1945 by applying modern knowledge of explosives to add the fact that a large gunpowder explosion creates fiery gases which sweep upward and then back in a circular course along the ground as atmospheric pressure pushes air and gas back to fill the vacuum created by the explosion. The violent rush of hot gas along the ground would blow the nightwear of the king and his valet up their bodies. It would push over the chair and scatter the clothing in a line toward the house, and, finally, breathing the hot gas would kill both men without marking their bodies. And so the cause of death was convincingly determined about 400 years after the event.[3]

The story illustrates that occasionally relevant evidence may be gathered even without a theory in mind. Of course, the situation of a body is so notoriously relevant to the explanation of the death that the agent's careful drawing of the scene hardly was a random choice. Darwin was right in his protest against the idea that evidence should be collected without preconceptions. "How odd it is," he wrote, "that anyone should not see that all observation must be for or against some view, if it is to be of any service."

As evidence that seems relevant to the investigator is gathered, tentative theories will occur as possible explanations for the facts observed. A mark of an experienced investigator is to keep these initial hypotheses *tentative* so as to maintain an open mind for alternative explanations. It doesn't take long to fall in love with one's own theory and, as with marriage, the consequences of haste can be serious.

4. Testing Tentative Hypotheses

As soon as a theory is thought of, one begins to test it. One muses, "Is this idea consistent with all the evidence?" Any contradictory fact will discredit the theory while any diverging fact will weaken its support. An obvious caution, however, is to consider whether an inconsistent apparent fact is indeed a fact: observation can be faulty, witnesses sometimes are mistaken. Occasionally evidence is planted to mislead, and hoaxes occur. When the initial test of consistency with all the facts is passed, the theory may still have only meager support and, in any case, it is always good to have more supporting evidence. So the next step is to look for more.

The hypothetical syllogism is a tool to use systematically in seeking more evidence. "If *so and so*, then *such and such*" runs the major premise of the hypothetical. "If my daughter Frieda is eloping, she must be able to leave from the second story." Is there a way for Frieda to leave? "Why there *is* a way, a ladder!" "Aha, Frieda is eloping." Or is she? Not so fast. We have affirmed the consequent and that's a fallacy, for the rule is unvarying—affirm the antecedent or deny the consequent. It's embarrassing—not the elopement but the logic. Though it looks like a paradox, hypothetical syllogisms are a highly practical way of locating more evidence for a theory even though their use involves fallacy. And we can explain away the paradox. Fallacy means a mistake in reasoning, so we know a conclusion arrived at by faulty reasoning is not reliable. To say a conclusion is not reliable is to say that its truth is not properly established, and this is quite different from saying that it is false. It may be true and it

[3]W. J. Phythian-Adams, "How Darnley Died," *Juridical Review*, 47 (1945), 112–21.

may not, we don't know. All right. So I see the ladder and I still don't know for sure that Frieda is eloping. My neighbor may have brought it over this afternoon to get into the house when my wife forgot her key. "Phooey on logic! Why, the girl will be gone before you logicians have got through with your talk about validity!" Well, perhaps we'd better keep an eye on the ladder while we mull over just what is accomplished by proposing premises for hypothetical syllogisms which, as it turns out, are invalid.

When the thought occurred to me "If Frieda is eloping tonight, then she will have to leave by the second-story window," I checked the possibility of her leaving by the second story and what I discovered was *not proof* but *additional evidence*. All the facts supporting the elopement theory—love letters, scene with the family, secretly packed suitcase, and now, the ladder—may be true without Frieda intending to elope. Maybe, unknown to me, she has had a terrible fight with her erstwhile swain and plans to run away from her whole horrible life. No matter how many or what the facts, induction never asserts that its conclusion is certainly true. So when deduction is used to discover a new fact that fits into the inductive process of theory building, one can expect it to no more than increase the reliability of the theory. And, when you think about it, one should not expect the hypothetical syllogism to stamp the conclusion "Frieda is eloping" as valid when, as we have seen, this conclusion is inductive and might, just possibly, not be true. But the new facts discovered will be useful whether they give further support for the theory or whether they weaken it, for in either case one is ahead in the search for truth.

We saw earlier that the same application of the hypothetical syllogism applies to a crucial experiment: If theory *so and so* is true, then *such and such* will occur. Where the predicted phenomenon occurs there is additional evidence supporting the theory even though this does not prove it to be necessarily true, while if the predicted phenomenon does not occur, then the theory is dismissed as false.

It will be worthwhile to look at some examples showing the use of hypothetical premises to gain additional evidence. The ponderous stones of Stonehenge seem to have been brought from Wales by water up the River Avon and thence overland 2 miles to the site. Whatever else, the builders did not scrimp on labor. Now if we have the habit of thinking about reasonable hypothetical premises, we can say, "If blocks weighing many tons were to be transported from the Avon River for 2 miles onto Salisbury plain, then a road or graded way would be an obvious help." So we look for the road and, thanks to the astonishing revelations of aerial photography, there it is! Faint scars on the landscape are traceable from the river to the vicinity of Stonehenge, indicating a wide and gently graded way. A new fact has been found adding strength to the theory that the stones for Stonehenge were brought by water.[4]

[4]Excerpt from *Stonehenge Decoded* by Gerald S. Hawkins and John B. White. Copyright © 1965 by Gerald S. Hawkins and John B. White. Used by permission of Doubleday & Company, Inc.

The origin of the Indians of Central America has been attributed variously to migrations in pre-Columbian times, including, among other theories, the Ten Lost Tribes of Israel. Setting up some hypothetical premises to get more evidence concerning this theory, we have: "If the Indians of Central America are descended from the Ten Lost Tribes of Israel, then their language will show some Semitic influence." But philologists find no Semitic influence in their language, so the Central American Indians are not descended from Israelites. Now here we have an interesting thing: the minor premise denies the consequent in this case, and this makes the syllogism valid. So here we know that *if the premises are true* the conclusion must be true and the theory of Indian descent from the Ten Lost Tribes of Israel is totally discredited. Again the result is what we should expect, for although finding an additional fact never can establish a theory with certainty, a single contradictory fact will falsify it while a diverging fact will reduce its credibility. Let's test the theory with another hypothetical premise. If the Indians of Central America were descended from the Lost Tribes of Israel, then they would have had knowledge of the wheel as a useful tool known to the Lost Tribes. But the pre-Columbian Indians used the wheel only in toys. So, they did not have contact with the Ten Lost Tribes. Again, a valid conclusion which, if its premises are true, destroys the theory.

The illustrations just given are not uncommon; ordinarily one can think hypothetically of not one but several situations which may reasonably be expected to exist if a tentative theory is true. Consider how the auto mechanic and the physician we mentioned earlier go about posing hypothetical situations and checking to see whether the evidence confirms them. Putting hypothetical premises to oneself—"If *so and so*, then *such and such*"—is the great resource of the detective, of the researcher, of anybody at all who wants to develop a theory.

5 & 6. Refinement of the Theory *and* Elimination of Rival Theories

We have seen that all truth is consistent with all other truths, so if enough evidence can be assembled, one theory will become reliably established and all other explanations will be struck down by evidence inconsistent with their truth. How can we be sure we have all the evidence? How can we know that the situation could not be as well or better explained by some rival theory we have not thought of? Well, we never have all the evidence and we can never be sure of not overlooking some rival theory. The best we can do is to understand this and to make a conscious effort to think of alternate explanations.

The possibility of overlooking a rival theory is an intrinsic weakness of theory building. In fact, this is the origin of the common prejudice against circumstantial evidence. The circumstances of a case—that is, the facts from which something is inferred—may seem to be very strong, and yet experience shows that occasionally strong circumstances have been misinterpreted to establish a wrong theory which seemed convincing because some other explanation that would fit the evidence went unnoticed. A famous English case illustrates the point well. A guardian was seen with his ward in a wood, having a heated quarrel in which the ward appeared to be pleading for her life. Furthermore, the guardian stood to gain some property in the event of the death of the ward. After the quarrel the ward was not heard of again, and the guardian was charged with her death. Years later the ward was discovered living in Holland; the quarrel was established to have concerned the ward's desire to marry one of whom the guardian disapproved; matters had come to such a pitch that the ward pleaded for her life. But no harm had come to her, and she had immediately eloped to Holland.

SUMMARY

"Hypothesis" and "theory" are not distinguished by any consistently followed usage. They are used as equivalent terms in this book.

A *general theory* states a universal law that has a general application. A *special theory* explains a particular set of facts and is without general application.

Any theory, general or special, will be reliable only if it meets the following requirements:

1. It must fit all the facts.
2. It must be supported adequately by a number of facts.
3. No reasonably possible rival theory may exist.

A fact is *contradictory* to a theory when the nature of the fact makes it impossible for the fact and the theory to be simultaneously true.

A fact is *divergent* from a theory when it renders the theory less likely, although it is not impossible for both the fact and the theory to be true.

Every fact in the world is consistent with every other fact. Consequently, if enough evidence is forthcoming, any false theory will sooner or later encounter a contradictory fact. Conversely, no true theory will encounter a contradictory fact, though if a falsehood is mistakenly accepted as a contradictory fact, then as a consequence of human error a true theory will be discredited.

Some principles of theory building are:

1. *Simplicity*—A theory that provides a simple explanation is more likely to be true than one that is complex or requires any unusual assumptions.
2. *Capacity to predict*—A theory gains impressive support if the assumption of its truth leads to the discovery of further facts.
3. *Testability*—A theory must be capable in principle at least of being confirmed by experience in the space–time world.

There are six steps for forming a theory or hypothesis:

1. Formulate a question answerable in the space-time world
2. Gather evidence
3. Formulate tentative hypotheses
4. Test all tentative hypotheses
5. Refine the hypothesis as the facts require
6. Eliminate all reasonably possible rival hypotheses

Formulating hypothetical syllogisms on the premise "If this theory is true, then..." is a fertile way of obtaining additional evidence. An additional fact discovered in this way adds support but does not prove the theory because it is an affirmed consequent. If the additional fact is a denial of the consequent, then the theory is disproved—assuming that the premise is true.

EXERCISES FOR CHAPTER 15
pages 237–252

I. Answer **T** for "true" or **F** for "false":

_____ **1.** A theory never is certainly true.

_____ **2.** If it is correct that a theory never is certainly true, then no theory can be viewed as reliable.

_____ **3.** The statement "That is all right in theory but it won't work in practice" points out a fundamental shortcoming of constructing theories.

_____ **4.** A hypothesis is even more doubtful than a theory.

_____ **5.** In general, the more facts a theory can explain, the greater its reliability.

_____ **6.** Some hypotheses which explain only a few facts are nevertheless highly reliable.

_____ **7.** No hypothesis is reliable if a reasonably possible rival hypothesis can be formed.

_____ **8.** Every fact in the world is consistent with every other fact. As a consequence of this, no fact ever is contradictory to a true theory.

_____ **9.** A diverging fact shows that the theory cannot be true.

_____ **10.** When a theory can be applied to predict a fact, that shows that the theory must be true.

_____ **11.** Some theories are not testable in fact, but all theories conforming to the criteria of logic must be testable in principle.

_____ **12.** Asking the right question is often the key to solving a problem because it focuses attention upon what is relevant to the answer.

_____ **13.** Proposing hypothetical syllogisms is a way of proving a theory is true.

_____ **14.** Proposing hypothetical syllogisms is one way of finding more evidence which may either strengthen or weaken a tentative hypothesis.

_____ **15.** The possibility of overlooking a rival theory is a weakness of all theory building.

_____ **16.** A contradictory fact shows that a theory is not true.

_____ **17.** Logic makes its greatest contribution when it shows reliable support for theories concerning values and answers to philosophical problems.

_____ **18.** Economy, testability, and predictive capacity are notions all of which apply to the general theories of science.

_____ **19.** If a general theory is not testable, at least in principle, then it cannot be true.

_____ **20.** Only if a general theory is testable, at least in principle, will it be possible to determine whether or not the theory is reliable.

_____ **21.** Occult influences are not testable in principle and therefore cannot be shown to be either true or false through the application of evidence and sound logic.

_____ **22.** A theory which in principle is not subject to falsification is not to be accepted as reliable in logic.

_____ **23.** When an alibi is established, usually it will constitute a contradictory rather than a diverging fact.

_____ **24.** According to the principle of simplicity, a theory that does not construe the facts as occurring in their most usual manner is false.

_____ **25.** A crucial experiment can eliminate one of two rival theories as false, but it cannot prove the surviving theory to be true.

II.   Without referring to the text, state or write down the three requirements for a reliable theory.

III.   Provide short answers for the following questions:

1. Explain the difference between a general theory and a special theory. Cite an example of each.

2. State the difference between a divergent and a contradictory fact. Give an example of each.

3. Explain how framing hypothetical premises about a situation helps to locate further facts bearing upon the problem. Make up an example of such a hypothetical statement.

4. Although formulating a hypothetical syllogism running "If this theory is true, then so and so" may lead to a conclusive showing that the theory is false, it never can produce a conclusive showing that the theory is true. Explain why this is so.

5. What is the *principle of simplicity* in theory building?

6. What is the *principle of economy* applied to the general theories of science?

7. What is a *crucial experiment* in science?

8. What does it mean to say that a theory is "testable in principle"? Why must a theory be testable in principle if it is to be accorded serious attention in the field of science?

9. Give an example of a theory that is testable in principle but not at the present time testable in fact.

IV.   The Lindbergh Case[5]

This exercise is based upon the trial of Richard Bruno Hauptmann for the kidnapping and murder of the Lindbergh baby. The defendant is to be found guilty only if it is shown beyond a reasonable doubt that he participated in the crime. Imagine yourself to be on the jury. Rate the reliability of each hypothesis presented according to the following scale:

1. Certainly true
2. True beyond a reasonable doubt
3. More probably true than not (i.e., true according to a preponderance of the evidence)
4. Indifferent
5. More probably false than not
6. False beyond a reasonable doubt
7. Certainly false

The baby was taken at about 9:30 P.M. on March 1, 1932 from its bedroom on the second floor. At the scene of the crime a ladder made of scrap wood was found.

    a. *The wood in the ladder had been dressed by a plane with nicks and unevenness in the blade that matched the marks made by a plane in Hauptmann's garage.*

---

[5]Winston W. Little *et al., Applied Logic* (Boston: Houghton Mifflin, 1955), pp. 203–205. Adapted by permission of Mrs. Winston W. Little.

b. *One side of the ladder was made from a piece of wood having tree rings and nail holes that matched a place where a piece of wood of that size had been sawed and taken from the floor of Hauptmann's attic.*

c. *Nails in the ladder had been made by the same nail-making machine that made nails in Hauptmann's garage.*

d. *The ladder was constructed in three pieces that locked together when assembled for use. It would take knowledge of carpentry to make such a ladder. Hauptmann was a carpenter.*

1. Which of these facts gives the strongest support to a hypothesis that Hauptmann made the ladder? Which gives the weakest support?

Strongest _____   *Weakest* _____

2. Rate the reliability of the hypothesis "Hauptmann made the ladder."

_____

3. Propose a hypothesis in which Hauptmann makes the ladder but is innocent of the crime.

_____

_____

e. *Left in the baby's room was a note demanding $50,000 in ransom. At the bottom of the note were two interlocking blue circles, a red oval, and three square holes. The note concluded: "Indication for all letters are singnature [sic] and three holes."*

f. *Fourteen kidnap notes containing several hundred words in all were received with this identifying mark.*

g. *The notes had many misspellings:* anyding *for anything,* boad *for boat,* ouer *for our,* where *for were,* note *for not,* someding *for something,* singnature *for signature. The letters* g *and* h *were regularly transposed so that light was written* lihgt *and right was* rihgt. *A hyphen was inserted in New-York, and the $ symbol always followed the number (50000 $).*

h. *A writing test was given to Hauptmann after his arrest. Both the writing test and letters written by Hauptmann showed the same misspellings found in the ransom notes.*

i. *Paper in Hauptmann's house was of the same kind as that used in the ransom notes. It was a widely distributed brand.*

j. *Handwriting experts studied the ransom notes, the writing test, and letters written by Hauptmann. Seven handwriting experts for the prosecution tes-*

tified that Hauptmann wrote the notes. One expert for the defense testified that he did not write the notes.

   k. *Hauptmann denied writing the notes.*

4. Which facts given above are the strongest support to the hypothesis that Hauptmann wrote the ransom notes?

_____

5. Cite those facts which diverge from this hypothesis.

_____

6. Rate the reliability of the hypothesis "Hauptmann wrote the ransom notes."

_____

   l. *Dr. J. F. Condon, who acted as intermediary, testified that he sat on a bench in a cemetery and talked from 9:30 to 10:45 P.M. to a man who had come to collect the ransom. No ransom was paid at that time.*

   m. *Dr. Condon testified that at another meeting on the night of April 2 he delivered $50,000 ransom in exchange for the baby's nightgown which was produced to show that the man was not an imposter. The numbers of the bills had been recorded.*

   n. *Dr. Condon testified that Hauptmann was the man with whom he dealt at both meetings.*

   o. *Colonel Lindbergh, who sat in a car beside the cemetery fence while Condon negotiated, testified that Hauptmann's voice sounded like the voice of the man in the cemetery.*

   p. *Dr. Condon testified that he gave his address and unlisted phone number to the man in the cemetery.*

   q. *This address and phone number was found penciled on a closet wall in Hauptmann's closet.*

   r. *One of the ransom bills was found in Hauptmann's wallet at the time of his arrest.*

   s. *A search of Hauptmann's garage turned up $19,700 of the ransom bills hidden in various caches.*

7. From the facts given above, rate the reliability of the hypothesis "Hauptmann was the man to whom Condon gave the ransom money."

_____

t. *Hauptmann testified that the ransom money had been left with him for safekeeping by a deceased friend named Fisch.*

u. *Hauptmann testified that he had spent some of the money because Fisch owed him $2,000.*

v. *Hauptmann's accounts showed that Fisch had at one time borrowed $2,000 which he had later repaid.*

w. *Hauptmann testified that quitting his job, buying a new car, and going on expensive vacations soon after the date the ransom money was paid was made possible by profits from the stock market.*

x. *Examination of the brokerage records for Hauptmann's transactions revealed a net loss of $9,132.29.*

y. *An estimate of Hauptmann's expenses for the 2 1/2 years between the delivery of the ransom money and his arrest, the net loss in stock investments, and the amount of ransom money recovered totaled approximately $50,000.*

z. *Three months before the kidnapping, at a time Hauptmann claimed to have had $4,000 on hand in a box, he wrote requesting postponement of a $74.89 bill which he was being pressed to pay.*

aa. *Hauptmann testified that on March 1, 1932, the date of the kidnapping, he was working as a carpenter on the Majestic Apartments.*

bb. *The contractor's payroll records for the Majestic Apartments showed that Hauptmann began work March 21, 1932 and quit April 1, immediately before the ransom was paid.*

cc. *Hauptmann denied guilt.*

8. From the above evidence, rate the reliability of the theory that Fisch or some party other than Hauptmann committed the kidnapping.

9. Consider the evidence as a whole. Do this by reflecting upon whatever reliability you have attached to the hypotheses (1) that Hauptmann made the ladder, (2) that he wrote the ransom notes, and (3) that he was the man to whom the ransom was paid. After determining the degree of reliability with which these three hypotheses *together* establish that Hauptmann was the kidnapper, then consider whether Hauptmann's testimony creates an alternate hypothesis having sufficient reliability to raise a reasonable doubt about whether he was the kidnapper.

V.   The Sacco and Vanzetti Case[6]

This exercise is another case for your evaluation. Use the rating scale in Exercise IV to judge the reliability of the hypotheses presented.

At about 3:05 P.M. on April 15, 1920, a paymaster and his guard were carrying a payroll of $15,776.51 to the Slater & Morrill shoe factory in South Braintree, Massachusetts. As they walked along a sidewalk they were suddenly fired upon and killed by two men armed with pistols. As the murders were being committed, a car occupied by three men drove up. The murderers threw the two payroll boxes into the car, jumped in, and were driven away.

Previously, on December 24, 1919, a shoe factory payroll holdup had been attempted in Bridgewater, Massachusetts. In the Bridgewater incident three men got out of a parked car and fired upon a payroll truck. In this case, the guard returned the fire, whereupon the assailants fled in their car.

On April 17, 1920, a Buick later identified as the car used in both holdups was found abandoned in a wood. Leading away from the Buick were the tracks of a smaller car.

The chief of the Bridgewater police suspected one Boda of involvement in the Bridgewater crime, and when he learned that on April 19, 1920, Boda had had his small Overland car towed to a garage for repairs, the police chief arranged for the garage to report who should call for that car. On May 5, four men appeared: Boda, Orciani, Sacco, and Vanzetti. When the Overland was not delivered, Boda and Orciani left on a motorcycle while Sacco and Vanzetti took a streetcar. Boda never was apprehended and Orciani was not indicted for either crime because his punched timeclock showed him to have been at work at the time of the Bridgewater crime and there was not sufficient identification to charge him with the South Braintree murders. Sacco and Vanzetti were arrested on the streetcar.

Arrest and Interrogation

The arrest and interrogation of Sacco and Vanzetti revealed the following facts:

   a. *At the time of the arrest, Sacco was carrying a .32-caliber Colt pistol with ammunition. A .32-caliber Colt pistol had been used in the South Braintree murder.*

   b. *At the time of the arrest, Vanzetti was carrying a loaded Harrington & Richardson .38-caliber revolver. No shots from this type of pistol had been fired in the murder. The slain guard, Berardelli, customarily carried a Harrington & Richardson .38-caliber revolver. After the murder, Berardelli's revolver had not been found on his person or at the scene.*

[6]The material for this exercise is taken from Felix Frankfurter, *The Case of Sacco and Vanzetti* (Boston: Little, Brown, 1927) and from Osmond K. Fraenkel, *The Sacco-Vanzetti Case* (New York: Alfred A. Knopf, 1931).

    c. *Both Sacco and Vanzetti told several falsehoods concerning their acquisition of the pistols and ammunition, and both denied knowing certain people that they did know, including Boda.*

    d. *Neither Sacco (age 29) nor Vanzetti (age 32) had any previous criminal record.*

1. On the basis of the possession of arms and the telling of falsehoods in the interrogation, the prosecution argued that Sacco and Vanzetti had given evidence of "consciousness of guilt" of the Bridgewater and South Braintree hold-ups. From the evidence that you have at this point, rate the reliability of the inference that Sacco and Vanzetti's conduct showed "consciousness of guilt."

———————————————————————

    e. *The police interrogation of both Sacco and of Vanzetti began with questions about their political opinions and whether they belonged to certain radical groups including the Communist Party and the IWW. In neither interrogation was mention made of the holdups at Bridgewater or South Braintree.*

    f. *Both Sacco and Vanzetti were Italian immigrants, and both were anarchists who actively associated with radical groups.*

    g. *Boda was a Communist.*

    h. *The Department of Justice was engaged in a campaign to round up and deport aliens holding Communist or other radical views. Sacco and Vanzetti both had radical friends who had been deported.*

    i. *In January or February 1920, Sacco's employer had told him that he was under investigation by the Department of Justice.*

    j. *Both Sacco and Vanzetti were pacifists and draft-evaders.*

2. On the basis of this evidence, rate the defense hypothesis that Sacco and Vanzetti exhibited "consciousness of guilt" relating to draft evasion and political activities which could result in the Department of Justice bringing deportation proceedings against them or their friends.

———————————————————————

3. Since (1) and (2) present alternative hypotheses, rate degree of confidence you have in whichever theory you regard as the better supported. If you regard the theories as equally supported, then give your rating concerning either one being true.

———————————————————————   ———————————————————————

Prosecution's Eyewitness Identification of Sacco and Vanzetti

k. *Lillian Splain testified that she saw the getaway car from a second-story window as it was being driven away from the scene of the crime. She identified Sacco as standing between the front and back seat of the car.*

l. *Frances Devlin testified that she saw the getaway car from a second-story window along with Splain. She identified Sacco as in the car.*

m. *Carlos Goodridge testified that a man in the getaway car had poked a gun at him during the getaway; he identified Sacco as the man.*

n. *Michael Levangie, the gate-tender at the railway crossing which the getaway car passed over, testified that Vanzetti was the driver of the car.*

Defense Cross-Examination of the Eyewitness for the Prosecution

o. *Lillian Splain, according to her own testimony at the trial, had 1 1/2 to 3 seconds to observe a man previously unknown to her who was 60 to 80 feet away and was moving 15 to 18 miles per hour. Yet she claimed to recall twelve features of the man's appearance, including the size of his hand and the color of his eyebrows.*

p. *Neither Splain nor Devlin had been certain of their identification of Sacco when first questioned, nor had they been required to pick Sacco from a lineup when they were first introduced to him.*

q. *Goodridge had a poor reputation for veracity, had been convicted of several petty thefts, was wanted on an indictment for theft in the State of New York, and used the name "Carlos Goodridge" as an alias, his real name being Erastus Whitney.*

r. *All accounts except for that of Levangie agreed that the driver of the car was a light-haired, sickly-looking man. Vanzetti had black hair. The prosecution agreed that Levangie was mistaken in placing Vanzetti as the driver and argued that his testimony should be taken as an observation of Vanzetti in the back seat.*

4. On the basis of the eyewitness evidence, state your assessment of the reliability of the hypothesis that

Sacco was in the getaway car. _____

Vanzetti was in that getaway car. _____

Ballistics Testimony by Expert Witnesses

s. *The marks a bullet receives as it passes through the barrel of a pistol often are distinctive enough to determine the particular pistol to which the bullet is linked. But this type of identification is not always clear and undisputable. Two witnesses for the prosecution were taken as testifying that one of the bullets that killed Berardelli came from Sacco's Colt .32-caliber pistol, while two witnesses for the defense testified that the bullet had not been fired through that pistol.*

t. *No .38-caliber bullets, the type fitting Vanzetti's gun, were used in the crime.*

u. *The other five bullets used in the crime came from a Savage .32 automatic pistol.*

5. Assuming that as a juror you consider the ballistics testimony as establishing beyond a reasonable doubt that one of the bullets that killed Berardelli came from Sacco's pistol, and considering all the other evidence in the case, rate the strength of your conviction that

Sacco participated in the South Braintree holdup. _____

Vanzetti participated in the South Braintree holdup. _____

Opportunities to Commit the Crime

v. *Sacco was regularly employed, but on the date of the South Braintree murder, April 15, he had taken the day off. He testified that on April 15 he had gone to get a passport to visit Italy, but the passport had not been issued because his pictures were too large.*

w. *Vanzetti was a fish peddler in Plymouth and claimed to have been engaged in this occupation on April 15.*

x. *A number of witnesses for the defense supported Sacco and Vanzetti's alibis given in (v) and (w) above.*

y. *Other witnesses for the prosecution testified to having seen Sacco or Vanzetti in South Braintree on April 15 at various places and times before the holdup.*

z. *Neither Sacco nor Vanzetti was shown to have had any previous connection with or knowledge about the operation of the Slater & Morrill Shoe Factory. Neither were shown to have received any money of unaccounted-for origin or to have changed their living style after the holdup. Neither had a car.*

6. For each of the three possibilities given below, state how the testimony reported in (v)–(z) above affect the hypothesis that Sacco and Vanzetti participated in the South Braintree holdup.

If you accept the defense witnesses as correct.

If you accept the prosecution witnesses as correct.

If you conclude that the testimony is in such conflict that it is impossible to determine which set of witnesses is correct.

Confession of Celestino Medeiros[7]

aa. *In November 1925, after Sacco and Vanzetti had been convicted, one Medeiros voluntarily wrote a note: "I here by confess to being in the South Braintree shoe company crime and Sacco and Vanzetti was not in said crime." [sic]*

bb. *At the time of writing this note, Medeiros was awaiting the outcome of an appeal from his conviction for murder during a holdup in Wrentham.*

cc. *Medeiros gave as his motive for making the confession that he was sorry for Sacco's kids who he saw visiting in jail, and that he did not like to see two innocent men go to the electric chair.*

dd. *Medeiros steadfastly refused to reveal the identity of others associated with him in the South Braintree holdup.*

ee. *In response to questioning, Medeiros did indicate that three of his associates were of Italian origin and the driver of the car was "Polish or Finland or something northern Europe."*

ff. *Besides refusing to identify any associates, Medeiros' description of the holdup was vague on many points, wrong on a detail about which Medeiros had expressed uncertainty himself, and right in stating that the escape car had stopped to ask directions at a house at the corner of Oak and Orchard St., a previously unknown detail.*

gg. *Shortly after the South Braintree crime, Medeiros had $2,800 in the bank, an amount approximately equal to one participant's share of the South Braintree holdup. (Undisputed evidence established five participants and $15,800 taken.)*

[7]The Medeiros confession was unknown to the jury since it came after Sacco and Vanzetti had been convicted. Since the presiding judge denied a motion for a new trial based upon the confession, the many leads that it opened up were never properly investigated.

hh. *Medeiros had a long record of crime including theft, robbery, and murder. His reputation for veracity was extremely poor.*

ii. *James F. Weeks, an associate of Medeiros in the Wrentham holdup, signed an affidavit stating that Medeiros had several times told him that the South Braintree holdup was done by the Joe Morelli gang. This gang consisted of the five Morelli brothers—Joe, Mike, Pasquale, Fred, and Frank—and Billy Barone.*

jj. *John J. Richards, U.S. Marshall for the District of Rhode Island and active in the prosecution of the Morellis, confirmed Weeks' account of the membership of the gang and added Tony Mancini and "Steve the Pole."*

kk. *The Morelli gang members were professional criminals well known to the Providence and New Bedford police. In April 1920, several members of the Morelli gang were under indictment for theft of shoe shipments from the Slater & Morrill Shoe Factory in South Braintree. All members of the gang except Fred Morelli and Billy Barone were at liberty on April 15, 1920.*

ll. *Several who had been witnesses identifying Sacco or Vanzetti at the trial declared that pictures they were shown of Joe Morelli looked like Sacco. Pictures of "Steve the Pole" showed him to be a blond of slight physical stature fitting all descriptions of the driver of the getaway car except for Levangie's identification of Vanzetti as the driver.*

mm. *Joe Morelli had a .32 Colt pistol and Tony Mancini had a pistol of the type and caliber of the other five bullets used in the crime.*

nn. *In April 1920, the Morelli gang had a need for a substantial sum of money to pay the expense of their defense against their indictment for theft.*

oo. *The Morelli gang had a Buick of the type used in the South Braintree holdup. The tracks of the smaller car that led away from the abandoned Buick were not made by Boda's car.*

7. Accepting as true the material you have concerning the Morelli brothers and their associates, compare the hypothesis that this group committed the South Braintree holdup with the case the State presented against Sacco and Vanzetti. Make your comparison in two columns covering the aspects listed below and any other aspects of the case that you care to add. For each aspect of the situation, check the hypothesis which better accommodates the facts. Be prepared to defend your choices.

	S. & V. Hypothesis	Morelli Hypothesis
Character of the accused		
Motive		
Opportunity to commit the crime		
Possession of money		

	S. & V. Hypothesis	Morelli Hypothesis
Completeness of explanation	_____	_____
Additional comparisons:		
_____	_____	_____
_____	_____	_____
_____	_____	_____

chapter 16

Analogy

In discussing the fallacy of false analogy we noted that analogy is one of the most common and one of the most abused ways of thinking. Here we will take a closer look at the subject. What we seek is to develop standards for fairly evaluating analogies so that we will neither make the mistake of pooh-poohing sound ones nor be taken in by comparisons that do not support any conclusion.

When are two things or two situations analogous? We may set down that a sound analogy exists where the comparison shows:

1. A number of essential similarities within the area of the comparison
2. An absence of essential differences within the area of the comparison

Two situations are analogous whenever these requirements—presence of essential similarities and absence of essential differences—are met. Reasoning by analogy, however, involves one more step. This step is to notice a characteristic found in one of the things or situations compared which is not known about the other. On the basis of the similarities and the absence of differences, one reasons that the pattern of similarity is likely to continue so that the feature known to exist in the first situation may be found in the second also. No one can be sure that the analogy will continue to hold, but a strong analogy does create a likelihood of further correspondence. Granted, it will take confirmation by observation or other evidence before the expectation of further correspondence will become reliable.

Let's apply the criteria for a sound analogy as given above to the proverbial try-it-on-the-guinea-pig analogy. Even though you may feel that the answer is fairly obvious, we will take a step-by-step approach to create a clear illustration. We will assume that our problem is to assess the effect a new drug is likely to have on humans by applying it first to guinea pigs.

Step 1 is to identify the area of comparison. In this case, the area of comparison is guinea pig and human responses to drugs.

Step 2 is to consider whether there are essential similarities which make it likely that guinea pigs and human beings will exhibit similar physical responses to drugs. Both are mammals. Placing both in the class "mammals" means that they have many essential physical similarities: warm blood, heart, circulatory system, lungs, kidneys, liver, nervous system, etc.

Step 3 is to consider essential differences in the area related to physical responses. For one thing, the guinea pig is herbivorous, while man is omnivorous, so the analogy may not hold well in the area of digestion. Size is a difference that has to be compensated for by proportional doses. Other differences exist.

So, how strong is the guinea pig/human being analogy in the area of physical responses? Strong enough to create a reasonable expectation that physical responses obtained in guinea pigs are likely to occur similarly if a comparable treatment is applied to a human being. As you know, guinea pigs, rats, mice, dogs, chimpanzees, rhesus monkeys, and many other species serve as laboratory animals to reach conclusions which, if the results are satisfactory, eventually will be applied to people. Obviously, some of these laboratory animals have greater essential similarity to a human being than do others. Why, then, use such a range of animals? Well, expense and space are factors favoring small animals; further, their quick reproduction may be a positive advantage in the study of eugenics. Work started with small animals may be checked on the rhesus monkey or some other primate more closely analogous to a human being before undertaking a potentially dangerous application to a human volunteer. The history of the Salk vaccine against polio is a case in point. For the ten years that medical researchers worked identifying the virus and developing a vaccine, they checked the immunization on monkeys and chimpanzees. Initial application of the vaccine to humans was on a limited scale, and there was division in the medical profession as to whether the testing had been sufficiently exhaustive before widespread inoculation was undertaken. There is a case for caution even when the analogy is a close one, as in moving from one human being to another. Individual reactions to food or drugs may differ. Since the closest of analogies may break down, conclusions reached by analogy have to be kept tentative.

Before leaving the guinea pig example or, better, the laboratory animal example, we should face up to one question: How does one know which similarities are essential and which are not essential within a particular area of comparison? This question has to be answered through knowledge of the material. Very often there is no difficulty over the point—for example, no laboratory technician would consider that the color of a guinea pig's fur made any difference to most experiments he might devise. Sometimes it takes special knowledge of the problem to realize which similarities are and which are not essential to the comparison being made.

Analogy is much used. The mechanic is using analogy when he seeks to repair a lawnmower by applying his knowledge of some other lawnmower that operates on similar principles. Or, to take an intangible situation, the legislative committee considering a statute revising automobile insurance requirements in its state may study the insurance laws and the kind of results arising under them in a neighboring state. Or, again, the realtor who is listing a house for sale will review prices recently obtained for property of similar quality in the area, and will use analogy to recommend a price in line with those sales. Indeed, everyone uses analogy in trying to figure out something about new problems on the basis of knowledge of some similar situation.

Even though using analogy to reach tentative conclusions about new problems is a common and useful way of reasoning, many seem inclined to downgrade the method. "That is only an analogy" crops up as a charge in discussion. Logic books, too, sometimes give the subject cursory treatment after toiling long and earnestly with that haven of certainty, the syllogism. Why so? Well, analogy is the weakest type of induction and even a strong one is not anywhere near as reliable as a well-supported generalization or theory. A conclusion reached by analogy should always be confirmed by an observation if it is feasible to do so. Further, analogies run through a range from strong to useful and on to a point of weakness where no inference is justified. Moreover, far-fetched comparisons sometimes are urged where lack of essential similarities makes it fallacious to reason from such a comparison.

To develop a feeling for the relative strength of analogies, we will examine a set of analogies that run from strong to weak. Suppose you have a Ford V-8 that won't run, little money, and several good friends. Your friends all like to tinker with their cars, and each has become thoroughly acquainted with the engine of his own vehicle. These vehicles are: a blue Ford the same year and model as yours, which is red; a Volkswagen one year newer than yours, a motorcycle the same age as your car, and a Stanley Steamer which your best friend resurrected from his grandfather's barn and rebuilt. You regard all your friends as equally competent. Since you want to get your car back on the road, you've made the coldblooded decision to call your friends in the order of which one is most likely to get the job done. In what order would you make your calls?

It certainly isn't taxing to pick out the best order. What we want to think about is how we explain the choices in terms of analogy. The friends are being called to work upon an "internal combustion gasoline Ford automobile engine." Clearly, the friend who will have the advantage of the greatest number of essential similarities and the fewest differences is the one who owns another Ford of the same model.

What about the Volkswagen? It, too, has an "internal combustion gasoline automobile engine." But it's a *Volkswagen*. Please don't be too negatively impressed by this difference—some of my students seem to react as if I might as well have suggested calling an experienced camel driver. The friend who understands his Volkswagen engine is dealing with a situation having many essential similarities to the functioning of a Ford. He is a reasonable choice to call and his chance of successful use of analogy is considerable. There is more chance of encountering differences; for example, he will discover that the Ford engine is water-cooled rather than air-cooled.

Now for the motorcycle friend. He is familiar with an "internal combustion gasoline engine." This is relevant to the problem. Pity it isn't an automobile engine, though. So the analogy is weaker and the points of breakdown—of lack of correspondence—greater.

The Stanley Steamer owner? There's no useful analogy here with respect to how the engines run, for the principles are different. Might as well head for the garage as take up the time of this fellow.

Analogy and generalization work together. In practice, knowledge limited to a single analogous case is the exception rather than the rule; for example, it is unlikely that the friend who tinkered with his car would work on the Ford from a knowledge of his car alone, having had no experience with any other car. Likewise, the medical experiment performed with rats hardly will be applied by analogy to humans after testing on a single rat! The researcher will experiment with a group of rats sufficient to form a reliable generalization about the reaction *of rats.* Then comes the step taken by analogy whereby it is proposed that the rats and a human being are essentially similar within the respect compared, say in their reaction to the lack of a certain vitamin, so that the human being subjected to conditions similar to those of the rats probably will exhibit a similar reaction. Does it make any difference whether the conclusion drawn is limited to a particular human being or extends to human beings as a class? Clearly not. *It is projecting from one class to another upon a foundation of essential similarity and absence of essential differences which makes an argument analogical.* This is not affected by whether the comparison relates to a group or to a particular instance only.

In law, arguments often take the form of showing that a given case falls under a precedent, or, in other words, that the case is analogous to some previously decided case. And the courts commonly decide the meaning of a statute by examining whether or not a particular situation is analogous to the situation with which the statute was designed to deal. The case of *Omaha and Council Bluffs Street Railway Company* vs. *Interstate Commerce Commission* (230 U.S. 324) will illustrate this use of analogy. The Supreme Court had to decide whether the statute granting the Commission jurisdiction to regulate interstate "railroads" applied to a streetcar line that crossed a state border. Some state courts had previously held that streetcar lines were "railroads" in the sense of the statute; others had held that they were not. Mr. Justice Lamar gave the Supreme Court's decision as follows:

> This conflict of state court decisions is not so great as at first blush would appear. For all recognize that while there is similarity between railroads and street railroads, there is also a difference. Some courts, emphasizing the simi-

larity, hold that in statutes the word "Railroad" includes Street Railroad, unless the contrary is required by context. Others, emphasizing the dissimilarity, hold that "Railroad" does not include Street Railroad unless required by the context. . . .

Mr. Justice Lamar then proceeded to examine whether the similarities of street-car lines and railroads made the two analogous *for the purpose of regulation by the Interstate Commerce Commission.* He pointed out that railroads were not characteristically local in their business; they connected with other lines to move freight across the country; they were prone to engage in rebating, pooling, and discrimination (which the statute was designed to regulate); they operated elaborate stations and terminal facilities. Streetcar lines, on the contrary, were primarily local; rarely connected with other lines covering widespread areas; did a passenger business unsuited to rebating, pooling, or discrimination; and generally picked up and deposited passengers on the street. Noting these differences, the Court decided that a streetcar line could not be included by analogy as a "railroad" subject to Interstate Commerce Commission regulation.

This decision is typical of the careful application of analogy in legal reasoning. The comparison is limited to similarities and differences which are relevant to the question at hand. It is quite possible that on the next day the Court might have considered a streetcar line included by analogy as a railroad for the purpose of taxation or for some other purpose in which the similarities might be more relevant than the differences.

Most of the analogies we have examined so far have involved concrete or easily visualized situations. Analogies may also be drawn in situations that are not tangible, and they may be proposed even though there are more differences than we would like. Historians and economists sometimes bring out parallels between one set of circumstances and another, seeking to reach conclusions from past experience. The analogies are weak where, as usually happens, the differences are great; the very use of analogy may be in desperation because numerous identical "cases" are unavailable to give firm support for generalizations in these fields. Very likely, applying analogy to areas in which close parallels are hard to come by has contributed to the downgrading of the method which we mentioned earlier. Yet if one does not utilize generalizations and analogies more tenuous than one would like, the alternative may be simply to reach conclusions on unsupported hunches that are worse than an attempt to sift the evidence into a rational argument. So I will illustrate the use of analogy in a social science problem by discussing a question that confronts us all—the question of world order. You may not agree with the conclusions. That is not the point. What I want to focus on is the evaluation of similarities and differences in a problem not so obvious as a Ford car.

For thousands of years, whether humankind has been organized into tribes, city-states, feudal entities, monarchies not conforming to ethnic lines, or modern national states, people have fought with other people organized in other independent groups. As long as the means of force have been institutionalized in some group independent of any control, there always has been war. Here is one historical generalization we can surely make: Groups possessing uncontrolled power to wage war get into conflicts and do so. White Europeans, yellow and brown Asians, red American Indians and black Africans—all have done this repeatedly.

Is there any way to control war in human society? Clearly, an absence of control—that is, an anarchy of unrestrained states—does not produce peace. What about a collective organization such as the League of Nations? As a device for preventing international war, the League's twenty-year struggle was largely in vain. Its membership was not universal, it lacked power to make its own members follow its decisions, it lacked a judiciary with compulsory jurisdiction over international conflicts, there was no force to carry out its recommendations, no revenues could be raised by the organization directly, its personnel could be and were sometimes prevented from making inspections, armaments mounted with the League powerless to limit them. Wars were waged which the League could not prevent. So low did League prestige sink that when Hitler launched World War II, no state even bothered to officially inform the League or lodge a protest.

Though stronger than the League, the United Nations is dismayingly close to it in powerlessness. We will only have to change tense. Though membership in the United Nations, unlike the League, is nearly universal, still the United Nations lacks power to make its members follow its decisions, it lacks a judiciary with compulsory jurisdiction over international conflicts, there is no force to carry out its recommendations, no revenues can be raised by the organization directly, its personnel can be and sometimes are prevented from making inspections, armaments mount with the UN powerless to limit them. Wars are waged which the UN cannot prevent. So low is UN prestige that when World War III breaks out. . . . This analogy is getting uncomfortable.

To know what won't work is to know something. Possibly historical analogy can give us ideas beyond this. Looking at our own history, we see that in 1781 the thirteen original states adopted the Articles of Confederation, a scheme of government in which the central authority could only act indirectly through the member states. It could enforce no measure upon any individual through its own officials nor require that any state give effect to its policies where that state proved unwilling to do so. Other shortcomings soon became evident: treaty making was impaired as the leaders of foreign states began to question, "Are you one government or thirteen?", inadequate taxing power made the government's credit weak, lack of power to regulate tariffs and a chaos of state currencies hampered trade, inability to provide for an armed force made the national defense inadequate.

Profiting from the mistake of attempting government without needed powers, the leadership of the nation met and devised a federal plan which still functions as one of the oldest and most stable governments in the world. It is fair to say, however, that the United States Constitution never could have been written or agreed to without the experience of the Articles of Confederation. We will take time only for the essentials of the federal plan:

1. The federal government is limited to delegated powers, with all other powers reserved to the states. The delegation made was broad, including power to enforce federal law against individuals directly.
2. Executive, legislative, and judicial branches were created in a form practical to operate and with power shared under a system of checks and balances.
3. Certain civil liberties were enumerated and the government was barred by law from infringing upon them.

Is there a useful analogy between the experience of the United States under its federal plan of government and the possible experience of the world should it adopt a federal plan? Rather obviously, both are human organizations subject to all the loyalties and all the dishonesties of which human beings are capable. It is clear also that the notion of a world government on a federal basis is a long step from where the world is at present, and that no plan that was close in detail to the government of the United States would be suitable. The question is whether the broad principles stated under (1), (2), and (3) above are applicable by analogy to a world situation.

I propose to leave this analogy here with the suggestion that it be neither accepted uncritically nor dismissed offhand. Look for similarities and differences within the area of what makes viable government possible. Some of the factors to consider are:

- Does the selfishness and aggressiveness of man operate in both situations?
- Does the great diversity of culture throughout the world compared to the relative uniformity of language and culture within the USA invalidate the comparison?
- Does the more limited scope of jurisdiction that presumably would be suitable for a world government invalidate comparison?
- Insofar as public support is essential to the success of any plan of government, is there any reason to believe that public support such as now stabilizes the U.S. Constitution could develop to stabilize a world government?
- Does the American Civil War illustrate anything?
- Has it been feasible in the United States to maintain the system of checks and balances?
- Is it possible to accommodate both democratic and nondemocratic societies in a federal government?

There is much to think about. One may consider also the Common Market, the Swiss Federation, and a dozen other governments. The idea of applying analogy to a question so enormous and so novel may seem farfetched. Certainly, the similarities between past historical experience and a projected world government will be less and the differences greater than with some close-knit class such as cars or primates. Indeed, the application of analogy to a not-so-certain area in social science is what we are illustrating here. If the analogy is not strong, is it altogether worthless? Evaluations will differ here. Still, if you are to reason about the future you must apply the experience of the past. To use that experience you must support premises, form theories, make generalizations, or draw analogies. Though the desire to find evidence does not make the past relevant if it is not, at least one should not be in haste to exchange some evidence for none at all.

So far we have defined the elements for sound argument by analogy, discussed some analogies that are simple and clearcut, and ended with the sort of historical analogy that is provocative and debatable. In the section on fallacies we mentioned another type of analogy, sometimes called figurative analogy, which is in reality no analogy at all. As the name suggests, in a figurative analogy the resemblances are merely *figurative*. Since the requirement of *essential similarities* is lacking, no further correspondence can be expected from a mere figurative resemblance, and it is a fallacy to hold that such a comparison is support for a conclusion.

It is remarkable how often figurative comparisons have been confused with literal ones. Here is a gem from the writings of Paracelsus as presented by Aldous Huxley:

> It is worth remarking parenthetically that Paracelsus . . . owed his enthusiasm for antimony to a false analogy. "Just as antimony purifies gold and leaves no slag in it, in the same form and shape it purifies the human body." The same kind of false analogy between the arts of the metal worker and the alchemist on the one hand and the arts of the doctor and the dietician on the other led to the belief that the value of foods increased with their increasing refinement—that white bread was better than brown, that a much-stewed bouillon was superior to the unconcentrated meats and vegetables of which it was composed. It was assumed that "coarse" foods coarsened the people who ate them. "Cheese, milk and oatcakes," Paracelsus says, "cannot give one a subtle disposition." It was only with the isolation of the vitamins a generation ago, that the old false analogies with alchemy ceased to play havoc with our theories of diet.[1]

Figurative comparisons, however, have their legitimate place as colorful illustrations. They can be effective in getting a point across, particularly when an abstract situation can be explained in familiar terms that are easily visualized. Take this introduction to an essay on the law of contracts:

> The existing law of contracts with its four and seven volume treatises, and its supplementary treatises on insurance, negotiable instruments, and sales, ap-

[1]Aldous Huxley, *The Devils of Loudun* (New York: Harper & Row, 1952), p. 170.

pears not dissimilar to the reciprocating steam engine at the height of its perfection thirty years ago. Like that engine, it represents a century's refinement upon a single valuable idea. Like that engine, it has developed its idea into a complex instrument of tremendous power. Like that engine, it has evolved forced draft, feed-water heaters, super-heaters, triple expansion cylinders, condensers, and differential valve gears. To study it is an education. To drive and contemplate it is an unalloyed delight. But its designer will ultimately turn from contemplating its perfections to reflecting upon its irreducible defects. He will think of the inherent wastefulness of its heat cycle, of its bulk, of the growing difficulty of securing competent operation. He will toy with ideas of an internal combustion engine, where the fire will strike directly on the pistons, and which anyone can drive. His fingers will reach and find a pencil. He will begin to draw.[2]

Legal literature would be the poorer without this passage. The tangible intricacies of the steam engine make a vivid image with which Professor Gardner seeks to awaken his readers to the possibility of a fresh approach to the intangible, less easily visualized but equally ponderous details of the law of contracts.

Likewise, parables, fables, and cartoons are figurative analogies to illustrate the points they make, not prove them. So we see, figurative analogies make good comparisons for illustration. Danger lies in accepting them in the wrong spirit—that is, in confusing superficial resemblances with essential similarities and thereby being carried on to a conclusion. To pursue a figurative analogy as if it were a support for argument is to be taken in by a mirage. The safeguard against being misled is simple: it is the habit of putting the question whether the parallel proposed concerns things *essentially similar* within the area of the comparison.

SUMMARY

For a sound analogy to exist there must be:

1. A number of essential similarities within the area of comparison
2. An absence of essential differences within the area of comparison

Reasoning by analogy involves noting that two things or situations possess a number of essential similarities and an absence of essential differences within the area of comparison. Then, one feature *known to exist* in one situation is taken as *likely to exist* in the other. In other words, within the area of similarity the pattern of similarity is expected to continue.

[2]George K. Gardner, "An Inquiry into the Principles of the Law of Contracts," *Harvard Law Review*, 46 (1932), pp. 2–3. (copyright 1932 by The Harvard Law Review Association).

Analogies range from strong down to negligible in strength. Any analogy may break down, and it is always desirable where possible to check a conclusion based upon analogy with an observation or by other evidence.

Figurative analogies, as the name implies, lack essential similarity and therefore are useless as a basis for expectation of any further similarity. Figurative analogy may provide a colorful comparison for illustration; it should be sharply distinguished as not supporting any conclusion, even tentatively.

EXERCISES FOR CHAPTER 16
pages 266–275

I. Answer **T** for "true" or **F** for "false":

_____ 1. Whenever there are essential similarities within the respect compared, there is a sound analogy.

_____ 2. Reasoning by analogy never supports a conclusion with more than a high probability.

_____ 3. A figurative analogy is not a proper basis for argument.

_____ 4. The strongest analogies exist between members of a close-knit class because this means that there are many characteristics in common.

_____ 5. Since members of a close-knit class have many characteristics in common, such a class can have only a few members.

_____ 6. The truth of conclusions suggested by analogy should be checked in other ways.

_____ 7. Two situations which offer a strong analogy must be closely similar in all ways.

_____ 8. A comparison for illustration usually is a sound literal analogy.

_____ 9. Things analogous in some respects may differ widely in other respects.

_____ 10. Any analogy may break down.

_____ 11. For an analogy to be sound there must be not only a number of essential similarities but also an absence of essential differences within the area of comparison.

_____ 12. Historical analogies generally are weak because historical situations always present numerous differences.

_____ 13. The "area of comparison" for an analogy is the respect in which the comparison is being made.

_____ 14. One human being is closely analogous to another in the area of response to medical treatment, so that it is likely that a treatment successful with one human will succeed with another.

_____ **15.** Analogies drawn in the fields of history and economics embody so many essential differences that they are best set aside as not providing support for any conclusion.

_____ **16.** In law, to say that a precedent is to be "distinguished" from a situation at hand, is to argue that the two situations are not analogous because of some essential difference affecting the legal principles to be applied.

_____ **17.** Figurative analogies are deceptive and never should be employed.

_____ **18.** An analogy may rest upon a comparison of the characteristics of two particular cases, or it may rest upon characteristics exhibited by a group of cases.

_____ **19.** Sometimes analogy is utilized in supporting a conclusion because of the difficulty of finding clearcut cases that will support a reliable generalization on the subject.

_____ **20.** No conclusion can be supported by a figurative analogy.

II.   We read in the paper, "_The play 'Trees are Green' is a lively farce about bachelors which has been tremendously popular with both the reviewers and theater-going public here in Boston. Producer and cast alike are confident of a good reception when they hit Broadway next month. And with reason, too._"

1. What is the area of comparison?

2. Make a list of similarities between Boston and New York which are essential similarities within the area of public response to plays, or, in other words, things you think would make public reception of a play similar in the two cities.

3. Make a list of differences between Boston and New York which you consider would make the public reception of a play different in the two cities.

4. Look over your lists for essential similarities and essential differences. As you know from the information given, "Producer and cast alike are confident of a good reception when they hit Broadway next month." Evaluate the degree of support that you consider the analogy gives to this conclusion:

    a. Strong support
    b. Fair support
    c. A slight support
    d. Not worth considering as support

Defend your choice.

III.   Identify the area of comparison for each of the following proposed analogies. Then point out the similarities and differences that should be considered in making an evaluation for each. In the blanks provided, enter the letter corresponding to your evaluation on the (a) through (d) scale listed above. Defend your choices.

_____   **1.** The fossil bones of the Great American Cat show it to have stood 3 feet high at the shoulder, possessed teeth suited to grip prey and tear flesh, and had a leg structure that made it capable of fast running. The animal appears to have been a predator subsisting on large game much as do modern lions and tigers. (Bones of the Great American Cat recovered from the La Brea tar pits are on display at the Los Angeles County Museum.)

_____   **2.** Paul, age 12, is being taken to an evening movie while his brother Peter, age 8, is being left at home. "If Paul goes, I should get to go, too," wails Peter.

_____   **3.** Sound financial policies for a nation are comparable to the prudent management of a household. The prudent householder saves up a bit for a rainy day, and he most certainly does not go into debt year after year because that will end in bankruptcy. States, too, should accumulate a surplus where possible and always be ready to try hard to avoid a deficit.

_____   **4.** A dangerous criminal, like a wild beast, threatens the security of the people. Society gains when a dangerous beast is destroyed, and so it must gain when criminals are exterminated.

_____   **5.** The State of Washington distributes liquor through state-operated stores. Public bars are prohibited; only a private club may supply drinks to its members at a bar. In my opinion, the state monopoly of liquor dispensing has worked well in Washington and the problems in liquor control there are the same problems we face in California. Therefore, I favor California adopting a liquor control law similar to the Washington statute, except that the clause permitting "clubs" to maintain bars should be changed, since it has led to abuses. California liquor control should then be as good as liquor control in Washington and, as far as the phony "club" situation is concerned, it might be better.

_____   **6.** In (5) substitute "Pakistan" for "California." Evaluate the strength of this new analogy.

IV.   In a sandy bank you discover six white objects, cylindrical in shape but with rounded ends, similar to some large pills. Each object is about 1 1/2 inches long and its covering is leathery, strong but pliant. You have never seen anything like these objects before, so, your curiosity aroused, you take them home and place them in a shoebox. Next day you are pleased to find a small turtle, a bit of shriveled-up shell, and five of the white objects in your box.

1. What do you now expect is contained in the other five white objects?

2. Are you using analogy to reach your conclusion?

3. Are you using a generalization to reach your conclusion?

V. A series of cases known to lawyers as the "turntable cases" has established that a railroad will be liable for damages if a child is injured when playing with a turntable that has been left unlocked or otherwise unguarded. Posting a "No Trespassing" or other warning sign is not sufficient to avoid liability. The theory is that a turntable is an "attractive nuisance" which tempts trespassing children to turn it in play and, thereby, run a risk of injury.

A child entered the property of a chemical company and discovered a large abandoned quarry filled with apparently clear water. The quarry was distinctly posted "No Swimming." The child went swimming and was injured by chemical wastes that had been disposed of in the quarry.

Should the theory of the "turntable cases" be applied to hold the chemical company liable for damages? Argue the case on both sides. Use analogy to the "turntable cases" when arguing for liability. Distinguish the "turntable cases" when arguing against liability.

VI. The following exercise describes a situation which, incidentally, I have twice put to practical use. *Answer the questions as if you were living in the early years of World War II.*

> **a.** *Besides the loss of life, the participation of the United States in World War I was attended by huge expenditure, unbalanced budgets, scarcity of labor and materials for civilian needs, economic dislocation, and inflation. Inflation continued after the war in all nations that participated actively in the war. Houses and buildings of all kinds rose in price.*
>
> *With the advent of World War II, the United States again undertook huge expenditure and unbalanced budgets. Labor for civilian needs was curtailed to an even greater extent in order to fill military requirements.*

1. Are the situations similar enough to make a useful analogy supporting the conclusion that World War II will be attended by inflation so that during and after the war the price of houses and buildings of all sorts will rise?

> **b.** *In the course of the war you learn that the government is establishing a rationing system, price control for many materials, and rent control. These measures were not undertaken during World War I.*

2. Are these essential differences between the two situations? How do they affect the strength of the analogy?

    c. *Add to the above information that you have learned in a history course that after World War I there was serious inflation in every nation that participated in that war.*

3. Does this information provide you with a sufficient number of similar cases to support as a generalization the statement "War stimulates inflation"? Comment on the problems encountered in making such a generalization and on the degree of its reliability. Is the proposed generalization empirical or explained?

    d. *Thinking about the matter further, you recall an economics course in which you learned that purchasing power in the hands of consumers at a time when consumer goods are in short supply tends to produce inflation as consumers compete to buy the few goods available. Channeling labor into the production of war materials while reducing the production of consumer goods creates—in the absence of heavier taxes, bond buying, or other offsetting possibilities—a situation in which consumers have money to spend on a reduced supply of goods. Therefore, unless effective controls are introduced, war will be attended by inflation.*

4. How does this information bear upon the generalization suggested in (c) above?

    e. *Musing further about your history course, you recall that price control was tried during the decline of the Roman Empire, following the Black Death in the Middle Ages, during the French Revolution, and by numbers of modern states during and after World War I. Though one cannot readily estimate what effect these various attempts to prevent inflation may have had in reducing its rate, one can say that considerable inflation did continue in all cases despite the legislation against it.*

5. Does this knowledge affect your evaluation of factor described in (b) above?

part four

Language

chapter 17

Nature and Uses of Language

All or, at the very least, almost all reflective thinking is carried on in language. In fact it is difficult to imagine thought going on without words to think with. When we pointed out that symbolic logic gained freedom from the "distraction" of meaning by employing symbols, we were not implying that symbolic logic is divorced from language: all the symbols of mathematics, chemistry, symbolic logic—such as $\div$, xy, CO_2, or $\not>$—are a special language for designating concepts with economy and clarity. In sum, reasoning regularly involves using the symbols of some sort of language.

Tracing the pitfalls of language can lead to becoming overimpressed with its inadequacies. Even though language is an imperfect medium for thought and though it plagues us with difficulties, I want to make a positive and rather obvious beginning: more often than not, language serves its purposes well enough and without misleading. At the same time, it is possible to speak a language for a lifetime without fully realizing its uses or its limitations. Only in recent times, with Alfred Korzybski (1879–1950) as its most outstanding exponent, has semantics (the study of the relationship between language and thought) received widespread attention.

WORDS SHOULD NOT BE CONFUSED WITH THINGS

Words are symbols. *Just symbols.* Obvious though this seems, probably every child starts off by believing that the things with which he becomes familiar are extensions of the words which he has learned to designate them. Many peoples take words to have a magic influence, so that the mere saying of a name or a charm formula is believed to influence events. The ancient Egyptians believed the doors to heaven could be opened by a recitation of the names of all the parts of the door: its handle, boards, spikes, hinges, etc. Widespread among primitive peoples is the taboo against using one's own name, which rests upon belief that knowledge of a person's true name will give the possessor of that knowledge the power to work evil against the named individual. Mystic confusion connecting words with the things they stand for is especially strong in young children. Words are not things, and as adults, we need to break that lingering link from childhood when we believed them to be associated with things. Whether expressed in written marks or sound or Braille dots, words remain merely symbols. A language is just a particular set of symbols. And, the symbols may outrun the things in the real world. Thus we have plays and novels dealing with fictitious characters who, sometimes, are placed in fictitious places.

SOME WAYS IN WHICH LANGUAGE SHAPES THOUGHT

Many people who are aware that language is said to influence thinking could not explain the ways in which language does direct the mind. Here are some of the ways:

Words direct thought into the classes they suggest.   In studying deduction we had to consider exactly what each term designated. We noted also that language generally evolves single words for the things or situations that are most important to its users or that are obvious "natural" classes—dog, cabbage, frozen. Whatever words a language generates, concepts outrun them and are described with phrases—second-hand furniture, and so on. The words and phrases that make up a person's vocabulary direct his thinking to the situations they describe. "Teenager" is a good example. The word is a comparative newcomer to English and with its coming we have in a sense created the group, now much attended to, but not so much thought of in days when no word suggested the notion. Again, as was remarked earlier in this book, it is useful to have descriptive names for the most common fallacies because the terminology alerts one to be on the lookout for the kinds named.

Words may suggest the existence of what they describe.   Everybody is aware of fiction. So, we can dismiss the occasional character who, like Don Quixote, has trouble distinguishing fact from fancy. When a situation is understood to be imaginary, then no confusion results. We saw with *Word Magic,* however, that some words or phrases may have nothing in the real world behind them—like "unicorn." And we discussed that greatest joke of all, words that defy investigation of whether or not they refer to anything that exists—like "destiny." Yet words like *unicorn* and *destiny* and many others do on occasion suggest the existence of what they describe. They can become decoys to lead us astray. It is not our purpose here to identify any particular word or notion as an instance of Word Magic, but we make the point that the coining of a word or phrase does not assure that the designated notion relates some reality.

Words influence observation.   As well as directing thought into the classes they suggest, the terms a person commands influence the observations he makes. The artist with a well-developed vocabulary for colors is led to observe color carefully enough to select the appropriate word from the rich variety of choices his vocabulary permits. Benjamin Lee Whorf provided a much-cited example of the Eskimo language containing many words for various conditions of snow. It's plausible enough that the importance of snow to an Eskimo would lead to a refined classification in his language, and the ample vocabulary in turn would direct the user of that language to observe *which* of his several available word choices was appropriate.

Influence of the emotive element in language.   The emotive power of language is, in my opinion, the most pervasive kind of influence that language exerts over thought. Everyone is constantly exposed to descriptions in which emotive overtones are put to work to encourage acceptance or to rouse hostility. This subject has been discussed already and can be reviewed at pp. 27–31.

Terminology contributes to—or hinders—thought processes.   We introduced this chapter by noting that the symbols of mathematics, chemistry, and symbolic logic are shorthand ways for setting down what it would be more cumbersome to express in words. A good terminology may assume a power of its own by enabling people to manipulate values and to penetrate to areas of knowledge that would be unreachable without the special terminology. One thinks at once of the invention of the zero, and of the limitations that would burden mathematics if Roman numerals had been retained. Likewise, symbolic logic permits the relationships of a complex sentence to be reduced to a single symbol that is not only concise but also far easier for the mind to follow.

Now that we have seen a number of ways in which language influences thought, let's take a look at some of the different purposes for which language is used.

THE DIFFERENT USES OF LANGUAGE

The most prosaic phone call ordinarily illustrates several distinct uses of language.

Henry: "Hello, John, how are you?"

John: "Fine. How are you?"

Henry: "I can't complain. Isn't it nice weather we're having?"

John: "It certainly is."

Henry: "I called up about the plan to widen Washington Street, which means cutting down those magnificent elms near Upland Road. It will be a pity if everybody rests on his oars until it's too la... Damn! Excuse me. The phone book slipped off my lap and I jiggled the coffee on the table. Well, where was I? Oh, I don't want those fine elms to go to the buzz saw."

This will do for a start. The conversation begins with an attention-getting word followed by an enquiry, "How are you?" This greeting does not seek information about health—rather its purpose is to maintain good relations by saying in effect, "I hope that you are getting along all right and I am taking the trouble to politely inquire about your welfare." John interprets the remark correctly and returns the polite form to Henry, who proceeds to prolong this phase of the conversation by remarking about the nice weather, a bit of information that John presumably knows. John comes through with agreement as expected. So far, language has been employed to express polite respect and common ground, and no serious exchange of information has taken place. Now Henry gets down to the true purpose of his call, to enlist John's support of a move to prevent cutting some trees. A minor accident intervenes, drawing an expletive mild enough not to be deleted. Expletives are largely habit, a response used to relieve frustration. After communicating to the presumably curious John what has happened, Henry returns to the subject of his call. One can't say whether the words "Well, where was I?" are used as a stall for Henry to gather his wits or are a device to reorient John to a return to informative discourse. Perhaps this has been enough to show language put to a variety of uses even in the simplest exchanges. Now we will take a brief look at these uses, one by one.

Informative Use

There is no need to make the case that conveying information is the chief function of language. What one needs to become aware of is language functions in addition to this.

Interrogative Use

Obtaining information is the chief purpose of questions, obviously. Questions also have a use keeping communication channels open by exhibiting a polite regard for others. "How are you?" "It's a nice day, isn't it?" are questions in form only and seek no serious answer. Occasionally a question is rhetorical, in which case it amounts to an assertion.

Directive Use

A command is the obvious case of directive language. "Stop pushing." Very often one is not firmly set in a driver's seat that will permit issuing blunt commands, and even where authority exists, tact may recommend minimizing this fact by ostensibly nonimperative forms. "Would you work on the windows today." may be a directive properly punctuated with a period. Directive situations range from situations of legal obligation to circumstances lacking any formal obligation at all. Regardless of whether there is any sort of obligation to obey, there are numerous times when we would like others to follow our suggestions, and we adopt various directive devices in the hope that they will. Pledges of allegiance and oaths are devised to assure conformance to the norms desired by those who frame them. Mottoes such as Wellesley College's *Not to be served but to serve* are directives pithily expressed and, it is hoped, remembered and followed. Ceremonies and prayers often have the purpose of impressing the participants with rules of social conduct. "I, Will Willoughby, do take you, Madeline Swan, to be my lawful wedded wife, and foresaking all others, to love, honor, and keep until death do us part." Creeds are recited and hymns sung to remind the faithful of the beliefs that are to be upheld. A threat may help matters a bit, whether it be hellfire, a reminder about the pangs of conscience, or "Keep out—trespassers will be prosecuted."

Promises are one of the more effective ways of getting directive language followed. The bank promises to pay a favorable interest rate to lure in deposits, colleges have popularized an implied promise by publicizing the material success of their graduates compared with groups with less schooling, advertisers will promise the moon to the one who buys the antiperspirant, takes the medicine, purchases the car. As we know all too well, sometimes these promises are kept and sometimes not. Unkept promises erode trust between human beings, as is testified to by the widespread skepticism with which the promises of advertisers and politicians are received. In *Language in Thought and Action*, Hayakawa makes a moral point of the obligation not to utter directives supported by promises that arouse false expectations and end in disillusionment. "*Each of them* [disappointments over a broken promise] *serves, in greater or less degree, to break down that mutual trust that makes cooperation possible and knits people together into a society."* (Hayakawa's italics)

Language to Arouse Emotional Response

We use language to create states of mind. Who has not recited a bit of poetry to enjoy the sweet melancholy that it creates, or the laughter, or the indignation. ... One applies terms of endearment to family members or sweethearts: honey, dearest, or, perhaps some special term generated by the family. Linguistic extravaganzas can be fun: "You fill the horizon of my desire," "When the burnt-out sun drives on through darkened skies, still I will love thee," to cite a couple of my own. So we see, language has a use as a source of emotional enjoyment as well as to inform or direct.

Language to Prevent Friction and to Maintain Good Relations

When one accidentally touches another he says immediately, "Excuse me." We have many polite greetings: "How do you do," "Thank you," "You are welcome," "Have a nice day." If we go to a party there will be a lot of small talk exchanged, talk that cannot be explained as uttered for its value as information, directive purpose, or creating some emotional response. Though the conversation that never gets beyond small talk will be dull, still it would be a mistake to judge all trivial observations made at social gatherings as mirroring the intelligence of the participants. The purpose of much of the communication on such occasions is maintaining good relations, and this is no mean purpose but, rather, an important function of language which must be recognized to understand what goes on.

Language to Give Vent to Feeling

Cheers, catcalls, and expletives function chiefly as means for venting feeling. Words like "damn" and the stronger expletives are understandable; apparently they exist in all languages since all people experience life's frustrations. Unfortunately, the use of expletives can become a habit, as was illustrated by the appalling speech in the Nixon tapes. Despite this sorry example in high places, the level of taboos a person applies to his choice of expletives reflects his origins and social aspirations. No one could possibly live in soldiers' barracks and then in officers' quarters without noticing the difference in the use of profane speech.

Cheers, catcalls, hisses are interesting. Their obvious purpose is to encourage or harass, though they may be resorted to so that somebody will "get the message" in an informative or directive sense. An organized cheer is a wonderful thing, a final specimen to show the venting of feeling through language.

Though we have discussed the different functions of language under distinct subtitles, the various uses merge into one another: informative language also may have a directive purpose, language to arouse emotional response can include a measure of directive or informative intent. Nor is there a claim to completeness in this brief discussion: what about the language of deliberate insult, and what about prayer?

ABSTRACTION

To many people the word "abstract" carries the connotation of being vague, intangible, and unspecific. The rejoinder, "That's only an abstraction" crops up occasionally as if somehow abstractions were weak or unrelated to down-to-earth situations. Such a general distrust of abstraction shows ignorance about what the process is all about, for language necessarily involves forming abstractions. Yet one can overdo the process by presenting ideas at too high a level of abstraction without mentioning more specific applications, and no doubt this abuse accounts for some of the popular misgivings. Let's have a look at how the process works.

Imagine we live in a fishing village in which every family has a boat—"Gull," "Storm King," "Shangri-la;" "Lucy II," and so on. Imagine for a moment an absurdity: we have no word for boat. Now this is inconvenient. When the chief wants to give an order for no boats to go out today because of a storm or some chiefly whim, he has to enumerate "Gull" and "Storm King" and "Shangri-la" and all the others. When we discern an object out at sea that can't be identified for sure as "Gull" or "Lucy II," we are hard-put to designate the object. Our linguistic fantasy won't last long, for very soon we will generate some noise, "boat" or any other sound we decide to use to refer to the important qualities which "Storm King," "Lucy II" and the rest have in common. In creating the term "boat" we have resorted to an abstraction.

The process of abstracting is simply selecting certain qualities in common which are designated by the new term. "Boat" refers to all objects possessing certain well-known qualities, and heaven help you if you don't know what a boat is. Granted, defining a boat or anything else isn't so easy; for the moment we will let the chief call the villagers together and do some pointing and explaining about what particular features he wants to bundle together in the new word "boat."

Alfred Korzybski worked out a detailed explanation of the process of abstracting, and his work was adapted by S. I. Hayakawa in a readily under-

ABSTRACTION LADDER

Start reading from the bottom *UP*

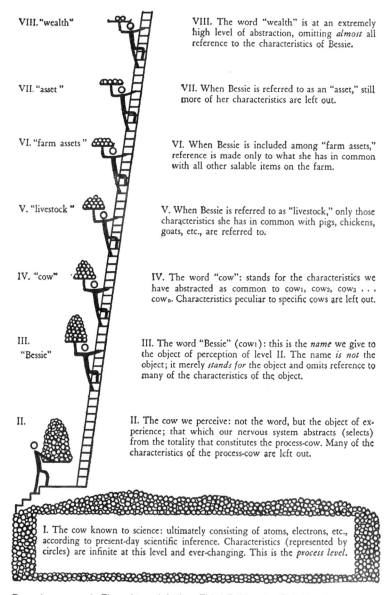

VIII. "wealth"

VIII. The word "wealth" is at an extremely high level of abstraction, omitting *almost* all reference to the characteristics of Bessie.

VII. "asset"

VII. When Bessie is referred to as an "asset," still more of her characteristics are left out.

VI. "farm assets"

VI. When Bessie is included among "farm assets," reference is made only to what she has in common with all other salable items on the farm.

V. "livestock"

V. When Bessie is referred to as "livestock," only those characteristics she has in common with pigs, chickens, goats, etc., are referred to.

IV. "cow"

IV. The word "cow": stands for the characteristics we have abstracted as common to cow_1, cow_2, cow_3 ... cow_n. Characteristics peculiar to specific cows are left out.

III. "Bessie"

III. The word "Bessie" (cow_1): this is the *name* we give to the object of perception of level II. The name *is not* the object; it merely *stands for* the object and omits reference to many of the characteristics of the object.

II.

II. The cow we perceive: not the word, but the object of experience; that which our nervous system abstracts (selects) from the totality that constitutes the process-cow. Many of the characteristics of the process-cow are left out.

I. The cow known to science: ultimately consisting of atoms, electrons, etc., according to present-day scientific inference. Characteristics (represented by circles) are infinite at this level and ever-changing. This is the *process level*.

From *Language in Thought and Action, Third Edition*, by S. I. Hayakawa, copyright © 1972 by Harcourt Brace Jovanovich, Inc. and reproduced with their permission.

standable form, the *abstraction ladder,* which we reproduce here. With the abstraction ladder one proceeds from the bottom and goes up—just as with a real ladder.

The first two steps are called "subverbal levels" which, as your examination of the ladder will show, are (I) What Bessie actually is, and (II) What we perceive her to be. The Bessie that exists is not a word; rather, according to science, she is an ever-changing dance of whirling electrons. Instead of being static as we generally think of her, Bessie really is *a process* of growth, decline, and eventual fading out of existence. So the first subverbal step of the ladder stands for what Bessie actually is—a whirl of matter that follows a slowly changing process of growth, decline, and decay.

In Level II we have Bessie as we perceive her with our sense organs. Sense organs miss a lot: they give no inkling of atoms or of the electrical impulses that make Bessie's nervous system work, etc. What sense organs report are bright colors and shades which experience has enabled us to interpret, a range of sound waves which probably will cover any sound Bessie may emit, impressions of heat and smell. So, the Bessie we perceive is just that—an impression in the mind gained from the sensory organs we happen to have. This is subverbal, a mental impression and not a word.

Now we come to words. The first verbal level is "Bessie," the name applied to this one individual cow, unique and separate from all other things in the world. The word "Bessie" is a symbol for the object and will be applied to designate the object through all its changes until one day the changes become so great that it is inappropriate to consider that the entity continues to exist.

Mounting the abstraction ladder from here on is easy. The word "cow" refers to cow_1, cow_2, cow_3 ... cow_n. All the special characteristics of Bessie and other individual cows are left out; only those properties required for membership in the class "cow" are referred to. With "livestock" one mounts to a still higher abstraction, since this word leaves out reference to the characteristics of particular animals and refers only to the quality of usefulness as an agricultural product that is common to cows, horses, sheep, and other farm animals. For further levels of abstraction, refer to the diagram and observe the constantly shrinking number of characteristics referred to as one journeys upward to high abstractions.

Applying the Abstraction Ladder

When our chief invented the word "boat," a step some prehistoric genius must have taken at some point in human development, he made it easier to carry on affairs and he began to stretch people's minds. All sorts of objects could be classified and talked about. The process is virtually endless, and the languages of primitive peoples have many high-level abstractions. More sophisticated cultures carry their linguistic abstracting further and further, and this process is both necessary and a temptation to lose touch with the real world. Here is a pronounced example of writing at too high a level of abstraction:

> Thus the concrete and qualitative reciprocities that characterize the relationships of primitive societies are replaced by the "mere form" of abstract and quantitative exchange relations of the market. And while in primitive societies the "forms" of reciprocal exchanges are closely interwoven and are virtually inseparable from "contents," from the real life—processes of the community, in modern capitalist societies the apparent "forms" of exchanges are contradicted by "contents."[1]

This sort of overabstracting sometimes develops in the work of experienced writers, making it uphill work to figure out the meaning. What has gone wrong? The trouble is that sentence after sentence consists of very high-level abstractions without any relief in the way of examples at lower levels which might give an idea of what sorts of things the writer has in mind. Even if we read the whole article we would not learn what this is all about unless at some point the high-level descriptions are related to familiar cases of the phenomena. This writer is circling around in the clouds.

It is possible to be too earthbound, too. When too many particular facts are recited, one gets in effect a description of tree after tree until one longs for a higher level of abstraction that will point out what kind of forest the trees create. As an example of this fault, consider this passage describing the financial situation of the French government in the years before the French Revolution:

> In 1775, under Turgot, the expenses are estimated at 414 1/2 millions, the receipts at 377 1/4, and the permanent debt charge at 235 1/4 millions. In 1776, under Clugny, the expenses were 402 1/2 millions and the receipts 378 1/2, while expenses charged upon future budgets amount to 50 1/2 millions. Calonne places the deficiency in this year at upwards of 37 millions. In 1784 Calonne sold to Burgundy the privilege of exemption from the *aides;* and it is estimated that, out of the total borrowing of 1647 millions between 1776 and 1786, Calonne alone borrowed 650 millions and a half, at an annual cost of 45 and a half millions, in 41 months of peace. In 1786 the expenses amounted to. . . .[2]

Here we are drowning in facts, clumsily presented, and their meaning further obscured by lack of adequate rounding, tabulating, or a graphical presentation that would help to show the overall situation. I have spared you from the much longer enumeration of assorted facts before the author finally arrives at the significance of all the details—"These figures sufficiently show the desperate financial position of the French monarchy on the eve of the Revolution. . . ."

Writers who have learned to make their meanings clear constantly vary

[1]Emil Oestereicher, "Praxis: The Dialectical Source of Knowledge," *Dialectical Anthropology*, 1, no. 3 (May 1976), 233.

[2]F. C. Montague, "The Government of France," in *The Cambridge Modern History*, Vol. VIII (New York: Macmillan, 1904), p. 74.

their levels of abstraction, using higher-level abstractions to give their statements a broad scope and lower levels to illustrate the broad assertions in action. I hope you have noticed this being done on many occasions in this book. Lest I use myself as a model, here is a sample of effective varying of abstraction levels:

> It is important to realize that vague words can be very useful. In fact, some of them are useful *because* they are vague: it is handy to be able to report that the room was "crowded," without having to calculate the number of people per square foot. . .[3]

Perhaps we have said enough to show that frequent moving up and down the abstraction ladder is the way to clarity. General assertions have many applications; examples show the kinds of things they refer to. And examples have another advantage: they add interest. Notice how attention often increases when a lecturer illustrates his point with an anecdote. Concrete situations are visualized readily because it is easy to imagine some of their many characteristics, while high-level abstractions with their nearly empty tray of common characteristics are less likely to kindle mental pictures. Test your own reaction to "Bessie," "livestock," and "asset."

Avoid using higher levels of abstraction than are needed to cover all the situations in mind. This simple rule for writing increases precision and develops clear thinking. For example, do not use the word "law" if what you mean is "statute." When you are justifiably unable to work because you are ill, the boss will be better informed (and likely more satisfied) if you name the actual physical disorder than if you merely assert, "I'm sick today." Of course, "law" and "sick" have their purposes. The word "law" is broad enough to cover constitutional provisions, statutes, legal precedents, and municipal ordinances and this is fine when the assertion applies to all these things. "Sick" may be useful when one does not care to be precise. On the other hand, accurate communication is obtained by using the lowest level of abstraction covering all the characteristics in mind.

I have a final idea about abstraction and maybe it's wandering away from the subject of *About Thinking*. I don't know. My idea is *a plea not to allow abstraction to cause a failure of imagination* as it invariably tends to do. I have had the experience of being in a German concentration camp while a steam shovel was excavating mass graves. Few Germans, I firmly believe, ever would willingly have worked in such a camp or personally abused other human beings in such sadistic ways. Unfortunately, millions of Germans worked for, voted for, cheered for a leader whose policies, whose openly proclaimed hatreds, brought about the isolation and extermination of these people. "Jew," "Pole," "Russian" are all abstractions of medium level, but a faceless man or woman or child never passed into the gas chamber. I think we all need sometimes to check ourselves, whether

---

[3]Monroe C. Beardsley, *Thinking Straight*, 2nd ed. (Englewood Cliffs, N.J.: Prentice-Hall, 1956), p. 169.

as decision makers or followers of decision makers, to ask of our abstractions, "What does this mean in lower-level terms?"

Vagueness

Who has not witnessed an attack on the vagueness of some ideal? Or of some proposal? There certainly is need to question whether terms are too vague in the use made of them. But is vagueness always objectionable? If not, *when* is vagueness objectionable? How precise is it possible to be?

Let us start with physical science as a model of the elimination of vagueness. One of the first things that impresses the beginning student of science is the difference between scientific and ordinary vocabularies. Vague terms like "warm" or "far" or "soon" are not allowed in the laboratory; they are replaced by exact measurements of temperature, distance, and time. "Mass," "energy," "velocity" have meanings specified in mathematical equations. The laws and observations are expressed in terms as free from vagueness as it is possible to make them, the language of measurement and precise definition. Compared to that vapor of vagueness which we use in the language of ordinary affairs, scientists use a language that seems a relatively perfect instrument of communication. The precise determination of categories becomes possible in science because the phenomena dealt with are concrete: physical substances can be identified beyond question and points along a continuum can be measured exactly. Degree by degree temperature rises, centimeter by centimeter distance increases, even earthquakes have their Richter scale.

The material with which social scientists are concerned is not so easily classified and measured. It is difficult to make up categories that are cleanly drawn and free from marginal cases. Think of all the treaties that have foundered on the word "aggression," a state of affairs that never can be reduced to some measurement that all nations will accept. Sometimes the diplomats do not or will not recognize whether a "war" is going on or not. Social scientists labor unsurely to determine the cause of a strike, the effect of a contraction of credit, or any number of other questions. The material resists measurement; more often than not experiment is impossible because the situation can neither be controlled nor produced again.

Social scientists are of course aware that their field is clouded by imprecise categories and many have made great efforts to devise standards that can be measured objectively. For example, though intelligence tests with their numerical results are an improvement over earlier estimates in rough categories such as "bright," "ordinary," or "slow," their limitations are widely discussed and no one supposes, even when better tests are devised, that measurement will approach the accuracy of a thermometer. Rewarding as has been the work of economists in assembling data and formulating laws, the economy remains subject to so many influences, including mass psychology, that there is no wonder when the projections fail. History is in the most trouble of all. It deals with events as amorphous as they are huge, while the evidence concerning them may be too abundant to survey or, for earlier times, it may be scanty odds and ends that have survived by happenstance. No field gives greater rein for prejudice—prejudice in the reports of the sources as well as bias in the historian trying to make sense out of it. No field offers less chance for meaningful measurement. When we say, vaguely, "History repeats itself," we do not mean like a chemical experiment. And the saying itself is only a half-truth, for the historian needs to recognize where features are unique to an age and will not repeat. In spite of the difficulties, history has lessons for those who will listen, and there is justification, it seems to me, for George Santayana's observation, "Those who do not learn from history are condemned to repeat it." Nothing is gained by deprecating the findings of social science, for people must do the best they can to resolve the problems that affect them. What we have to consider here is where vagueness in social science is permissible and where it is not. We will begin with law.

First, consider the broad scope of some terms in the United States Constitution. The Congress is given power to "regulate commerce with foreign nations and among the several States." It is declared that "The United States shall guarantee to every State in the Union a Republican form of government," and the Fourteenth Amendment provides that no state shall "deprive any person of life, liberty, or property, without due process of law." These are just a few important clauses of the constitution—notice how vague they all are. Of course, to specify all the situations that should come under them would be impossible. The point is that no attempt was made to define more precisely the application of these clauses, and well so, for a constitution should be a broad grant unfettered by descriptions so specific as to prevent interpretation to cover the unforeseeable development of society.

More commonly, however, legislatures and lawyers are concerned to avoid vagueness. In fact, when a criminal statute is vague enough to leave doubt about just what sorts of acts it prohibits, it will be declared unconstitutional because one necessary protection of civil liberty is that no one shall be punished for an act not clearly specified to be illegal. Punishment for acts prescribed in sweeping terms such as "enemy of the people" in the French Revolution, or "social parasite" under the Nazis, leaves far too much to be filled in by judicial interpretation. For this reason our legislatures and courts make a great effort to define crimes so that each offense will consist of categories which can be accurately determined with as few marginal cases as possible. "The people of the State of N charge that on or about 7:00 P.M. EST, November 4, 1978, at 100 First Street, City of X, County of Y, the accused John Doe did commit an act of burglary, to wit. . . ." The dates and times, the names of the people and places are, of course, almost always unmistakable. What of the definition of the crime, in this case burglary? The law defines this as exactly as possible so that even though, unavoidably, there can be marginal cases, still such cases are held to a minimum. A court applying common law will instruct the jury to find the accused guilty if and only if the prosecution has proved that at the times and places specified the accused did in fact (a) break and enter (b) the dwelling of another (c) in the nighttime (d) with intent to commit a felony (not necessarily theft). All these four elements are, in turn, defined to make each concept as precise as possible. To "break and enter" refers to any entrance without authority even though no door or window is moved and even though the accused only reaches in with an arm or hook; "dwelling" refers to any place of abode and its immediate outbuildings; "nighttime" receives a statutory definition as so many minutes after sunset; while "felony" is generally defined by statute as applying to any act punishable by a certain penalty, commonly over one year imprisonment. The trial will involve attempting to prove that the accused committed certain acts (as specified in the dots following "to wit" above) which fall within the legal category of burglary.

Many crimes and many civil rights are defined in ways that reduce vagueness successfully, but it would be a mistake to overlook intractable situations that cannot be made satisfactorily precise. Difficulty in defining "obscene" or "libelous" makes for endless dispute in those areas; key concepts such as "negligence" or establishment of guilt "beyond a reasonable doubt" are little aided by further definition. We are back where we started—much can be done to eliminate vagueness but, at other points, neither care nor willingness to concede an arbitrary definition for the sake of preciseness seems to work. In such cases one will be forced to use standards that are themselves subjective and vague. The judge who must decide whether a motion is "frivolous" or the jury member who must decide whether a party acted with "due care" are examples of the problem.

We will bring together the notions of permissible and impermissible vagueness:

1. In general, vagueness is to be avoided when clear categories are available. Science is insistent upon this. And in ordinary affairs it will be more informative not to employ higher levels of abstraction than are needed: avoid "tool" if "hammer" is appropriate.

2. Continuum situations by their nature contain clear extremes and marginal cases as well. (a) *When the problem to be decided involves placing a marginal case*, then an arbitrary definition will be required. "Poor" will not do for a welfare official who must have a standard to go on. (b) *Where the problem to be decided involves a clear case*, then determining a precise definition is unnecessary. No need to define a "beard" in a discussion about Henry, who obviously has one.

3. Some terms resist precise definition even though their general areas of meaning are understood well enough. Plato's "The good, the beautiful and the true" contains such terms: meaningful and yet undefinable in any precise way. Generally, it is not useful to set up standards for notions of this sort, and to insist upon an unattainable exactness is obscurantist.

SUMMARY

Some ways in which language shapes thought are:

1. Words direct thought into the classes they suggest.
2. Words may suggest the existence of what they describe.
3. Words influence observation.
4. The emotive overtones of language influence thought.
5. Terminology sometimes assumes a power of its own which contributes to—or hinders—thought processes.

Among the uses of language, one may distinguish:

1. Informative use
2. Interrogative use
3. Directive use
4. Arousing emotional response
5. Maintaining good relations
6. Giving vent to feelings

The most concrete term on the verbal level is the word that names a single specific object—"Bessie." The process of abstracting involves selecting certain qualities and referring to these qualities with a new term. "Cow" represents certain qualities Bessie has in common with other females of her species; "livestock" represents certain qualities a cow has in common with certain other farm animals, etc. (see the "Abstraction Ladder" on p. 290).

Clear writing involves varying the levels of abstraction so that highly abstract notions become illustrated by familiar or easily visualized examples. In like fashion, concrete instances may need higher-level abstract statements to show the general significance of what would otherwise be a series of particulars.

In thinking about policies concerning people, it is desirable to check any failure of imagination by climbing down the abstraction ladder to the point at which one perceives the effect of the policy upon a concrete human being. Visualize a particular concentration camp inmate, welfare recipient, farmer, etc.

Vagueness has both its permissible and impermissible applications. Vagueness is useful in giving general directives when a precise statement would be difficult and would unduly limit discretion. Vagueness is unavoidable in many important notions that cannot be exactly defined—e.g., "liberty," "joy." Vague terms for different ranges in a continuum—"tall," "medium stature," "short"—may inform well enough. But if a decision is to be made, then the uncertainty of vagueness needs to be overcome so far as possible by setting up precise standards as a foundation for action. Some notions simply cannot be reduced to a precise standard—e.g., "negligence."

EXERCISES FOR CHAPTER 17
pages 283–297

I. Answer **T** for "true" or **F** for "false":

_____ 1. If there is a word for a thing or a concept, then that thing or concept must exist somewhere.

_____ 2. The nature of abstraction makes abstractions vague.

_____ 3. Varying the level of abstraction is a device permitting broad statements with wide applications to be made more understandable through citing one or more concrete examples.

_____ 4. Wherever action is to be taken, generally it is best for directives to be vague.

_____ 5. One way language influences thought is by suggesting the classes in which thought takes place.

_____ 6. It is objectionable to overcome vagueness with distinctions that are arbitrary.

_____ 7. Some arbitrary lines are poorly selected.

_____ 8. The vocabulary at your command influences what you observe with your senses.

_____ 9. The connotations of words—i.e., the "emotive" element in language—is the most pervasive way in which language influences thought.

_____ 10. Since every continuum has borderline cases, whenever one wishes to discuss any case in the continuum his first effort should be to set up a standard for placing the borderline cases.

_____ 11. Precise definitions are sometimes neither necessary nor useful.

_____ 12. Sometimes making a decision according to vague criteria is a practical necessity.

II. Cite three ways in which language influences the thought of its users. For each one, point out a way by which a user of the language may counter the particular influence. If you consider that sometimes there is no satisfactory way to wholly overcome the influence of language, point out why you consider that the influence of language on thought is unavoidable.

III.   "The impressions which language conveys result from a never-ceasing mixture of connotations and denotations of words." Is this statement justified? Support your answer.

IV.   Some of the following terms can be confirmed practically, some are confirmable in principle though we are not able to confirm them at the present time, and some are not confirmable in principle. Fill in the blanks with **a**, **b**, or **c** as appropriate.

>   **a.** Can be confirmed in practice
>   **b.** Confirmable in principle
>   **c.** Not confirmable in principle

———— **1.** mermaid   ———— **7.** natural rights

———— **2.** psychic powers   ———— **8.** love

———— **3.** Timbuctoo   ———— **9.** life in other solar systems

———— **4.** persecution   ———— **10.** predestined

———— **5.** haunted   ———— **11.** flying saucer

———— **6.** George Washington   ———— **12.** omen

V.   **1.** Which notions given in the list for Exercise IV are definitely not *word magic*?

         2. Which notions given in the list for Exercise IV can never be established so as to be free from the possibility of being mere *word magic*?

VI.   Clarity in communication is much aided by varying levels of abstraction. Explain how this works.

VII.   **1.** Why does a statute defining a crime endeavor to avoid vagueness as far as practical?

         2. Why do articles of incorporation under which a corporation receives its authority to carry on business normally employ many sweeping, i.e., vague, terms?

         3. An arbitrary standard is a way of breaking into a continuum situation and permitting cases to be placed according to the standard. Cite five such arbitrary standards of your own knowledge. Do not cite more than one each which employs height, length, or age.

4. To say that a standard is "arbitrary" does not mean that it is "unfair." What does it mean?

5. Explain what is a permissible and what is an impermissible type of attack on an arbitrary standard.

chapter 18

Definition and
Interpretation of Meaning

As Felix Frankfurter was fond of saying, "Accuracy in the use of words is the basis of all serious thinking." Though this is a reasonable statement, we have just seen that accuracy in the sense of eliminating vagueness isn't always possible. Nevertheless, attention to terms is fundamental to clear thinking. One of the benefits fairly claimed for the study of deduction is its contribution in developing a habit of considering carefully the scope of the terms used. In fact, the giant minds in any field are the most incisive in defining terms, which confirms Frankfurter's dictum.

DEFINITION

Definitions are of several kinds. *Lexical definition* is the kind supplied by a dictionary whenever a synonym for the word defined is given. *Definition by example* is just that. Then there is the *stipulative definition*, which is a statement that a term will be employed in a certain way. Natural science offers *theoretical definitions* to define a phenomenon in terms of its properties; e.g., "heat" is defined as the "velocity of molecules." None of these concern us here. We mention that definitions are of several kinds because this may help to avoid confusion.

Analytical definition is the main concern of logic. Sometimes this is called definition by *genus* and *differentia*, and the meaning of these notions is best shown by tracing them in some examples.

1. *A "bachelor" is an unmarried man.* The *genus* is the most general class to which the term being defined belongs—in this example "man"—while the

differentia are characteristics cited to differentiate the term being defined from those members of the general class to which the term does not belong—in this example "unmarried." In this clearcut case the application of the differentia "unmarried" to the genus class "man" produces a precise equivalent for "bachelor." *Genus* in logic refers to the broadest class found in a definition, while in biology *genus* refers to a fixed level in the classification system of forms of life. Though it is a pity that two differing uses of *genus* have developed, the usage is well entrenched and is continued here.

2. A *"novel"* is a book-length story related in prose about fictional characters. The widest class used as the genus here is "story," and three differentia are cited to differentiate the novel from stories of other types—namely, it must be "book length," "related in prose," and "about fictional characters." If the definition is successful, then it will be exactly equivalent to the concept "novel"—that is, all stories that are novels will satisfy the three differentia, and no story that does satisfy the differentia will turn out not to be a novel. (Is this a good definition? What about plays?)

3. A *"government"* is an organization for the administrative control of society which commands significant obedience to its laws by a population. Here we have a definition studded with vague terms which are defensible only if greater precision is not possible. The genus is "organization," while the differentia are "administrative control," "society," "commands significant obedience," "laws," and "population." The first test for this analytical definition is to check whether it *includes* everything that is a government. Does the definition include all the things we recognize as governments—namely, the United States, the State of Pennsylvania, the City of Portland, Vietnam, the Tonga Islands, etc.? Can you think of anything that *is* a government and yet does not meet the differentia? If so, the definition is too narrow. Next, check whether the definition *excludes* every organization that is *not* a government. Do one or more of the differentia exclude all nongovernments such as General Motors Corporation, the French Army, a pirate's nest, a terrorist organization, a primitive band of Australian aborigines, a "government" in exile, etc.? If not, the definition is too broad.

Now that we have had a go at applying the terms *genus* and *differentia*, it will be well to list all the requirements for sound analytical definition. These requirements appear in most logic books, and with reason, since without consciously following them it is impossible to propose definitions that hold up or to reject inadequate definitions when they are encountered.

A sound analytical definition must satisfy the following tests:

1. The definition must be properly inclusive.
2. The definition must be propertly exclusive.
3. The definition must not repeat the term defined.
4. The definition must not be wholly negative.
5. The definition should not be expressed in figurative or metaphorical language.
6. The definition should be stated in language that is appropriately simple.

Now we will take up each of these tests. It seems best to combine the discussion of requirements (1) and (2).

A definition must be properly inclusive and exclusive.   These two requirements are Siamese twins, and a difficult pair they are. We touched on the
problem already as we labored to define "government." As we have seen, to
meet these requirements a definition must be wide enough to include every case
that is an instance of the thing defined, and it must be narrow enough to exclude
all situations that are not instances of the thing defined. One can visualize the
problem with a figurative analogy. Suppose you have on your desk a piece of
red paper cut out in an irregular shape and you wish to cover this piece of paper
exactly with a piece of white paper. Your problem in definition is to cut the white
paper out with words, so to speak, so that it makes a perfect match over the red
paper. If the white paper allows a bit of the red to show, then the definition is
too narrow; if the white covers all the red but you discover by peering under the
edges that it extends beyond the red at some point, then the definition is too
broad. Sometimes it isn't easy to match the defining words to the thing defined.
And this is all the more reason for making a habit of applying these tests of
inclusiveness and exclusiveness which will expose faulty definitions.

There is the classic story of the scholars of the School at Athens who
labored to construct a definition of "man." They decided upon "featherless
biped." Thereupon Diogenes tossed a plucked chicken over the school wall and,
after further pondering, the scholars countered by adding "with broad nails."
It's odd that the joke jarred the learned man into a change. After all, a plucked
chicken remains a chicken just as a man who lacks legs through accident remains
a man; both are simply maimed or imperfect specimens. Definitions are not
disturbed by maimed specimens or freaks. We can pardon the good scholars for
their ignorance of gorillas and other primates which more legitimately embarrass
their definition. Let's go along with the scholars' approach, however, and define
"man" as a "featherless biped with sparse hair." Maybe you will allow that the
differentia of "featherless," "biped," and "with sparse hair" successfully limit
the genus "animal" to what we recognize as "man." Yet the definition strikes
one as absurd. Why? Well, in choosing differentia such as "featherless" or
"having sparse hair," characteristics not essential to the nature of "man" were
selected. Though it is extremely hard to define—let alone crisply define—just
what an essential characteristic may be, still, everybody has a feeling that some
characteristics are more vital than others. Here we stand at the edge of a perplex-
ing problem. Although, in a way, any definition that succeeds in including all
members of the class defined and in excluding all other matters cannot be called
wrong, it is also necessary for definitions to rest upon fundamental characteristics if they are to build upon one another in a logical pattern. What is fundamental varies with man's knowledge. A more sound analytical definition for "man"
is "a primate distinguished for high mental development exceeding any other
known animal."

The definition should not repeat the term defined.   This simple requirement cuts out circular definitions. Not only does it forbid any exact repetition of
the term but also it applies against using any form incorporating the root of the

term defined. One cannot define, for instance, "chivalry" as the "code prescribing chivalrous behavior."

The definition must not be wholly negative. This rule is rarely violated. The requirement arises from the fact that to state what a thing is *not* ordinarily leaves so many possibilities open that it is not satisfactorily informative. To say, "A reptile is not a vegetable or a mammal" is patently inadequate, leaving open the possibilities that a reptile is a fish or an invertebrate or, for that matter, a house. Even if the negatives succeeded in excluding everything in the world except for reptiles, such a wholly negative definition still would remain unsatisfactory because it would give no information about what affirmative qualities reptiles possess. Some terms incorporate a negative idea as part of the meaning. It causes no difficulty for one of the differentia to be negative, as "bankrupt" means "a property-owning entity not possessing sufficient assets to meet obligations that are due," or "widow" means "woman whose husband is not living." The requirement bars only definition by negative conditions alone.

The definition should not be expressed in figurative or metaphorical language. Again, this requirement is unlikely to be violated by one who seeks to work out an analytical definition according to genus and differentia. Metaphors and figures of speech are cited as definitions often enough, so it is well to bar them from acceptance here. "Life is a flicker in an infinite night" may express somebody's feeling, cry of despair, or whatnot, but it does not define "life."

The definition should be stated in language that is appropriately simple. The requirement of language as simple as possible does not rule out technical language or suggest that all definitions be simple. A complex notion may resist simple characterization, and technical terms—say in medicine—may best be defined by using other technical terms which are accurate and understood by those in the field. On the other hand, if a doctor informs his patient of the technical name for his condition (which he may well do) and then explains that term with other medical terminology, he would do well to consider whether his explanation was *appropriately simple*.

Whether or not to spell out the definition of a term is a practical decision. For an example of a situation absolutely requiring careful definitions, take a look at an insurance policy in which every term will be defined—"fire," "loss," "assured," and so on. Statutes sometimes begin with a section devoted to stipulating the meanings for various terms employed in the statute. Though such lists make tedious reading, their evident purpose is to make the meaning unmistakable to those who take the time to scrutinize them, and this has a good result if lawsuits are avoided or if those who must apply or follow the particular document are aided in their task. On the other hand, presenting a list of definitions at the beginning of a speech or nontechnical paper may be worse than boring; it may be ineffective. It is simply unrealistic to expect numerous definitions to be kept in mind unless there is a writing which one can read and reread. Yet not a few times I have witnessed speakers—as a result of training in definition, I fear—dutifully presenting definitions without thought about their need or of the audience's ability to digest them. As a matter of strategy, not logic, the number of terms given special explanation in ordinary discourse should be few, and those that do require explanation are best defined at the point when they are first introduced.

The ability to define something does not necessarily indicate that one understands it or even can identify it! If knowledge were obtainable merely by learning a definition, then legal training, for example, could be reduced to learning definitions for "contract," "libel," "easement," and so on. Alas, definitions tell us only what words mean, a mere beginning in the task of comprehending what sorts of situations fall under them. So it is that law schools use the case method to teach concepts like "contract" by having students read numbers of cases, in some of which the facts were held to be a contract while others were held not to have created a contractual obligation. Gradually the student acquires a notion of the requirements for a contract and a feeling for where the line runs between situations which do and those which do not fall within the term. He may even know a good deal about contracts without being able to give a ready definition of the word "contract."

Popular semantics has produced exaggerated claims about the part language has in disagreements. Everyone has had the experience of contending with some party only to discover in the end that the disagreement arose because language had not conveyed the meaning supposed. If this is the problem, then defining terms will end it. Although awareness of the possibility of semantic disagreement is valuable in prompting an effort to look for ambiguity or definition of terms as a source of misunderstanding, many disagreements are real. In such cases the parties understand each other perfectly well or, if there has been some element of misunderstanding, it is not the basic problem. The use of the word "democratic" in the Yalta Agreement toward the close of World War II is a classic and much-cited case in which the disagreement was, in my opinion, not semantic. Granted that the Soviet Union and the Western powers make different uses of the term "democratic," this difference hardly could have escaped notice at the time by the participants to an agreement every word of which must have been sifted by experts. Diplomats, particularly when an appearance of harmony is sought, sometimes leave undecided issues papered over with vaguely expressed agreement which can turn out to be no agreement at all. Certainly the Soviet Union, a dictatorship that has never allowed either representative government or civil liberties to its own people, had no interest in setting up Western-style democracies on its doorstep. Its refusal to create such institutions is the natural consequence of Communist ideology and of Russian conceptions of self-interest, not misunderstanding arising from a choice of words. We may hail those whose skill in language helps preserve us from unnecessary friction grounded in misunderstood terms; it is too much to ask mastery of the art of definition to save us from whatever follies we persist in.

INTERPRETING THE MEANING OF LANGUAGE

A problem about meaning is not a problem of logic. After all, to resolve a question of meaning is to answer the question, *What is asserted?* Until this question is resolved, no one can know *what* the argument is. Settling any question about meaning has to be done before the argument can be known and analyzed from a logical standpoint. We can imagine a logician declaring in a lordly way, "I stamp with the word 'valid' those deductive arguments that conform to the rules of logic, and I stamp with the word 'reliable' those inductive arguments which appear well supported. It is bad enough to have to admit the uncertainty of induction. Thank heavens, it's not my province to get bogged down in all the nuances of language or in squabbles over its meaning." The logician is right for logical analysis begins only after the meaning is settled. With all the good will in the world, the best a logician could do *as a logician* would be to say, "If the meaning is this, then the argument is valid, but if you take this other meaning, then. . . ."

Dividing the spheres of the logician and the semanticist does not affect the importance of either one, of course. It is just a matter of noticing whose territory is whose: one needs to attend to both fields in order to apply logic to problems which come, necessarily, expressed in language.

How can one go about deciding how to interpret a passage that leaves us uncertain about its meaning? We will describe several approaches that can be thought of as tools. No single tool will apply to all problems, nor does the use of one tool at one point preclude the use of another later on. Likewise, meaning may be determined by applying one or several of the following methods:

1. Ask the source for clarification.   This works well if the source is handy, and referring to the source is exemplified every time a participant in discussion is asked to explain his meaning. Obviously, this solution won't work where writing is involved and the author is not around. Further, if a dispute has arisen—for instance, where two parties are contending over the meaning of a sales agreement they signed—then one can hardly trust self-serving explanations by the parties.

2. Take the grammatical meaning of the language used as a guide.   This will resolve many problems. In fact, one normally assumes meaning to be what the application of grammar implies. Yet not everybody is a competent grammarian, and not everything asserted is intended to be taken literally. The speaker who declares, "I ain't never been there" makes a plain meaning contrary to grammar. "*That* was a fine thing to do" may be sarcastic and not a statement of approval. Nevertheless, in the absence of some reason found in the nature of the speaker or the situation or the context, there is a presumption that the grammatical meaning is intended.

3. Determine the intention of the source as a guide to meaning.   When one can perceive the intention, the battle is more than half won. After all, the meaning will align with the intention, and this usually will settle the matter.

It may be of interest to notice that law runs into some thorny problems when it comes to allowing intention to "cure" or override the normal meaning of the language used. This is because law must guard other interests as well as give effect to intentions of parties. For instance, if committee hearings and debates of a legislature show the purpose of a statute but the language used fails to express this purpose, should an individual be held to comply with the intention of the drafters rather than with the apparent meaning of the language they adopted and published? If Party A to a contract intends a provision to have a certain meaning, but the contract is poorly phrased and Party B signs unaware of A's intentions, then can A enforce his intention or rescind the contract? If a layperson draws his will and uses a technical word having a well-defined legal meaning with the intention that the word indicate something other than its usual legal consequences, can his heirs show the intention in order to have the will construed in a way varying from the legal force of its wording? In answering these questions the courts have to consider whether too tolerant a reception for argument seeking to explain the intended meaning of the language used will not endanger civil rights or encourage litigation or make law uncertain. However, where argument has none of these constraints, then one is free to accept whatever meaning was intended by the source.

4. Use the context as a guide to meaning.   Isolated sentences may mislead, and "lifting out of context" is one of the commonest modes of distortion. Pursuing the opposite course, a study of context may make the intended meaning evident even when it is ambiguous or unclear or misstated at some restricted point. Context involves, of course, surveying the meaning of the surrounding sentences and paragraphs. More broadly, context includes all types of circumstances bearing upon meaning, and this can take one far afield. An atmosphere of joking can reduce a remark to a harmless jibe when the same words would be insulting if the mood were serious. The character of the source may shed light on meaning, as we acknowledge when making allowances for somebody who has a weakness for extravagant language which we have learned not to take literally. Cultural background, too, may modify meaning. For example, when a Chinese host deprecates his obviously elegant house he is not implying that the house falls short of his personal standards, but following a cultural form to put guests at ease.

5. Consider whether tone or stress play a part in the meaning.   Tone plays a part in communicating meaning, and so does the stress placed upon one part of a sentence or another. Try emphasizing first one and then another of the words in the sentence, "I didn't invite him to the party." Depending upon which word is stressed, five different implications emerge. *The same can be done for almost any sentence.* Wherever speech is reduced to writing, the nuances of tone and stress generally are lost. Courts are well aware of the problem, so judges on appeal often note the disadvantage of trying to determine meaning from written transcripts stripped of the cues of tone, stress, and demeanor of witnesses. Unfortunately, it is easy to raise more difficulties than answers. Nevertheless, a search for meaning may need to consider what, if anything, can be done to rediscover the manner in which the words were uttered originally.

6. Apply an appropriate presumption to determine the meaning.   There are times when none of the approaches mentioned so far will satisfactorily determine what the meaning is. Sometimes at such a juncture one can throw up his hands, declaring it to be an unresolvable riddle like the sign "Croatoan" left by the vanished Roanoke colonists. Sometimes, however, one has to make a decision and to do this some sort of presumption about the meaning will have to be used. Different disciplines have different presumptions. A presumption favoring a sensible result is widely applied: where of two possible interpretations, one produces a sensible result while the other produces an unlikely or foolish situation, then the sensible result is preferred. Perhaps this could be called a variation of gathering meaning from context. Another presumption favors grammatical interpretation of the language over any interpretation contrary to normal operation of grammar—unless there is some reason for overriding a grammatical approach. In logic a presumption is made that "all" is the quantifier intended when no quantifier is stated. Another presumption of logic favors an interpretation that results in a valid argument rather than one which renders the reasoning invalid. In law there is a parallel presumption favoring an interpretation that provides for lawful conduct over any that would make a provision contrary to law. A rule of parsimony applies to interpretation of meaning as well as to evidence. In effect, this is a rule against making unnecessary assumptions or, to put the matter another way, the rule holds that a simple interpretation requiring few assumptions is more apt to be correct than a complicated one that requires more assumptions. We may never know what Shakespeare "meant" by a certain passage, yet according to the law of parsimony the simplest explanation is most likely to be right. All these presumptions are ways of dealing with Gordian knot situations which nobody really can untie. Where no one has to make a decision it may be best simply to point out that the meaning is unclear and leave it at that. But sometimes a decision has to be made even though the source did not foresee the situation and had no meaning in mind concerning it. In such cases, presumptions are a necessary expedient for reaching a decision.

SUMMARY

An analytical definition must meet the following requirements:

1. It must include all cases that belong under the concept defined.
2. It must exclude all cases not belonging under the concept defined.
3. The definition must not repeat the term defined.
4. The definition must not consist wholly of negative statements.
5. The definition should not be stated in figurative language.
6. The definition should be stated in language that is appropriately simple.

The various devices for interpreting meaning can be thought of as so many tools. More than one tool may be used on a problem, and there is no assurance that every problem can be solved. Problems of meaning are not problems of logic, for only after the meaning is known can the standards of logic be applied. Finally, in logic and in most matters, one is interested only in determining the meaning intended. The construction of language in a legal situation sometimes presents a sort of special case, although courts, too, usually seek the intended meaning. On some occasions, however, a court will refuse to look beyond the clear meaning of the language used when to do so might encourage fraud, undermine the certainty of law, or erode the construction of a technical term. These problems are peculiar to courts; the ordinary concern in interpretation is to determine the intended meaning, whatever the imperfection of its expression.

Approaches useful for determining meaning are:

1. Ask the source for clarification.
2. Accept the grammatical meaning of the language used.
3. Determine the intention of the source in using the language.
4. Refer to the context in which the language is used.
5. Consider whether tone or stress play a part in the meaning.
6. Apply an appropriate presumption to determine the meaning.

EXERCISES FOR CHAPTER 18
pages 301–309

I.   Answer **T** for "true" or **F** for "false":

_____ **1.** The ability to define something is not assurance that one understands the notion or even that one could identify the thing defined.

_____ **2.** Many conflicts are real and not to be overcome by definitions or by semantics.

_____ **3.** An analytical definition never is by example.

_____ **4.** An analytical definition must not be too broad or too narrow.

_____ **5.** Any good analytical definition is in simple language.

_____ **6.** Sometimes it is proper to use a negative idea as one of the differentia.

_____ **7.** Determining meaning is a part of logic.

_____ **8.** One can always be sure of determining the true meaning by consulting the source, when available.

_____ **9.** Following grammar is always the best way to determine the meaning.

_____ **10.** In logic, at least, the intention of the source is the best guide to meaning when this can be determined.

_____ **11.** Some definitions are not analytical.

_____ **12.** The considerations applied in determining meaning for legal purposes are not always the same as the determination of meaning for nonlegal purposes.

II.   Each of the following definitions fails to comply with one of the requirements for a sound analytical definition. State the weakness of each in the space provided.

1. A "hero" is one who performs a heroic act.

_____

2. "Poetry" is the liquid silver of language.

_____

3. A "motorcycle" is not an automobile or a truck.

_____

4. "Network" is "Anything reticulated or decussated, at equal distances." (Famous definition from Samuel Johnson's Dictionary)

_____

III. The requirements for a sound analytical definition that are most difficult to comply with are that (1) the definition must be properly inclusive, and (2) the definition must be properly exclusive. Explain the meaning of each of these requirements.

IV. Each of the following analytical definitions is either **too narrow** or **too broad.** State which each one is and your reason on the line provided.

1. A "pipe" is a hollow tube made of metal or clay.

_____

2. A "restaurant" is a place where the public may buy food.

_____

3. To "murder" is to kill a human being without legal excuse.

_____

4. "Caution" means an unwillingness to take chances when physical injury is involved.

_____

5. A "chair" is an article of furniture designed for sitting.

_____

6. A "work of art" is a painting.

_____

7. A "charitable organization" is an organization formed to serve a public purpose.

_____

8. "Theft" is taking the property of another without the owner's consent.

_____

V.   Make up an analytical definition for each of the following terms. Note how often you have to amend your first try.

1. shoe   3. careless   5. robbery
2. automobile   4. drunk   6. kindness

VI.   **1.** "A problem about meaning is not a problem of logic." Define the field of "logic" and show how it is that meaning is not included in it.

2. Explain how it is that a book that focuses on applying logic has to consider questions concerning meaning.

3. As far as an intellectual grasp of meaning is concerned, one seeks only to determine the intended meaning as exactly as possible. A legal interpretation of meaning, however, is a sort of special case, for courts do not invariably seek to find and follow the intended meaning. Why so?

VII.   Point out one or more practical difficulties that may be met in the attempt to determine meaning according to each of the following:

1. Ask the source for clarification.

2. Apply the grammatical meaning of the language used.

3. Determine the intention of the source.

4. Use context as a guide to the meaning.

5. Consider the part played by tone and stress.

6. Apply a presumption to establish meaning.

part five

Evidence

chapter 19

Observation and Inference

Logic is a procedure for making valid or reliable inferences. It can be called the science of inference. Now we step into another world, the world of evidence. Our interest here shifts from logical procedure to the substance upon which belief is justifiably based. What can we say to some purpose about this new world of evidence?

All have encountered that refuge of the individual who cannot support his stand: "I have a right to my opinion." People believe all sorts of things for all sorts of reasons, true enough. To the rational person, however, there is no justification for opinions held without evidence. Though the ideal of fairly assessing evidence is a praiseworthy goal, I must say that my own life experience convinces me that inability to look at evidence objectively is a human failing shared, on occasion, by all of us. Even the best-trained minds can find it hard to hew the line of assessing evidence impartially: all have egos to protect, beliefs that have become sacred cows, and special interests to guard when a problem comes close to home. It is surprising how the most educated, who should know better, will warm to debate and drop a balanced view of evidence in favor of seeking to make the material support some position. Another tack taken in human weakness is to refuse to be convinced, throwing up impossible standards for reliability, or to fall back on the nothing-but-objections fallacy. These sorts of reactions cross the line between scholar and advocate: ideally, the scholar views evidence impartially and seeks only to find the truth, while the advocate seeks to persuade by construing evidence to support his claim. In a way, scholarship and advocacy complement one another; scholarship is a basis for understanding while advocacy leads to action. In any case, evidence is the stuff for thought, and assessing its quality is part of effective thinking.

What is evidence? *Evidence is the factual basis for belief.* Anything at all may be evidence shedding light on some subject. In order to sort out the problems met in evaluating evidence, we will distinguish several types:

1. Direct observation
2. Observations by others—i.e., witnesses
3. Opinion of experts
4. Circumstantial evidence

This chapter takes up direct observation only, leaving the three remaining types to be dealt with in Chapter 20.

DIRECT OBSERVATION

Seeing is believing. And so is hearing, smelling, touching, tasting—the impressions from all five senses. Whoops, there's a sense of balance, complete with its own organ, so we haven't even sensed our own senses correctly! Best we start with a look at human sensory equipment through which must come all observation of the outside world. It's often remarked that human senses aren't very acute and, although I would rate human beings well endowed as a whole, it is true that they don't take any first places. Personally, I'm happy to give first place for smell to the dog and to call him home, if he'll come, with a whistle too shrill for the neighbors to hear. People see a more colorful world and see it better than a dog does, though. But the hawk is incredible. Imagine being able to spot a quarter on the sidewalk from the top of the Empire State Building! No less refined is the rattlesnake's infra-red sensing organ, alerting it to the possibility of dining on a mouse located out of sight 20 yards away. What's really intriguing, though, is to fancy having sonar such as bats use to fly in the utter darkness of a cave or to time a crazy dodge from the clear-visioned hawk. Yes, human senses have their limits both in capacity and in what sorts of phenomena they can record.

Human beings have the senses they have, no more. For thousands of years this simple fact was an enormous barrier to human understanding, since man's idea of reality remained limited to what he could sense. George Sarton's fine sentence, "No mountains or seas or desert sands equal the barriers of the mind" applies equally well here: there is nothing so hard to grasp as the fact that the impressions of the senses are not what IS in the world. One step in breaking the bonds of human sensory limitations came with the invention of instruments to extend the power of our senses: the telescope and the microscope. Since that not-so-long-ago time, we have learned of a host of forces which our senses do not record: electricity, magnetic fields, X-rays, infra-red rays, cosmic rays, radio waves, germs, viruses, galaxies, and more. Understanding these unobservable forces has led us on to all sorts of useful accomplishments such as polio inoculation and electric lights. Or, H-bombs, if you please. Whatever else, I hope these comments highlight the limits of man's unaided senses. The possibilities are far too many for the seeing-is-believing assumption.

Perhaps you're becoming a bit impatient with me. "See here—you're implying that my own senses can't be trusted, and if I really believed that I'd never be sure of anything. I know about this desk when I thump on it, and I know, too, that it probably is a whirl of electrons. So what? I never claimed to observe everything, but I certainly can observe what I do." Clearly, it is time to take a look at how direct observation works.

An "observation" is made up of two elements: (1) receiving a sensory impression, and (2) giving an interpretation to that impression. Observation is not limited to the sense of sight; it may be any of the senses, of course. Since sight is the most important sense in human beings it will be used as the base for most of our investigation of observation here. The first thing to notice is that one does not "see" all of a phenomenon. The lens in the eye focuses the light, which creates a pattern of shades and colors on the retina. It's a rich upside-down pattern recording the whole spectrum of the rainbow. Rich though human sight is in color perception, it has limited strength, which means that we need a fair amount of light and smaller details escape perception. Further, the pattern on the retina does not include sensory information about *where* things are, and the brain has to rely on experience with the outside world to decide which parts of the pattern are to be interpreted as small but close and which parts are large but further away. Scale is achieved by interpreting the pattern in harmony with the object or objects which happen to be of familiar size, and everybody understands the purpose of the ruler, geologist's hammer, or person appearing in a picture to give it scale. Pictures are interesting devices to fool the eye or one should say, perhaps, to challenge the mind to make "sense" out of the picture. Most animals are reputed not to interpret pictures but to look at them more literally, seeing in them only what they are. Cinerama—I regret its passing— created the ultimate optical illusion so that on the famous roller-coaster ride the audience swayed to bank the curves, the pit of the stomach felt that sinking feeling when the track dropped steeply, and everybody laughed as he sensed himself gliding to a slow stop at the end of the ride.

I apologize to the eye. It serves us marvelously, and usually the mind isn't deceived by the sensations it records. Yet we often strain to interpret sensations that are barely perceptible, momentary, or otherwise difficult to make out. Everyone has plenty of this kind of experience, so to avoid elaborating the obvious we will list the factors for reliable observation with only the briefest comments. As you peruse the list, however, remember that trial lawyers are well paid for questioning witnesses about the reliability of their observations, and many of their questions simply go over the appropriate points of this list.

Requirements for Reliable Observation

1. *Ability of the sense organ to perceive.* Do the thick glasses give 20–20 vision? How's your hearing? Consider, in short, how well the observer can perceive.

2. *Proper conditions to observe.* Was there enough light? What about distance? Were there competing noises?

3. *Background knowledge relating to the event observed.* Was it like the sound from a burnt-out connecting rod? Generally the casual observer who doesn't know what to look for either does not notice or does not remember the things essential for understanding the situation.

4. *Mental capacity.* Children fantasize, though they may observe correctly things within their grasp. The same goes for the mentally disturbed. Normal adults vary enormously in ability to observe carefully and report accurately what sense impressions they received.

5. *Attention.* How well can you describe the face of your watch? Ninety-nine percent of what can be seen isn't focused on, remaining in peripheral vision; most sound is quickly classified as harmless and is disregarded. Attention varies from close concentration to none at all, with equivalent fluctuations in perception.

6. *Absence of preconceptions and bias.* Since the mind has to interpret the sensory data it receives, if it has any preconceptions these can influence the interpretation it makes. Do you catch all errors when proofreading? Have you ever misidentified something for the object you were anxiously expecting?

7. *Freedom from disturbance.* Excitement and fear create gross errors in observation. How large was that bear that fiddled with the latch to our cabin? Experiments staged to present an unsuspecting group with a contrived argument, pistol firing, and flight *always* produce all kinds of mistakes in observation: gun attributed to the wrong person, wild misdescriptions of the people involved, errors in comprehending the few words spoken.

Reliable observation requires favorable conditions. Consequently, those who must evaluate reports probe as a matter of course the conditions surrounding reported observations. Especially trial lawyers, journalists, and intelligence officers make constant use of these requirements.

OBSERVATION AND INFERENCE

As we have seen, the brain has to interpret the sensory impressions it receives, a job it does pretty effectively despite occasional mistakes. The interpretive element within sensory experience means there is a certain amount of inference within the process of observation itself. In the discussion here, however, the phrase "interpretation of sensory impressions" is used to describe this action of the brain, while the word "inference" is reserved for interpretations that go *beyond* sensory impression. Inferences going beyond sensory impression constantly round out our observation: they are so commonplace that usually one is not aware of the line between what is observed and what is inferred. Let's start with the head-and-wall example.

I observe my neighbor's head above the garden wall, smiling and talking pleasantly to me. So I *infer* his body is attached to the head. I'm not joking! Seriously, it is an inference, however safe in this case, for *I do not observe* the body. So we see, the rejoinder "That's only an inference," standing by itself, at least, isn't justified if it is a protest against inferences in general. Of course, if the intent of the "only an inference" remark is to object to some shaky inference, then one might accept it without cavil as meant to protest, "That is a *doubtful* inference." Still, we need to make the elementary point that there is nothing uncertain about inferences as such. Each particular inference has to be evaluated with the judgment of common sense gained in life experience.

Many things commonly spoken of as "observed" are, actually, inferred. Maybe you can see the "lovelight in her eyes" but you can't see love. Nor hate, nor anger, nor any other emotional state. All conditions of this sort are inferred from various observed cues including, sometimes, knowledge of background situations that seem to support the interpretation. Again, many concepts are states lacking physical existence and are thus not capable of being observed. Some intangibles of this sort are work, carelessness, help, fault, skill, superiority, diligence, deceit, or any number of other intangible concepts. One who says, "I saw John steal the bicycle" is not reporting an observation of "stealing" although he may, of course, have seen John take the bicycle. Whether or not the taking is a theft depends upon several conditions: ownership of the bicycle, absence of permission, mistake or a lawful justification for the taking, and the existence of an intent to steal. In any trial, lawyers will be found holding witnesses to recount only what was observed directly and not to add their interpretations—that is, their inferences from the facts. The objection "that is a *conclusion* of the witness" is one of the most common objections raised; its meaning is precisely that the witness is straying from what he has observed and is adding material that he has inferred about the situation. It is for the jury to draw its own inferences from the evidence which is, ideally, either factual or the opinion of expert sources.

Sometimes, however, it is impossible to communicate effectively if one is held to wholly disentangle observation from inference. For instance, a charge of drunkenness could not be made out practically if the witnesses were strictly held to describing the unsteady gait, gyrations, or whatever from which the witness had concluded that the subject was drunk. Since recounting the observed facts alone might be confusing or leave the meaning unclear, a witness would be allowed to testify to his opinion that the subject was drunk along with a description of the facts he observed and upon which he based his conclusion. This is a compromise solution—and a whole lot better than permitting a naked statement "John was drunk" to appear as if it were a fact observed by an eyewitness instead of the inference based upon other observations, which it is. It is well for the jury or whoever is determining the facts to know just what was observed and to be in a position to evaluate whether the observations afforded convincing support for the conclusion. Notwithstanding the unfeasibility of sharply separating observation from inference at all times, the difference between the two is fundamental, so fundamental that any probing investigator keeps it in mind. It's easy to forget and to overlook just where one's observation ended and inference began. I'll illustrate the point with an anecdote from personal experience.

Some years ago a business concern in my neighborhood set out three shade trees, each supported by a post and heavy wire. The trees thrived until the wire around one of them began to choke it and it started to die. I happened to know one of the employees, so I telephoned the suggestion that the supports and wires needed to be removed, particularly the one on the dying tree. My friend would see it done. Fine. Since I often pass close to the trees, I watched for a sign of action. Nothing happened. Meeting my friend one day, I remarked that the wires remained; he declared he would call the Grounds Department again. A little later I reflected that I had not closely inspected the wire: the posts remained by the trees and from this I had inferred that the wires remained also. Inspection of the distressed tree showed the wire cut and, embarrassed, I phoned my friend to head off the effect of a wrong report. "The wires have been cut," said I—using the plural. This, too, turned out to be an error. Though one might expect the gardener to have cut all three of the harmful wires, my conclusion that he had done so was another inference, for I had inspected only the choking tree. I didn't bother my friend again. As the story illustrates, observation is the best foundation for belief. This is why courts and investigators seeking the most reliable evidence will dig down to the bedrock of observation. And then they will want to know how favorable were the conditions for that observation.

SUMMARY

Evidence is the factual basis for belief.

Direct observation is made up of (1) the sensory impressions gathered from the senses, and (2) the interpretations which the brain adds to those impressions.

The physical world contains many phenomena beyond the capacities of human observation and, basically, the acuteness of human sense organs is limited within the areas in which they operate. Still, direct observation ordinarily is highly satisfactory when conditions are favorable. Everyone has enormous experience with observation, so the conditions affecting it are common knowledge—provided one takes time to reflect on the subject. The requirements of reliable observation are:

1. Normal ability of the sense organ to perceive
2. Proper physical conditions to observe
3. Background knowledge relating to the event observed
4. Mental capacity
5. Attention
6. Absence of preconceptions and bias
7. Freedom from emotional disturbance

The brain rounds out sensory impressions to interpret size and distance that sight does not record directly; also direction that is not recorded adequately by hearing. Thus some inference is involved in the process of perception.

Beyond the inference involved in perception itself, we constantly round out observation with inferences that go *beyond* our sense experience, as in the head-and-wall example. Some of these roundings may be correct and some not—the point is that recognizing them as inferences is a basic step in assessing evidence. This is the line referred to by courts when admonishing witnesses to recount their observations without adding any "conclusions."

EXERCISES FOR CHAPTER 19
pages 315–321

I.   Answer **T** for "true" and **F** for "false":

———— 1. Sensory observation involves inference as well as the sensory impressions received.

———— 2. The "bedrock of observation" implies that observation always is reliable.

———— 3. The real world is what human senses report it to be.

———— 4. Observation involves giving an interpretation to the sensory impressions received.

———— 5. Many inferences are extremely reliable.

———— 6. A fact established by a reliable inference is still much more doubtful than it would be if directly observed.

———— 7. The amount of observation varies with the amount of attention paid.

———— 8. Awareness of what has been observed and what has been inferred is necessary for a competent investigation.

———— 9. Reports of observations stripped of inferences may be hard to understand or misleading.

———— 10. Nobody can observe "sorrow."

II.   1. List as many requirements as you can that should exist if there is to be reliable observation.

2. After looking over your formidable list of requirements, explain how it is that observation often is highly satisfactory and reliable.

III.   1. Explain, by giving an example, how the process of sensory perception may contain an element of inference.

2. The notion of "inference" in connection with observation usually refers to concluding that additional facts exist beyond any sort of sense impression. Give an example.

3. In a careful examination, why does the investigator want, as far as possible, to dig down to the "bedrock of observation"?

IV.

1. Explain how the expression "That's only an inference" shows—if taken literally—a lack of understanding of what inference is all about.

2. Rephrase the expression in a way that makes a justifiable assertion.

V.

1. List five conditions that are incapable of being observed directly.

2. Why bother to notice whether something can be observed directly or not?

chapter 20

Witnesses and Circumstantial Evidence

WITNESSES

Everyone prefers his own observations to those of others. But since we must make great use of reports by others and of circumstantial evidence too, this chapter will discuss those sorts of evidence. All that has been said about observation and inference applies to the testimony of witnesses as well, and there are additional problems from the possibilities for conscious or unconscious distortion and from misunderstandings rooted in the use of language.

Often the evidence at hand is not as reliable as one would like. So, we shall begin by taking a look at the degrees of reliability. These degrees can be set down as follows:

1. Certainly true
2. True beyond reasonable doubt
3. More probably true than not
4. Indifferent
5. More probably false than not
6. False beyond reasonable doubt
7. Certainly false

It's a simple list. "Certainly true" is in a sense unattainable, but in practical affairs sometimes one does feel certain. I'm certain no cow ever jumped over the moon. "True beyond a reasonable doubt" and "more probably true than not" are common standards constantly used in law. For a criminal conviction the evidence must establish guilt "beyond a reasonable doubt," and whatever this vague phrase may mean, it does *not* permit the existence of any significant ground for doubt. All can agree that a very high level of reliability is needed before criminal action should be sanctioned. Recovery of damages or other relief in a civil suit requires only that the plaintiff establish his case as "more probably true than not"—a far lower standard. "Indifference" is so evenly balanced that there is no choosing a heavier side, while "more probably false than not" and "false beyond reasonable doubt" are obvious counterparts to the strength with which positive reliability may be established. The symmetrical scheme is but a verbal description of a few points along the continuum of conviction that runs between certainly false and certainly true. Notice that the limits of points (3), (4), and (5) are separated by but a hair's-breadth. Still, the scheme is useful if it brings to mind two questions: How reliable is this evidence? and How reliable should the evidence be in this situation?

Sometimes it's important to consider how reliable the evidence should be. To cite an example from a newspaper squib, a father came home to find his son making a repair under his car. "The jack isn't very secure," commented the father as he walked into the house. Since the affair got into the newspaper, you can guess the answer. The son was crushed because neither father nor son recognized where reliability beyond a reasonable doubt was required absolutely. In less simple situations one must grant that a high degree of reliability may not be obtainable even though the question is important. Should I take this job? Engage this surgeon? Make this investment? All one can say is the obvious— appropriate effort should be made to obtain evidence so that the conclusion becomes supported to whatever degree of reliability is practically obtainable. The poor innocent who buys land that he has never seen or invests in stock after a telephone sales pitch will pay for his gullibility. Then there is the other extreme of the intellectual who requires a degree of reliability not to be found in many business situations and who is, therefore, incapable of decisions involving risk. Now we will turn to the reliability of witnesses with the attendant possibilities of willful or of unconscious distortion.

Willful Distortion

No rule will unravel this topic. Perhaps there is not a greal deal to add beyond the lessons of life experience which, it seems to me, is the indispensable teacher in learning to assess the likelihood of lying. Yet a few points are worth mentioning. One is that neither a poor reputation for veracity nor a motive to distort will in itself justify a conclusion that there has been a departure from truth. It may be prudent at times not to accept—that is, *not to believe* uncorroborated statements from unreliable people or from those with a motive to falsify. This suspension of belief does not label such assertions "false," it simply requires more supporting evidence before accepting them as true. A second point is that where testimony turns out to be wrong, one should not be quick to conclude that there is an intentional falsification. Right enough, there may have been an intent to deceive. Yet it is more charitable and often more accurate to seek an explanation in simple error or in unconscious distortion which can arise in many ways. One of the more painful aspects of the courtroom scene is the blowing up of minor discrepancies in testimony with the implication that the conflict shows intentional falsehood making the testimony as a whole unreliable. The fact that people observe different details or retain different memories of them makes it in no way surprising to find minor differences in two accounts of the same event. The grossly erroneous statement which a normal person would not make without intent to deceive is another matter, and a falsehood of this sort rightly discredits a witness.

Unconscious Distortion

In addition to the possibilities of an error in observation or of failure to distinguish inference from observation, unconscious distortion may be grounded in the vagaries of memory or in a misunderstanding of language. Since observation was taken up in the last chapter, we will discuss here only distortions attributable to memory and to the use of language.

Memory is notorious for the tricks it can play. Everybody has struggled with faded memory and has found how inaccuracies creep in with the passage of time. Painful truths and facts contrary to self-interest tend to be suppressed, while other scenes may become exaggerated and glamorized. Many things that are unimportant or that are part of a common routine are quickly forgotten. Then there is the long unsought memory revived by a cue. How, then, can one get the greatest and most accurate recall?

An observer may recall his observations in his own narration. The advantage of this kind of an account is that the narrator is not confined to questions asked, nor is he influenced by the framing of the questions themselves. The disadvantage of spontaneous recall is that the detail reported is always less than the observer has observed and can recall under questioning. The spontaneous report habitually passes over details through oversight or because they seem unimportant to the narrator or, possibly, because the narrator considers that the detail is better left unsaid. Narrations in response to questioning have an opposite set of strengths and weaknesses. Questioning has the great advantage of increasing the amount of detail recalled and produced. Assuming that the questioning is competently conducted, not only will relevant matters be discovered and brought out, but also the limits of what was observed will be determined so that additions made by inference will be identified. Also, the possible distortion from questioning will be minimized where there is not a spirit of advocacy seeking to bring out only one side. Mention of the virtues of questioning implies some of its weaknesses, for in the real world questioning may not be impartial or skillful, and these shortcomings may increase distortion. Further, the observer can be asked to recall too much and may produce inaccuracy by straining to get beyond the bounds of clear memory. It follows that maximum recall is best achieved by both methods: a free narrative by the observer followed by scrupulous questioning designed to discover added details and assess the reliability of the observation reported.

Language is another common source of distortion. No matter how large one's vocabulary may be, one still must choose the word that best fits the meaning intended, and usually the choice is made quickly. Sometimes it is made unskillfully and a square verbal peg gets thrust into a round hole. Further, a word carrying one meaning for its user may carry a different shade of meaning to others. Relative terms are notorious for indicating different degrees to different people: everybody has had tangles over large, small; steep, gentle; new, old; and many more. I will supply an illustration from personal experience. In the course of a will contest, three witnesses were asked to describe the signing of the will, an event that had taken place in a small hospital room not many weeks before. The conditions for observation were ideal, the witnesses honest, and they testified separately without opportunity to hear the testimony of others. The first witness declared that the testatrix (female who signs a will) signed "sitting up" in bed; the second stated she was "lying down"; while the third provided a more accurate choice of words, saying "she was sort of reclining on her elbow." A more simple case would be hard to imagine. It makes the point that conflicting observations may turn out to be merely variant choice of words and that this possibility should be explored. After all, there may not be a third witness to come to the rescue.

Memory and language combine to produce a steady loss of accuracy as reports pass from one party to another. Twelve bishops presumably do not distort intentionally, but if information is passed between them the final account may be pretty well garbled. No second-hand source is apt to be more accurate than the original, and it certainly may be a lot less. Hence historians prize the accounts of original observers and courts exclude "heresay" whenever witnesses who can recount direct observations are available.

EXPERT OPINION

So far we have been discussing the evidence of witnesses who observed something that we did not observe ourselves. In relying upon their reports, we have had to think about whether their observations are likely to be accurate and whether their accounts are reliable. So far as possible we have desired to *exclude the opinions of ordinary witnesses* in favor of factual reports that we can evaluate for ourselves. In considering the opinion of an expert witness, however, our approach becomes quite different. We will want to be satisfied that the expert is personally reliable, just as we considered personal reliability of ordinary witnesses. In addition, before accepting an opinion as coming from an expert we will want to be satisfied that the source is indeed an expert, or, in other words, that he or she is professionally qualified. If we are satisfied on both scores, then we will *accept the opinions of the expert* as a sort of reasonable delegation of our judgment to one who has special knowledge of the problem.

To be *professionally qualified*, an expert source must meet the following tests:

1. The source must be identified.
2. The source must have professional standing.
3. The source must be current—i.e., not be obsolete.
4. The opinion given must be within the field of special competence.

These requirements are listed easily enough; the real difficulty is to determine how well a proposed authority satisfies them. So we will look at the tests with the problem of satisfying them in mind.

1. Identification of the source gives no trouble, for this is merely the name of the source, a necessary beginning point for considering its claim as an authority.

2. Finding out what sort of recognition peers in the field accord to a proposed authority may not be easy, since doctors, architects, paperhangers, and others may not willingly discuss the merits of their colleagues even though they know them. One can fall back upon other signs of recognition by peers, such as holding prestigious positions in the field, possessing licenses or special certifications, writing, or winning awards within the field.

3. The requirement that an authority be current relates chiefly to written material, for writing preserves beyond the powers of Egypt's embalmers. It is hard to know which parts of a book have become obsolete; one avoids old books in rapidly changing fields and, when the importance of the matter justifies the effort, one can consult a living authority in the field to certify that a written opinion still is current.

4. Finally, the field of the authority shades off into other areas beyond his area of special competence, making the bounds of expert knowledge hard to set. Into what sorts of matters does the president of a steel company gain experience and special insight? How much exposure to matters of diet or vitamins is included in a doctor's medical training or his reading?

Questions about the quality of an expert source are indeed more easily raised than answered. But answers are needed, and courts insist on having them. Before receiving testimony as coming from an expert, a court requires evidence that by education or life experience the source has acquired a knowledge of the field in which his opinion is sought. To prevent use of obsolete statements in books, in court a witness who is qualified as an expert in the field will have to examine the passage and testify that it is a statement of current opinion. Should questioning stray outside the field in which a witness has been qualified as an expert, the attorney on the other side will be quick to challenge the admissibility of his testimony on the point. So we see, legal proceedings in their formal attempt to reach reliable conclusions have framed rules to assure that expert opinions come from qualified sources.

In most ordinary matters when one turns to others with special knowledge—getting the car fixed, for example—there is generally neither time nor readily available information to be sure of the qualification of the "expert." Though it would be nice to know the "peer judgment" about the source, most of the time one has to make do with some slender information, such as the recommendation of a friend or the mere fact that the garage is handy and in business. Still, when you are faced with a problem of special importance, then you will do well to make a time-consuming attempt to procure a qualified expert. Conceivably, your action could save your fortune or your life.

Some years ago I faced the family crisis of moving to a new town and at the same time having to secure good medical care for my seriously sick wife. She was not responding to the treatment prescribed before the move and had reached the point of sleeping up to 22 hours per day, barely being able to stay awake to eat. How could we best choose a new doctor? Any of my few acquaintances in the new town might have been glad to help with a recommendation, very likely of his own physician. But experts are qualified by the recognition of their peers who can judge their work, not by laypersons. Well, a librarian is an expert on finding material and maybe she could direct me to material about the local medical profession. "Why, yes, you might try the *American Medical Directory.* It lists the doctors for each state broken down into the areas where they practice." So I turned to the *American Medical Directory,* which, though no mine of value judgments, is at least factual and well organized. In addition to listing all doctors in the area, it states the medical school attended, dates of admission to practice (from which one may infer years of experience and approximate age), type of practice, specialty ratings held, positions held on the staff of hospitals. So we chose an endocrinologist (the proper specialty) ten years out of medical school (hoping to satisfy the idea of current training plus experience and vigor) who had a specialist rating from the American College of Physicians and Surgeons (a qualification by peers beyond the state requirements for a license to practice). Next came a check beyond the printed page, carried on to the best of my limited ability. Asking acquaintances for their recommendations and mentioning my selection turned up no special information—most especially, it uncovered no criticism. So we had done what we could and made an appointment. "Who referred you to us?" asked the secretary. "Well, we located you in the *American Medical Directory."* "I never heard of that before." I think the doctor was pleased to have been an intellectual choice in competition with his colleagues. And there's a happy ending. The doctor went to work with X-rays and many tests not given before, completely revised the diagnosis, and, after some months, my wife was well. Fortunate were we.[1]

This discussion has dealt so far with the requirements by which an expert is deemed to be *professionally qualified,* and with the practical difficulties in applying those standards. In addition to this, an expert must be *personally reliable* like any other witness. "Personally reliable" refers to the source being unbiased, willing to tell the truth, disinterested or able to rise above self-interest, free from duress, and conscientiously attending to the problem. Professional competence, unfortunately, is not proof against human weakness; authorities may be biased, selfish, swayed by conceit, lazy, even dishonest. No mind is more unreceptive than the mind that already "knows." How else can one explain the professional hostility that greeted Lister's antisepsis or the opposition provoked by Colonel Mitchell's demonstration of the potentiality of air power? No one lives long without coming up against the expert who is not diligent or has a closed mind or some other human weakness. The layperson is competent to judge human failure, and he acts rightly when he seeks on his own assessment to protect himself from it.

We need to look at expert opinion with a new stress—expert *opinion.* We have seen already how an investigator seeks to identify inferences and cut them out as much as possible; he seeks to reach the "bedrock of observation." Instead of seeking opinions, the investigator asks witnesses to recount their observations, stripped of inferences, so that he can draw his own conclusions. All this contrasts with the *opinion* of an expert, which rests upon a different basis. One turns to the expert precisely because he has special knowledge to apply to the problem. The expert is called to make needed observations, draw the proper inferences, and give an opinion in a matter which those seeking the advice are not qualified to form for themselves. So the expert is to give an opinion. Should, then, the layperson accept whatever opinion the expert gives? This isn't a nice question to answer.

Here is my answer to the practical problem of laypersons passing judgment upon expert opinion. Though the opinion of a qualified authority is not reasonably laid aside on the basis of lay common sense, it is unwise also to receive expert advice with a passive or unquestioning attitude. After all, the original qualification of the authority as *professionally qualified* and *personally reliable* was a judgment that could be misplaced. And even the best authority may be mistaken. So in a serious case—a major medical decision comes immediately to mind—one should seek the safeguard of a second opinion by an expert chosen independently of the first. That most people fail to do this has been brought out in the report of a congressional subcommittee which estimated that some two million unnecessary operations were performed in the United States in 1977. The subcommittee pointed out that patient use of a voluntary second-opinion

---

[1]Another approach to a serious medical problem is to go to a diagnostic clinic that is well regarded in reputable medical circles.

program has so far been low.[2] Other safeguards are to request justification for the opinion by a factual explanation in terms understandable to the layperson, a possibility which experts often provide along with their opinion anyway and which usually can be provided except for very technical matters. Finally, when expert opinion concerns an ongoing problem so that a prediction is in order, then a prediction should be called for and a re-evaluation made if subsequent events do not bear it out.

Need an expert hold representative views in accord with others in his field? The slightest glance at history provides an answer, for history is replete with instances in which experts have clung to the prevailing practice and have resisted new views that turned out to be correct. For example, most of the medical treatments used today were not accepted practice a hundred years ago, and there is no reason to suppose that the process of change is at an end. Yet as long as conflicting views are held by authorities in a field, one cannot regard the views of either side as established. This makes it improper to cite an authority holding unrepresentative views without acknowledging the fact that there is conflict in the field. The same ethic should bind the authority; he should not give advice without pointing to the existence of other views if professional opinion on the matter is split seriously. Where expert opinion is divided, the layperson is in a quandary: he may do the obvious things such as seek additional opinions, try to determine which view enjoys the better-qualified support, or examine the arguments offered to support the differing opinions. A division of expert opinion spotlights the risk of error.

Before leaving the topic of the maverick expert who does not follow along with his peers, I wish to suggest the wisdom of hearing unorthodox views with respect, particularly if they come from a person of outstanding ability or if evidence of their successful application is at hand. Most authorities in any field are not remarkable as original thinkers; rather they are people who have made that field their specialty and source of livelihood. Experts do not differ from ordinary people in their tendency to accept what they have been taught and to believe what others around them believe. Further, respectability and security may depend upon doing what everybody else does. The doctor who follows "generally accepted procedure" will not be controversial and will be safe in a suit for malpractice. All these influences explain why great innovators such as Louis Pasteur or Linus Pauling are met with opposition from their colleagues. Dr. Carlton Fredericks has this to say about the problem:

> The weight of the consensus in medicine is formidable. It salutes a practioner who uses the "accepted form" of treatment even if this treatment does little or nothing for the patient; it condemns and may even punish a physician who uses an "unaccepted form" of treatment, even if that treatment

---

[2]"10,000 people died in 2 million unnecessary operations in 1977," *Boston Herald American*, December 27, 1978, reporting the findings of a subcommittee report of the U. S. House of Representatives.

may help a patient. There is even a motto perpetuating this philosophy: Be not the first by whom the new is tried nor yet the last to lay the old aside![3]

The expert is sought for his knowledge. His opinions are entitled to weight because they are based upon knowledge that others do not have. But this clear-cut notion that the opinion of an expert is to be accepted when it is based upon knowledge runs into two difficulties.

First is the difficulty of the relative certainty of some fields as compared to others. Expert opinion works best in matters that are subject to objective analysis. One thinks at once of engineering and the natural sciences, for in these areas laypersons lack the knowledge and even the vocabulary to discuss the problems technically. These are matters in which solutions are most generally tangible and undeniably workable or not workable, a natural check which imposes caution and a healthy humility.

In contrast, one may cite other areas in which clear measurements are hard to come by and the subjective values of the investigator are not so easily excluded. One thinks of history, economics, and the social sciences generally. Let's take the investment counselor as a clear and, perchance, a practical example. Conceding him to be qualified in his field, one can yet realize that particular business concerns and the stock market generally are subject to so many variables that *any* opinion will be tainted with a substantial risk of error. "The expert is sought for his knowledge," as we said, but what becomes of expert opinion where all knowledge is more or less unsure? Clearly, when a field is plagued with uncertainties it doesn't improve matters to cast aside whatever knowledge there may be and boldly implement lay opinions. On the other hand, the evidence of expert opinion in matters in which subjective influences can't be excluded and in which there is a high risk of error has to be viewed like any evidence that is not as reliable as one would wish.

A second limitation on expert opinion arises from the limits of knowledge itself. Since the expert is sought of his knowledge, his opinion will not resolve the many matters of philosophy, taste, and social policy which elude definitive answers through a reservoir of knowledge. A decision to follow the lead of a person or organization in matters of faith, moral values, political ideology, or standards of beauty is a philosophical commitment. Here there may be wisdom but not an objective weighing of evidence in the light of knowledge.

The democratic process allows to every layperson his tiny tug on the throttle of government policy, with the expectable consequences that democracies pursue erratic and sometimes unenlightened courses. Would we be better governed by experts? One thinks of Winston Churchill's dictum, "Democracy is the worst form of government—except for all the others." No, determining basic policies is not a function for experts. The fact that sound policy is a mixture of

---

[3]Carlton Fredericks and Herman Goodman, *Low Blood Sugar and You* (New York: Grosset & Dunlap, 1969), pp. 44–45.

philosophical commitment and knowledge creates a dilemma that democracy has to live with by accepting whatever errors of uninformed direction are mixed into the control of policy. Were I asked to cite such a cost born of primitive public attitudes, I would cite the prisons of America, most of which are schools of crime for reasons that criminologists well understand.

CIRCUMSTANTIAL EVIDENCE

Any fact may be circumstantial evidence for something: a valentine, a fingerprint, borrowing a dime. Though circumstantial evidence often is spoken of as if it were an unsatisfactory and dubious kind, in reality it is like inference in varying through a whole spectrum, from facts of undeniable significance down to those that are worthless as evidence. So if you have a prejudice against "circumstantial evidence," shed it. The form as such should not be condemned. After all, whole fields of knowledge rest largely upon circumstantial evidence: geology, paleontology, and archaeology, to name three. Further, whenever no one is available to give a direct observation of an event, then inferring what happened from circumstantial evidence is the *only* way to determine what occurred. Even if there are many eyewitnesses, this is no reason for not using pertinent circumstantial evidence too. In short, circumstantial evidence is a large part of all evidence, and the question is not whether to use it but how to use it best.

Let's begin with the strong points of circumstantial evidence. "Facts don't lie," the saying goes—and all facts are circumstances. A Doubting Thomas will note, however, that facts can be tampered with or arranged to mislead. For instance, when George Rogers Clark put his snowshoes on backward to avoid the unpleasant consequences of the Indians tracking him down, he arranged the circumstantial evidence so ingeniously that it still makes a good story. Yet deliberately manipulating the facts to mislead is exceptional, and the notion holding circumstances more dependable than the accounts of witnesses is often justified. Crime and conflict, for all their notoriety, are exceptional, and even in these areas in which a motive to tamper with evidence exists, most of the facts will be thought insignificant at the time, or not discoverable, or simply unchangeable. We need to focus on the mainstream, which clearly is that circumstances often support a conclusion very reliably. Not only may circumstances be strong in their implications; they often may be examined at leisure so that any chance of error in observation or in the memory of witnesses is eliminated.

Circumstances are like the strands of a cable. Each single circumstance standing alone may be weak, yet when the circumstances are woven together they may fasten a conclusion with enormous strength. For instance, one issue in the perjury trial of Alger Hiss was whether or not Hiss knew Chambers in 1937 and 1938, which Hiss denied. Chambers' former maid testified that Alger and Priscilla Hiss visited the Chambers' house during that time; Chambers testified that Hiss loaned him $400 to buy a car in November 1937, and bank records showed a withdrawal of $400 from the Hiss account a few days before the car purchase. Chambers produced four notes in Hiss' handwriting dated in the first three months of 1938, together with typewritten copies of forty-two government documents which he claimed Hiss had delivered to him. Study of the typing characteristics of the copied documents showed them to be the same as the typing produced by an old Woodstock typewriter in Hiss' possession in 1938. (All typewriters have their own characteristic peculiarities: irregularities in slant, alignment, or spacing of the letters is sometimes visible to the eye, while nicks and flaws in the type show up under microscopic examination.) Taken together, this evidence points to Hiss knowing Chambers—unless the testimony is part of a plot to frame Hiss, as he contended.

What about the weaknesses of circumstantial evidence? Is there a basis for the popular prejudice against it? Indeed there is. Nothing is worse than weak circumstantial evidence, and even circumstances that at first sight seem clear in their implication can turn out to have been misinterpreted. I still remember a scene from a movie which tortured the audience with this problem. Flash: a beautiful child, a mere toddler, drops mother's golden locket into the laundry hamper. Next, the washwoman, honest as the day is long, is striding down a sun-drenched street, the laundry basket perched on her head. Arriving home, she puts down the basket, discovers the locket with wonderment—and you have it, in come the police. The audience knows what has happened, yet somehow the police can't see it and it takes reels of film to straighten matters out. The great weakness of circumstantial evidence is the same as the great weakness of hypothesis: it is that the circumstances may be consistent with either of two explanations, but one of these explanations is not thought of. The facts observed are correct as far as they go, while the inference drawn from them is not. So long as other possible explanations go unnoticed, the circumstantial evidence may seem to give strong support for what is in fact a false theory.

Now we come to the ideal evidential situation: where direct observation and circumstances confirm one another. The direct observer cuts out all other possible explanations, for he observed the event himself. And the circumstantial evidence confirms the observation which, standing alone, might be an instance of misobservation or of willful distortion. Nor is it rare to have a combination of direct and circumstantial evidence; indeed, the availability of both types is commonplace. For example, Norse sagas tell of voyages to Greenland and Vinland. But where was Vinland? It wasn't until 1959 that a Norse settlement identified by numerous artifacts was discovered on Epaves Bay, Newfoundland. The area of the settlement possesses many features mentioned in the sagas: a shallow tidal bay, a cape jutting North, islands to the North of the cape, and an abundance of salmon and sea birds. The circumstances confirm that the sagas report truly of voyages to a settlement in the New World.

SUMMARY

When a witness has a poor reputation for veracity or has a motive to distort, these conditions in themselves do not justify concluding that the witness' statements must be false. Such conditions may justify not accepting the account given as true unless it is corroborated.

Minor discrepancies in the accounts of witnesses are a natural outcome of the fact that different witnesses observe different details and retain different memories of them.

The maximum recall generally is obtained by a free narrative from the observer, followed by questioning.

An expert source should be (a) *personally reliable,* and (b) *professionally qualified.* The notion of personal reliability applies to all witnesses and includes matters such as willingness to tell the truth, absence of bias, freedom from duress, and conscientiously attending to the problem. The requirements for being professionally qualified as an expert are:

1. The expert source must be identified.
2. The source must have professional standing.
3. The source must be current—i.e., not obsolete.
4. The opinion given must be within the field of special competence.

The expert is sought for his knowledge. From this it follows that although an expert may be asked to state the basis for his opinion, still his opinion as such is evidence.

Since knowledge is the basis for expert opinion, matters of faith, taste, or social policy involving philosophical commitments or value judgments are beyond the sphere of expert opinion.

An expert opinion is not entitled to uncritical acceptance. The personal reliability or professional qualifications of an authority are always subject to re-evaluation, and since all opinion is subject to error one may seek the added evidence of another authority to guard against this possibility.

There is no satisfactory way for a layperson to choose between conflicting expert opinions. Only common-sense precautions can be taken. Whenever a substantial conflict exists on the point, an expert should reveal this fact along with his opinion.

Circumstantial evidence is neither strong nor weak as such. Some strengths of circumstantial evidence are:

1. Circumstances may be distinctive and numerous, making their implication highly probable.

2. Some circumstances cannot be tampered with, misobserved, or distorted; often circumstances can be observed carefully and at leisure.

Some weaknesses of circumstantial evidence are:

1. Occasionally circumstances are arranged to mislead, or they may be tampered with, misobserved or distorted.
2. Circumstances which appear to support one conclusion may support another conclusion equally well. Yet if the alternative interpretation is not thought of, then the circumstances may be taken as convincing support for a wrong conclusion.

The ideal evidential situation is a combination of direct observation and supporting circumstances. The direct observation confirms that the circumstances are not misinterpreted and the circumstances confirm that there is no error in the observation.

EXERCISES FOR CHAPTER 20
pages 324–336

I. Answer **T** for "true" and **F** for "false":

_____ **1.** A strong motive to falsify justifies a presumption that the source is not telling the truth.

_____ **2.** If there is any conflict between witnesses, at least one of them should be discredited.

_____ **3.** Questioning almost always produces a greater recall of a situation than is obtained from an unrestricted narration by the observer.

_____ **4.** John testifies, "James said he was tired of the job." This is hearsay evidence.

_____ **5.** Those who look at evidence critically realize that hearsay evidence is always unreliable.

_____ **6.** Direct observation is by nature more reliable than circumstantial evidence.

_____ **7.** A fact is most reliably established when there is both direct observation and circumstantial evidence.

_____ **8.** Evidence inadmissible in court may or may not be reliable evidence from the viewpoint of one seeking to determine the truth.

_____ **9.** The text admits that it is hard to know how to qualify an authority in his field.

_____ **10.** At least the text has to concede that often it is difficult in practice to be sure a particular individual is especially competent within his field.

_____ **11.** A reference librarian is an expert in finding written information.

_____ **12.** A careful investigation of a technical matter admits the opinions of experts and avoids relying upon the opinions of laypersons.

II. Provide short answers to the following questions:

1. The greatest possible recall is usually obtained by a combination of free narration followed by interrogation. Explain why this is so, regardless of whether the witness is willing or reluctant.

2. "No two people do or ever can speak the same language, exactly. This makes a certain amount of semantical misunderstanding unavoidable." Agree or disagree. Then explain your position.

3. What does it mean to say that an expert should be (a) "professionally qualified" and (b) "personally reliable"? In your answer, cite several specific requirements that are needed to fulfill (a). Cite others needed to fulfill (b).

4. In what kinds of fields does expert opinion work most satisfactorily?

5. What kinds of questions are in general not satisfactorily resolved by reference to expert opinion?

6. What is circumstantial evidence? Give an example.

7. Make two lists, one showing the strengths or advantages of circumstantial evidence, and one showing its intrinsic weaknesses or disadvantages.

8. "A number of different circumstances, no one of which is unusual or strong in itself, may when taken together become extremely strong evidence for the conclusion that they imply." Justify this assertion by providing an appropriate illustration.

9. In an ideal evidential situation, direct observation and circumstances confirm one another. Explain what makes such a combination "ideal."

III.   Refresh your recollection of the Lindbergh Case on pages 255–258, and then answer the following questions:

1. Did the state's case against Hauptmann rest principally upon direct observation or on circumstantial evidence?

2. Did the circumstances in connection with one another make a strong "cable of evidence" supporting a conviction of Hauptmann?

3. Though no such testimony was available, what sort of testimony would convert the state's case against Hauptmann into what the text termed an "ideal evidentiary situation"?

chapter 21

Judging Statistics

Statistics are facts expressed as numbers. Reducing the bulk of innumerable observations to a few faceless numbers is absolutely necessary to make many kinds of material usable. Yet the manipulation of numbers, unfortunately, is both technical and easy to abuse. In this chapter we take a look at some ways to check statistics. Though our approach is akin to the treatment of fallacy in stressing the possibility of flaws, still the object isn't negative, since one wishes to accept sound work just as much as to guard against being taken in.

"Statistics are no substitute for judgment," remarked Henry Clay.[1] Turn around the comment and it remains apt: "Judgment is no substitute for statistics." Taking Clay's comment in the spirit intended, one can acknowledge that there are many decisions that cannot be made mechanically according to some statistical analysis. At the same time, statistics has been developed into an essential tool in numerous fields to the point where only reference to statistically organized data makes an effective decision possible. For example, a police blotter sets down crimes in the order reported, but only organizing this record according to type, area, and time will give the useful overall view of crime statistics. Sampling procedures, a comparatively recent development, can give sound support for generalizations used in public opinion polls and marketing. Correlations observable in organized data help point the way to the discovery of causes. Probability theory underpins the insurance industry by assessing the probability for the occurrence of events of various types when there is no way of

---

[1]Stephen K. Campbell, *Flaws and Fallacies in Statistical Thinking* (Englewood Cliffs, N.J.: Prentice-Hall, 1974), p. 152.

knowing when a specific event of the type described will occur. Government and business are future-oriented: they habitually plan their operations on the basis of statistics showing present situations and future trends. It simply makes no sense to deride statistics as a subject.

What is needed and practical within the brief treatment of this book is to look at some standards that should be applied in judging whether a particular set of statistics is worthy of confidence.

WHERE DO THE FIGURES COME FROM?

Unfortunately, inadequately explained statistics may make superficial or dishonest work appear significant and accurate. For this reason, no statistician will accept figures without knowing the source, just as no one should credit an opinion as coming from an expert unless the authority is identified. With figures, there are two kinds of sources: there is the source that originally recorded the data, and there is the party responsible for the use being made of it. Where the data was assembled originally to provide general information or, at least, was assembled without reference to the particular use being made of it, then there is obvious relief from the rankling suspicion that surrounds figures gathered by a party with an axe to grind. Nobody misses the purpose of the claim "based on figures from the U.S. Census" or any other source of known thoroughness and reliability. Whatever the original source for the material may be, one must know and evaluate also the party presenting the material in argument. Here one comes to that not-to-be-avoided question, "Is the source reliable?" Though there is no certain answer to this query, a good deal can be learned from the quality of the presentation of the statistics themselves. A good presentation will describe the amount and the reliability of the data, frankly conceding limitations as well as pointing out strengths. A source that does not trouble with these details is in effect asking for trust without bothering to describe the evidence. Statistics resting on unknown data have not earned trust.

WHAT UNIT IS EMPLOYED?

Statistics concern units: "students," "unemployed," "major distributors," and so forth. It is surprising how terms that seem clear enough at first glance have a way of becoming uncertain when one gets down to dealing with them.

Does the term "students" include part-time students, auditors, enrollees in any institution that calls itself a school? Are the criteria for being counted as "unemployed" the same in the United States and Italy? Unless "major distributor" is defined in some way, any talk about such a unit will be meaningless. At least a tolerably clear notion of what the unit includes is central to understanding what is being claimed. When we cited in the last chapter a congressional subcommittee's report alleging that some 2 million "unnecessary operations" were performed in the United States in 1977, did you wonder what the term "unnecessary operations" included? You should have. The committee included as unnecessary those operations performed without appropriate medical treatment being tried first and separate operations performed on the same patient within days of one another when no medical justification existed for not doing both during the initial surgery.

Sometimes the unit changes. For example, a sales manager may note that sales of electric mixers have declined and wonder if changes are needed in his sales force or advertising budget. He knows also that on May 1 the company discontinued giving discounts and that on August 15 a new model was brought out. Where the unit changes, results will not be strictly comparable, and only knowledge of the situation can tell whether the differences are great enough to vitiate statistical comparisons that include as the same unit cases with minor differences. Finally, there is the blatantly undefined class which will mask any sort of chicanery, as in a claim that "37 out of 43 professional tea tasters recommend Winchett's." Here we have an incomplete term. "Recommended Winchett's" *for what*? Best buy for the money? Best-tasting to Chinese consumers? Best quality in its class? In short, the unit is fundamental; to be unclear about the unit is to be unclear about what the figures deal with.

Whenever the unit cited does not fairly cover the situation to which it is assumed to apply, a distorted impression results. *The Washington Monthly* gives this example:

> If you've always questioned in your heart those defenses of the federal bureaucracy that cite how little it has grown since World War II, Spencer Rich of *The Washington Post* recently confirmed your doubts. While the federal bureaucracy has grown by only a third to 2.8 million since 1950, the number of people who work for universities, research organizations, and state and local governments who are paid by the federal government has grown to between three and four million. HEW, for example, in addition to paying its 144,000 regular employees, has 980,000 others whose salaries it pays through other organizations. So ask the real HEW to stand up and you'll see over a million people rise.[2]

---

[2]Charles Peters, "Tilting at Windmills," *The Washington Monthly*, September 1978, p. 8. Reprinted with permission from *The Washington Monthly.* Copyright 1978 by The Washington Monthly Co., 1028 Connecticut Ave., N.W., Washington, D.C. 20036.

HOW WAS THE SAMPLE OBTAINED?

Since an enumeration of all the data often is impractical or impossible to make, statistics must report the results of sampling. The U.S. Census of 1970, for example, used an intermediate form for 15% of the population and a still longer form for 5%, thus securing information beyond the questions of the basic form with less expense and trying of the patience of citizens. Samples are notorious for sometimes being of inadequate size or biased in some way. Since samples that are too small or skewed are unreliable, it's necessary to have a description of the size of the sample and how it was obtained if one is to have at least a sporting chance for assessing its reliability. Responsible sources *invariably* supply this information, and where results of sampling are supplied without a description of the procedure used, there is good reason to doubt the results and withhold judgment. After all, painstaking and scrupulous work will hardly be presented without mention of careful sampling procedures which would give impressive support. The shallowest assertions of all are those supplying a mere ratio: "Four out of five dentists recommend. . . ." If we are to believe there ever was an actual count behind such statements, there is no knowing whether the ratio rests on five dentists or five hundred, let alone how the sample was chosen. Ratios resting on unidentified or inadequate samples should be rejected out of hand.

Though sampling is a large subject, a few paragraphs may show some of its characteristics. We will start by noticing the difference between dependent and independent events. Suppose there are ten pennies on the floor, five heads up and five tails. You are to pick them up without looking at them and, obviously, the initial chance for your picking up a head is even with the chance for a tail. The first one you pick happens to be a head. Since you are not to return it to the floor, the chance for picking up a head the next time is now 4/9 while the chance for a tail is 5/9. Assume you happen to pick another head: the chance for yet another head on the next draw becomes 3/8 vs. 5/8 for a tail. Here you are dealing with dependent events, for the odds of future drawings are influenced by the outcome of previous drawings.

Now let's take a different situation. Suppose six fair tosses of a penny happen to give you six heads. Each toss is independent of the others and the odds remain even for heads or tails on the next toss. Some people believe in a sort of mystical "law of atonement" whereby they conceive that after a long run of heads or of poor hands at cards or whatever, the odds change against a continuation of the experience. Not so if the events are independent. With dependent events, as we have seen, the odds do change.

The so-called "law of averages" is a different situation. This notion takes no position about what the chance relating to the *next* case in a series may be. The law of averages notes that experience in the long run will tend to come closer and closer in percentage to whatever dispersion truly exists. For example, the following records the result of 100 fair tosses with a quarter:

No. of Tosses	Heads	Tails	Percentage Excess of Heads
10	7	3	40%
20	15	5	50%
30	17	13	13%
40	22	18	10%
50	26	24	4%
60	31	29	3%
70	37	33	6%
80	40	40	0
90	48	42	7%
100	50	50	0

We were fortunate in having this particular series start with an inequality that registered a large percentage of excess heads at the outset. The somewhat uneven reduction of the disparity as tosses proceeded is characteristic of the tendency of larger numbers to come closer in percentage to whatever dispersion truly exists. A deficit of heads never did develop in the series as it might easily have done, while the end on an exact 50–50 balance was unusual.

In a heads or tails example one is dealing with the simplest of situations in which the two possibilities are equiprobable. However, it does not matter what kind of dispersion the subject may have so far as the tendency of larger numbers of an unbiased sample to approximate more and more closely whatever the true dispersion is. Another way of stating this tendency is that the larger the number of instances in an unbiased sample, the more reliable the sample will tend to be.

Sampling does not work well in identifying relatively small numbers of cases among a large population. To take the example of an oyster bed of 1,000 oysters with only one having a pearl, no sample could show accurately the ratio of the pearl to the non–pearl-bearing oysters. A sample of 300 oysters, whether it included the pearl or not, would in any case not be a reasonably accurate measure of the situation. If interest were in the size of the oysters and if we assume that 40% of them are under 8 ounces in weight, a random sample of 300 probably would approximate the 40% figure satisfactorily. In short, sampling works best in measuring situations common enough to be represented numerous times within the sample taken.

Sampling works exceptionally well when the cases are homogeneous—that is, when all cases in the population measured are the same. In fact, in a perfectly homogeneous situation any sample will be perfect. One sip of milk will determine whether the whole jug is sour, one cup of grain may be enough to assess the quality of the whole bin. In this kind of instance the reasoning is deductive rather than inductive, for everything rests upon the premise "This is a homogeneous situation." As situations vary from being perfectly homogeneous to situations containing more and more diverse cases, then larger samples are needed. How large? The answer cannot be precise. In principle, the sample needs to be large enough to give all situations within the population sampled a chance to turn up in substantial numbers. For example, a sample of 500 might be adequate to forecast the voting patterns for a town election of 5,000 voters, while a sample of the same number would be wholly inadequate in forecasting a national election. This is because the number 500 is insufficient to measure with approximate accuracy the many diverse areas and interests involved in a national election.

When an adequate number of cases are examined, still the result will be unreliable if the sample is biased in some way. To avoid a biased or loaded sample one must devise a way that allows every member of the population an equal chance of being selected in the sample. Achieving randomness requires some knowledge of the situation. Frequently names can be taken at intervals from an alphabetical list. Or, any procedure will do as long as it assures that no factor other than chance will influence the selection of cases.

One way of checking whether a sample is biased is to take another sample selected by a different method. If both samples yield approximately the same results, probably there is no serious bias in either, though it remains possible for the same undetected bias to be present in both. This appears to be what happened in the famous *Literary Digest* poll of 1936 which predicted victory for Alf Landon in what turned out to be a landslide vote for Franklin Roosevelt. The *Digest* was aware that canvassing undue numbers from lists of its subscribers, telephone directories, and city directories (some people do not even make the city directory) might bias the sample. As a check, the *Digest* sent its straw ballot to every registered voter in Allentown, Pennsylvania—yet lo and behold, the Allentown results turned out to have the same inaccuracy as the poll at large. "Do Democrats live further from mailboxes than Republicans?" editorialized the bewildered *Digest*. No, but present-day analysis is that Democrats had slightly less of the white-collar "clerical habit" of filling out forms and mailing them, and this unthought-of bias affected both the survey as a whole and the Allentown survey designed as a check.[3]

When a population is heterogeneous, there will be a greater chance of securing a representative sample if its strata are identified and a sample is taken for each stratum. The strata are the various features within the population which seem likely to bear upon the generalization. For example, if one wished to generalize about public attitudes in the United States toward abortion, one would have to recognize as strata the different age groups, religious affiliations, social levels, geographical areas, and whether an individual is male or female. A stratified sample would be subdivided into samples for each of these strata

---

[3]"What Went Wrong with the Polls?" *Literary Digest*, 122 (November 14, 1936), p. 7.

weighted according to the proportion of each class of strata found in the population. Assuming that sex may have a bearing on attitude, the proper proportion of males to females should be applied for each stratum. In effect, stratified samples break down a population into subgroups that are more uniform and, as was noted before, the more homogeneous the group the better the chance a random sample has of being representative.

WHAT'S IN AN "AVERAGE"?

An average is a tremendous simplification. Unfortunately, the word "average" is applied in different ways so that a figure referred to as an "average" may not be the result of the process the audience has in mind. Statisticians avoid the term for this reason, preferring instead to speak of the *mean*, the *median*, or the *mode*. These concepts are easy and much used.

The word "mean" ordinarily refers to "arithmetic mean," which is obtained by adding the values for the units together and then dividing by the number of units—the process generally in mind when one speaks of an average. Arithmetic means are useful when the range of values is reasonably narrow so that the resulting mean is fairly typical of the situation. For example, if the average or arithmetic mean wage for carpenters in Miami is $10.94 per hour, this can be taken as a fair indication of carpenters' wages at that time and place, since carpenters' wages do not vary tremendously. But where six stockbrokers in an office earn commissions of $5,000, $15,000, $20,000, $20,000, $20,000 and $90,000 then it makes no sense to declare that the average is $30,000, a result influenced by the earnings of the extraordinary successful broker to the point that it distorts the situation. In short, an average or arithmetic mean is a proper simplification. where the result represents the situation fairly, but it should be avoided where extreme values create a meaningless and misleading picture. Even when an arithmetic mean fairly represents the group, it is a most naive error to expect it to reflect the nature of any particular member. The day when the stocks of the Dow Jones average have risen 15 points may be the day your particular stock has gone down 2 points on a frolic of its own. Yet the Dow Jones "average" is an arithmetic mean and it is meaningful in indicating whether the day's sales produced a rising or a declining trend.

A *median* is used to avoid the distortion which an arithmetic mean produces when it is influenced by a few extreme values. To obtain the median, all values are arranged in order of magnitude and then the central value is selected as the median. If the number of values is an odd number, then the central figure is the median; when there is an even number of values, then the median is the midpoint between the two values which are the central pair in the sequence. The result in any case is that half the values stand above and half below the median. Obviously, the median will not be influenced by the size of the extremes, and this is its advantage. Whenever there is a considerable scattering of values, resort to the median is most apt to produce a typical figure. One might, for instance, be interested in the median time for a power failure uninfluenced by occasional breakdowns of exceptional duration.

The *mode,* another way of avoiding the influence of untypical extremes, is the value that occurs most frequently. The approach is useful only when there is a definite clustering around the modal figure so that it represents a common occurrence which some reason makes helpful to identify. For example, a manufacturer might find the frequency with which orders of a certain size are received more enlightening than either the arithmetic mean or the median. Though the mode is not a rare approach and it seems well to identify it, the most common problems arise with arithmetic means and medians. So we will return to them.

The object of any sort of average should be to gain a useful simplification without misleading. One way to do this is to accompany the average, be it arithmetic mean, median, or mode, with a statement of the range of the figures so that one can perceive where the extremes lie. The range is simply the difference between the highest and the lowest figure. A baby book is a good illustration of the need for the range; statements that a baby walks at 15 months or weighs so much at age 4 will worry mothers whose children do not conform to the oversimplified figure that is taken as "normal." Stating the range over which those events may take place gives a much better picture of the situation. Sometimes the range, too, suffers from the presence of a small scattering of extremes that are far removed from the great majority of values. For instance, a test might have a 10 from a student who had given up and a 100 from the class genius, so that the range is 10 to 100 with not many grades approaching either extreme. In fact, since the range is determined by subtracting the smallest from the largest value, large numbers of cases tend to turn up more extremes and thus to produce an enormous range. To deal with this, statisticians have devised the *10–90 percentile range,* which is computed by disregarding those cases which fall below the 10th percentile or above the 90th percentile. Percentile simply means percentage; thus the 10th percentile has 10% of the cases falling below it while the 90th percentile has 90% below it and, naturally, 10% above it. To calculate percentiles, all the cases must be arranged in order of magnitude, while the range is more easily arrived at by simply picking out the lowest and highest values, a fact that may contribute to the greater popularity of the range even though the 10–90 percentile range has the advantage of not being influenced by a few uncommon extremes.

To conclude, all averages are enormous simplifications. Consequently, no sort of average can portray the *nature* of a diverse group and there simply is no such thing as an "average student," "average teacher," or average anything else that can be taken to represent the situation.

OF WHAT IS THE PERCENTAGE GIVEN?

Percentages are a handy way to express the size of one thing relative to something else. "Interest at 6% is included in the monthly installments," "The supermarket makes only 1% profit on sales," "Our prices on closed-out items have been slashed 50% and now we are cutting them 30% again." All these seem clear enough and indeed they are, for those familiar with the arithmetic of percentages. Every percentage depends for its meaning upon *what it is a percentage of*. In some situations it is easy to make a wrong assumption about the figure to which a percentage applies and, in fact, confusing ways of calculating interest have been used so repeatedly by credit departments and loan agencies that some states have adopted laws requiring the effective rate of interest paid on an annual basis to be stated on the face of installment contracts and loan agreements. After all, interest at 8% per year on the unpaid balance of an installment loan may be described as 8% interest, but where interest is calculated on the original amount of the loan until the whole is paid off, then the effective interest rate is increased. Assuming that the loan is paid in twelve equal monthly installments, then the average balance will be approximately half of the original balance, making an effective interest rate close to 16%. The supermarket that makes only 1% on the total amount of its sales may appear to be doing its customers a favor. But the percentage of profit on total sales is not same as the profit realized on an annual basis, for a supermarket inventory sells rapidly and hence it turns over many times in a year. Nor is percentage of profit on sales a measure of the cost of distribution to consumers, because all the costs of the business, whatever they may be, have been added as costs before profit is computed. In the case of prices slashed 50% and then 30%, the reduction from the original price is 65%, not 80%. Each percentage reduction (or increase) is calculated on its own base, and a second percentage cannot be added to the first. Thus the dollar item that is reduced 50% becomes priced at 50¢, and a further markdown of 30% will be applied to the new 50¢ base to make the price 35¢.

Unless one starts with the same or, at least, comparable bases, it will be misleading to compare changes expressed as percentages of growth or decline. For example, fears of the United States falling behind in technology or productive capacity have been fed by quotations of startling percentage increases of production in other parts of the world. Though the percentage of a change may be great, before assessing its significance one must know the size of its base. After all, an increase in bicycle production from 15,000 to 60,000 units is a 400% increase, while an increase from 2,000,000 to 2,500,000 units is only 25%. At the same time, adding 500,000 units is a greater change in absolute numbers than adding 45,000 additional units. A look at U.S. population statistics provides a dramatic illustration of the need to attend to absolute numbers as well as growth rates. The United States was the first modern nation to initiate a regular and detailed census. Here are some highlights:

Year of Census	Population Rounded to 100,000	Increase from Previous Census	Percentage Increase to Nearest % Point
1790	3,900,000	—	—
1800	5,300,000	1,400,000	36%
1810	7,200,000	1,900,000	36%
1880	50,200,000	11,600,000	26%
1950	150,700,000	19,000,000	14%
1960	179,300,000	28,600,000	19%
1970	203,200,000	23,900,000	13%

Source: U.S. Bureau of the Census, as published in *The World Almanac and Book of Facts 1978* (New York: Newspaper Enterprise Association, Inc., 1977), pp. 190–91. Numerical increase and percentage increase computed by Harold N. Wells.

Note that the rate of increase has fallen from 36% to 13%, a reduction of nearly two-thirds. Yet despite the greatly diminished rate of increase expressed by the percentages, the lower rates operating upon a mass base produce large increases in absolute numbers. Inspection will show that the increase during the twenty years, 1950–1970, equals the entire population in 1880.

WHAT ABOUT ROUNDING?

Rounding figures helps to make large numbers easier to grasp. The population figures just cited wouldn't be improved by dropping the rounding—how long did the United States continue to have the 203,235,298 people officially reported by the 1970 census? Corporations regularly report their activities to their shareholders rounded to the nearest thousand. Splendid. Figures in round numbers should have—and usually do have—a note stating the degree of the rounding. What if the rounding isn't noted? At best this is sloppy work and at worst the figures are mere estimates or guesses without benefit of counting any data at all. Obvious common sense rejects figures given in unexplained round numbers for a situation one would not expect to come out even if counted. Then there is the apparent guess expressed in statements like "nine out of ten guests do not steal hotel towels." Such an assertion quantifies the estimate; its a useful device but not a statistic.

Sometimes a sort of false accuracy is suggested by carrying a statistical result to several decimal points. If the material contained borderline cases or if the calculations are based upon assumptions or on a sample, then the results can be approximate only. In such situations it makes no sense to present computations down to digits or decimal points suggesting an accuracy exceeding that of the original material. One can laugh off the occasional claim of a 3.027% increase in efficiency as naiveté or, more likely, a transparent attempt to impress with fictitious accuracy.

HOW ACCURATE ARE THE FIGURES?

The preciseness of numbers suggests exactness even when the original information may be questionable or its classification subjective. It's a disturbing thought and one apt to be put aside for the lack of anything else to go on. The best we can do here is to point to sources of difficulty which have to be mulled over if one is lucky enough to have a glimpse of how the figures were obtained. Public opinion polls are a good example of the difficulty of getting information that is sound in the first place. Beyond the problem of getting a representative sample, all sorts of influences come to play in the answers: the wording of the question, reaction to the interviewer on a personal level (including reactions to the social or ethnic group he seems to represent), irritation aroused by the questions themselves, or desire to please the interviewer by giving the "right" answer. Again, one can't take at face value what people choose to respond about their racial prejudices, sex life, income, reading habits, or anything else when they may feel that a true answer would fall short of the culturally approved ideal. Even in so cut and dried a matter as marital status, as Reichmann points out, the census regularly reports slightly more women claiming to be married than men!

In addition to the truth of the original data, the use of subjective judgment in classifying the material may be a major influence over the picture that emerges. Yet subjective judgments are unavoidable in situations having borderline cases that are hard to classify; for instance, a hospital administration seeking to rate cases as "critical," "serious," "ordinary," and "minor" would surely find the resulting record influenced by the outlook of whoever made the evaluations. One way to reduce the affect of individual judgment in such situations is to employ several individuals, rotating them to see if they produce similar evaluations for the same or similar groups. It isn't comforting to doubt the accuracy of the original data or its measurement, and yet, unless one has a gullible faith in whatever comes expressed in figures, the problem is real. Further, one has to consider whether the data supports the interpretation placed upon it: Do the figures represent "crimes" or "reported crimes" in Philadelphia? Is this the median income of a college class or is it the median answer of those who answered at all?

THE USE OF GRAPHS AND VISUAL DEVICES

Just as statistics simplify raw data, graphs have the purpose of making data comprehensible at a glance. And they should do just that—inform quickly and accurately. Here we will have some fun spotting flaws; fortunately, they're easily spotted when one is aware of them.

Though bars and line charts can show the relative size of numbers clearly, they are drab things compared to a picture. So an eye-catching way for contrasting numbers is to draw pictures of two bags of money or sheafs of wheat or ships or whatever. Such picture charts appear only in popular writing and are a mark of propaganda. Though the height of the pictures reflects relative numbers correctly, their area increases roughly as the square of the height, so that the result is an exaggeration of the difference between the numbers rather than an aid to grasping the true situation. In Fig. 1, the gray bull stands for a value that is twice the amount of the white bull—$25,000 to $50,705. Not bad for ten years investment. But I must confess that the magnificent gray bull whetted my greed to expect more than a mere doubling—which is exactly what the advertiser wanted. How did you fare?

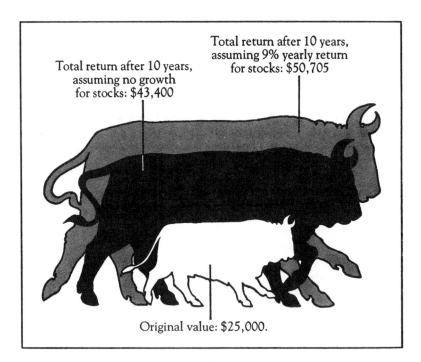

Total return after 10 years, assuming no growth for stocks: $43,400

Total return after 10 years, assuming 9% yearly return for stocks: $50,705

Original value: $25,000.

FIG. 1

Source: Advertisement in *Forbes Magazine*, January 15, 1977, p. 4.

If one wants to catch the eye with pictures and yet not misrepresent, then one may use a standard figure for a certain number of units and arrange the figures in lines to give a visual impression of the relative numbers. The final picture is split as the numbers dictate. The result is essentially a bar chart.

Bar charts indicate relative differences by columns or bars which properly start at line zero so that each column has a height and an area proportional to the numerical differences represented. For example, the International Planned Parenthood Federation illustrated with the bar chart shown in Fig. 2 the varying degree to which fertile couples practice contraception in the different areas of the world, China and the USSR excluded.

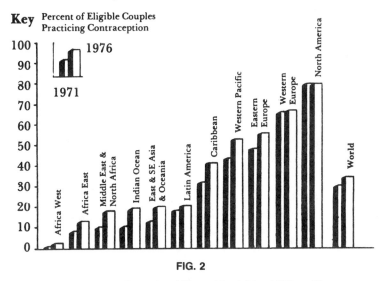

World Contraceptive Practice Levels: 1971 and 1976

FIG. 2

Source: Planned Parenthood News, March/May 1978, p. 15.

The form of this chart is good. It permits one to see at a glance and without distortion the widely different degree to which contraception is practiced in various areas of the world. The accuracy of the data, which was secured by a survey of family planning organizations, is hard to assess.

Those presenting charts, however, sometimes want to exaggerate the impression they make by showing things as looking better—or scarier—than they are. It's the easiest thing in the world to do. All it takes is truncating—that is, cutting off the bottom of the chart, preferably not making this too obvious, so that what is left will be bars heightening the impression of difference. For instance, Fig. 3 shows a graph published by the Rhode Island Department of

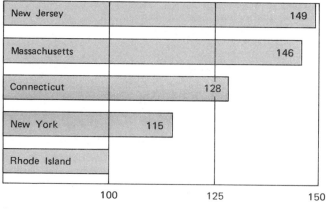

Of the five most industrialized states in
the northeast, Rhode Island may now be the
smallest–*tax* state.

Comparison of business taxes for a general
manufacturing company using a tax ranking index
with Rhode Island equal to 100.

FIG. 3

Source: Advertisement in *Forbes Magazine*, April 15, 1975, p. 27.

Economic Development seeking to impress readers that business taxes in Rhode
Island are lower than those of neighboring states. Note that the bars do not
begin at zero but at a point it apparently did not seem worth numbering as 75.
The result is what Darrell Huff calls a "gee whiz graph" with bars suggesting
Rhode Island taxes one-third those of New Jersey, while the figures show Rhode
Island taxes to be two-thirds of the New Jersey level. Not bad for advocacy.
Is there deception or isn't there? Well, one can say the eye is deceived but not
the mind—that is, not the mind of one who looks closely at the figures. Yet if the
purpose of a chart is to facilitate getting an impression of a situation, then this
one fails by creating a misimpression. Still, there's no saying the information is
false. It isn't. Saving space is the invariable defense for cutting off the bars or
not showing the space down to point zero. When a chart or graph is truncated,
good practice requires a broken line or some device to call attention to the omis-
sion. Figure 4a is a chart showing the presence of truncating, properly indicated.

The very nature of truncating exaggerates fluctuations. By charting the
material of Fig. 4a without truncating, Fig. 4b gives the mind's eye a more
accurate impression of the change in earnings.

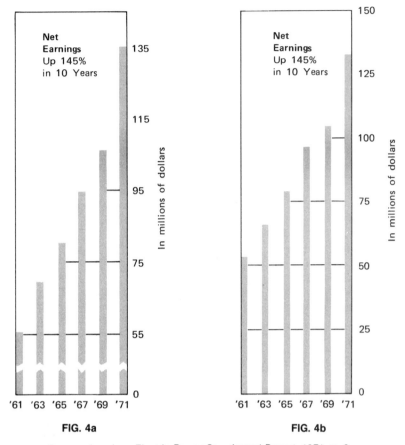

FIG. 4a   FIG. 4b

Source: American Electric Power Co., *Annual Report*, 1971, p. 3.

Figure 4a is something of a model in indicating the truncating with such eye-catching clarity. Many graphs are published with but a scanty indication—such as an inconspicuous jog in the axis line near point zero. This sort of treatment preserves the principle more than it provides any practical warning to those approaching the graph without the possibility of truncating in mind. So, make a habit of examining the values along the axis to protect yourself from the exaggerated impression that truncating creates.

Any failure of a graph to identify the units along both axes should be taken as a red-flag warning for fraud. Figure 5 on the next page illustrates a bit of this tomfoolery published by a company that wanted to exaggerate the subliminal impression of its rising earnings.

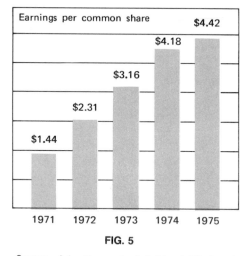

FIG. 5

Source: Advertisement of Ashland Oil, Inc. in
The Wall Street Journal, July 15, 1976.

What is represented by the unidentified lines which the mounting profits are so successfully overtaking? 75¢—of course!

Line graphs are common. They are a great convenience in showing the trend over a period of time. Figure 6 is an example in good form.

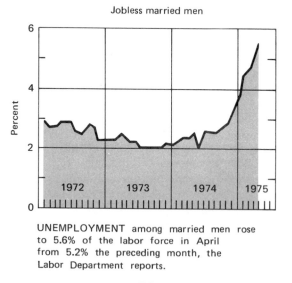

UNEMPLOYMENT among married men rose
to 5.6% of the labor force in April
from 5.2% the preceding month, the
Labor Department reports.

FIG. 6

Source: The Wall Street Journal, June 4, 1975, p. 1.
Reprinted by permission of *The Wall Street Journal* ©
Dow Jones & Company, Inc. 1975. All Rights Reserved.

Note that this graph runs down to point zero, and that its simplicity enables one to perceive quickly and accurately the result of a great amount of data. Most line graphs, like the one here, represent time periods marked off at equal intervals horizontally along the X-axis while quantities or percentages rise vertically along the Y-axis. If the data is incomplete and does not cover all intervals in the time sequence, then a line graph is inappropriate. The spacing chosen for a line graph has a great deal to do with the impression the graph will make. Figure 7 shows the same values charted according to different spacing.

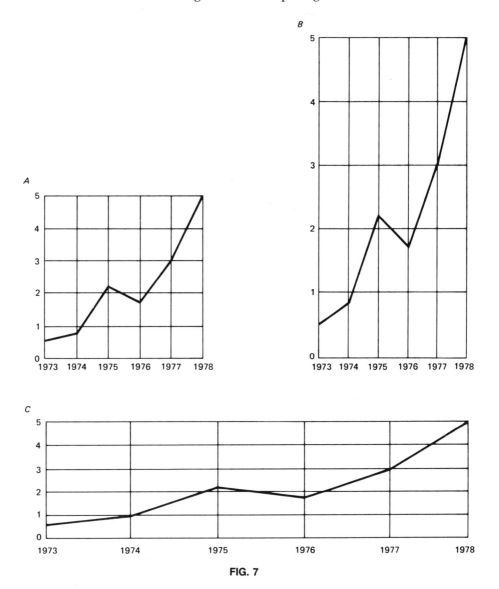

FIG. 7

Numerically the lines tell the same story; visually they do not. What is proper practice? Is there a principle that the spacing of values along the coordinates should be scrupulously unexciting, neither emphasizing nor lessening the impression of change? And, since the same issue happens to be involved, is it bad practice to truncate a graph? The answer for both questions is "no." Proper form depends most importantly upon the audience for which the graph is designed. Charts to communicate to an audience meeting a situation for the first time and having only a general knowledge of it should avoid any form apt to create a false impression by misleading the eye. Advertising, a textbook, or any nonspecialized writing is of this sort. On the other hand, charts designed for those in more or less regular contact with the situation may legitimately omit unneeded areas that are familiar to those using the chart. Figure 8 is an example from *The Wall Street Journal* showing daily fluctuations of the stock market for an audience that presumably knows the market's general level.

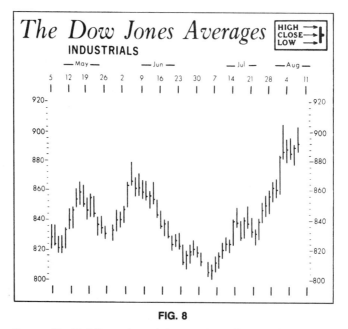

FIG. 8

To print the values on down to zero on the graph shown in Fig. 8 either would take an impractical amount of space or it would require a very fine calibration of values along the vertical axis, resulting in a graph that was not only flattened but hard to read. Since those using this graph presumably are following the market, they will not be deceived by a form showing variations in a pronounced way that clearly indicates even minor fluctuations.

Sometimes one is not so much interested in the amount of change as in the rate of change. When a line runs from low to much higher values, then an ordinary graph with equal space for each unit along the vertical axis does not indicate the rate of change in a uniform manner. Particularly when a graph ranges from low to comparatively high numbers—say from 50 to 1,000—the same slope of line at various points on the graph will indicate quite different degrees of change. For instance, a fifty-unit rise from 50 to 100 is a change of 100%, while moving from 1,000 to 1,050 units is but a 5% change. Evidently, when examining the rate of change is the chief interest, something other than ordinary graph paper is needed in order to represent equal amounts of change by an equal rise along the vertical axis. The semilogarithmic chart has been devised to meet this problem of making the slope of the line stand for the same rate of change at any point on the chart. It isn't necessary to understand logarithms to use such a chart. All that is needed is to understand the purpose of the chart and to realize that the spacing of the horizontal lines of the semilogarithmic chart varies so that the same *rate* of increase or decrease is reflected by the same angle at all points on the chart. Figure 9 uses a semilogarithmic chart to show the increase of the Gross National Product of the United States and of Monetary Interest Paid within the American economy between 1947 and 1972. Both lines show a rising pattern at a fairly constant rate.

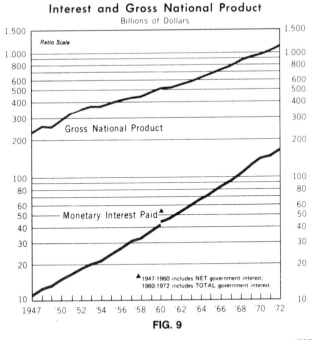

Interest and Gross National Product

Billions of Dollars

FIG. 9

Source: The Conference Board, *Road Maps of Industry*, no. 1732, February 15, 1974.

If a semilogarithmic chart were not used, both lines of Fig. 9 would curve up-ward as they moved from left to right, suggesting an accelerating rate of growth. The accurate impression of the rate of change which a semilogarithmic chart gives is bought at the expense of uneven spacing along the axis. This is no great disadvantage, assuming the reader notes the values along the spacing.

PROJECTIONS ON GRAPHS

Business and government must anticipate needs and prepare for them. What are the future prospects for this product? What traffic growth should be anticipated? In any number of situations, interest is in where trends are leading. One of the uses for statistics and graphs is to show factual developments that may reveal a trend. An obvious requirement for any sort of projection is that it be labeled as such, either by words such as "estimated" or symbolically by intro-ducing broken graph lines or changing color where projected values start. The reliability of projections is technical and varies so greatly with subject matter that we won't attempt a discussion here beyond a reminder about two common-sense points: (1) consider whether the projection is subject to any "all bets are off" conditions, like war or depression, and (2) remember that the reliability of most projections diminishes rapidly with time.

I hope this short chapter is useful as far as it goes in identifying some of the simple deceptions and elementary problems met when statistics are offered as evidence. The goal is well-balanced evaluation. Yet, if the scales cannot be balanced perfectly, one is more apt to be deceived and to misapply his energies through overcredulity than through overdoubt.

SUMMARY

Both the source for the data used in statistics and the name of the party compil-ing the statistics should be known.

The unit employed in statistics must be clearly defined and constant or, if it is subject to any variation, then the differences must be minor enough for fair comparisons to be made.

An average is a simplification. Its usefulness depends upon whether the kind of average employed is suited to the material. Three kinds of average are:

1. An *arithmetic mean*, obtained by adding the values of the units together and then dividing by the number of units

2. A *median*, the mid-figure in which all values are arranged in order of magnitude

3. A *mode*, showing the value that occurs most frequently

If one is interested in the *rate* of change, then one may compare percentages that rest on bases of different size. Such a comparison does not indicate the amount that *volume* has changed. For most purposes, percentages computed on small bases produce results that are valueless and apt to mislead. Therefore the size of the base should be revealed, along with any presentation of percentages.

Rounding is desirable both to aid in the grasping of large numbers and to avoid the false accuracy resulting from giving unrounded numbers for situations that cannot be measured with the accuracy the numbers suggest.

Some questions to ask about graphs are:

1. Do any pictures used exaggerate the relative size of the material compared?

2. Does the graph start at base-point zero or is it truncated?

3. Does the spacing chosen for a line graph either exaggerate or minimize the impression of change?

4. Is the graph on ordinary or semilogarithmic paper?

EXERCISES FOR CHAPTER 21
pages 339–359

I.　　Answer **T** for "true" or **F** for "false":

_____　**1.** Statistics can be true and misleading at the same time.

_____　**2.** Statistics will pick out causes.

_____　**3.** The source of material used in statistics should be identified.

_____　**4.** Statistics based upon vague, undefined units are valueless.

_____　**5.** An average will reflect the nature of at least one member in the group.

_____　**6.** The data has to be arranged in order of magnitude for the mean to be determined.

_____　**7.** The 10–90 percentile range is not influenced by extreme cases that are unusual.

_____　**8.** "Interest at 6%" has to mean "6% per year."

_____　**9.** A percentage standing by itself gives no idea of the numbers upon which it is based.

_____　**10.** Rounded figures are best viewed with suspicion, because they indicate inaccurate work.

_____　**11.** Rounded figures may be a sign of inaccurate work.

_____　**12.** It is generally misleading to carry the mathematical result to more decimal points than the least accurate figure used in the computation.

_____　**13.** It is not proper to employ a truncated graph, which necessarily results in an overemphasis on the amount of change.

_____　**14.** A graph may permit comparisons to be made at a glance.

_____　**15.** Graphs that distort by exaggerating the area or volume never are justified.

_____　**16.** It may be useful for a graph to emphasize fluctuations.

_____　**17.** Ordinary graph paper shows the rate of change via the same slope of line throughout the graph.

_____ **18.** It is necessary to know something about logarithms if one is to use a semilogarithmic chart.

_____ **19.** A semilogarithmic chart reflects the rate of change by a slope that is constant for the same rate at any point on the chart.

_____ **20.** The reliability of most projections diminishes rapidly with time.

II. Some of the following materials can be sampled satisfactorily with fewer cases than others. Rate the situations **a, b, c, d,** or **e,** with **a** standing for the situation you consider _least_ in need of a large number of cases and **e** standing for the situation needing the _most_ cases for a satisfactory sample. Be prepared to explain why you place the situations in the order you choose:

_____ **1.** The proportion of rotten apples in a bushel basket

_____ **2.** Proportion of Republicans and Democrats among students in a college of 2000

_____ **3.** Degree of salinity in Monterey Bay

_____ **4.** Proportion of students at Columbia University with IQ ratings in excess of 140

_____ **5.** Quality of peaches in a truck carrying 500 boxes (consider each box as a "case")

III. **1.** In conducting a student opinion poll you have obtained responses from 100 students waiting in line for dinner at the school cafeteria. It occurs to you that this location might be a biasing factor. Devise a check which would have at least fair prospects for success in determining whether your sample is biased.

2. State as many obstacles as you can that affect the reliability of public opinion polls.

IV. The text states, "The law of averages notes that experience in the long run will tend to come closer and closer in percentage to whatever dispersion truly exists."

1. What does the notion of the "law of averages" tell about the nature of the next case to be encountered (e.g., the next penny tossed, etc.)?

2. Does the "law of averages" mean that in 200 tosses of a penny there will be a more even division between heads and tails than for 100 tosses?

V.   **1.** You are struggling with 1,000 test scores. Explain what you have to do to determine:

    a. The arithmetic mean

    b. The median

    c. The mode

    d. The range

    e. The 10–90 percentile range

  2. Point out an appropriate use for and describe one problem that may arise in connection with each of the five items in (a) above.

VI.   The percentage of increase or decrease may be misleading unless the absolute numbers involved are considered also. Make up an example that illustrates this point.

VII.   **1.** Truncating or cutting off the bottom part of a graph is sometimes a legitimate practice, and sometimes it is not.

    a. Describe how truncating is properly carried out.

    b. Describe some devices used in truncating when the intention is to mislead.

    c. When is a truncated graph useful? When is it of doubtful propriety?

  2. The spacing along the coordinates will have a marked influence on whether a line graph rises and falls sharply on the vertical scale or is relatively flat. What considerations should govern the spacing chosen?

  3. Explain what a semilogarithmic chart is and what special purpose this sort of chart has.

chapter 22

Reasoning in Physical and Social Sciences

This chapter shows logical reasoning in action. To do this, I have taken two cases that were consequential for the world. The first case, Semmelweis' discovery of the cause of puerperal or childbed fever, is presented as an example of logical reasoning in a physical science problem, while the second case, Malthus' theory concerning the tendency of populations to increase to the limit of the available food supply, is an instance of a serious effort to investigate evidence bearing on a social science theory.

SEMMELWEIS: LOGICAL REASONING IN PHYSICAL SCIENCE

Ignaz Philipp Semmelweis[1] was a young doctor employed as an assistant in the maternity division of the Vienna General Hospital. For over twenty years before 1846, when he began his internship, the hospital had been disturbed by mortality among maternity cases ranging from 2 to 15 percent of all cases delivered. The maternity division was divided into two wards: one served as a clinic for training medical students and the other as a clinic for training midwives. These wards were in identical wings of the same building, their food came from the same kitchen, they served the same population assigned to one ward or the other by chance, and yet the rate of mortality in the ward for doctors usually was

[1] I am indebted for many facts concerning Semmelweis' life to William J. Sinclair's *Semmelweis: His Life and His Doctrine* (Manchester: University Press, 1909).

three times the rate in the ward for midwives. The situation can be seen from a table covering the years 1841–1846:

Year	Ward for Doctors (Ward 1)			Ward for Midwives (Ward 2)		
	Number of Lying-In Women	Number of Deaths	Percent of Women Dying	Number of Lying-in Women	Number of Deaths	Percent of Women Dying
1841	3,036	237	7.7	2,442	86	3.5
1842	3,287	518	15.8	2,659	202	7.5
1843	3,060	274	8.9	2,739	164	5.9
1844	3,157	260	8.2	2,956	68	2.3
1845	3,492	241	6.8	3,241	66	2.03
1846	4,010	459	11.4	3,754	105	2.7
Total	20,042	1,989	9.92	17,791	691	3.38

Source: Ignaz P. Semmelweis, *Die Aetiologie, der Begriff und die Prophylaxis des Kindbettfiebers,* reprinted from 1861 ed. (New York: Johnson Reprint Corp., 1966), p. 3.

Why? Why should nearly three times as many women die in the doctors' ward? Why should so many women die at all?

The fact that childbed fever was a steady inhabitant of the Vienna General Hospital was well known. From time to time the state had appointed commissions of enquiry to determine the cause of the high mortality. None had been successful. Some authorities believed the disease was epidemic from the air; some thought that the roughness of student examinations accounted for the high mortality; some asserted milk was the agent spreading the disease; others alleged fear on the part of the patients was predisposing them to infection; and so on. Semmelweis addressed himself to the question with the fervor of a good man and with one great advantage over many of his colleagues—he had the habit of testing theories by checking them against the facts. He soon saw that all of the generally accepted explanations failed to fit the evidence; this spurred him to look for further possibilities. (We should note here that Semmelweis' work was just before bacteriology produced the germ theory and the general introduction of sterile procedures.)

The arrangement of the maternity division into two identical wards was a fortunate chance, since it provided a number of constant factors—population served, atmosphere, ventilation, food. This apparent identity of the two wards convinced Semmelweis that the mismatched results must be a consequence of some unobserved internal difference (for the Method of Difference, see p. 220). Perhaps the cause could be found by close examination of the evidence.

Circumstances Apparently Unrelated to the Disease

- Seasonal influences were not significant, since the high mortality did not occur at the same season in each year.

- Diet, overcrowding, and washing seemed unrelated, since changes in these factors did not influence the frequency with which the disease occurred.
- Difference of race, occupation, or standards of living of the patients were not a factor, since patients were assigned to the two divisions without discrimination.

Circumstances Revealing Unaccountable Differences that Might be Related to the Disease

- Ward 1 was used for training medical students and Ward 2 was used for training midwives.
- Patients in neighboring beds frequently died so that sometimes, out of a whole row of patients, all or all but one or two contracted the disease; on other occasions a single patient would contract the disease while others remained unaffected.
- Patients who gave birth before arrival at the hospital, the so-called "alley births," rarely contracted the disease.
- Patients who underwent long labor in Ward 1 very often contracted the disease, though long labor in Ward 2 presented no special hazard.
- Infants born to mothers suffering from childbed fever generally died from the same disease, but when the mother became afflicted *after* delivery, then the infant usually remained unaffected even though handled or nursed by the mother.

The year 1846, when Semmelweis began his service, was a year of tragedy. As the table on page 364 shows, in that year the death rate was 11.4% of all admissions to Ward 1 (doctors' ward), and 2.7% of all admissions to Ward 2 (midwives' ward). In figures, there were 459 deaths in Ward 1 and 105 deaths in Ward 2. On an average of once every nineteen hours throughout the year, the bell tolled for the priest to administer extreme unction to a dying woman in Ward 1. Semmelweis pursued his work with unusual zeal, inspected every patient as was his duty, and performed autopsies regularly. But he made no progress beyond noting the baffling facts around him.

An incident occurring in March 1847 gave Semmelweis insight into what the nature of childbed fever *might* be. Professor Kolletschka, a teacher of anatomy at the medical school associated with the hospital, cut his finger while demonstrating on a cadaver. Kolletschka's wound became infected, and he exhibited the symptoms of lymphangitis and phlebitis. He died of pleurisy, pericarditis, peritonitis, and meningitis, and a few days before his death, metastasis occurred in one of his eyes. Semmelweis was struck by the similarity of Kolletschka's symptoms and those of the many women he had seen die of childbed fever. In his words, "it impressed itself on my mind with irresistible clarity that the disease from which Kolletschka had died was identical with the one from which I had seen so many hundreds of lying-in women die. Indeed, the lying-in women died also with phlebitis, lymphangitis, peritonitis, pleurisy, pericarditis, meningitis, and also with the lying-in women metastasis formed."[2] The source of Kolletschka's infection was known: it was the introduction of cadaveric matter into a wound. Could the lying-in women have received their infection from a similar source? (Here Semmelweis was applying analogy—see p. 266.)

As soon as Semmelweis put this question, he saw that the possibility of infection was present in the physical examinations made by doctors and medical students whose hands had been contaminated in the anatomy class by their work on cadavers. Although the hands had been washed with soap, still was it not possible that the infection had been introduced in this way? In May 1847, Semmelweis introduced washing with *chlorina liquida* as a way of destroying infection through cadaveric material adhering to the hands. The disinfecting agent was soon changed to chloride of lime to save expense. Mortality in Ward 1 fell at once to one-third of its former level and for the following year it approximated one-ninth of the former level. The figures are displayed in the table on the next page.

The maternity division of the Vienna General Hospital had not produced a record equal to this for over twenty years. In fact, a review of the record going back to the opening of the maternity division in 1784 clearly showed the correlation between the introduction of anatomical instruction on cadavers and the gradual rise of childbed fever cases.

As months passed and the precautions to prevent the transmission of infectious material to the bloodstream of lying-in women were accompanied by a sustained reduction of childbed fever, evidence that the cause of the disease had been found accumulated. Of course, if Semmelweis' theory were sound, then it should be consistent with all the hitherto baffling facts observed in Wards 1 and 2. And a moment's reflection shows this consistency spreading out and fitting every detail. None of the factors that had *not* seemed significant—the season, overcrowding, diet, washing with soap, and so on—were significant conditions under the theory. On the other hand, the facts that had seemed to be associated with the disease in some unknown way all became explicable. Ward 1 had a far higher incidence of the disease because the medical students' hands had become contaminated by their work on cadavers; the midwives seldom worked on cadavers. The occurrence of the disease in rows of beds through part or all of the ward bore out the theory of contamination by examination, because students and doctors moved from one bed to the next. Patients who had had "alley births" before arrival in the hospital were not infected by prenatal examinations, while those who suffered long labor in Ward 1 were prone to the disease because they were almost sure to undergo several examinations. Infants born to mothers suffering from the fever almost always contracted the disease during birth, but when the mother's infection followed the birth, the child usually remained unaffected. All these facts fell into place. (For the requirements for a sound hypothesis, see pp. 238ff.)

[2]*Ibid.* p. 53.

Ward for Doctors (Ward 1)

Record for 1847
(after chloride of lime washing)

	Births	Deaths	Percent
June	268	6	2.38
July	250	3	1.20
August	264	5	1.89
September	262	12	5.23
October	278	11	3.95
November	246	11	4.47
December	273	8	2.93
Total	1,841	56	3.04

Record for 1848

	Births	Deaths	Percent
January	283	10	3.53
February	291	2	0.68
March	276	0	0.00
April	305	2	0.65
May	313	3	0.99
June	264	3	1.13
July	269	1	0.37
August	261	0	0.00
September	312	3	0.96
October	299	7	2.34
November	310	9	2.90
December	373	5	1.34
Total	3,556	45	1.27

Source: Ignaz P. Semmelweis, *Die Aetiologie, der Begriff und die Prophylaxis des Kindbettfiebers,* reprinted from 1861 ed. (New York: Johnson Reprint Corp., 1966), p. 56–57.

As a further check on his conclusion, Semmelweis conducted some animal experiments; he introduced cadaveric material into the uteri of rabbits that had just borne litters. In nine experiments, all but two of the rabbits died, and dissection revealed the rabbits exhibited same types of changes as were found in the bodies of the women who had died of childbed fever.

One might think that such a pronounced reduction of mortality following immediately upon the introduction of a simple technique would have brought quick recognition to the process and fame to its discoverer. Quite the contrary: owing partly to Semmelweis' habitual tactlessness and partly to the blind jealousy of Dr. Klein, head of the maternity division, Semmelweis was denied the customary extension of his assistantship and he was obliged to return to Pest in his native Hungary.

The details of the controversy that arose over Semmelweis' discovery are too tortuous to follow here. It is fair to say that some medical authorities at once saw the significance of the discovery, while others allowed personal considerations, tradition, or the distorted accounts which controversy engenders to block their reception of the new idea. Identifying childbed fever as a systemic infection conflicted with other theories to which some doctors had committed themselves. Controversy obscures sound reason by turning people's minds to justifying their position rather than to looking at evidence dispassionately—even a matter of life or death may not be an exception. Unluckily, those opposed to the new theory were soon able to point with satisfaction to the fact that the maternity ward in the hospital at Pest where Semmelweis was employed had a poor record for childbed fever. Semmelweis traced the infection to poorly washed bedlinen which was made lethal by commingling it with linen from other wards of the hospital so that it became fouled with all sorts of infectious material. Classification and proper washing soon brought the disease down to "normal" proportions, so the evidence fitted the theory when objectively examined.

Probably nothing impaired acceptance of chlorine disinfection so seriously as reports of its trial without result. A hospital is an affair of many people working at all times of the day and night. Thus, the half-hearted compliance of a scoffer could undo the prescribed antiseptic methods and lead to outbreaks of the disease although a "systematic and diligent" trial of the prophylaxis would be alleged when reporting undiminished mortality. Semmelweis had trouble with his own staff at Pest on this account, and a Scottish student at the Vienna General Hospital in the 1860s has left an account of how students still came direct from the dissecting room merely washing in cold water and dipping their hands in a weak solution of permanganate of potash which was never changed. Persistent perversions of the doctrine had the good effect of inducing Semmelweis to undertake a full exposition of his findings in his *Aetiologie* published in 1861.

Having followed this incident so far, it is perhaps of interest to mention its historical conclusion. Frustrations from apathy, disobedience of his own staff, and the resistance and misrepresentations encountered by his doctrine may have contributed to unsettling Semmelweis' mind. At any rate, he was committed to an insane asylum in Vienna in 1865. He entered with an unobserved cut on the finger, probably incurred in one of his last operations, and, as a result of infection in this wound, he soon died of the very disease it had been his life work to combat.

Semmelweis' dream that his colleagues would one day recognize his work is now universally fulfilled, and those of his associates who ignored the findings or permitted their egos to rule their judgment are now remembered for their folly. In his lifetime, Semmelweis confirmed the theory by animal experimentation (analogy), and the development of bacteriological science has given further confirmation (direct observation). The clinical evidence justified an empirical generalization (see p. 206) sufficient to identify the causal factors and indicate the effectiveness of the prophylaxis. The victory of Semmelweis' idea, though it took a quarter of a century, has been complete.

MALTHUS: LOGICAL REASONING IN SOCIAL SCIENCE

Now we turn to a consequential social science question: the relation of population to poverty. In 1798 a small book was published anonymously under the cumbersome title *An Essay on the Principle of Population as it Affects the Future Improvement of Society, with Remarks on the Speculations of Mr. Goodwin, M. Condorcet, and Other Writers.* This book advanced the notion that the vice and misery of humanity result from a disparity between people's power to increase their numbers and their power to increase production, particularly production of foodstuffs. Here is a social science problem *par excellence.* Does the mass of humanity condemn itself to poverty by increasing its numbers to the point where production can provide only subsistence-level living and further increase becomes impossible? Is the misery and distress of the world of 1798 or of today or of the future attributable to overpopulation? The Reverend Thomas Robert Malthus, the author of the essay, took the view that this was so. He devoted the rest of his life to accumulating evidence to support the notion. His original essay grew into a lengthy work in which he examined population trends in many regions and for many periods of time.

One can explain Malthus' notion by comparing human existence on the earth to life in a fishpond.[3] A certain number of fish and plants will live happily in the pond. If the food is ample, disease infrequent, and the depredations of enemies slight, then the fish will increase until a point is reached at which all begin to suffer certain hardships and disadvantages. It becomes difficult for them to find a living in the limited space of the pond; their condition deteriorates, and they become more subject to disease. Left to themselves, some fish will die until their numbers return to a level the pond can support. If we suppose that the ingenuity and charity of man is applied to provide food from sources outside the capacity of the pond, then the fish may multiply further until lack of oxygen or crowded conditions become a problem. In any case, the fish possess a capacity to go on multiplying without limit, and they actually do go on multiplying until their further increase is checked, owing in one way or another to the limited size of the pond.

It is undoubtedly true that the enormous capacity of living things to reproduce would, if unchecked, rapidly overcrowd the whole earth. Malthus illus-

---

[3]The analogy of the pond is not mine: I have forgotten where I first encountered it.

trated this with two famous examples. First, he assumed that if wheat returned the low yield of six grains for one and that all of it were saved and sown, then "it might safely be calculated hypothetically, that if, setting out from the produce of one acre, land of the same quality could be prepared with sufficient rapidity, and no wheat were consumed, the rate of increase would be such as to completely cover the whole earthly surface of our globe in fourteen years."[4] Wheat has a relatively rapid capacity to increase: it can register an annual sixfold increase, or, in other words, it increases *annually* in the geometric progression running 1, 6, 36, 216, 1,296, 7,776, etc.

Turning to sheep for a second example, Malthus noted that their natural rate of increase will double their numbers every two years, and so he calculated hypothetically that starting with the sheep supported on one acre of good land, in 76 years the whole earthly part of the globe would be covered with sheep to the density with which sheep inhabit good pasture. With sheep the increase every two years runs on the geometrical progression 1, 2, 4, 8, 16, 32, etc.[5] The point is undeniable: no living thing can realize its *capacity* to increase over any protracted period of time.

Turning now to the case of human beings, Malthus calculated from the United States census that it took just under 25 years for the population of the United States to double. Critics pointed out, rightly, that early census figures did not report immigration, so that this had to be estimated, and that the age composition of the population was unknown. Still, granting a fine degree of accuracy to be impossible, Malthus' reference to the mechanics of reproduction as following a geometric progression is correct; whether more accurate statistics would have established 22 or 32 years as the time for doubling is beside the point. The United States initiated the first nationwide, accurate census in modern times and Malthus placed much reliance on the evidence that it provided up to his death in 1834. We can test his theory more fully by taking advantage of the fact that we live later and have access to more evidence. The table on the next page gives the census figures down to our time. I have rounded the figures to the nearest 100,000 and added computations for the *rate of increase* for each decade, and the *time to double* at that rate.

Now we come to the other side of the Malthusian equation: How rapidly can production, particularly of foodstuffs, be increased? Here we will let Malthus answer:

> If I allow by the best possible policy, by breaking up more land, and by great encouragements to agriculture, the produce of this Island [England] may be doubled in the first twenty-five years, I think it will be allowing as much as any person can well demand.[6]

[4]Thomas Robert Malthus, *A Summary View of the Principle of Population* (London: John Murray, 1830), pp. 2–3.
[5]The series starts with "1" for one *unit* of sheep, not one sheep!
[6]Thomas Robert Malthus, *An Essay on the Principle of Population . . .* (1798). Printed by The Macmillan Company, New York, 1906, p. 10.

		Numerical	Percentage	Years to
Census	Population	Increase	Increase	Double
1790	3,900,000	—	—	—
1800	5,300,000	1,400,000	36%	23
1810	7,200,000	1,900,000	36%	23
1820	9,600,000	2,400,000	33%	24
1830	12,900,000	3,300,000	34%	24
1840	17,100,000	4,200,000	33%	25
1850	23,200,000	6,100,000	36%	23
1860	31,400,000	8,200,000	35%	23
1870	39,800,000	8,400,000	27%	29
1880	50,200,000	10,400,000	26%	30
1890	62,900,000	12,700,000	25%	31
1900	76,000,000	13,100,000	21%	37
1910	92,000,000	16,000,000	21%	36
1920	105,700,000	13,700,000	15%	50
1930	122,800,000	17,100,000	16%	46
1940	131,700,000	8,900,000	7%	99
1950	150,700,000	19,000,000	14%	51
1960	179,300,000	28,600,000	19%	40
1970	203,200,000	23,900,000	13%	55

Population Increase in the United States, 1790–1970

Source: U.S. Bureau of the Census, as published in *The World Almanac and Book of Facts 1978* (New York: Newspaper Enterprise Association, Inc., 1977), pp. 190–91. Numerical increase and percentage increase computed by Harold N. Wells.

Using this assumption as his basis, Malthus argued that keeping pace with a geometric progression which required quadrupling the food production of England in the second 25-year period would be impossible, so he concludes:

> Let us then take this for our rule, though certainly far beyond the truth; and allow that by great exertion, the whole produce of the Island might be increased every twenty-five years, by a quantity of subsistence equal to what it *at present produces.*[7] (Italics supplied.)

Now this kind of assumption would not be allowed in science, nor would social scientists of today readily take it for granted. Can one say that addition to the English food supply was limited to an increase of no more than the volume produced in 1798 being added every 25 years? If this were in fact true for England, would it be true for the United States, China, and everywhere else on earth? As Malthus recognized, so long as new land was available, as in the United States, then food production could be increased as needed without either

[7]*Ibid.,* p. 11.

new technology or more intensive cultivation. When the special condition of new land should come to an end, as it inevitably must, is there then any ground for saying *what* rate of increase for foodstuffs can be achieved through improved technology and intensive cultivation? We are not making the point that the rate should be more or less than Malthus envisioned but that it cannot be established. Nor is there any evidence to establish a *uniform* rate at which man can succeed in increasing the production of food or any other product. Malthus's postulate of a capacity to increase food production on an arithmetic progression that would add the product of 1798 every 25 years is an assumption of what he considered as an outer limit *in a matter that could not be established by evidence*. The assumption was not justified, nor was it necessary to his theory. The situation which one must acknowledge in theory is that the potential capacity to reproduce runs according to a geometric progression and this has the potential to outpace the resources of a finite world. In other words, though the fish may be few and the pond large, the fish have the *capacity* to fill up the pond no matter what.

The capacity to increase and actual increase are different things. Why doesn't the world fill up with wheat or sheep or, for that matter, people? The restraints to the spread of wheat or sheep are apparent, and that people, too, are subject to restraints is becoming more and more apparent. Malthus considered population growth as slowed or even stopped by "misery and vice." "Misery" referred to the positive checks on population growth such as mortality induced by poverty, famine, malnutrition, wars, epidemics, and so on. Under "vice" he included birth control and abortion. As the one way to prevent undue growth of population without either misery or vice, Malthus urged "moral restraint," by which he meant abstaining from marriage, late marriage, or choosing not to have children. Now it makes no difference whether or not we agree with this classification of actions into "misery," "vice," and "moral restraint"; the possibilities classed under these heads are the factors that prevent the capacity to increase population from being realized.

Malthus did not write to prepare the world for a crisis in the long run. More than most theorists, he was a practical man and his aim was to find the cause of the poverty that afflicted much of the English population of his own day. Having shown the factors that gave population the potential to outrun food supply, he *assumed* that it was doing so, or, in other words, that the low living standards of the English working class were caused by overpopulation. Moreover, he contended that nothing could raise those living standards above a subsistence level so long as population increased as rapidly as production.

Malthus spent over 30 years assembling facts and applying his idea of population pressure as the fundamental explanation for the conditions he found. His examples range over the whole earth and they extend backward into ancient history: he interpreted the history of Greece and the fall of Rome in the light of the population factor; he discussed the population situation of teeming China and sparse Siberia, of American Indian tribes and Norwegian fishermen.

All this earned Malthus a place as a pathmaker in the application of inductive methods to social science problems, and yet—to me at least—it is a most "unscientific" path that he beats. One must forgive his not traveling over the whole world, and none denies that the masses of statistics and reports available today were nonexistent aids for Malthus. Still, he interpreted his evidence by conjecture and his bias consistently led him to declare population to be the explanation of whatever he found in a most diverse world.

A single example will have to stand for the innumerable instances in which Malthus' supporting facts are interpretations rather than measurements. When Malthus visited Norway he concluded by inspection that the farmers of the interior had higher living standards then the fishermen of the coast. Very likely his assessment was correct, though he gives no reference to records or measurements of income to support his conclusion. He describes the difficulty in acquiring farms and asserts that this difficulty imposes a preventive check to population via a tendency to late marriage among farmers. Then he continues:

> On the sea-coast, where, on account of the hopes of an adequate supply of food from fishing, the preventative check does not prevail in the same degree, the people are very poor and wretched; and, beyond comparison, in a worse state than the peasants in the interior of the country.[8]

So Malthus finds the circumstances confirm his theory. But do they? If we visit Iowa and then visit the Maine coast, we might well conclude that Iowa farmers as a group enjoy greater prosperity than Maine fishermen. Could we then set down with confidence that the cause of the difference is a matter of population pressure?

Lack of adequate records dogged Malthus in most of the cases he investigated and he could not possibly supply the deficiency. For example, the mortality rate for the years 1775–1794 is the only statistical tabulation he cites concerning Norway. Though the rate varied enormously, here is what he makes of it:

> It is also without doubt owing to the prevalence of the preventive check to population, as much as to the peculiar healthiness of the air, that the mortality of Norway is so small.[9]

We noted that Malthus was interested in the condition of society in his own day; he did not look upon his writings as a warning for the far future and he took an active part in urging political decisions in accord with his population theory. His influence contributed to repealing the English "Poor Laws," the welfare system of his day, on the ground that supporting the poor led to still greater numbers of surplus population through natural increase. That many En-

---

[8]Thomas Robert Malthus, *An Essay on the Principle of Population* (London: Ward, Lock & Co., 1890), p. 146.
[9]*Ibid.*, p. 147.

glishmen of the time were paupers was undeniable; that their impoverishment was due to overpopulation remained an unproved assumption. Could not the explanation have been in some malfunctioning of society rather than overpopulation? Was society in England or Norway or any other place so well organized with regard to distribution of wealth, access to education, and economic opportunity that the only explanation for the presence of poverty lay in overpopulation?

Whether Malthus was right or wrong in his assertions is not our concern. What is important here is to recognize the shortcomings of proofs of the sort he offered. Though he should be credited with making greater efforts to support his views than did most thinkers of his day, the evidence is of doubtful reliability, hard to measure, and impossible to properly ascribe to any single causal element. Although the particular arithmetic progression Malthus assumed as an upper limit to productivity was surpassed by modern technology for many decades, and though much of his evidence fails to prove his point, we wish to acknowledge his epoch-making merit. In a world that gave little heed to the matter, he pointed out the disparity between "potential production and potential babies." The problem is real. The world is finite. He gave a rough formula for a situation that could not be established exactly, and he too easily assumed that his theory explained the existing evils of his time. Yet the technological advances of the Industrial Revolution, including the related advances in sanitation and health care, have been attended by rapid increases in population that accord with the Malthusian analysis, and the increases are more impressive for their universality than for their differences in degree. Despite technological advances, enormous numbers today live at a subsistence level—or fall below it.

How different the outcomes of Semmelweis' theory and that of Malthus! Embittered in his lifetime, Semmelweis did not live to see the general acceptance of his work. But within a decade after his death his discovery was universally acclaimed to the benefit of humanity. Malthus was more honored in his day and for many years his supporters held the upper hand in the debate over his theory. Demography or the study of population, though it has added much knowledge about this field, has yet to produce a single accepted theory about the limits to population increase. Religious beliefs, emotional commitments, political considerations—all engender attitudes interfering with the objective evaluation of population policy, Malthusian theory included.

We should recognize that social science today enjoys the aid of statistical methods, computers, and records unavailable in earlier times. So our illustration does not do justice to the evidence that can now be amassed concerning problems in the social sciences. Yet there is a continuing contrast between the success with which logical criteria can be applied in the physical and social sciences. Indeed, the security of conclusions necessarily is limited wherever phenomena are, as in the social sciences, difficult to classify, measure, and evaluate objectively.

SUMMARY

In 1847 Semmelweis, a young doctor at the Vienna General Hospital, discovered by empirical causal generalization that childbed fever could be prevented by sterile procedures. He was led to his discovery by a literal analogy between the symptoms of childbed fever patients and the symptoms of a man dying of infection known to have originated in an unsterile wound. Semmelweis' theory concerning the origin of the infection was consistent with numerous facts observed at the hospital in connection with the occurrence of the disease. Introduction of a sterilizing agent under conditions satisfying the Method of Difference immediately confirmed that contamination through unsanitary conditions was the cause. Further confirmation was secured by literal analogy when Semmelweis infected pregnant rabbits. Though professional jealousy and reports that perverted the facts retarded the adoption of Semmelweis' discovery for more than twenty years, ultimately the theory was universally accepted. Modern bacteriology has converted Semmelweis' empirical generalization into an explained generalization confirmed by direct observation and by other theories.

In 1798 Malthus published his famous essay in which he asserted that population expanded according to a geometric progression while food supply could be increased only on an arithmetic progression. Since any geometric progression will outrun any arithmetic progression, Malthus concluded that poverty whereby many people live at a subsistence level is the result of population increasing up to the limits of available production, particularly production of food.

Malthus was able to establish with satisfactory evidence that the population of the United States was at that time doubling on a 25-year geometric progression, and that various European states were doubling at a slower rate. It is not possible to project any rate of increase for production and since increased production does not follow a constant rate, but Malthus simply assumed as an outer limit that the food production of Britain could be increased to *add* every 25 years the amount produced in 1798. This assumption was a rough rule to permit calculations to demonstrate his point of a difference between "potential babies and potential production."

Malthus devoted his life to evaluating many societies from the standpoint of population pressure. His work made him a pathmaker in applying observation and inductive methods to support a social science conclusion. Though plagued by the scantiness of records available, the difficulties he faced were only in degree different from those hindering firm conclusions about many social science problems today. Characteristically, the data was not available in the form needed, it was difficult to classify or measure, laboratory experiments could not be made, the facts established were open to many interpretations that could be influenced by preconceptions or bias, and causal relationship could not be established by controlling the various possible causal factors.

Malthusian theory still has its supporters and its critics. Looking at the theory with the evidence available today, one can say that the development of production has exceeded Malthus' assumption, and that attributing poverty in a given society to population pressure is a matter requiring proof in view of other possible explanations in a malfunctioning social order. On the other hand, rapid increase of population in a world of finite resources is beginning to vindicate the Malthusian thesis over the long run.

EXERCISES FOR CHAPTER 22
pages 363–376

I.   Answer **T** for "true" or **F** for "false":

_____   **1.** Prior to Semmelweis' work at the Vienna General Hospital, all the theories brought forth to explain the high incidence of childbed fever in the maternity ward had failed to fit the known facts.

_____   **2.** Semmelweis applied logic to reject all previous theories alleged to explain the high incidence of childbed fever.

_____   **3.** An analogy gave Semmelweis insight into the likely cause of childbed fever in the ward.

_____   **4.** When the practice of washing hands in _chlorina liquida_ was followed by a dramatic and prolonged drop in the occurrence of childbed fever in Ward I, it was possible, by the Method of Agreement, to identify the cause.

_____   **5.** All the apparently unrelated facts such as alley births and long labor were consistent with Semmelweis' theory of the origin of the disease.

_____   **6.** The occurrence of some cases of childbed fever in Ward I after Semmelweis' prophylaxis was introduced shows that the facts did not conform to Mill's canons.

_____   **7.** When the Vienna General Hospital abandoned Semmelweis' prophylaxis and higher mortality rates returned to the ward, the Method of Difference should have been applied.

_____   **8.** The development of bacteriology has now confirmed Semmelweis' theory by providing direct observation of the causal agent.

_____   **9.** The fact that there no longer is professional disagreement over the utility of Semmelweis' prophylaxis is the usual though not universal outcome of a scientific controversy.

_____   **10.** The reproductive capacity of living things provides a potential increase along a geometric progression.

_____   **11.** Malthus demonstrated that increased food supply must follow an arithmetic progression.

_____ **12.** When Malthus checked his theory by examining contemporary societies in all quarters of the world, he was using inductive methods to determine a social science truth.

_____ **13.** The great mass of material concerning population levels and economic conditions that Malthus assembled enabled him to rely upon objective measurements uninfluenced by interpretation.

_____ **14.** So carefully and well did Malthus support his theory that any fair-minded person will agree with his conclusions.

_____ **15.** Semmelweis found little difficulty in keeping his preconceptions from influencing the interpretation of the facts he observed.

_____ **16.** Malthus carefully observed the requirements of Mill's Methods to demonstrate that the poverty he observed in England was caused by overpopulation.

_____ **17.** Semmelweis' evidence does identify the cause of childbed fever by evidence that conforms to Mill's Methods.

_____ **18.** A geometric progression is a series obtained by multiplying the base number indefinitely by any number; an arithmetic progression is a series obtained by adding any number indefinitely to the base number.

_____ **19.** The world has many societies and, further, all history is available as a source of cases showing the effect of population on poverty. So at least it should be easy to construct reliable empirical generalizations from this material.

_____ **20.** There is a literal analogy between the problems confronting fish if their numbers overexpand in respect to fish food in a fish pond and the problems confronting humans if they overexpand their numbers in relation to the food supply they utilize on the earth.

II.   Provide short answers for the following questions:

1. Apply the definition for analogy (See p. 266) to the situation Semmelweis noticed when he compared the symptoms leading to Dr. Kolletschka's death with the symptoms exhibited by the women dying of childbed fever.

2. If a theory is true, all facts will be consistent with it. Show how Semmelweis' explanation made understandable a number of hitherto baffling facts that had been noticed about the occurrence of puerperal fever.

3. What was the contribution of the record kept of deaths occurring in Ward 1 and Ward 2—i.e., statistics—in enabling Semmelweis to demonstrate causal relationship between contamination and the occurrence of the disease?

4. When a causal factor is correctly identified and removed, the effect will no longer occur. After Semmelweis' prophylaxis was introduced, deaths from childbed fever did continue to occur, though at a reduced rate. Does this not show that Semmelweis had not fully identified the cause? Explain.

5. The germ theory had not been developed at the time Semmelweis was employed at the Vienna General Hospital. How did the later development of this theory contribute to Semmelweis' work?

6. It took some twenty years for Semmelweis' prophylaxis to gain general acceptance in the medical world. Yet the procedure was a testable physical science problem. Why did general acceptance take so long? Do you consider that the need for changes in procedure in accord with evidence concerning a physical science problem is, as a rule, recognized more rapidly today? Defend your answer.

7. Malthus showed that population has a potential to increase beyond the availability of food on a finite planet. Did this establish that the subsistence-level standard of living of many Englishmen in Malthus' time was a result of inability to produce food? Justify whatever answer you give.

8. Propose some standards according to which you can decide whether or not an area possesses a population in excess of its capacity to produce food.

9. Describe your difficulties in establishing the standards you used in answering (8).

10. Describe any points at which your own value judgments entered into your answer to (8).

11. No nation is an island in today's world. In fact, there are only about a dozen countries in the world that are net exporters of food. Subsistence standards of living are widespread in the world. Do these facts establish that Malthus' reasoning was correct?

12. Evaluate the evidence upon which your answer to (11) rests.

III.   It is easy to make noisy demands for more evidence than can be produced. Gathering support for Malthus' theory is a good example of the difficulty of demonstrating a cause–effect relationship in social science. If logical requirements are so hard to satisfy in a problem such as the one Malthus dealt with, of what use is a knowledge of logic when evaluating Malthusianism?

IV.   Try solving this not-too-difficult riddle:[10]

There is a pond of limited dimensions where water lilies grow.

Each day the lilies double, so that there are twice as many as the day before.

At the end of 30 days the lilies occupy the entire pond, crowding each other out, using up the sunlight, air, and water, and they die.

Question: When was the pond just half full, so that the gardener still had time to do the pruning and provide for the health and survival of the lilies?

[10]The answer is printed upside down:

The riddle is from Gene E. Bradley and Edward C. Bursk, "Multinationalism and the 29th Day," *Harvard Business Review*, 50 (1972), 37. The answer is 29 days.

chapter 23

Logic and the
Scientific Method

Surely the story of the *Bounty* goes deeper than the dream of a secluded life hidden away in the South Seas. After all, the men of the *Bounty* were more than cut off from the civilization in which they had been born; as their children grew up they faced the realization that they, and they alone, would be the transmitters of whatever of their European background was to survive on their island. I suppose that most of us have toyed with some form of this same situation in our daydreams: "Were I the sole representative of my civilization, what could I transmit about it?" It's a fascinating speculation. Here is my answer:

> I could transmit to others but the tiniest bit of the accumulated knowledge of our civilization. If, however, I could transmit the notion of the scientific method and if that approach to truth could resist beguilement by superstition, then in a comparatively short time the knowledge of the natural order that underpins the material accomplishments of our civilization would be rediscovered.

Are there good grounds for such a bold assertion? This chapter will attempt to show that there are.

To start, let us distinguish four broad bases upon which human beings have and still do rest their beliefs:[1]

1. Reference to the supernatural
2. Reference to authority and tradition

[1]Discussions of the basis for belief following slightly different lines may be found in Morris R. Cohen and Ernest Nagel, *An Introduction to Logic and the Scientific Method* (New York: Harcourt Brace Jovanovich, 1934), pp. 191–96 and in Stuart Chase, *The Proper Study of Mankind* (New York: Harper and Row, 1948), pp. 8–11. One may add "psychologically based belief" as a fifth source. Beliefs inspired by rationalization, wishful thinking, hatred, ego protection, etc. are not taken up here.

3. Common sense
4. The scientific method

Reference to supernatural spirits appears as man's earliest attempt to answer the more difficult questions of the world around him. So long as people cannot conceive how events occur in the physical world while at the same time they demand answers to questions about creation, disease, success or failure in hunting or some other activity, then resorting to supernatural explanations appears as the universal human practice. The method has the nice advantage of resolving every possible question for those who accept the spirit theory. As a means for discovering true explanations, however, the approach is useless. A profusion of myths and spirits contradict one another, and they fail to supplement each other in a coherent system. This is not the way human knowledge about the natural order has advanced.

Authority and tradition are long honored foundations for belief, and they account for many beliefs in any group, from primitive to modern. For the tribe one thinks of the taboo and the culturally accepted norms, for more modern societies one thinks of commitments to Marx or Mao, of resort to passages in the Bible, the Koran, or the Bhagavad Gita. Regarding political and religious creeds as sources of belief not to be reviewed critically by their followers is a widespread situation. Occasionally, the mistake of regarding some authority as final has been made even in the area of beliefs about the physical world as, for example, when the works of outstanding scientists such as Aristotle and Galen went unquestioned. Viewing authority as beyond question can be worse than being wrong; those overimpressed with authority are discouraged from inquiry and those attempting to preserve it repeatedly oppose change. Because of this approach to truth, new ideas have had to battle until old beliefs are thoroughly discredited. Moreover, there is no reason for believing that any person or any age has discovered final truths, or that any tradition is beyond question.

To determine truth according to common sense is to follow a standard too completely reflecting the current state of the culture. Common sense gives no inkling that our sensory equipment is incomplete. It gives no notice of magnetism, x-rays, sonar and the like, nor does it suggest that the structure of matter or the immensity of the universe is not as sensory perception seems to report. Nor is common sense a good psychologist or economist or sociologist, or, in fact, an adequate master of any field. No wonder that for centuries common sense told most people that matter was solid, that the earth was flat, that slavery was necessary, that poverty was unavoidable, that prison life should be punishing. Much of what we encounter daily was below the low horizon of common sense a century ago. In fact, the developments of physical science have so often transcended our common-sense notions that people today, unlike those in the past, hesitate to declare limits for what may be physically possible in the future. Not so in the social sciences, however, where many accept their notions of common sense as a satisfactory guide to truth. Yet the milestones of human progress do not mark triumphs of common sense; rather they are monuments to original thought that went beyond contemporary beliefs, often disregarding what seemed obvious to less open minds. While common sense can be acknowledged as a virtue, it is neither innovative nor a reliable sanction for truth.

We have seen that beliefs based upon supernatural explanations, authority, and common sense have time and again led people down false paths. Recognizing the weakness of these methods, however, does not establish the scientific method as a reliable alternative. We have yet to find suport for my daydream about the scientific method as an underpinning by which the material features of our civilization could be rediscovered. So I will seek to give this support first by drawing a thumbnail sketch of the accelerating pace of European civilization, the force that now spreads through and revolutionizes the world, and second, by presenting the scientific method as a way of thinking.

The dying tribesman of earlier times looked out on the morning of his death to observe his associates performing the same tasks, either wholly or almost wholly in the same way they had in his childhood. Change was slow, mythical explanations and traditions held sway over the tribal beliefs. As we noted, so long as the tribe's accumulated knowledge was unequal to the task of explaining the phenomena of nature, the human desire for explanation created a fanciful world of spirits and myths. Rich and colorful myth is a literary delight: Aaron's rod becomes a snake, the shaded area on the moon is made by groves of katsura trees, and so on. Myths also are a monument to a way of thinking, for in myth there is no apparent order, and insofar as myths pass as explanations they obscure the natural order. One can sympathize with primitive people for their inadequate knowledge and their beliefs studded with superstitions; personally, I can only wonder at those inhabitants of our great cities who, though they have attended schools and live in the presence of libraries, still pay attention to astrology, the signs of the Zodiac, and other occult explanations of events experienced in this world.

The ancient Greeks developed interest in pure science and made serious attempts to understand natural phenomena. Aristotle, scientist as well as logician and philosopher, pointed out the importance of observation, though occasionally he failed to make use of it. In biology he developed a classification of species. Other Greek contributions were made in medicine, mathematics, astronomy, and geography, while the Roman contribution to scientific theory was slight outside the work of Galen and Ptolemy, both of whom happened to be Greeks. The purely scientific accomplishments of the ancient world, however, never equaled the advances made in literature, history, philosophy, law, public administration, engineering, and religion. Nor is the reason for the limited scientific development of the ancient world hard to perceive: science was hampered by the slight accumulation of knowledge, by the bounds of sensory observation, and by lack of a clear perception of the need to separate the results of observation from philosophical and mystical influences. Even so great a mathematician as Pythagoras mingled mysticism with his work, "justice" being associated with the number 4, and so on. But we should not be stinting in praise for the ancients; after all, not for over a thousand years was the work of Greek scientists and mathematicians surpassed.

Medieval thinking was essentially theological. The world was simply assumed to have been created and guided by God for the benefit of man. Philosophy was used as a handmaiden for theology, serving largely to reconcile all knowledge with the doctrines of the Church. Questions about the natural world were resolved by philosophical argument buttressed by citing authorities, especially Aristotle and the authority of the Scriptures. Above all, medieval preoccupation with philosophical disputation and other-worldliness was unfavorable to developing understanding of the material world. We owe much to the Middle Ages. Europe was dotted with monasteries and cathedrals, schools and universities were organized, the revival of classical literature began. There were some practical innovations—particularly printing and gunpowder—which hastened the period's end. Yet in increased *understanding* of natural phenomena the Middle Ages offered little, and this lack of progress is testimony to the influence of its outlook and the deficiency of its methods.

The world view of the European Middle Ages received blow upon blow after the fifteenth century. First, the lusty attitudes of the Renaissance bade man exchange medieval other-worldliness for the savor of life in this world. Then came Luther. With the unity of Christendom in disarray, philosophy was put in a position to become more independent.

During this religious upheaval, Europe was overflowing its bounds physically as well as intellectually. The list of giant strides made at this time shows technical accomplishment and changing intellectual concepts stimulating one another. For example, we rightly praise Columbus for seeking trade on the theory that the earth is round; perhaps we should attend more to the evolution of his ship and the navigational instruments that made the voyage possible. A few years later, the remnant of Magellan's crew came home, demonstrating that the world was indeed a sphere and, incidentally, whetting earthly ambitions by marketing the cargo of 22 tons of spices for enough to cover the expenses of the whole voyage, including the loss of four of the original five ships of the expedition. Less immediately practical was a theory suggesting that the world was a planet, a view Copernicus got up his courage to publish in 1543, the year of his death. Why so much concern over a new theory? The problem was that the Church, relying upon the conception of the solar system and universe which Ptolemy had formulated in the second century A.D., had elaborated a theology in which Ptolemy's scheme supported the view of man as God's central concern. Copernicus' theory shook a point in the foundations of established theology: the shock to the Church was one it has experienced many times since as scientific knowledge moves on to new explanations. Much remained to be done, however, before Copernicus' theory would be refined and given convincing support. Few adopted the theory immediately as their belief, and one of the most celebrated incidents in the history of science occurred when the Inquisitors ordered

Galileo to deny his acceptance of the Copernican view. But listen to Martin Luther:

> People give ear to an upstart astrologer [sic] who strove to show that the earth revolves, not the heavens or the firmament, the sun and the moon.... but sacred Scripture tells us that Joshua commanded the sun to stand still, and not the earth.[2]

Calvin, too, disposed of the theory with a biblical quotation. Clearly these leaders had no inkling of the fact that questions about the physical world are not settled by citing theological positions.

The hundred years following Copernicus' death saw remarkable extensions in the frontiers of knowledge. Galileo gained fame by applying the principles of optics to construct a telescope which, by piercing space further than any human vision, revealed that Jupiter had moons, Saturn rings, the moon had mountains, and the sun harbored blemishing spots. A little later Leeuwenhoek and others developed a microscope to uncover a new living world of such fantastic smallness that everyone assumed it to be harmless. Man's broadening horizon was supplemented by a new method for determining truth. Though the picturesque scene of Galileo dropping weights from Pisa's leaning tower may be apocryphal, the legend of the crashing weights demolishes belief in philosophical speculation as the means to confirm truths about the natural world. Galileo not only made observation the base for his investigations but he also expressed the results in mathematical terms. Naturally enough, he was not immediately successful in getting his contemporaries to change their ways of thought; there were those who refused the evidence of their senses and continued to discuss the nature of the physical world without examining its characteristics. Still, the observational approach had been launched for others to develop into the modern scientific method. Sir Francis Bacon wrote an account of the means for establishing truth which, because of its emphasis on observation, earned him recognition as one of the founders of modern inductive science. Complementing Bacon's use of induction is the work of René Descartes, who emphasized deduction and sought to reduce physical phenomena to mathematical expression.

Sir Isaac Newton (1642–1727) brought together the work for his predecessors and thus provides an appropriate conclusion for the transition from the time when science was held to confirm theological beliefs to the time when the scientific method was realized. Newton stressed both the application of mathematics and the need for observation, and his approach to truth was rigorously scientific. As he observed:

> Analysis consists in making Experiments and Observations, and in drawing general Conclusions from them by Induction, and in admitting of no Objections

---

[2]T. Walter Wallbank et al., *Civilization: Past and Present*, 6th ed., Vol. I (Glenview, Ill.: Scott, Foresman, 1970), p. 554. In Luther's time the distinction between astronomy and astrology was not as sharp as it is today.

against the Conclusions, but such as are taken from Experiments, or other certain Truths.[3]

Perhaps the flashing of these highlights will be enough to indicate this period, roughly the sixteenth century, as the time when people began to acquire the instruments and the method to examine the world.

Why does knowledge advance at such an accelerated rate today?[4] Undoubtedly, part of the credit must go to the cumulative effect of the background knowledge humankind has at last amassed. When a jigsaw puzzle begins to take shape, the general relationships begin to emerge and there are more cues for inserting further pieces; work proceeds upon an expanding front. So it is with knowledge; its accumulation affords new cues so the opportunities for discovering further principles and further applications fan out.

Important though the influence of accumulating knowledge is, the heart of man's extraordinary advance since the sixteenth century stems from a way of thinking, the scientific method. The method eludes crisp definition, for it is a product of several perceptions and attitudes working together. Succinct statements such as "systematic doubt" or "the method of observation" point to some characteristics without touching others, so we will begin by setting down a list of factors which, taken together, comprise the notion of scientific method:

1. Application of logic
2. Seeking evidence for all facts and labeling assumptions as such—i.e., "systematic doubt"
3. Accepting observation as the best confirmation of truth
4. Rejecting philosophical requirements for the natural order
5. Laying aside bias and personal or social interest as far as possible
6. Fidelity to truth
7. Open-endedness—that is, willingness to consider any conceivable solution and to discard previous belief whenever new evidence renders the earlier view untenable

Any application of the scientific method must begin with a question that is answerable in the space–time world. This limitation is important. To understand it is to understand that *science and religion are not rivals for the same crown.* Thus questions such as "What is the purpose of life?" or "Is it wrong to steal?" are not matters answerable by the scientific method. The method applies only to matters in which, ultimately, observation can confirm truth. The scientific

---

[3]*Ibid.*, p. 558.

[4]Harvey C. Lehman contends that plotting the "outstanding creative contributions" in chemistry, geology, medicine, and ten other fields reveals that for 25-year periods beginning at various times about 1500 and ending in 1900, contributions in each field tend to approximate a geometric progression with 2 as the constant factor. This cannot go on forever, but it is an interesting attempt to indicate the situation in which we are now living. See Harvey C. Lehman, "The Exponential Increase in Man's Output," *Social Forces*, 25 (March 1947), 281–90.

method does apply throughout the social sciences although, as we saw in Chapter 22, the practical obstacles to its application are considerable.

Investigation under the scientific method complies consistently with all logical requirements; no conclusion is accepted unless it is allowable as a reliable inference. And since the object of the method is to determine factual truth and not mere formal validity, unsupported premises are not accepted in support of conclusions. Hypotheses are advanced as hypotheses only, and are taken to be satisfactorily confirmed only when borne out by observation. Nothing is accepted as self-evidently true. This approach, often referred to as "systematic doubt," is not an indiscriminate skepticism; it is a realization of the need to subject *all* belief to confirmation, preferably by observation. By systematic doubt the investigator seeks to test every fact and expose every assumption.

Viewing the natural order as being in harmony with philosophical requirements has proved to be an obstacle to understanding in the past. The order of nature is as it is. So, also, bias and human will are irrelevant to truth and, as far as possible, to be kept from deflecting investigation. Nor is personal or social interest relevant to truth, which is to be pursued apart from these influences. Taken together, one can say that the scientific method involves a fidelity to truth which places truth above whatever may be its human consequences. To me the method appears both moral and amoral. It is moral in the sense of fidelity to truth: to yield to bias or self-interest, to distort facts through fabrication or doctoring an experiment, to misuse logic by resort to fallacy—to do any of these things is to violate the method and incur censure from those who accept its discipline. On the other hand, the method is a procedure not concerned with content; it is neutral and amoral in the sense that the pursuit of truth is disconnected from human welfare.

The scientific method is ready to revise any concept in the light of new evidence. Thus, the method admits correction. By not taking any findings as absolute but holding them only to be the best-supported conceptions of the time, the scientific method has a flexibility which other systems of belief do not. Science proposes no belief for acceptance as truth, but it proposes instead criteria for judging the reliability of its theories. This open-endedness, which acknowledges and anticipates changing belief, is an immense advantage over closed systems that commit themselves to certain conceptions and are embarrassed whenever new evidence suggests revision. Surely the evolution of human understanding throughout time and in all fields illustrates the baselessness of human claims to any final perception of truth. Further, even though the questioning of basic conceptions may be rare, the willingness to look on any conception as open to question can be a stimulus to creative thinking.

The search for truth by means of the scientific method is a cooperative venture. Information is shared, ideally at least, and the publication of conclusions serves as a practical invitation to all humankind to produce further evidence or counterevidence bearing upon the problem. The history of science is filled with long chains of contributions by people from different nations which, taken together, have advanced the frontiers of knowledge. Human development rests upon human intellect and cooperative nature, not upon the noise of history with its emphasis upon frictions and wars that have changed governments or shifted ethnic groups on the map. Important as such events are as sources of national pride or as upheavals in the lives of those who experience them, they do not account for man's place upon the earth today. The late Judge Learned Hand expressed this perception well:

> Most issues are not decided; their importance passes and they follow after. But in their day they rack the world they infest; men mill about them like a frantic herd: not understanding what their doctrines imply, or wither they lead. To them attach the noblest, and the meanest, motives, indifferent to all but that there is a cause to die for, or to profit by. Such habits are not conducive to the life of reason; that kind of devotion is not the method by which man has raised himself from a savage. Rather by quite another way, by doubt, by trial, by tentative conclusion.[5]

This chapter began with a daydream proposing that if the scientific method could be imparted to a group of human beings unfamiliar with the material knowledge of our civilization and if this group could adhere to that method in their thinking, then in a relatively short time the knowledge of the *physical* world that now exists would be rediscovered. I hope that reviewing the alternative sources of belief—explanation by the supernatural, authority, or common sense—has shown their inadequacy, and that the thumbnail sketch of the mounting surge of knowledge that has followed upon the realization of the scientific method is enough to identify it as the base for our present knowledge of the natural world. Already people everywhere are wondering if the human race has unloosed a Frankenstein for, as George Sarton put it, "Science is the most revolutionary thing in the world."

Loud though our praise has been for the methods of science, we must end by acknowledging *ethical* values that lie beyond the truths that science can reveal. We live in a paradoxical age which combines the moment of man's greatest understanding of the material world with dangers to his very existence. During the last few moments of history, so to speak, a select few of humankind's keenest minds have been applying the scientific method to systematically discover the powers of the natural world. But the means of discovery stand in sharpest contrast to social control over humankind's newfound power. Controls—whether they be over nuclear energy or unrestrained population growth—rest upon judgments that embody ethical perceptions. And to put into effect whatever controls may be devised requires the understanding assent of millions, even of billions of ordinary people. Is the population of a world riven with hatreds for other races, other classes, other religions, other social systems mature enough to control the powers that the scientific method will continue to unleash?

[5]Learned Hand, *The Spirit of Liberty* (New York: Alfred A. Knopf, 1952), pp. 74–75.

SUMMARY

Four broad bases upon which human beings rest their beliefs are:

1. Reference to the supernatural
2. Reference to authority and tradition
3. Common sense
4. The scientific method

Reference to the supernatural, though it may undertake an "answer" to any question, does not provide a coherent system for understanding the physical world. Later knowledge provides an imposing record of disproved supernatural explanations.

To accept authority or tradition as an unquestioned source for truth is to endow the source with infallibility. There is no reason for supposing that any human being is infallible.

Common sense reflects the current state of knowledge of its time. This is no guarantee of truth; great ideas repeatedly have been original thoughts transcending the common-sense beliefs of the day.

The scientific method is a procedure for marshalling the available evidence to judge the reliability of an idea. The method does not involve a final commitment to any idea as "true" but stands ready to reconsider any belief and to discard it whenever new evidence renders it untenable. Thus the method is self-correcting.

The scientific method is a procedure; it is not definable in any single statement. The factors which, taken together, make up the scientific method are as follows:

1. Application of logic
2. Seeking evidence for all facts and labeling assumptions as such—i.e., "systematic doubt"
3. Accepting observation as the best confirmation of truth
4. Rejecting philosophical requirements for the natural order
5. Laying aside bias and personal or social interest as far as possible
6. Fidelity to truth
7. Open-endedness—that is, willingness to consider any conceivable solution and to discard previous belief whenever new evidence renders the earlier view untenable

The scientific method applies only to questions answerable in the space–time world. It does not undertake to answer ethical questions or philosophical questions such as those regarding the purpose of life. The method does apply to social science problems although, as often remarked, the practical difficulty of making use of the method in social science often is much greater than is its application to physical science.

Over the past several centuries, the application of the scientific method with gathering intensity by some of humankind's most able minds has produced a tremendous expansion both of knowledge of pure science and of technological applications. Social control over the consequences of the new technology is hard to achieve because controls require policies that can win support from the whole mass of humankind. A Canadian newspaper put the problem succinctly: "If we can't save the whale, maybe we can't save ourselves."

EXERCISES FOR CHAPTER 23
pages 381–390

I. Answer **T** for "true" or **F** for "false":

_____ 1. Supernatural explanations for phenomena do not supplement one another to provide a coherent system for understanding the natural world.

_____ 2. Very few people of today are influenced in their beliefs by either authority or tradition.

_____ 3. Common sense is not innovative.

_____ 4. Decisions about social problems often rest upon ethical perceptions that elude the scientific method.

_____ 5. Many of the material consequences of technology can be controlled only with the understanding assent of the mass of humankind.

_____ 6. The scientific method applies only to questions that are answerable in the space–time world.

_____ 7. The discipline of science does not relate to one's mental attitude toward truth.

_____ 8. Science is not committed to the view that the existing beliefs about the physical world are necessarily true.

_____ 9. Correct use of both inductive and deductive procedures are an unvarying part of the scientific method.

_____ 10. If an idea cannot be verified according to the scientific method then it is not true.

II. Describe the elements which together make up the scientific method.

III. It was stated (p. 387) that "Science proposes no belief for acceptance as truth, but it proposes instead criteria for judging the reliability of its theories." Of what importance is this?

IV. Explain the place of logic in the scientific method.

V. Knowledge gained by the scientific method cannot assure that social problems will be resolved. Why not?

appendix

Checklist of Fallacies

This list is for reviewing the fallacies we have discussed. I suggest going over the list to see if each name suggests a faulty argument that you can describe. Being familiar with the names helps to make one aware of the various fallacies. But I do not suggest memorizing these names or that other names you may know will not serve just as well.

GROUP I

PSYCHOLOGICAL FALLACIES

1. PERSONAL ATTACK: *ad hominem* **argument**   page 8

Seeking to discredit the source of argument by charging *irrelevant* personal shortcomings.

2. DAMNING THE ORIGIN, CEREMONY, AND SETTING   page 9

"Damning the origin" suggests dismissing argument because the origin is unimpressive—e.g., inexperienced, unsuccessful, radical, and so on. "Ceremony" and "setting" refer to the psychological influence which these factors have in swaying the audience's receptiveness toward argument.

3. MISUSE OF AUTHORITY   page 11

Authority is a counterfeit whenever any one of the following requirements is lacking: (1) identification by name, (2) recognition by others in the field, (3) current in the sense of not obsolete, (4) opinion expressed within the authority's field.

4. IMPRESSING BY LARGE NUMBERS: bandwagon   page 12

The belief of numbers of people who are not specially qualified to judge the problem is not an argument.

5. APPEAL TO TRADITION: tried and true   page 13

Repeating the tradition and implying that departure therefrom would be scandalous without showing why the tradition should be followed on its merits.

6. POPULAR APPEALS: *ad populum* argument   page 14

Seeking to gain support by announcing agreement with ideas that are popular with the audience.

7. FORESTALLING DISAGREEMENT: poisoning the well   page 15

Presenting argument in a way that makes disagreement embarrassing.

8. CREATING MISGIVINGS   page 16

Playing on fears by making unfounded innuendos or distorted charges.

9. APPEAL TO PATHETIC CIRCUMSTANCES: crybaby   page 17

Seeking to influence action by pointing to personal hardship either in a way that is overdrawn or in a situation in which personal circumstances are beside the point.

10. THE ARGUMENT FROM IGNORANCE   page 10

Arguing that since something cannot be proved, the opposite should be taken to
be true.

11. MISUSE OF HUMOR AND RIDICULE: lost in the laugh   page 23

Distracting thought with humor or ridicule.

12. OBFUSCATION, PETTIFOGGING, AND
CLAMOROUS INSISTENCE ON IRRELEVANCIES   page 23

These fallacies do not define neatly. Unclear discussion and urging trivial matters will obscure argument whether intended to do so or not.

13. THE BARRAGE OF OBJECTIONS and THE CALL FOR
PERFECTION   page 24

Overemphasis of objections makes a distorted argument.
A call for perfection suggests that practical action should await ideal conditions
or that a solution should await the perfection of human beings themselves.

14. POINTING TO ANOTHER WRONG   page 25

Claiming that one wrong justifies another wrong. Where the actions are related
the situation may be murky. See text.

15. ARGUMENT OF THE CLUB: *argumentum ad baculum*   page 26

Substituting a threat, either of physical harm or of loss of some other interest, for
argument.

16. EMOTIVE LANGUAGE: colored words   page 27

The connotative suggestions of words, rhythm, and dramatic arrangement in
sentences often sway the reception of argument. Fallacy exists wherever these
factors influence thought.

GROUP II

MATERIAL FALLACIES

17. FAULTY GENERALIZATION   page 36

1. Hasty generalization rests on too few cases.
2. Unrepresentative generalization rests on cases that are not typical.

18. ASSUMING THE CAUSE: *post hoc* reasoning   page 39

Taking the *mere* fact that one event precedes another as sufficient proof of causal relationship.

19. MISUSE OF HYPOTHESIS CONTRARY TO FACT   page 40

Treating as certain the outcome of a hypothetical situation when in fact the outcome is subject to a reasonable doubt.

20. FALLACIOUS EXTENSION   page 41

An extension is fallacious where the extended position does not fairly come under the argument originally stated. Note that an extension is legitimate when the argument involves a principle that must apply to the extended position also.

21. FALSE ANALOGY   page 42

A comparison of things or situations which lack essential similarity within the area compared may be made for the purpose of illustration. It is a fallacy to suggest such a comparison as a support for argument.

22. COMPOSITION and DIVISION   page 48

The fallacy of composition assumes that the characteristics of the parts will be found in the whole to which they contribute.
The fallacy of division assumes that the characteristics of an organized whole will be possessed by each part.

23. FALSE DILEMMA   page 48

A dilemma is false when there are more alternatives than it proposes, or when one of the alternatives is not a disadvantage.

24. BLACK-OR-WHITE FALLACY: the great either . . . or   page 49

This is presenting a situation in simple all-or-nothing terms when there are other possibilities in between.

25. ARGUMENT OF THE BEARD: one more doesn't matter   page 51

When a line has to be drawn in a continuum, it is a fallacy to either ridicule the fine distinctions that necessarily result or to argue that "one more doesn't matter." It is in order to argue before a proper authority that the cutoff point in the continuum is a poor choice or that circumstances make it desirable to depart from the rule.

26. LEADING QUESTIONS   page 53

A leading question is calculated to influence the answer. (See text for four common kinds of leading questions.)

27. BEGGING THE QUESTION   page 54

A question is begged by assuming what should be proved. (See text for three ways in which questions are begged.)

28. OVERSIMPLIFICATION: tabloid thinking   page 55

When a complicated situation is presented in simple assertions to the point of serious inaccuracy there is oversimplification.

29. WORD MAGIC   page 56

Assuming that words or phrases assure the existence of the notions they describe.

NOTE ON "BARE ASSERTION" page 58

Since a bare assertion offers no evidence and no argument, it cannot contain a mistake in reasoning. Upon realizing that an assertion is "bare," one is on his own to decide whether or not to accept it.

GROUP III

LOGICAL FALLACIES

30. FALLACY OF FOUR TERMS* page 96

Violating the rule that "a syllogism must have exactly three terms each used exactly twice."

31. FALLACY OF FAULTY EXCLUSIONS page 98

Violating the rule that "a syllogism must either have no exclusion or two exclusions, one of which must appear in the conclusion."

32. FALLACY OF THE UNDISTRIBUTED MIDDLE TERM page 99

Violating the rule that "the middle term must be distributed at least once."

33. FALLACY OF ILLICIT DISTRIBUTION page 100

Violating the rule that "any term distributed in the conclusion must be distributed in the premise where it appears."

34. FALSE CONVERSION page 113

Violating either of the rules for conversion produces a false conversion. The rules are:

1. The converse must retain the same quality as the orignal—i.e. both affirmative or both negative.

>*Note:* Fallacies #30–33 concern categorical syllogisms.

2. No term may be distributed in the converse unless it was distributed in the original.

35. FALSE OBVERSION   page 117

Violating either of the rules for obversion produces a false obversion. The rules are:

1. An inclusion in the original is changed to an exclusion, or vice versa.
2. The second term is negated.

36. INVALID HYPOTHETICAL SYLLOGISMS   page 132

Any violation of the rules for the hypothetical syllogism is a fallacy. The most important rule for a valid hypothetical is that the minor premise must *affirm the antecedent or deny the consequent.*

37. INVALID DISJUNCTIVE SYLLOGISM   page 145

Any violation of the rules for the disjunctive syllogism is a fallacy. The important rule for a valid disjunctive is that the minor premise must *affirm one disjunct.*

38. INVALID ALTERNATIVE SYLLOGISM   page 147

Any violation of the rules for the alternative syllogism is a fallacy. The important rule for a valid alternative syllogism is that the minor premise must *deny one alternate.*

Index